D1217703

MILTON STUDIES
57

~ MILTON STUDIES ~

Volume 57

Edited by Laura L. Knoppers

DUQUESNE UNIVERSITY PRESS
Pittsburgh, Pennsylvania

Milton Studies is published annually by Duquesne University Press as a forum for Milton scholarship and criticism. Essays submitted for publication may focus on any aspect of John Milton's life and writing, including biography; literary history; Milton's work in its literary, intellectual, political, or cultural contexts; Milton's influence on or relationship to other writers; or the history of critical response to his work.

Manuscripts should conform to *The Chicago Manual of Style* and be approximately 8,000–12,000 words in length. Authors should include a written statement that the manuscript is being submitted exclusively to *Milton Studies*. We encourage electronic submissions in Microsoft Word format, sent to Laura.L.Knoppers.3@nd.edu, followed by one hard copy (printout) of the essay sent by regular mail to Laura L. Knoppers, Editor, *Milton Studies*, Department of English, 356 O'Shaughnessy Hall, University of Notre Dame, Notre Dame, IN 46556.

Milton Studies does not review books.

Milton Studies may be ordered from Duquesne University Press at www.dupress@duq.edu.

Copyright © 2016 Duquesne University Press
All rights reserved

Published in the United States of America by
DUQUESNE UNIVERSITY PRESS
600 Forbes Avenue
Pittsburgh, Pennsylvania 15282

ISSN 0076-8820
ISBN 978-0-8207-0701-3

∞ Printed on acid-free paper

CONTENTS

Language and Sound

Readers in (Literary) History

PREFACE:
BEYOND MISPRISION

Sympathize as we might with the forlorn Creature in Mary Shelley's *Frankenstein*, most of us would not consider ourselves to share his mode of reading Milton. When the Creature fortuitously finds in the woods a leather portmanteau containing a copy of *Paradise Lost*, he evinces the Romantic fascination with the rebel Satan, struck with "wonder and awe" at "the picture of an omnipotent God warring with his creatures."[1] The reader might smile knowingly as the Creature takes the action of *Paradise Lost* to be a true history, along the lines of the human history he has heard while eavesdropping on the DeLacey family through a chink in the wall of his hovel. The Creature's bitter ruminations, as he compares and contrasts the "several situations" of Milton's characters to his own, might seem both unique and unpromising as a reading strategy. Like the newly awakened Adam, he has no links to any other being; yet Adam was "a perfect creature, happy and prosperous, guarded by the especial care of his Creator," while the Creature finds himself "wretched, helpless, and alone." Indeed, he many times considers "Satan as the fitter emblem of my condition." Learning about Eve both torments the Creature ("no Eve soothed my sorrows nor shared my thoughts") and inspires him to demand his own companion, one "as deformed and horrible" as himself, again a seemingly unique readerly response.[2]

Yet it is worth considering further how the Creature uses Milton in a struggle with his Maker. As the Creature self-consciously quotes *Paradise Lost* to contest and rewrite Frankenstein's implicitly Miltonic narrative, his reading practices might be seen as a type of what Harold Bloom has defined as strong misreading or misprision.[3] The Creature, after all, uses *Paradise Lost* against his own precursor and progenitor, Victor Frankenstein, striving to replace Frankenstein's self-absorbed narrative of himself as doomed and his Creature as unredeemable with a narrative in which the fallen Creature is an Adam who belatedly gets his Eve and turns away from evil. When Frankenstein abruptly ends that narrative, tearing the almost-completed mate into piece, and not recognizing the Creature's human longings and capacity for good, the Creature seems to embrace his role as malignant devil, killing off Frankenstein's loved ones in a protracted and vengeful battle against his Creator.

In this agonistic struggle, Frankenstein's Creature parallels Milton's Satan, whom Bloom views as the paradigmatic misreader and first modern poet.[4] Arguing in *The Anxiety of Influence* that Milton's Satan "begets" himself as a poet through misprision of the divine decree exalting the Son, Bloom (echoing the Romantics) is as sympathetic with Satan as he is unsympathetic with Milton's God: "Satan is that modern poet, while God is his dead but still embarrassingly potent and present ancestor, or rather, ancestral poet."[5] Bloom expands on the point in *A Map of Misreading*, declaring the proclamation of the Son to be "the ultimate Scene of Instruction," a poetic version of the oedipal primal scene, and suggesting that "Satan, like any strong poet, declines to be merely a latecomer. His way of returning to origins, of making the Oedipal trespass, is to become a rival creator to God-as-creator."[6] Mary Shelley's own reading of *Paradise Lost* has been similarly seen in Bloomian terms as a "despairingly acquiescent 'misreading'" that seems to repress Eve but in fact turns her into the monster that Milton implies she is.[7]

Yet I would suggest that both Mary Shelley and her Creature, in the end, use Milton to move beyond anxiety and misreading toward something more constructive and enabling. In a final swerve from Frankenstein's narrative, and an embrace of Miltonic reconciliation, the Creature comes to the deathbed of his Maker, weeps, and asks for forgiveness. The Creature rewrites the end of his own story, moving past the satanic role to become a repentant Adam, albeit one who, without his Eve, can only despair and embrace death. This is no Bloomian swerve. Rather, the Creature recounts to a listening Walton the exquisite self-torments caused by his opposition to his maker, voicing remorse and self-recrimination rather than resentment. Unlike Keats on Milton, not the life but the death of his precursor is death to him,[8] and he ends by fleeing the scene and jumping on an ice raft to seek out his own death. In terms of reading strategies, the Creature has moved from misreading to acknowledgment and self-recognition. In turn, the Creature's reading might well warrant more sustained reevaluation of Mary Shelley's own reading of Milton as distinct from the Bloomian (male) Romantic strivers in her more positive use of the Miltonic domestic.[9]

Explicitly cited (and challenged) by Paul Stevens, and implicit in several of our other essays, Harold Bloom's paradigm of strong misreading or misprision provides a useful heuristic for mapping the conversation on Miltonic reading, readers, and adaptations offered in 11 fresh and groundbreaking essays in this volume of *Milton Studies*. As these essays show, we are in an exciting period that has moved well beyond Bloomian misprision. For Bloom, Milton's precursors are Spenser and Shakespeare, the latter of whom he engages in a relationship marked by anxiety and repression.[10] Milton as reader in our volume emerges not as agonistic but as one who delights in difference (John K. Hale), self-reflectively worries about carnal readers (Raphael Magarik), acknowledges the power of reading models unlike his own (Alexandra Reider), or reworks Aristotelian natural philosophy (Charlotte Nicholls) and philosophy (Ayelet Langer, Christopher Koester). If for Bloom Satan becomes the first modern poet, refusing his belated status in a struggle with a dominating God the Father,[11] the Satan who emerges in this volume is one of a number of voices in a crisis of representation that reflects on literary forms (Andrew S. Brown), an organic and mechanical crafter of sound and language (Katherine Cox), or one whose fallen mind cannot interact with the world or understand the time and sequentiality essential to morality (Langer). If Bloom articulates a psychodynamic process of misreading,[12] contributors to this volume situate readers (and rewriters) of Milton in precise biographical, historical, and literary historical contexts: Robert Graves in England works through his own World War I and class experiences (Paul Stevens), Isaac Asimov writes during and after World War II in America (Ryan Hackenbracht), and Milton's contemporary John Dryden works in the Restoration cultural milieu (Diana Treviño Benet). Questions of Milton's reading and readers in this volume, then, open up into biography, history, and literary history, into constructive interrelationships, and into complex generic reworking and adaptations.

In our first group of essays, "Misreading and Representation," Paul Stevens examines how Robert Graves exorcises his own past self through the "monstrous" Milton. The younger poet's extraordinary antipathy to and sustained misreading of the elder, particularly in his brilliant if notorious *Wife to Mr. Milton,* tells us more about Graves than Milton, his war-induced neurasthenia and longing for intergender openness. In turn, Raphael Magarik investigates how, in his uses of phylacteries, Milton takes Protestant iconoclasm one step further to worry about the possibility of textual idolatry, given that bibliophilic Protestant readers, in rejecting objects and ritual for the text itself, might hence reify the biblical word. Milton's concern about a specific Jewish practice represents a persistent concern about interpretation and hermeneutics that could undermine, in the end, the textual authority of the Bible itself. In the third essay in this section, Andrew S. Brown reexamines the much-debated exaltation scene as a crisis of heavenly representation; the juxtaposition of the Father's decree with the hymns of the angels and Satan's solitary dissent initiates a broader pattern of reflection on the capacity of forms, and the closely related genre of the lyric, to serve political ends.

Opening the second group, "After Aristotle," Ayelet Langer shows how Milton uses and revises Aristotle's concept of the *now*; in the moral universe of *Paradise Lost,* only the unfallen mind evinces an Aristotelian interaction with the world through the now—a capacity unavailable to the rebellious and fallen Satan, although regained by the repentant Adam and Eve. Second, Charlotte Nicholls suggests that Milton draws productively on current experimentation and chemical innovation in his animist materialism, particularly the Creation scene. The work of Francis Glisson and others offers Milton a scientifically progressive version of transformative material spirit that prompts a reconsideration of Aristotelian theory of cause. Third in this section, Christopher Koester argues for the importance of solitude in Milton's concept of the human, a move away from Aristotle's view that solitude makes one a God or a beast. Rather than the Aristotelian foregrounding of the self-sameness and likeness of male-male friends, Milton depicts a marriage defined by difference within likeness and solitude within companionship, with consequences for our understanding of Adam's nativity and of the separation scene.

In our third group of essays, "Language and Sound," John K. Hale explores how Milton values the difference and otherness of Greek. Suggesting that something Greek, and especially Homeric, lies at the root of Milton's sense of what poetry is, Hale shows how Milton turns to Greek poets, dramatists, and critics for instruction and delight. In the essay that follows, Alexandra Reider offers a new interpretation of Milton's staging of the gawking and misreading passersby in Sonnet 11: rather than simple nostalgia for classic learning, Reider argues that Milton here (and elsewhere) registers the problem of linguistic "purity," even as he famously inflects his own English with foreign influence. In turn, Katherine Cox offers a new explanation of how Satan vocalizes the serpent, by tracing how the manufacture of instrumental sounds in heaven and hell leads to a mechanized and embodied satanic acoustics linked with Satan's power as "Prince of the air"; the corrupt sounds that Satan produces to beguile Eve disclose Milton's anxiety about his own readers.

In our final section, "Readers in (Literary) History," Diana Treviño Benet examines how an anxious Dryden strives to construct a literary history in which Milton belongs to a prior, earlier age by rewriting Miltonic epic and theodicy in *The State of Innocence*. Benet also shows, however, Dryden's self-conscious attention to literary genre and questions of gender as he converts *Paradise Lost* into heroic drama. Finally, Ryan Hackenbracht explores how Isaac Asimov's *Foundation* series self-consciously strives both to correct and outdo Miltonic myth, rewriting satanic disobedience as key to humanity's salvation and liberating what he sees as the puritanical Milton's oppressed Eve. Yet Hackenbracht also points out how Asimov's rewritings are shaped by his own historical moment, with fears of Nazism, Cold War anxieties, and 1950s "second sex" gender values.

By modeling Mary Shelley's own approach to Milton and rejecting the more negative reading of his flawed and human Creator, Frankenstein's Creature evinces a move beyond Bloomian anxiety and misprision that resonates with scholarly conversations on Milton in this volume and beyond. Admittedly, in his misery and commitment to internecine warfare, Frankenstein's Creature is no unequivocal role model for Miltonists, old, new, or otherwise. Yet as we recognize more fully the complexities of Milton's own literary and philosophical interrelationships and move into the brave new world of Miltonic adaptations, we might have something more to learn not only from our Shakespearean colleagues and precursors but also from Mary Shelley's monstrous readings.

Laura L. Knoppers

NOTES

1. Mary Shelley, *Frankenstein; or, The Modern Prometheus*, ed. Maurie Hindle (1992; rev. ed. New York, 2003), 132.

2. Ibid., 132, 134, 146.

3. Harold Bloom develops his theory of influence as dynamic psychic drama in which every strong poet, knowing that he is "belated," engages in a kind of oedipal struggle with a precursor in *The Anxiety of Influence: A Theory of Poetry* (New York, 1973); *A Map of Misreading* (New York, 1975); *Poetry and Repression: Revisionism from Blake to Stevens* (1976);

and other texts. Key to this struggle is what Bloom labels poetic misreading or misprision, a necessary swerve away from the original (as with Lucretian atoms) to open up a space for creativity. Milton is for Bloom the paradigmatic precursor poet, against whom the Romantic poets struggle.

4. For a consideration of Milton's Satan that engages and qualifies Bloom's comments, see Danielle A. St. Hilaire, *Satan's Poetry: Fallenness and Poetic Tradition in "Paradise Lost"* (Pittsburgh, 2010), 21–34.

5. Bloom, *Anxiety of Influence*, 20. As William Giraldi writes in "Bloomian Stride," *Kenyon Review* 35, no. 2 (Spring 2013), "Milton's Satan, paragon of poeticism and seditiousness, supreme abider of the self, is of course, one of Bloom's heroes" (175).

6. Bloom, *Map of Misreading*, 37. Such ruminations continue. In his more recent *The Anatomy of Influence: Literature as a Way of Life* (New Haven, Conn., 2011), Bloom writes that "the God of *Paradise Lost* is a nightmare of bad poetry and evil religion, vindicating everything Shelley and Blake said about him" (101). He goes on to add that "the alert reader's sympathies are with Satan, particularly when he regards God as a usurper, Christ as an upstart, and Abdiel as a timeserver" (101).

7. Sandra Gilbert and Susan Gubar, *The Madwoman in the Attic: The Woman Writer and the Nineteenth-Century Imagination* (New Haven, Conn., 1979), 189; see their chapter 6, "Milton's Bogey: Patriarchal Poetry and Women Readers," 187–212, and chapter 7, "Horror's Twin: Mary Shelley's Monstrous Eve," 213–47. This much-reprinted account has had considerable influence. See, for example, John B. Lamb, "Mary Shelley's *Frankenstein* and Milton's Monstrous Myth," *Nineteenth-Century Literature* 47, no. 3 (1992): 303–19. Bloom himself discusses the doubling and complicated Prometheanism of *Frankenstein* as a Romantic reading of *Paradise Lost*, in his introduction to *Mary Shelley's Frankenstein: Modern Critical Interpretations* (New York, 1987), 1–11. See also Joseph Wittreich's more positive account of Milton's early female readers, *Feminist Milton* (Ithaca, N.Y., 1987); Lucy Newlyn's reading, in *Milton and the Romantic Reader* (Oxford, 1993), of Mary Shelley as not so much competing with or misreading Milton as "us[ing] the radical indeterminacy of *Paradise Lost* as a way of...exploring the interface between politics and religion" (138); and Ana Acosta's account of Mary Shelley's Creature as critiquing Enlightenment utopian rewritings of Genesis (including Milton's) in *Reading Genesis in the Long Eighteenth Century: From Milton to Mary Shelley* (New York, 2006), chapter 6.

8. John Keats, "Life to him [Milton] would be death to me," in *The Letters of John Keats, 1814–1821*, 2 vols., ed. Hyder E. Rollins (Cambridge, Mass., 1985), 2:212.

9. For one such approach, see my "Miltonic Loneliness and Monstrous Desire from *Paradise Lost* to *Bride of Frankenstein*," in *Milton in Popular Culture*, ed. Laura L. Knoppers and Gregory M. Colón Semenza (New York, 2006), 99–112.

10. In his *Anxiety of Influence*, Bloom argues for Milton's "transumptive style," which transforms his own belatedness into precedence, particularly over Spenser as his rival and precursor as English's epic poet. Nearly four decades later, in *Anatomy of Influence*, Bloom focuses on another primary precursor for Milton, discussing Milton's struggle with, and creative repressions of, Shakespeare.

11. See Bloom, *Anxiety of Influence; A Map of Misreading*.

12. The revisionary moves made by inevitably misreading belated poets are analogous to the defense mechanisms (repression, selectivity) in Freudian psychology.

MISREADING AND REPRESENTATION

Reading Graves Misreading Milton

Paul Stevens

Nothing can make me like, admire, or even pity John Milton. That was my earliest judgment and the more I read the sounder it seems.

—Robert Graves (1941)

Robert Graves is notorious among Milton scholars as the author of the popular 1942 novel *Wife to Mr. Milton*. The novel is relentless in its representation of Milton as the most abusive of husbands, egotistical and cruel: in the words of one recent scholar, the seventeenth century poet is made to appear "pedantic, self-absorbed [and] callous."[1] By any measure, whatever the very real failings of the historical Milton, Graves's representation of the poet is so extreme that it beggars belief. But Graves was no hack: he was immensely talented, one of the greatest English poets of the twentieth century, and his novel is a disconcertingly brilliant piece of work. The principal topic of this essay is, then, the mysterious relationship between these two great poets, Graves and Milton—specifically the problem of the younger poet's extraordinary antipathy to and sustained misreading of the elder. One way to understand this, both the antipathy and the misreading, is to begin with Graves's approach to audience.

3

Misreading and Graves's Sense of Audience

There is a sense in which all reading is, of course, a form of misreading, but there are degrees of misreading and some are obviously less knowing or self-aware than others. Despite his insistence on clarity, Graves himself, certainly in his prose, is very easy to misread and this, so I want to suggest, is central to my main concern because his lifelong misreading of Milton has a lot to do with Graves's indistinct or unfocused sense of a reading public. That is, while his indifferent sense of audience often encourages us to misread him, it also enables him to persevere in what Harold Bloom would call his "strong" misreading of other writers, not least Milton. "Poetic strength," Bloom claims, "comes only from a triumphant wrestling with [that is, misreading of] the greatest of the dead, and from an even more triumphant solipsism."[2] This is helpful but not entirely so. Solipsistic or self-absorbed as Graves's motives might be, Bloom's formulation does not really capture the singularity of Graves's relationship with Milton, for his motives were considerably more inchoate and less straightforwardly literary than those imagined by Bloom. His relationship with Milton involved so much more than proving that he was the stronger poet.[3]

As everyone familiar with Graves knows, the writer had very decided views about his reading public. "Never use the word 'audience,'" he says in a 1969 interview. "The very idea of a public, unless a poet is writing for money, seems wrong to me. Poets don't have an audience: they're talking to a single person all the time."[4] With prose it seems to be a bit different. While he writes poetry for poets and satires for wits, Graves declared a little earlier in 1946, he writes prose for what he called "people in general." And as far as these people are concerned, he continues dismissively, I am "content that they should be unaware that I do anything else."[5] The serious work of poetry should not be wasted on them, for the "common people," he says on another occasion, "do not understand poetry."[6] While Graves's unfocused sense of audience cannot be explained entirely in terms of class and his own privileged upbringing, it clearly has something to do with it, for despite his assertion to the contrary, even in his prose he often seems to be talking to a single person—and that person a member of his own class.[7] When I first read Graves as a boy I found all this very confusing, so let me illustrate the effect of Graves's insouciance with an example from my own early misreading of his prose—an example of what happens when he's read by a single person not of his own class.

Reading Milton and Graves as a working-class schoolboy in South Wales in the 1960s had some powerful but unexpected results: while the one poet inspired an academic career, the other led me into the army. In the sixth form, I was reading *Paradise Lost* and Graves's *Proceed, Sergeant Lamb* at almost exactly the same time. Graves's historical novel is the story of a young British soldier in the American Revolution, and largely because of this prose adventure, not to mention Graves's idealization of Lamb's regiment (which was his own in the First World War), I joined the Royal Welch Fusiliers as soon as I could. On leaving school, against the wishes of my parents, I enlisted in the regular army and for three years in Cyprus and Germany and the West Country I lived out a fantasy life as a latter-day Sergeant Lamb. Only when I became an officer did I realize the degree to which my narrative had been scripted by Graves's unreflective, upper-middle-class idealization of what a working-class NCO should be. To resort to a cliché like "life imitates art" is to understate the potency of the art. Althusser's notion of interpellation comes nearer the mark: I felt as though I had been called into being—that is, the narrative gave me an extraordinary sense of identity, purpose, and self-worth, however lowly my rank. I'm sure I wasn't the reading public or particular "people in general" Graves had in mind, but his novel, specifically Sergeant Lamb's ideal of "proud subordination," knowing one's place, loyalty, and love of regiment, blinded me to the limitations of the life I'd chosen and encouraged me to invest, as ideology does, in what might well have become my own unhappiness. In retrospect, seen much more darkly, Graves's novel seems to have encouraged something like the commitment John Carey attributes to Christ Church college servants in the 1950s: "I got the impression they would have gone to the stake to defend the right of their employers to exploit them."[8] Graves's art was as potent as it was for many reasons but especially because its authenticity was guaranteed by the ethos of the artist. The author of the Sergeant Lamb novels was the sensitive but tough-minded hero of *Good-Bye to All That*, Graves's unsparing memoir of the First World War. Thus, it came as a surprise to discover that this wonderfully intelligent man despised Milton and, even more so, that he himself was despised by most of his fellow officers for lacking precisely the quality I most admired in him, his sensitivity or thoughtfulness. It is this last paradox that most immediately illuminates his problem with audience and suggests that his weakness is not simply a function of class.

One of the most familiar but still arresting accounts of Graves in the trenches is Siegfried Sassoon's portrait in his brilliant 1930 novel, *Memoirs of an Infantry Officer*.[9] Graves appears there as David Cromlech, "knobby-faced and gawky," big, impulsive, and untidy, a slack-looking young officer remarkable for his opinionated views on literature and complete indifference to those of others (231). He "was a positive expert at putting people's backs up unintentionally," says Sassoon's own character, George Sherston (78). A chorus of other witnesses, young and old, finds him unbearable: a "queer bird," butting in where he's not wanted, a "bumptious young prig," "never satisfied unless he's turning something upside down." Indeed, "it's about time," says one exasperated colonel, that "he gave up reading Shakespeare and started using soap and water." For all his privileged background, courage, and cleverness, there is something ungentlemanly about him—for many of his own class, he is a "rotten outsider" (78–79). Even the long-suffering Sherston finds his views on poetry irritatingly dogmatic: "He made short work of most books which I had hitherto venerated, for David was a person who consumed his enthusiasms quickly, and he once fairly took my breath away by pooh-poohing *Paradise Lost* as 'that moribund academic concoction.' I hadn't realized that it was possible to speak disrespectfully about Milton. Anyhow John Milton was consigned to perdition, and John Skelton was put forward as 'one of the few really good poets.' But somehow I could never quite accept his supremacy over Milton as an established fact" (106). What other people venerate is of little consequence to young Graves, and Sassoon's quiet irony would have been lost on him, for both Graves's abiding contempt for Milton and his curious indifference or only fitful ability to sense the feelings of others persisted throughout his life. Far from being limitations, however, these failings seem to have enabled him to develop his formidable powers of self-expression, his ability to turn his inner life into art.

In Graves's world, while Milton increasingly became the touchstone for both bad poetry and much more, the writer's indifference to audience, his "defensive exuberance," was turned to advantage as he increasingly came to represent its faux pas as positives—that is, as manifestations of an independent mind, a *contra mundam* disposition or willingness to defy the world for personal principle. If his 1929 masterpiece, *Good-Bye to All That*, best exemplifies this *contra mundam* stance, not surprisingly his 1942 novel, *Wife to Mr. Milton*, best allows us real insight into his abhorrence of Milton. My argument is that the one enables the other; that is, the "cheek" or *contra mundam* stance that is of such value in his war memoir encourages defiance and leads Graves to valorize his early prejudices, transmuting them into something rich and strange and so giving his historical novel the unusual power it has. Uninhibited by any sharp sense of the reading public as the reader over his shoulder, dismissive of academics and contemptuous of "people in general" (certainly as they appear in the popular press), he turns Milton into an image of something deeply hateful, and it is on the significance of this terrifyingly overdetermined figure that I wish to focus. My point here is that if Graves's Milton has little to do with the historical Milton, he has a great deal to do with Graves's enduring struggle to articulate and master some terrible darkness within himself—a process, it needs to be emphasized, facilitated by deliberately occluding audience. Before I turn to the novel, I need to say something about Graves's Milton in the context of the poet's experience in the First World War.

"Monstrous Milton" and the Great War

Graves's war poetry has considerably more unity than is usually allowed, and one of the images that gives his three books of war poems their metaphoric coherence is that of giants.[10] In the matrix or dark dream world of this poetry, as in Milton's phantasmagoric hell, nothing is stable. Everything can change shape and suddenly become gigantic—large, ugly, and threatening: in the trenches even tiny lice can change and suddenly become "Something bloody and big" (*CP* 15); on patrol the silver moon with all its magical childhood associations can suddenly turn "stony" and become "dreadful," dangerous, "cruel and round and bright," so much so that now "you can't make out the marks on its stupid face" (*CP* 17). Most pointedly, when Graves rewrites and reverses Scripture's parables of faith, it is the giant Goliath who first comes to mind. For Wilfrid Owen, unlike Graves, it might be a father-figure like Abram, the patriarch who when told to sacrifice the "Ram of Pride" instead of his son Isaac refuses: "the old man would not so, but slew his son, / And half the seed of Europe, one by one."[11] But for Graves, it is Goliath, the giant who together with a stupidly silent God, eyes "dim" and ears "shut," conspires to murder the nation's seed, the "Goodly faced" David (*CP* 24). The young boy's pebbles are no match for the giant's machine-made armor, his brazen shield and steel sword. Goliath laughs like Yahweh, his breath like that of Milton's God, scattering "chariots like blown chaff" (*CP* 24):[12] he straddles the corpse of David, looming and completely loveless, "Steel helmeted and grey and grim" (*CP* 23–24). The nightmare image of the looming giant reaches back into childhood and is given new life in the meaningless terror of mass industrialized warfare.[13] Throughout long nights in the nursery the menacing form stood:

> By my bed unwearying,
> Loomed gigantic, formless, queer,
> Purring in my haunted ear
> That same hideous nightmare thing,
> Talking, as he lapped my blood,
> In a voice cruel and flat,
> Saying for ever, "Cat!...Cat!...Cat!..."   (*CP* 50)

Now during the protracted bloodletting of the Battle of the Somme in 1916, as Graves lies wounded, the gigantic form returns "with straddling legs," his "black bulk darkening the day," repeating the same stupid, nonsensical words (*CP* 51).[14] As the image reaches back into childhood, so it also seeps outwards to animate all that is hateful in the world. Although war is always at the center, the image is inflected through a series of surprisingly unwarlike variations: most importantly, the grotesque giant figure does not materialize in the form of generals and politicians, as one might expect, but philosophers and critics, philosophers who would desiccate imagination and critics who would shackle the free play of poetry. Unlike Sassoon or Owen, Graves's satire even at its most defiant never quite becomes political; his poems seem to have no pragmatic purpose, or, as he himself would insist, no particular target or reading public besides his fellow poets.

The central drama of Graves's nightmarish war poetry is the infiltration and incremental corruption of all mental life. His subject is the internal disintegration precipitated by war and the pity of it; the poetry is not, however, in the pity but in the endless craft with which it is articulated. In his agon, the redoubts or crucial points of resistance are imagination and the skill with which its energies are sustained and turned into words. It is this life-giving articulate energy that is under siege. For the young poet, imagination is associated with innocence, children, play, fairies, and, somewhat curiously, fusiliers. Its magic first breaks into speech in nursery rhymes:

> Children are born of fairy stock
> Never need for shirt or frock,
> Never want for food or fire,
> Always get their heart's desire.   (*CP* 46)

Nursery rhymes and fairy stories allow the poet's voice a childlike authenticity, a truth beyond consciousness. "Fusiliers," as Graves's recurrent use of the antique term is meant to suggest, are not just soldiers but young men, usually officers and beloved poet friends like Sassoon or David Thomas, who retain this authenticity and who even in war remember their fairy stock—for their imaginations are untainted, and they still have the miraculous capacity to love and find "Beauty in Death, / In dead men, breath" (*CP* 31). It is this that ultimately explains the strangely affective dimension of his intense devotion to his regiment, the Royal Welch Fusiliers. The enemy of imagination is what Graves calls "wisdom" and its agent, the loud, Mr. Gradgrind-like philosopher who comes, "Making monstrous mouths" and "Braying like an ass" (*CP* 33). This giant-like figure is at his most dangerous when he invades the children's world and tries to co-opt their play:

> Old Mr. Philosopher
> Comes for Ben and Claire
> An ugly man, a tall man,
> With bright red hair.   (*CP* 33)

So over-bearing is his play, "Gambolling fiercely / Through brushes and grass," that Ben's legs turn unstable and "wingle" (*CP* 33). Wisdom at its most brutal appears in the poem "Babylon," a redaction of Psalm 137. Graves rewrites the terrible ending of the psalm from the perspective of Babylonian children, the "little ones" whose heads Israel will smash "against the stones" (Ps. 137:9). Since "the child alone a poet is," this atrocity against children is also an assault on the roots of imagination: "Banishing the Lords of Faery," wisdom, ratiocination, "Truth and Reason," made "a breach and battered / Babylon to bits." Even "Jack the Giant-slayer's gone" and we are left defenseless, weeping not for Jerusalem but for a "lost Babylon" (*CP* 25).[15] The philosopher's ally and the enemy of the poet's homely craft is the "ungentle critic" (*CP* 29). He appears only after *Over the Brazier* (1916) and *Goliath and David* (1916) have been published. He seeks novelty and despises playfulness, but most dangerously he becomes the poet's "familiar ghost" (*CP* 40), the reader over his shoulder, inhibiting and censoring. He is the "son of Conscious Brain," the monitor who listens, watches, and "takes no rest" (41). It is, then, the war poetry, so I want to suggest, that first gives us an idea of who exactly Graves's Milton is. He's not a poet at all but a peculiarly monstrous version of the old philosopher and critic, looming ungentle and loveless out of the Great War, epitomizing all its negation: he is the kind of rationalizing pragmatist who would shackle poetry by making it serve more than itself. In Graves's final book of war poems, *Fairies and Fusiliers,* Milton moves center-stage and appears as himself.

At the heart of this collection is Graves's poem on "John Skelton," the poem that elucidates his remarks to Sassoon about the respective merits of Milton and his Tudor rival. It is a brilliant poem written in the form of Skelton's own rapid-fire, playful meter. Skelton is very much a "fusilier," a poet whose delight in play remembers his fairy stock: "What could be dafter / Than John Skelton's laughter?" Graves asks (*CP* 43). He is Jack the giant-slayer reborn, the light-footed, life-giving antithesis of the war's ponderous, looming giants:

> But oh, Colin Clout!
> How his pen flies about,
> Twiddling and turning,
> Scorching and burning,
> Thrusting and thrumming!
> How it hurries with humming,
> Leaping and running
> At the tipsy-topsy Tunning
> Of Mistress Eleanor Rumming!
>   . . . .
> Sadly, madly
> Helter-skelter John
> Rhymes serenely on,
> As English poets should.
> Old John, you do me good!   (*CP* 44)

The most fearful of the war's nightmare giants is Old John's enemy, the figure Graves calls "monstrous Milton" (*CP* 43). Milton is not simply a fake poet or even a Bloomian precursor to be overcome; he is the inchoate horror of Graves's nursery nightmares reborn in the inner mental trauma of the trenches of the First World War: "I'd always hated Milton, from earliest childhood," he says in the 1949 *Paris Review.* Milton offers him none of the "pre-rational" truth he hungers for, no truth beyond consciousness. Milton has never "undergone the profound mental disturbance that calls poetry into being" (*Asphodel* 3)[16] and like the salesman that all rhetoricians really are he would make poetry work in the world, converting its art into so many public speech-acts to serve religion, politics, or his own vaulting ambition. Some may wonder at *Paradise Lost*, Graves says in his 1917 Skelton poem, long before Leavis and Eliot, but the truth is that it is a peculiarly un-English concoction or academic potboiler, "phrased so disdainfully" and "composed so painfully" (*CP* 43) that it completely lacks all honesty and spontaneity: Skelton "struck what Milton missed, / Milling an English grist / With homely turn and twist" (*CP* 43). What becomes increasingly clear is that Graves in 1917 is an intensely personal, late Romantic poet whose preoccupation with self-expression or what M. H. Abrams would call the "expressive dimension" of poetry is intensified by the war and renders him increasingly indifferent to the complex value of alternatives—most relevant here, that of seventeenth century public poetry.[17]

In Graves's sustained misreading of Milton, the elder poet becomes an emotionally charged, inhibiting obsession for the younger, contaminated by the monstrosity of the war and doing duty for ever more irresolvable negatives, specifically in terms of poetic practice, gender, and class. In Graves's mental landscape, Milton stands like Goliath towering "unhurt six cubits high" over a heap of "Goodly-faced" Davids (*CP* 23–24). He needs to be taken down. A quarter of a century later, the three-hundredth anniversary of England's civil war and Milton's first marriage gives Graves his chance. Inspired by the way Laura Riding in her 1939 *Lives of Wives* urges us to consider great men "as husbands rather than heroes,"[18] he will let us see Milton through his wife's eyes. He will let Milton's wife, Mary Powell, speak for him: like Tiresias he will change gender, he will appear "in woman's flesh and blood" ("The Pier-Glass," *CP* 102), and present his novel as her memoir. After all, as he had explained many years before, the true poet is as much a woman as a man—indeed, he is "a woman suffering all the hardships of a man; hardening her weak softnesses; healthy and clean, loving the elements, loving friends more than life itself, proud, whimsical, wise, simple."[19] As he begins work on Mary's story, "monstrous Milton" himself reappears as the author's familiar ghost: "I felt his ghost haunting my writing table with glowering eyes and minatory whispers," he says (*Asphodel* 315). He reappears as the reader over his shoulder, the ungentle critic who would sap all his articulate energy. But the old fusilier remains "undaunted" just as he did in the Great War. Determined to finally put this ghost to rest, the particular poet Graves calls to his aid is no longer Skelton but Shakespeare. As he does this, however, as he pursues his private struggle with Milton, he sows the seeds of considerable confusion among his reading public, "people in general," whether they be wartime academics, modern feminists, or working-class schoolboys.

Shakespeare and Milton's Wife

In *Good-Bye to All That*, Graves recorded that his first child, his daughter, the future actress and war correspondent Jenny Nicholson, was born on twelfth night 1919.[20] In 1941, as Graves began work on his novel, *Wife to Mr. Milton*, Jenny had put her life together, joined the RAF, and was remembered by her colleagues as "enchanting," "irresistible with her blonde hair (slightly longer than the approved length) shining eyes and vivacious mouth"; she had such intelligence, energy, and enthusiasm.[21] It seems no accident, then, that Graves's story of Mary or Marie Powell with her bright, fair hair, shining in the sun "like thin-drawn gold wire,"[22] should have a lot to do with his daughter—that the novel should begin with Marie's birthday on twelfth night 1641 and that it should be deeply engaged with Shakespeare's great play of the same name, *Twelfth Night; or, What You Will*. This seems especially likely since Graves, following the demands of middle-class taste and the elite literary criticism of Leavis and Eliot, increasingly feels comfortable in seeing Shakespeare as the antithesis of Milton, and the only point at which Milton seems overtly critical of Shakespeare is in a dispute over twelfth-night entertainments.

Shakespeare's play was performed twice at the royal palace of Whitehall during Milton's adolescence, once in April 1618 and once in February 1623. Charles I loved it, calling the play *Malvolio* in his annotated copy of the 1632 folio. At the height of the English revolution, Milton seems to remember the play in his 1649 pamphlet defending the king's execution, *Eikonoklastes*. Milton is at his most Gravesian or imperious in this work. There is no glory in writing against the king, he says disdainfully, for kings "most commonly," while strong in legions, are weak in arguments—indeed, since they are more practiced in the use of their will than reason, they "prove but weak and puny Adversaries."[23] The frontispiece of the late king's book, *Eikon Basilike,* is a case in point, he says. The image of the king kneeling piously in prayer, with its various mottos and cryptic symbols, looks all too theatrical, artificial, or inauthentic: "quaint Emblems and devices begg'd from the old Pageantry of some Twelf-nights entertainment at Whitehall," he insists, "will doe but ill to make a Saint or Martyr" (YP 3:343). By "Twelf-nights entertainment" he means masques like Jonson's *Masque of Augurs* or *Time Vindicated,* but it is hard to imagine that Shakespeare's play is completely out of his mind. Milton's apparent contempt for twelfth night and all it signifies seems to be the immediate trigger for Graves's satire against him. Not only twelfth-night festivities but Shakespeare himself, so it seems, is disparaged in the pamphlet: Shakespeare, not Scripture or any other kind of holy writing, was the king's closet companion in his solitudes, we are told, and the royal actor appears to have learned how to feign religion from Shakespeare's play, *Richard III.* But when read more carefully, the passage becomes increasingly conflicted.[24] Milton certainly appears to be criticizing the king for his association with Shakespeare, but he is also recognizing both the poet's power and his own long-standing admiration for England's great dramatist.[25] Most pointedly, for instance, the false king is not identified with Shakespeare so much as the king's own royal precursor, the Byzantine emperor, Andronicus Comnenus, a tyrant who had been a constant reader of Saint Paul and "by continual study had so incorporated the phrase & stile of that transcendent Apostle into all his familiar Letters, that the imitation seem'd to vie with the Original" (YP 3:361). Similarly, the king, a constant reader of Shakespeare, had incorporated the phrase and style of Shakespeare—but not so much of the dramatist himself as of his character, the tyrant Richard III. Thus, it might be argued that Shakespeare is to the king as Saint Paul is to the Byzantine tyrant, for as the emperor misuses Saint Paul, so the king misuses Shakespeare. Indeed, the playwright, like the apostle, leads us to the truth: as Shakespeare reveals Richard III "a deep dissembler," so, in Milton's text, he does Charles I (YP 3:362).

Even so, when placed in the context of Milton's apparent disparagement of twelfth-night entertainments, it is easy to see how Graves might miss the ambiguity, especially since he believes Shakespeare to be the very antithesis of Milton, the most important antidote to all that monster's bile: "With all possible deference to his admirers," Graves says in 1949, now trying hard to imagine his audience, "Milton was not a great poet, in the sense in which Shakespeare was great" (Asphodel 321). Poetry is ultimately about love, and while "Shakespeare loved greatly," Milton only hated: his sins may have been "petty by comparison with Shakespeare, but his lack of love, for all his rhetorical championship of love against lust, makes him detestable" (Asphodel 321). Accordingly, the most illuminating intertext for Graves's novel is not Miltonic, as one might expect, but Shakespearean. That is, Paradise Lost is less immediately helpful than Twelfth Night. In her understandable reliance on Milton's epic as the novel's principal intertext, even a critic as astute as Catherine Belsey is led astray by Graves's indifference to audience. Specifically, in Belsey's attempt to represent Graves's "irrepressible heroine" as what she feels must be "an unconscious repetition of the poem's own (unconscious?) account of Eve," her reading seems less than compelling.[26] Young as she is, Graves's Marie in her skeptical self-awareness, resourcefulness, and insistence on her genteel ancestry seems a long way from even an unconscious account of Milton's Eve in her naïveté and "unexperienced thought" (PL 4.457). Graves, unlike Belsey, it needs to be emphasized, is less interested in recovering or rehabilitating Milton than in crushing him. And so, since Shakespeare is the strongest weapon in Graves's armory, what he seems to offer in the novel is a new version of Twelfth Night, a version in which Marie plays a combination of Viola, Olivia, and Maria to Milton's Malvolio. This new play involves two key acts, one foregrounding a disturbing new fear of lower-class mobility and the other assuaging that fear by staging the trans-gendered resilience of art. In other words, Graves goes his own way, and, however inadvertently, a very real concern for gender equity or inter-gender openness is disconcertingly deployed in the service of reasserting class distinction.

Malvolio's Stockings and the Fear of Lower-Class Mobility

In defending the novel against the angry reaction of various academics, Graves insists that he had not recreated Milton as a stereotype or in the image of the "prick-eared Puritan of farce"; there is nothing "Hudibrastic" about his style, he argues (*Asphodel* 316). But then, of course, there is nothing Hudibrastic about Malvolio's style either. Shakespeare's Malvolio is certainly "a kind of Puritan,"[27] but more important, he's a social climber or upstart. The women whose remarkable agency drives the action of the play understand this straightaway. They are much more immediately perceptive than the men. While Malvolio's mistress, Olivia, has no difficulty identifying his "self-love" and "distempered" lack of grace (1.5.89–96), his fellow servant Maria is even more acute in recognizing his inordinate ambition: he is inconstant, "a time pleaser, an affectioned ass, that cons state without book, and utters it by great swarths" (2.3.146–48). Conning "state without book" means he has so incorporated the phrase and style of his superiors' authority into his everyday speech that his false imitation vies with the original. He is, however, so "affectioned" or self-absorbed that he misreads his social context every bit as much as he misreads the text of Maria's trick letter. That artful letter is itself a false imitation but one meant to disclose Malvolio's hypocrisy and the enormity of his secret desires. Its effectiveness is entirely contingent on the accuracy of Maria's insight, her precise reading of Malvolio. In other words, as Shakespeare's art reveals the king's political dissembling in *Eikonoklastes*, so Maria's art reveals Malvolio's social pretensions, and, most importantly, Marie Powell's art, specifically the insights and carefully constructed female perspective contained within her vellum-covered book, will reveal Milton's monstrous hypocrisy. He will be humiliated in the same way Malvolio is.

Both Malvolio and Graves's Milton are, then, inauthentic: they are described as renegades, turncoats who deny their faith or deepest convictions for advancement. When Malvolio reneges on his much-touted virtue, casts aside his godly demeanor and "respect of place, persons" (2.3.92–93) to betray his ludicrous fantasies in public, Maria can hardly contain herself: if you would "laugh yourself in stitches," she says to her confederates, "follow me. Yond gull Malvolio is turned heathen, a very renegado; for there is no Christian that means to be saved by believing rightly can ever believe such impossible passages of grossness. He's in yellow stockings!" (3.2.65–70). Similarly, in Marie Powell's eyes, says Graves, Milton is "a renegade Arminian and renegade Royalist" (*Asphodel* 316): she wonders why he befriends a scurrilous hack like Marchamont Needham, "with his leering looks and faithless heart"—unless, of course, she reflects, it is because he "himself has so often turned cat-in-pin, from Prelatist to Presbyterian, and from Presbyterian to Independent, that he sympathizes with all others of restless conscience" (*Wife* 379). More important than their inconstancy, or what Marie calls with such acid irony the "restlessness" of their consciences, is Milton and Malvolio's overweening desire for dominion. Before he makes an ass of himself in public, mincing and cross-gartered as he believes his mistress desires, Malvolio imagines himself "Count Malvolio": "Contemplation makes a rare turkey-cock of him," say those who overhear his reverie; it puffs him up and makes him strut "under his advanced plumes" (2.5.30–32). Having pleasured his mistress, leaving Olivia sleeping, so he fantasizes, he would "have the humor of state" and subject the household to the real authority he has so often only imitated (2.5.52). He would subject and humiliate all those around him. What arouses such intense antipathy, what makes him so abhorrent, is the threatening, invasive nature of the dominion he desires—he would take for himself what belongs to others. Social climbing is understood as a kind of theft, not only of property and status but also of one's very being. This is the source of Sir Toby's sense of outrage, and it is this that animates Graves's newly recharged hatred of Milton: the psychological danger "monstrous Milton" had come to articulate in the Great War is now reborn in terms of class. In the years between the First and Second World Wars, while Shakespeare increasingly came to represent the natural vitality and integrity of a middle-class English norm, Milton, through the criticism of Leavis, Eliot, Middleton Murry, Wilson Knight, and innumerable others, increasingly came to be seen not only as what Graves would call a "fake poet" but as a rank outsider, which is somewhat ironic for Graves, especially as he himself was seen as such in the trenches; much of Milton's verse, says Graves the officer and gentleman, is "downright vulgar" (*Asphodel* 321), not to mention peculiarly un-English.[28]

When "Mr. Melton the Younger," a wealthy scrivener's son with a coat of arms stolen from an old Shropshire family, comes to court Marie Powell, a gentleman's daughter of seven descents, he behaves exactly as Malvolio hopes to behave. "Melton" shows no sense of class deference, no respect of place or persons (*Wife* 144–45). Although only a "mushroom gentleman," he is every bit as self-assured as he was when he first met Marie many years before. At the entrance to the Royal Manor in Kidlington in 1636, so she records in her book, he wore "light grey silk stockings" (46) and assumed the humor of state: his face showed an inexpressible quality of "such haughtiness and conscious power that he seemed to stand there in arrogation of an ancient claim to be the rightful Lord of the Manor — even though the whole country acknowledged it to the King's own" (41). He is the social climber Graves imagines in his satire on Jacob Bronowski in "Dream of a Climber," a poem originally entitled "Jacob's Ladder" and published in 1942, the same year as *Wife to Mr. Milton*. Graves loathed Bronowski, a wealthy Jewish haberdasher's son and graduate, like "Melton," of Cambridge. Unlike the patriarch, this Jacob "raises his own ladder" whose "nosings," says Graves in an anti-Semitic aside, are "of pure brass" (*CP* 392). He is more than willing to push himself to the top and take what is not his own, his very masculine, "muscular broad hands a-glint in the sun, / And crampons on his feet" (*CP* 392). Similarly, young "Melton" would claw his way to the top, taking Marie Powell and her golden hair in repayment for a debt and destroying the middle-class idyll of England's organic Forest Hill. Graves's Forest Hill occupies the same place in bourgeois England's imaginary as Pook's Hill—Powell and Pressburger's Chillingbourne in *A Canterbury Tale* (1944), Eliot's East Coker in the *Four Quartets* (1944), or Evelyn Waugh's country house in *Brideshead Revisited* (1945), sacred places constantly threatened by lower-class, urban philistinism. It is associated with Shakespeare not only through the novel's engagement with *Twelfth Night* but also because it is redolent with memories of *A Midsummer Night's Dream*: it is the place where fairies "danced under the moon in our grandmothers' days," says Marie's real lover, "Mun," the fusilierlike Captain Edmund Verney (*Wife* 36). The metaphor that announces its destruction, the figure that assimilates social climbing, utilitarian ratiocination, and monstrous Milton, is grinding.

When Milton begins the actual process of courtship at Marie's uncle's house at Sandford on the Thames, he seems considerably older than his 33 years. In fact, he seems like "Old Mr. Philosopher" from the war poetry, "Making monstrous mouths" and "Braying like an ass" (*CP* 33). Like Ben and Claire, Marie and her brother James are subjected to his play. But his motives are anything but lighthearted: fun becomes intellectual labor, courtship debate, and what might have been an open-ended discussion of fossils becomes a matter of rational grinding. Milton pronounces "his *r*'s very hard" (*Wife* 47), just as he does in Aubrey's *Brief Lives,* and one of his favorite locutions is "I should have ground you to powder" had you made that argument (*Wife* 158).[29] When James has the temerity to disagree with Milton and imagine the scallop-shaped fossils as the imprints of oysters "driven outwards towards the outer rim of the Earth" by the backwash of Noah's flood, Milton turns on him. Misunderstanding James and mistaking the stone itself for the imprint, Milton crushes him: "Here, Sirrah, take this poor scallop as a gift," he says, offering James the stone fossil—"Eat, eat!

Break your teeth upon the sweet meat under shell!" As the conversation progresses, he appears increasingly overbearing, gigantic, a mighty "monologian" (*Wife* 161). In a wonderfully suggestive article, Ian McCormick is acute in noticing Milton's preoccupation with giants in this passage.[30] The great bone, unlike the fossils found at Headington quarry, is not, says Milton, a stone *sui generis* "naturally moulded by an extraordinary plastic virtue latent in the Earth" (*Wife* 155), but a real bone, the remnant of a giant like Goegmagog, so substantiating the truth of Geoffrey of Monmouth's *Historia regum Britanniae*, a history "so glorious to our nation" (*Wife* 160). Our giants, so it seems, are taller than Goliath and, as Marie observes, upstart Milton longs to join their company: by taking religion and grinding down all opposition, he hoped, she says, "to add four or five cubits to [his stature] and straddle any hall or court like a Colossus of Rhodes" (*Wife* 182). All rivals, intellectuals, and poets, including the "scandalous buffoon" Skelton, are dismissed out of hand (*Wife* 171). By the end of the novel, having ground down his wife, he triumphs over Europe's first scholar, the mighty Salmasius. Having reneged on true poetry for polemic, Milton becomes the Goliath he would slay: "my husband scorned the use of a sling-shot to sink him in cowardly fashion after the manner of David; but had come against him with the customary weapons of a scholar-warrior and beaten him at his own sword-play, piercing him through and through; and had, as it were, given the finishing stroke with Goliath's own tuck" (*Wife* 386). The gigantic figure of Milton, which had originally identified ratiocination and "fake poetry" with the horrors of war, now identifies them with the insidious threat of class mobility. In Graves's renewed but much less neurasthenic agon, the crucial point of resistance in *Wife to Mr. Milton* is the trans-gendered resilience of art, Marie Powell and the story she tells in her vellum book.

Marie's Hair and the Trans-Gendered Resilience of Art

The Shakespearean plot of *Wife to Mr. Milton* is intensified by Graves's complex engagement with Dickens's great 1850 novel,

David Copperfield. Despite the arrogance with which he dismisses Dickens's prolixity, Graves loved the novel and in 1933 he rewrote and published it as *The Real David Copperfield*.[31] The influence of the novel is immediately apparent in Graves's story of Marie Powell, even in details like the titles of chapters: Dickens's chapter 4, for instance, has the same deeply ironic title as Graves's chapter 8—"I Fall into Disgrace." More importantly, the influence is evident in the way Marie's unhappy marriage to Milton is imagined in terms of Clara Copperfield's doomed marriage to the monstrous Edward Murdstone, another nightmare figure, "deep mouthed and black haired," an upstart who would, like Malvolio, take for himself what belongs to others.[32] On arrival in London Marie and her faithful servant Trunco, a figure like Sergeant Lamb who knows her station in life, become prisoners in Milton's house just as Clara and her faithful servant Peggotty become prisoners in what soon becomes Murdstone's house. Just as Murdstone's sister Jane becomes the jailer in Dickens's story, so Milton's housekeeper Jane becomes the jailer in Graves's novel—Jane Murdstone appropriates the "management of the household" just as Jane Yates refuses to give it up.[33] There is nothing of the resilience of *Twelfth Night*'s female agents in the child-like Clara Copperfield, and she is ground down by the brutal "firmness" of her husband and his sister. Dickens's representation of the relentless way Clara's desire for affection is exploited by Murdstone is the stuff of great art. It transcends gender boundaries to suggest how a male writer might imagine the embodied experience of a woman's suffering. The pathos of the way Clara's body and spirit are broken by Murdstone's desire to train her as he would an animal, to possess her and the "bright curls" of her hair as his own, is unbearable (*DC* 28). But thanks to Shakespeare, Graves's Marie is made of sterner stuff.

Like Murdstone, but for different reasons, Graves's Milton is intensely attracted by his wife's hair: "Your hair delights the eye, pretty Child," says Milton. "Without doubt, Eve had tresses like yours" (*Wife* 173). But Marie is no child-wife, and from the beginning she senses that this attraction is obsessive, amounting to some peculiarly dangerous form of envy. He would have for himself what belongs to others. Marie records in her book "how angry a man he was," how "like an avenging angel's his face" was, and she remembers from an old sermon "how a woman's hair should be covered" for "fear of the angels" (57). This particular "angel-faced" young man, she says, "eyed my hair (which I wore naked of any hat or kerchief) with a certain hard fury as though it were of offence to him" (58). The specific text the old sermon recalls is Saint Paul's first letter to the Corinthians, a text in which the apostle is determined to assert the hierarchy of gender, the dominion of men over women: "Neither was the man created for the woman; but the woman for the man." For this reason, "the woman should cover her head"; she should, he says darkly, "have power on her head because of the angels" (1 Cor. 11:9–10). In the same way that *Twelfth Night* refuses any such hierarchy, so Graves's novel stages a rebellion against both it and the monstrous Bronowski-like angel who would enforce it. Both Shakespeare's play and Graves's novel produce art that is gendered or trans-gendered in the very specific sense that, like Tiresias, men become women and women men; they see the world in more than one dimension and expand the plenitude of human experience. This inter-gender openness is the point of Twelfth Night, both the feast and the play: that in turning the world upside down it opens it out and "sets it to rights." As some part of the real Milton, the Lady of Christ's, the complex and conflicted Milton unavailable to Graves, would do, twelfth night would undo custom and open "the womb of teeming Truth" (YP 2:224).

Like Viola, the intensely feminine, fairylike Marie is more than willing to play the man's part. At the beginning of the novel, she pointedly dares to appear in man's clothing on twelfth night: "I affected" the role of a cavalier, she says, "a modern godamme blade, wearing a tall ribboned hat with narrow brim and great plume" (*Wife* 15). As Viola's literal cross-dressing as Cesario renders Duke Orsino's insistence on gender hierarchy ludicrous, so Marie's figurative or authorial cross-dressing as an independent-minded memoirist who will not be limited to women's issues does the same for Milton's. Marie's vellum book is not simply an account of "the small particulars" that a "young gentlewoman" would write but the kind of grand-scale memoir her father would have her write—a history of her life and opinions, of England's "bloody Troubles," and the passing of an age, or what her father calls the "brave old days" (40, 12–13). When Orsino unclasps "the book even of my secret soul" (1.4.13–14) to the cross-dressed Viola, all he reveals is a mind full of fancy's shapes (1.1.14–15); but when Marie unclasps her book to us she reveals a mind every bit as acute as the trans-gendered mind of Viola/Cesario.

Both Viola and Marie are made to listen to their future husbands hold forth on gender relations. While Orsino lectures on the emotional inadequacy of women, Graves's Milton explains their moral limitations. Graves has learned from Shakespeare, and in both cases the acuity of the female listener ironizes and subverts the authority of the male speaker. When Viola (as Cesario) urges Orsino to see past gender difference and realize that Olivia might not love him just as he might not love a female suitor, he refuses. The parallel is impossible, he insists, talking man to man, because no woman could love as he does. Indeed, women in general cannot love as men do:

> There is no woman's sides
> Can bide the beating of so strong a passion
> As love doth give my heart; no woman's heart
> So big, to hold so much: they lack retention.   (2.4.94–97)

The irony is, of course, that the long-suffering Viola confounds Orsino's assertion by performing the very "retention" he speaks of *as he speaks*, sitting like "Patience on a monument, / Smiling at grief" (2.4.115–16). Similarly, when Marie suggests that Milton's representation of Eve in his projected epic denies her any kind of conscience or independent moral agency, the pattern repeats itself. Milton, like "Old Mr. Philosopher" or Murdstone, rounds on her: "Certain is it that a woman cannot be any better conditioned, as to her soul, than the man with whom she is united in flesh." A woman can only be as good as the man she marries—if he falls, she falls, but if she falls, he may save himself by separating from her, just as "Scripture requires him to pluck out an eye that offends him, or hew off an offensive hand" (*Wife* 180). Unlike Clara Copperfield,

Marie is unmoved by her husband's brutality, and her skeptical response undermines Milton's assertion by enacting precisely the independent moral acuity he claims to be impossible in a woman: "This is a hard conclusion," she says in disbelief, pointing to the ludicrous practical consequences of his assertion, "and a rough warning to fathers to marry their daughters to men of good principle" (180). Despite his protestations to the contrary in works like *The Common Asphodel*, Graves is, of course, cavalier in his reading, or perhaps deliberately willful in his misreading, of the real Milton. He is not constrained by the demands of audience, learned or otherwise. He writes as though he were talking to a single person, someone like himself, indifferent to the subtleties of class and knowing full well how much he will annoy academics. In doing so, however, he liberates Marie and establishes what is for him the larger principle of a Tiresias-like, trans-gendered art, the resilience of which paradoxically protects social distinction and puts upwardly mobile, lower-class masculinists, like his version of Milton, in their place.

The crowning, Malvolio-like humiliation of Graves's Milton is his wedding night in Reading on the way to London. Both Malvolio and Milton are the victims of their own self-absorbed ambition, and because of this their insensitivity to gender is exacerbated by misreading. In order to make themselves sexually successful they both go by the book. Malvolio, says Maria, appears like "a pedant that keeps school i' th' church," that is, he "does obey every point of the letter that I dropped to betray him" (3.2.72–75). Milton is equally pedantic following the letter of Scripture as though its poetry were a series of magical injunctions. He does not wear yellow stockings, but, as Marie reports, he sprinkles the wedding bed's coverlet with gold dust, lights a menorah, and fills the bridal chamber with wine and flowers from the Song of Songs. If he is to be a great epic poet, he tells Marie, he has to embrace the chastity of a scriptural marriage; Leviticus tells him his wife should be a virgin and the Song directs the performance of his love-making. He climbs into bed with a Bible and reads from Solomon, his holy manual. The effect is every bit as ludicrous as that of Malvolio's cross-gartered wooing. As he becomes excited, Milton speaks "very lover-like and sweetly" to Marie; unfortunately, it's "in some foreign language, which sounded so uncouth that I believe it to have been the Syriac or the Aramaic" (*Wife* 191). She is finally overwhelmed not by passion but by nausea, the sickening effect of the wine and the flowers' "heavy fragrance" (192). Her headache leads her to suspect the onset of her period, *the flowers,* and when she asks for water, the erect Milton is crushed: "he looked chapfallen and incredulous and knew not what to say" (192). The bathos of the scene is caught in her memory of coupling dogs doused with water: the "bitch's rut" is cooled in a moment, and "as for Jack the greyhound, he stood shivering in a foolish manner which made us all laugh, and then began to howl" (192). In the case of both Malvolio and Milton's foolishness, all the world holds its sides in laughter: "What could be dafter / Than John Skelton's laughter?" (*CP* 43) Graves might exult. His passion interrupted, the prescriptions of Scripture frustrated, and in fear of pollution from Marie's menstrual cycle, monstrous Milton is left in tears. "Very early in the morning," says Marie, "I was awakened by a sound which affrighted me, as of a man weeping" (194).

What we are offered here is not just the crushing of Goliath-like Milton or the exorcism of his ghost, but the triumph of an art that is Tiresias-like in its ability to embrace the experience of both men and women. As Graves heals himself, so he produces great art. While Graves succeeds in imagining the embodied experience of a woman, Milton fails. The monstrosity of Graves's Milton lies in the paradox that while he seems to understand Tiresias's virtues in principle, his own masculinist needs deny him any access to their fullness. When we first meet Milton, he identifies himself "as Tiresias" (*Wife* 48), but as he demonstrates his command of Echo's effects, the nymph becomes his solipsistic ideal, a travesty of cross-gendered discourse: "the nymph, being a woman," he says, "had the good manners neither to be the first to begin a conversation, nor to refrain from a reply when decently addressed" (47). Returning to the recurring topic of Marie's hair, he later explains his own curious boyhood experience of losing his hair: I became "feeble and womanish, with headaches, megrims, and ill vapours ascending from the stomach to the brain, and also I conceived strange amatory fancies for persons of my own sex" (176). He recognizes the practical value of this gender change: "Doubtless, the poet Tiresias," who "became for a while a woman in body was, when at last he was restored to masculinity, the better poet for his long unmanning; for the power to put apt speeches in the mouths of women is necessary for the complete poet" (176). But if this ability comes at the long-term expense of one's hair, he feels sure, it is extremely dangerous, for in the male's hair "resides the holy masculine virtue of man," his Samson-like vigor, boldness, and power to achieve (176). A woman's hair is similarly "her crowning glory," the guarantee of her femininity (177). Hair is, then, the marker of gender difference, but because it's the same for both men and women, it is a profoundly unstable signifier. Milton's problem is not "trichomania," as Graves routinely claims,[34] but the degree to which Marie's hair constitutes "an offence" (58). Her beautiful hair, like her bold spirit, compromises difference and undermines the integrity of Milton's existential commitment to Pauline gender hierarchy. Milton's marriage to Marie is the only way he can contain this threat: "your hair became an obsession of my mind," he says, "it wreathed itself between my eye and whatsoever book I read." Sensation obscured sense: its "gadding or serpentine motion" routinely choked "the sense of my reading," even of Scripture (174). Only by possessing Marie's hair in marriage, he continues, would it cease to plague him. This is why his wedding night humiliation is so important—it subverts his attempt at containment. Marie cannot be possessed and the deconstruction of gender hierarchy at the center of Marie's book cannot be constrained.

Graves's Milton

Who is Graves's Milton? It is surprising how little Graves's engagement with Milton tells us about the seventeenth century poet and how much it tells us about Graves. This paradox, so my argument seeks to suggest, is a function of Graves's indifference to audience and preoccupation with his own inner life. Graves's Milton is very much a projection of himself or, rather, those parts of himself that need to be exorcized. Graves's first biographer, his nephew, Richard Graves, is acute on this point: *Wife to Mr. Milton* displays "the kind of virulent hatred [toward Milton] that betrays some deeply personal motive."[35] Indeed, in expressing this hatred, Graves was "holding up a mirror to the dark side of his soul."[36] Graves's Milton has all the younger poet's own residual masculinism and arrogance: "With the poet," Graves confesses, "there is always the tinge of arrogance in the thought that his own poetry has a lasting quality which most of his contemporaries cannot claim."[37] Most importantly, however, Milton is a projection of Graves's inner wounds, of the trauma or "profound mental disturbance," the threat of mental disintegration he experienced in the First World War. Milton comes to represent all those forces that would destroy his inner life, that endanger his way of being in the world—the war itself, but also his own weaknesses, the consciousness that falsifies poetry, the ratiocination that stands in the way of his articulating his deepest feelings, the very means by which he might contest the destructive power of his war experience. Monstrous Milton is always with him. The elder poet's looming threat is reborn in the fear of an invasive class mobility, the specter of Bronowski and the upstart scrivener's son; it is a mobility that is routinely and confusingly identified with masculinism. Graves is an intensely male kind of feminist. The feminism is every bit as real as Catherine Belsey senses, but it is more conflicted. What is most liberating about *Wife to Mr. Milton* is this desire to see things through women's eyes—something deep in Graves that led him to Nancy Nicholson, Laura Riding, and finally to the White Goddess. It is difficult not to be moved by Graves's imagination of Marie's Shakespearean defiance of monstrous Milton. The crowning irony is, however, that while Graves's indifference to audience allows him to step outside his own masculinism and go some way toward becoming Tiresias, this extraordinary feat remains subtly but powerfully class-oriented. Graves's Marie, like Jane Austen's Elizabeth Bennet, is always already and emphatically a "gentleman's daughter."

University of Toronto / Jesus College, Oxford

NOTES

1. Douglas L. Howard, "*National Lampoon's Animal House* and the Fraternity of Milton," in *Milton in Popular Culture,* ed. Laura Lunger Knoppers and Gregory M. Colón Semenza (New York, 2006), 165.

2. Harold Bloom, *A Map of Misreading* (New York, 1975), 9.

3. Works like *Milton in Popular Culture* make it clear not only how limited Bloom's model is but just how rich and pervasive are the patterns of Miltonic adaptation and re-figuration in contemporary culture, everywhere from movies to graphic novels. They indicate the extraordinary strength with which Milton continues to live in this constant process of renewal and re-creation. See Paul Stevens, "Milton and the Marginalization of the Humanities," *Milton Quarterly* 50, no. 2 (October 2016).

4. "Robert Graves, "The Art of Poetry No. 11," interview by Peter Buckman and William Fifield, *Paris Review* 47 (1969), http://www.theparis review.org/interviews/4178/the-art-of-poetry-no-11-robert-graves.

5. Robert Graves, foreword to *Poems 1938–45,* qtd. in J. M. Cohen, *Robert Graves* (London, 1960), 1. Cf. John Carey, *The Intellectuals and the Masses: Pride and Prejudice among the Literary Intelligentsia, 1880–1939* (London, 1992), which analyzes the distinction between writing poetry for an elite and prose for the new mass audience produced by the introduction of universal education and the resultant rise in literacy.

6. Robert Graves, foreword to *Ha! Ha! Among the Trumpets,* by Alun Lewis (London, 1945), 7.

7. Consider how he describes the love life of working-class people in Lancaster to a close friend in a verse letter after first joining the army in 1914:

> The pale townsfolk
> Crawl and kiss and cuddle,
> in doorways hug and huddle;
> Loutish he
> And sluttish she
> In loathsome love together press
> And unbelievable ugliness.

Qtd. in Richard Perceval Graves, *Robert Graves: The Assault Heroic, 1895–1926* (New York, 1990), 116. My point is that even in the prose, and even in his "socialist" days, this basic distance from working-class people doesn't really change: Graves is always conscious of being a gentleman, of "being bourgeois myself" (209).

8. John Carey, *The Unexpected Professor: An Oxford Life in Books* (London, 2014), 150.

9. Siegfried Sassoon, *Memoirs of an Infantry Officer* (1930; repr., London, 1978); hereafter cited in the text.

10. See *Over the Brazier* (1916), *Goliath and David* (1916), and *Fairies and Fusiliers* (1917). Graves's poetry is quoted from *The Complete Poems,*

ed. Beryl Graves and Dunstan Ward (1995; repr., London, 2003); hereafter cited in the text as *CP* with page number.

11. Wilfred Owen, *The War Poems*, ed. Jon Silkin (London, 1994), 123.

12. Cf. *Paradise Lost* 1.304–13. Milton's poetry is quoted from John Milton, *Paradise Lost*, 2nd ed., ed. Alastair Fowler (London, 1998).

13. The giant is there as early as the *Red Branch Song Book*, poems composed by Graves's mother for her children. In one of these, "The Lost Child," a small boy with no clothes on is beaten savagely by a giant who "got tired of this very soon / And left him under the silver moon, / I need not say he ran home fast / And was safe in his mother's arms at last" (qtd. in R. P. Graves, *Assault Heroic*, 38). See also Frank Kersnowski, *The Early Poetry of Robert Graves: The Goddess Beckons* (Austin, Tex., 2002), esp. 44–46.

14. In *Poetic Unreason and Other Studies* (London, 1925), 139–55, Graves spends almost a whole chapter explaining the relation between his childhood cat dream, "the central terror of which is an enormous half-human cat" (142), and his war-induced neurasthenia.

15. On the significance of Babylon as "Babyland," see Graves, *Poetic Unreason*, 31–34.

16. Robert Graves, *The Common Asphodel* (1949; repr., New York, 1970); hereafter cited in the text.

17. Although Graves fully understands what he calls the public or classical "ideal of poetry," an ideal "which by conforming to system without losing its power of emotional appeal could be used for purposes of civic education," his romantic preoccupation with self-expression is intensified as he increasingly comes to see it as the poet's peculiar means of personal, psychological healing (Graves, *Poetic Unreason*, esp. 125–26).

18. Laura Riding, *Lives of Wives* (New York, 1939), 5.

19. Letter to Robert Nichols, February 2, 1917, qtd. in R. P. Graves, *Assault Heroic*, 169.

20. Robert Graves, *Good-Bye to All That*, ed. R. P. Graves (Oxford, 1995), 249.

21. Jenny's colleague Maureen Pilling qtd. in Richard Perceval Graves, *Robert Graves and the White Goddess, 1940–85* (London, 1995), 35–36.

22. Robert Graves, *Wife to Mr. Milton* (1942; repr., London, 1985), 35; hereafter cited in the text.

23. John Milton, *Eikonoklastes*, in *Complete Prose Works of John Milton*, 8 vols., ed. Don M. Wolfe et al. (New Haven, Conn., 1953–82), 3:337–38. Milton's prose works are from this volume, hereafter cited in the text as YP.

24. Nicholas McDowell, "Milton's Regicide Tracts and the Uses of Shakespeare," in *The Oxford Handbook of Milton*, ed. Nicholas McDowell and Nigel Smith (Oxford, 2009), 252–71.

25. Paul Stevens, "Subversion and Wonder in Milton's Epitaph on Shakespeare," *English Literary Renaissance* 19, no. 3 (1989): 375–88.

26. Catherine Belsey, "Reading Graves Reading Milton," in *John Milton: Language, Gender, Power* (Oxford, 1988), 58–63; and Paul Stevens, review of *John Milton: Language, Gender, Power, Journal of English and Germanic Philology* 89, no. 3 (1990): 404–07.

27. William Shakespeare, *Twelfth Night,* ed. J. M. Lothian and T. W. Craik (London, 2003), 2.3.140.

28. For Carey's instructive portrait of Graves in 1969, see *Unexpected Professor,* esp. 242.

29. John Aubrey, *Aubrey's Brief Lives,* ed. Oliver Lawson Dick (Harmondsworth, U.K., 1982), 274.

30. Ian McCormick, "Graves's Milton," in *New Perspectives on Robert Graves,* ed. Patrick J. Quinn (London, 1999), 136–45.

31. Robert Graves, *The Real David Copperfield* (London, 1933).

32. Charles Dickens, *David Copperfield,* ed. Jeremy Tambling (London, 2004), 55; hereafter cited in the text as *DC.*

33. Nothing is known of Milton's servant Jane Yates, but Graves seems to have picked up this way of representing her from an offhand remark by David Masson: Milton moved to "the house in Aldersgate with Jane Yates to keep it in order." David Masson, *The Life of John Milton,* 8 vols. (London, 1871), 2:208.

34. Buckman and Fifield, "Art of Poetry No. 11".

35. R. P. Graves, *Graves and the White Goddess,* 37.

36. Ibid., 39.

37. Qtd. in R. P. Graves, *Graves and the White Goddess,* 40.

Milton's Phylacteries:
Textual Idolatry and
the Beginnings of Critical Exegesis

Raphael Magarik

What does John Milton mean when he refers to phylacteries, as he does four times in his poetry and prose?[1] Editorial
glosses typically identify both the physical referent of this obscure
word and its symbolic significance. Here, for instance, is Martin
Dzelzainis's note on the mention of "phylactery" in *Tenure of Kings
and Magistrates*: "A phylactery is a small vellum box containing
four texts from Deuteronomy and Exodus worn by Jews at morning
prayer as a sign of strict obedience. For Milton it symbolizes the
ostentatious display of righteousness."[2] There are two problems
here. First, Dzelzainis's definition semantically fixes a word whose
meaning for Christians was changing in the seventeenth century,
its reference narrowing from an ill-defined and general category of
amulets to a specific Jewish ritual object. Closing off that history,
I claim, obscures the reasons why Milton chose such a recondite
and antiquarian metaphor. Second, Dzelzainis provides the entire
communicative sequence, clarifying both the material vehicle and
its symbolic tenor. But since phylacteries are worn as signs ("a sign

upon your hand" is the language used in Deuteronomy 6:8), the metaphorical use of "phylactery" is a sign about signs. It thus seems plausible that when Milton used the image of phylacteries, he intended to draw the reader's attention to the process of interpretation, to the work required to travel from signifier to signified. If so, straightforwardly glossing Milton's use of "phylactery" glosses over a thorny problem.

Milton's uses of "phylactery" reflect a deep theoretical worry about signs and interpretation. Radical Protestants typically privileged religious reading and interpretation, which offered both an alternative and a corrective to idolatrous religious practices centered on objects and physical ritual. But, I claim, both in his discussions of phylacteries and more broadly, Milton takes Protestant iconoclasm a step further, worrying about the possibility of textual idolatry.[3] That is, readers might reify the biblical word inappropriately and, suspending their critical reasoning faculties, essentially worship it as an object rather than interpret it intellectually. Milton thus uses phylacteries to name the danger that readers will confuse a text's spirit and its letter, falling into a carnal, fetishistic mode of interpretation. In its most radical form, this concept of a textual idol subjects even religiously revealed truth to a rigorous skepticism, producing from Protestant iconoclasm an epistemological caution against accepting the authority of the biblical text itself.

Thus, for Milton, a serious theological and exegetical error underwrites the deviant practice of phylacteries. My argument both builds upon and reorients existing scholarship on Milton and Judaism. The only study devoted to Milton's use of phylacteries is by Mathew Biberman, who recognizes the importance of the Hebraist context but, attempting to establish Milton's philo-Semitism, strays into speculative and ungrounded readings.[4] This temptation to render Milton a closet Jew has long haunted the study of his debts to the Hebrew Bible and rabbinic literature.[5] Critics naturally desire to cleanse the great poet of apparent, embarrassing prejudice and also to substantiate Matthew Arnold's famous, none-too-flattering characterization of Milton as a Hebraic Puritan.[6] And the unspoken goal of diagnosing Milton's Jewishness persists, even as scholars have grown more cautious in estimating Milton's knowledge of Hebrew literature and more sophisticated in their assessments of his "Hebraism." So, for instance, while Jason Rosenblatt has advanced our understanding of Milton immeasurably by identifying and studying in detail his key Hebraist source, the great English philologist and classicist John Selden, Rosenblatt's conclusions from those materials nonetheless often follow the basic structure of traditional studies of Milton and Judaism. By arguing, for instance, that Milton believed the Mosaic law was in harmonious application in prelapsarian Eden, Rosenblatt produces a far more convincing and sophisticated portrait of a nonetheless recognizable type: the Hebraic, or at least Hebraish, Milton.[7] Similarly, Jeffrey Shoulson, who is skeptical of any specific, direct links between Milton and a particular corpus of rabbinic texts, argues instead that Milton's thought, in its recombination of elements from multiple, conflicting cultures, its responses to theological-political defeat, and its emphasis on human-divine dialogue, is an "uncanny recapitulation" of the rabbinic intellectual program in midrash.[8] Substituting analogies for allusions offers a safer answer to the question, "How is Milton Jewish?"

But in the wake of Rosenblatt's research on Selden, and the broader resurgence of scholarly interest in early modern Christian Hebraism, we can abandon the search for the Hebraic Milton.[9] The establishment of Milton's interest in and engagement with Hebraist scholars has paradoxically undermined the validity of the Hebrew sources themselves as context for his work. Hebraism provides an alternate interpretive community and context for what an earlier, less historically sensitive criticism would regard as "Jewish" sources. Hebraists studied and constituted *their own* canon. When the great scholar Joseph Scaliger calls Maimonides *"solum illum inter Judaeos desiisse nugari,"*[10] or when the English Hebraist John Lightfoot frequently insults Jews,[11] they remind us that a fascination with and mastery of rabbinic texts need not imply any particular sympathy with Jews or even with the corpus of classical rabbinic literature. Hebraists need not be Hebraic.

Instead, we should investigate Milton's interest in Hebrew texts by asking why Hebraists and their readers turned to Jewish texts: Which *Christian* theological and cultural problems and practices made them useful? By reading phylacteries through Milton's larger concerns with interpretation and idolatry, we highlight the context Milton's contemporaries brought to their study of phylacteries.

My argument has three steps. First, I trace the history of phylacteries, focusing on questions of signification. Jewish phylacteries, referred to here as the Hebrew *tephillin* to distinguish them from the unstable English word, were foundationally about signification and become the subject of arguments about how to read the Bible. But Christians often understood phylacteries as either magical amulets or prideful displays. In seventeenth century England, the spread of exact knowledge about Jewish ritual due to Christian Hebraism made available the link between phylacteries and textual interpretation, as a Reformation-induced crisis of signification made that link compelling.[12] Second, I turn to Milton, particularly his use of "phylactery." After surveying the word's appearances in Milton's prose, I analyze its most vexed instance, in "On the New Forcers of Conscience under the Long Parliament," a sonnet I read as being concerned with the hermeneutic dangers in texts and words. Milton uses phylacteries to highlight the dangers of idolatrous reading. Finally, I argue that textual idolatry has a broader purchase in Milton's thought. What might seem to be Milton's narrow concern about a specific Jewish practice in fact represents a persistent Miltonic concern about interpretation that, in the end, undermines even the Bible's textual authority.

The Word Made Leather: Jewish Tephillin as Signs about Signs

A central theme surrounding Jewish tephillin is representation, and in particular the question: how do material signifiers represent religious ideas? This problem is implicit in the Pentateuchal texts that the rabbis understood to command the binding of tephillin: Exodus 13:9 and 13:16 and Deuteronomy 6:8 and 11:18. Here is the first such reference, given with its immediate context:

Seven days thou shalt eat unleavened bread, and in the seventh day shall be a feast to the Lord. Unleavened bread shall be eaten seven days; and there shall no leavened bread be seen with thee, neither shall there be leaven seen with thee in all thy quarters. And thou shalt shew thy son in that day, saying, "This is done because of that which the Lord did unto me when I came forth out of Egypt." And it shall be for a sign unto thee upon thine hand, and for a memorial between thine eyes, that the Lord's law may be in thy mouth: for with a strong hand hath the Lord brought thee out of Egypt. (Exod. 13:6–9)[13]

The basic problem is "it" in Exodus 13:9, which refers, according the canonical rabbinic reading, to tephillin.[14] Of course, bracketing that legal tradition, the referent seems more likely to be either the retelling of the Exodus narrative to one's child or the eating of unleavened bread. Thus, the sign on the hand would be not a physical sign but only a metaphor for a sign. But even in a minimalist reading, the passage plays on the idea of the sign, intermixing letter and figure. Exodus moves from using body parts figuratively ("a sign unto thee upon thine hand," and "a memorial between thine eyes,") to using them literally, since either the unleavened bread or the retelling would actually instantiate "the Lord's law ... in thy mouth." As such, the ambiguity between bread and words seems deliberate, running together a straightforwardly physical symbol and the embodied, quasi-material presence of language. Note that in the second possibility the passage presents a nested sequence of signifiers, since the unleavened bread signifies the content of the addressee's speech to his child, which then in turn becomes itself a sign. Finally, the addressee's hand is implicitly connected to God's, which can also plausibly be meant either literally or figuratively. Even as Exodus commands the creation of memorial signs, it suggests the complexity and potential confusions of signification.

In a sense, then, the playful nuances of the biblical verses anticipate the dispute between rabbinic readers, who took the verses literally to mandate tephillin, and a series of unorthodox readers who took them as figures. But even rabbinic literalists seem attentive to the meta-figural dimension of the purported tephillin verses. That is in part because, as Elizabeth Shanks Alexander shows, rabbis of the Tannaitic and Amoraic periods (0–200 and 200–500 CE, roughly) saw tephillin as part of a nexus of commandments that constituted "ritual Torah study." That is, wearing tephillin provided a nonintellectual, repetitive practice of performing a particular relation to biblical texts.[15] I will add a small example, useful in distinguishing rabbinic tephillin from traditional Christian ideas about phylacteries. For the passages in the tephillin amulets, the rabbis chose to include the four biblical passages that they interpreted to mandate tephillin.[16] Doing so is only one way to fulfill Deuteronomy 11:18, which commands, "Therefore shall ye lay up *these my words* in your heart and in your soul, and bind them for a sign upon your hand, that they may be as frontlets between your eyes."[17] By interpreting "these my words" to refer to the tephillin verses themselves, and thus placing them in the amulets, rabbinic readers made tephillin self-recursive signs about signs.

This peculiar metatextuality becomes clearest in challenges to the rabbinic interpretation of the purported tephillin verses. Non-Pharisaic Second Temple sects and, centuries later, Karaite readers presented elaborate arguments rejecting the practice of tephillin and favoring figurative interpretation of these verses.[18] Similarly, the iconoclastic, twelfth century "plain sense" interpreter Rabbi Samuel ben Meir (Rashbam)[19] advocated reading Exodus 13:9 figuratively, at least in theory: "'for a sign on your hand'—According to the depth of its plain sense, [the verse means] 'it will be to you for a memorial always, as if it were written on your hand,' along the pattern of 'as a seal upon thy heart, [as a seal upon thine arm]'" (Cant. 8:6).[20] Rashbam uses the curious phrase "the depth of its plain sense" because he recognizes the apparent irony in claiming that the verse's literal sense is figurative. Indeed, another twelfth century "plain sense" exegete, Rabbi Abraham Ibn Ezra, probably responding to Karaite readers, exploits this point to buttress the orthodox interpretation:

> There are those who disagree with our holy forefathers, who say "for a sign and a memorial" [i.e., they read "sign" figuratively], in the manner of "For they shall be a chaplet of grace unto thy head, and chains about thy neck" (Prov. 1:9). And also [they read] "And you shalt bind them for a sign upon your hand" (Deut. 6:8) like

"Bind them continually upon your heart, tie them about your neck" (Prov. 6:21).[21] ...And what does it mean that it will be "for a sign and a memorial"? That it will roll off your tongue that God took you out of Egypt with an outstretched hand. But this is not the correct way, for in the beginning of the book [of Proverbs] it is written, "the proverbs [or allegories] of Solomon," and thus everything he mentions is by way of allegory. But it is not written in the Pentateuch that it is by way of allegory, God forbid, only that it is according to its received sense, and thus we should not remove it from its plain sense, for its received sense does not contradict common sense, as does "and you shall circumcise the foreskin of your hearts" (Deut. 10:16), which requires fixing according to common sense.[22]

Ibn Ezra identifies the "plain sense" with the literal meaning of the words. Thus, only when the literal sense is nonsensical, as in Deuteronomy 10:16, does the text authorize metaphorical interpretation. Ibn Ezra's reading may reflect what Israel Baroway identifies as a medieval conception of biblical figures, in which allegories are seen as esoteric and independent hermeneutic structures opposed to the plain sense and requiring outside theological knowledge to understand, rather than being commonplace literary strategies for realizing the author's communicative intention.[23] But Ibn Ezra's inversion also grows out of the paradoxes of the verse, which intertwines bread and words, objects and ideas, signifiers and meanings.

"The soul is the best phylacterie": Shifting Christian Interpretations

But if the ambiguities of signification were crucial to the Jewish discourse surrounding tephillin, Christian theologians and readers only joined that conversation in the seventeenth century. Before then, "phylacteries" raised different questions for Christian readers: in particular, the sins of hypocrisy and pagan magic. This discourse began, as did the use of the Greek term "phylactery," with Jesus's critique of the Pharisees in Matthew 23: "The scribes and the Pharisees sit in Moses' seat: All therefore whatsoever they bid you observe, that observe and do; but do not ye after their works:

for they say, and do not. For they bind heavy burdens and grievous to be borne, and lay them on men's shoulders; but they themselves will not move them with one of their fingers. But all their works they do for to be seen of men: they make broad their phylacteries, and enlarge the borders of their garments" (Matt. 23:1–5). In Matthew's view, phylacteries are not inherently problematic nor are they especially distinctive. Rather, they present one more temptation to ostentatious and hollow display. Matthew critiques Pharisaic phylacteries, not hermeneutically, as did other rivals to rabbinic Judaism in antiquity, but on moral grounds, irrespective of the scriptural verses.

As a result, Christian discourse about phylacteries remained disconnected from the tephillin verses and questions of signification. In pre-modern English, the distinctiveness of Matthew's critique registers in the very language itself. The Oxford English Dictionary records specifically Jewish senses of "phylactery" and a wider usage to refer to "a container for a holy relic" or "an amulet. Also fig.: a charm, a safeguard."[24] But, of course, the wider usage also reflects the original, generic sense of the Greek φυλακτήριον. And even in the early modern period, a generic view of phylacteries was never eliminated but only supplemented by Hebraist scholarship. So, for instance, in 1647 an anonymous poet satirizing the *Directory for Public Worship* could oppose Jews and phylacteries unironically, writing,

> Produce the Alcaron, Ile be a Jew,
> Rather then keep this worship coyn'd by you;
> That Phylactery for a Pagans wrist,
> Convei'd unto us in a Scottish Mist.[25]

As this line suggests, "phylacteries" had come to include decidedly pagan objects. This connection goes back as early as John Chrysostom, who linked Jewish phylacteries with magical amulets.[26]

The looser sense of "phylactery" is also bound up with mistaken ideas of what Jewish phylacteries were specifically. Anonymous notes in the widely used medieval *Glossa ordinaria*, for instance, identified the contents of Jewish phylacteries as the Ten

Commandments. Concerning Deuteronomy 6:8, the *Glossa* comments, "The Pharisees, badly interpreting this, used to write the Decalogue (that is, the ten commandments) in *membranulis*."[27] This reading interprets Deuteronomy 6:6–8 reasonably but not, as the rabbis had, metatextually, and this mistake facilitates the *Glossa*'s assimilation of phylacteries into the broader category of superstition. The *Glossa* to Matthew 23:5 concludes its discussion, which also mistakenly ties phylacteries to the Decalogue by connecting them to contemporary deviant practices: "Today, in zeal for God but not according to accurate knowledge, common working girls do similarly with little Gospels and with the wood of the cross, and similar things, which is a superstition."[28] Unaware of phylacteries' specifically textual associations, the *Glossa* links textual amulets to cross relics and condemns both as irrational magic.

Early modern English writers often perpetuated these mistaken ideas about what Jews put in their phylacteries. A 1621 English dictionary of difficult words, for instance, defined "phylactery" as "a scroll of parchment which the Pharisees wore on their foreheads, having the ten commandements written in it."[29] The mistaken belief that Jewish phylacteries contained the Decalogue was widespread, as evidenced by a 1659 pro-ceremonialist tract that complained that radical reformers "cancell the Decalogue, as a Judaick phylactery, a legall prescription."[30] The clearest example of how far the diffuse, traditional Christian understanding of phylacteries was from the theme of meta-signification is the 1599 Geneva Bible's gloss on "phylacteries" in Matthew 23:5: "It was a thread or ribband of blue silk in the fringe of a corner, the beholding of which made them remember the laws and ordinances of God: and therefore it was called a phylactery, or as you would say, a container. (See Numbers 15:38; Deuteronomy 6:8), a commandment which the Jews abused afterwards, as those do today who hang the gospel of John around their necks, which was condemned many years ago in the Council of Antioch."[31] In Jewish terms, this commentary conflates *tephillin* and tzitzit, the latter being the ritual fringes prescribed in Numbers 15. Given such confusion, phylacteries cannot be expected to signify about signs because tzitzit have no special relationship to textual representation. The Geneva Bible also links phylacteries to amulets containing extracts from the Gospel of John, which were commonly used as a form of apotropaic magic.[32] For an authority like Augustine, similar amulets had been tolerable as a replacement for pagan practices.[33] As either a quasi-pagan magical practice or a simple badge of hypocrisy, the category of phylacteries extended well beyond the Jewish objects and did not focus on questions of scriptural interpretation or textual signification more broadly.

Beginning in the seventeenth century, Christian Hebraism made the more specific, Jewish tephillin available as a meaning for phylacteries, and the Reformation elevation of the biblical text made this meaning attractive. First, Hebraism. In 1603, Johannes Buxtorf published *Synagoga Judaica* in German, which shortly after became available in England in Latin and, by the middle of the century, in English.[34] Buxtorf included detailed information about Jewish laws, rituals, and custom, including a substantial chapter on phylacteries, which included the blessings recited, the cleanliness requirements for wearers, and numerous other specific details (83–88). Needless to say, Buxtorf knew exactly which verses were included in phylacteries, even discussing, for instance, a midrash on Exodus 13:9 excluding women from the commandment.

Buxtorf also highlights the centrality of text to the practice. He discusses, for instance, the particular knots on the hand, by which, "in sowing, folding, knotting, binding, they use so great art & industry, that by a singular kind of subtilty, they form the name Schaddai...according to the three Letters, Schin, Daleth and Iod, and that so exactly, that every Letter is placed in the right order, which is accounted as a most holy thing, producing hidden effects and comprehending mysticall significations" (83).[35] Christian kabbalistic ideas about the magical efficacy of language clearly inform his interpretation of this practice, but so does tephillin's hypertextuality. Buxtorf represents the use of tephillin as a devotional practice centered on language. Thus, he also discusses the importance of having a diligent scribe, since "if any Letter do either superabound or be deficient, the Phylacteries become unholy and polluted, and whosoever shal use them in time of prayers, prates in vain," and he elsewhere observes that as a consequence of phylacteries being a sign, they are not worn on the Sabbath, which "it selfe is a sign of the Jewish faith" (151). Whether intentionally or simply because he was so immersed in tephillin discourse, Buxtorf made possible for English readers—many of whom would have never seen a pair of tephillin—a newly Jewish and metatextual conception of phylacteries.[36]

If Buxtorf and other Hebraists offered new information, readers responded in part because phylacteries were useful tools with which to think through a new, post-Reformation problem. The doctrine of *sola scriptura* assigned to the biblical text a newly autonomous doctrinal authority.[37] As a result, Protestants intensely privileged the words and text of the Bible, relating to them as religious and devotional objects in their own right to an unprecedented degree. Luther, for instance, in advocating scriptural education, replaces not only intellectual subjects, but also devotional practices, with Bible reading: "Above all, in schools of all kinds the chief and most common lesson should be the Scriptures....In truth, schools, monasteries, and convents were founded for this purpose, and with good Christian intentions, as we read concerning St. Agnes and other saints; then were there holy virgins and martyrs; and in those times it was well with Christendom; but now it has been turned into *nothing but praying and singing.*"[38] More broadly, Bible reading replaced forms of Catholic worship understood as idolatrous. The Reformation spawned furious anti-Catholic idol hunting, turning inward a theological discourse previously oriented toward pagan outsiders.[39] On many levels, Bible reading as a devotional practice acquired a new importance for Protestants.

Inevitably, enthusiastic masses of lay readers not only scoured the Bible for its sense but also experienced it as a material object of force and power. Bibliomancy, for instance, is a distinctly Protestant superstition. When, in Luke 4, Jesus is handed a scroll of Isaiah, he finds his destiny prophesied in the text's content. By contrast, when Robinson Crusoe flips through a Bible at random, he trusts not in particular prophecies but in a magical property inhering in its very words and textuality. More suggestively for us, as Hugh Amory argues, English Protestants often used octavo Bibles as ritual fetish objects.[40] The tiny print in these Bibles was just as unreadable as scrolls would be when hidden inside tephillin cases, and as with tephillin, the ceremonious leather binding was more to the point. Through miniature Bibles and tephillin, two textually obsessed cultures materialized forms of their sacred texts that were paradoxically unreadable.

This phenomenon made phylacteries a newly compelling image for seventeenth century divines. Most basically, the change is registered in the frequency of use. Even controlling for the varying sizes of the relevant corpuses, the jump from two usages of the word before 1600 and fifty-seven usages between 1620 and 1700 is striking.[41] More telling and surprising are those moments in which Protestant writers actually express desire for phylacteries, using the term in a positive sense. In a late seventeenth century sermon, Oliver Heywood writes of the regenerated, new nature of the saved Christian, "The New Creature is as a Phylactery to prompt and put him in mind of God's Law, Numb. 15.39."[42] Though he makes the Geneva Bible's mistake of conflating tephillin and tzitzit, far more noteworthy is his positive orientation toward a clearly Mosaic directive to remember the biblical text. Even more striking is preacher William Smythies's suggestion in 1684: "It were well if every one, (especially those that want a Spirit of Meekness) had a Phylacterie with the Apostles words written upon it."[43] Here we find open enthusiasm, though certainly only in theory, for an actual physical phylactery containing a scriptural message.

We also see phylacteries employed positively as a metaphor. For instance, here is how John Johnson, minister of Methley, concludes a 1647 sermon on the civil war: "Let this Text therefore bee as a phylacterie on the garments of your honour, write it on the table of your hearts, let it bee ever in your eyes, in your ears, in your hearts, let it eat with you, and drinke with you, let it sleepe with you, and wake with you, let it sit with you, and judge with you; let conscience which is the cud of the soul, preach this over again to you, when my voyce shall be buried in silence."[44] The phylactery, which is a literalized metaphor or at least a materialized sign, is repurposed as a purely textual figure. Nonetheless, Johnson's pastiche of biblical allusions, which combines language from the properties of pure animals, the tephillin verses, Proverbs, and the tzitzit passages, demonstrates that the biblical text is indeed echoing in his ears. In an even more figuratively convoluted moment, an anonymous Oxonian writes in 1662, "Many Christians have the Word of God written in their Bibles, but they never (as St. John) swallowed the Book. The Laws of God are best inscribed in the Tables of the Heart, the soul is the best Phylacterie and Repository for them, and Practice the fairest Transcript of them. He is a good Text-man whose life is a comment on Scripture."[45] Promoting a typically Restoration-era spirituality, the writer suggests the priority of moral conduct over biblical learning.[46] Though the passage is notable as an instance of the positive use of phylacteries, it also suggests an irony in the Protestant privileging of the biblical text. As the spirit calcifies into the letter, the devotional Bible reading that began as an alternative to Catholic idolatry becomes its own impediment to true Christianity.[47] The conclusion cleverly dispels but also raises the suspicion that a man may devote himself to the text at the expense of the meaning. In a neat inversion in the figurative history of the phylactery, the anonymous writer can defuse these implicitly bibliolatrous rituals, which literalize fidelity to the Bible (swallowing a scroll, wearing phylacteries), only by reducing them to metaphors.

"Read This Clearly": Milton's Use of Phylacteries

With the anonymous Oxonian's suspicions, we come finally to what Milton made of phylacteries. Milton's phylacteries, though used in an entirely negative sense, definitely belong to the post-Hebraist period. His threat, in "On the New Forcers," that Parliament will "Clip your phylacteries, though balk your Ears" (17) shows clear knowledge about the physical characteristics of tephillin: at least, he knew that they had straps that were affixed close to the ears. More importantly, he consistently conjoins "phylactery" to a worry about the possibility of reading idolatrously, of attaching significance to letters and texts at the expense of the spirit. If the anonymous writer's gentle criticism sees a text fetish as a potential distraction to the real work of Christianity, Milton sees it as far worse—a radical threat to reformation. By reading Milton's references to phylacteries in his prose tracts and "On the New Forcers," I argue that Milton turns Protestant iconoclasm even further inward, directing it against reading itself.

While Biberman argues that Milton shifts from an early anti-Jewish usage of the word "phylacteries" to a mature "Hebraist" approach, in fact Milton's usage is consistent, though he grows more radical with time.[48] There is no conflict between his Hebraism and his anti-Judaism. The key similarity is the idea of a fetishized text, regarded as authoritative and adored rather than interpreted. For instance, in the 1642 *Apology for Smectymnuus*, Milton defends an earlier tract, in which he had vituperatively attacked Bishop Joseph Hall, against the objection that a layperson should not so abuse an ordained prelate:

> But markè, Readers, there is a kind of justice observ'd among them that do evill, but this man loves injustice in the very order of his malice. For having all this while abus'd the good name of his adversary with all manner of licence in revenge of his Remonstrant, if they be not both one person, or as I am told, Father and Son, yet after all this he calls for satisfaction, when as he himselfe hath already taken the utmost farding. *Violence hath been done*, says he, *to the person of a holy and religious* Prelat. To which, something in effect to what S. *Paul* answer'd of *Ananias*, I answer, *I wist not brethren that he was a holy and religious* Prelat; for evill is written of those who would be Prelats. And finding him thus in disguise without his superscription or *Phylactery* either of *holy* or *Prelat*, it were no sinne to serve him as *Longchamp* Bishop of *Elie* was serv'd in his disguise at *Dover*. He hath begun the measure namelesse, and when he pleases we may all appeare as we are. (YP 1:897)

Superficially, Milton defends himself on the grounds that he did not know it was Hall he was abusing. Just as the medieval Bishop William Longchamp, disguised as a prostitute, was legitimately beaten by a fisherman who mistook him for a whore, so too Hall (whose sexual morality Milton is implicitly mocking, as he does throughout the *Apology against a Pamphlet*) has no right to complain since he wrote anonymously.[49] But "*I wist not, brethren, that he was a holy and religious* Prelat," has a second, more radical, meaning in the context of the antiprelatical tracts. The force of the earlier *Animadversions*, which Milton is here defending, is that he does not believe "holy and religious" prelates exist at all since prelacy is unjustified by Scripture. Thus, even had Hall written under his true name, he would have no prelatic privilege. Like Ananias in Acts 5, Hall is lying to God in claiming that privilege rather than lying to humans by presenting himself anonymously. When we "all appear as we are," Hall will ironically remain without title.

In this context, "phylactery" is used not merely to refer to hypocritical pride, but in a specifically textual sense. From its conjunction to "superscription," which refers to the missing header with Hall's name, it is clear that "phylactery" also refers to a piece of text. Further, as Michael Komorowski notes, Milton repurposes the language of Smectymnuus's earlier attack on those "who justified episcopal hierarchy based on the spurious postscripts to 2 Timothy and Titus, which named the addressees of these letters as bishops."[50] Bemoaning the printing of these postscripts in larger, Scripture-sized fonts, they write, "our Episcopall men of late in newer impressions [of the Bible] have enlarged their Phylacteries...that the simple might beleeve they are Canonicall Scripture."[51] Still, Milton and the Smectymnuans use the word very differently. The Smectymnuans police the boundaries of biblical text, identifying as phylacteries texts spuriously added to it. Milton instead uses "phylacteries" to identify language, such as the word "prelate," that seems to signify but does not. "Prelate" is a title, an apparently important superscription that, on closer inspection, reveals itself to be meaningless or misleading. To be sure, Milton still argues his antiprelatical case from the Bible's authority. There is no sense here that the biblical text is idolatrous. Rather, phylacteries name a problem inherent to signification generally: the possibility of words seeming to signify but actually commanding assent solely based on their supposed authority.

The two other occurrences of "phylactery" in Milton's prose are related, and they reinforce the term's connection to a specifically textual error. Both turn on Milton's use of the collectively authored pamphlet *Scripture and Reason Pleaded for Defensive Arms; or, The Whole Controversie about Subjects Taking Up Armes* (1643), a tract that drew upon natural law arguments to support an oppressed nation's right to defend itself. Milton cleverly adopts arguments from *Scripture and Reason* to support conclusions that were anathema to its authors. In the *Tetrachordon*, Milton savages Presbyterian clergyman Herbert Palmer for attacking an earlier divorce tract. First, Milton responds to Palmer's attack on the supposed "impudence" of publishing a pro-divorce tract with one's name attached: "But if onely to have writ my name must be counted *impudence*, how doth this but justifie another, who might affirm with as good warrant, that the late Discourse of *Scripture and Reason*, which is certain to be chiefly his own draught, was publisht without a name, out of base fear, and the sly avoidance of what might follow to his detriment, if the party at Court should hap to reach him" (YP 2:581–82). Second, Milton claims his arguments for divorce follow "by inevitable consequences drawn parallel from [Palmer's] own principal arguments in that of *Scripture and Reason*," so that Palmer cannot negate them "without shaking his own composition to peeces" (YP 2:582). Thus, Milton dispenses with Palmer's censure: "The *impudence* therfore, since he waigh'd so little what a grosse revile that was to give his equall, I send him back again for a *phylactery* to stitch upon his arrogance, that censures not onely before conviction so bitterly without so much as one reason giv'n, but censures the Congregation of his Governors to their faces, for not being so hasty as himself to censure" (YP 2:582). The parallel between Milton's characterization of Palmer and of Hall is very strong. As the similarity to the *Apology* would suggest, "phylactery" here signifies more than just hypocrisy. Narrowly defined, a phylactery is a title page (as in *Tenure of Kings and Magistrates*), for Milton is returning the charge of impudent titling by identifying Palmer as one of the authors of *Scripture and Reason*. The "stitching" to which Milton refers probably does not reflect a Geneva-like confusion of phylacteries and tzitzit because

the metaphor does not quite work: in Matthew, the phylactery signifies pride, not attachment to it. Rather, stitching comes from the
material structure of books. In exposing Palmer, Milton is suggesting a title page be newly bound together, or stitched, to *Scripture
and Reason*.

But the pejorative "phylactery" also has the sense it has in
the *Apology*, namely of a text that proves meaningless or empty.
While Palmer attacks Milton for "setting his name to what he
had writt'n," Milton responds conditionally: *if* my naming myself
is impudence, *then* Palmer's anonymity is worse (YP 2:581). But
since Milton rejects Palmer's initial critique, the whole business
of anonymity or self-naming proves empty. Milton would happily
"pardon" Palmer's anonymity if the latter could escape the logical
incoherence and intellectual hypocrisy ("inevitable consequences
drawn parallel from his own principal arguments") that that anonymity obscures. Palmer is, as it were, name-calling, using linguistic canards to avoid the substantive questions of virtue and reason.
Without reasoned arguments, he has subjected Milton to a meaningless "censure," a word Milton repeats three times to mimic a
mindless reassertion of criticism "without so much as one reason
giv'n." Both "censure" and Palmer's authorship of *Scripture and
Reason* function, then, as textual idols. Intellectual examination
will "shak[e]...to peeces"—that is, iconoclastically smash—these
linguistic distractions.

In *Tenure of Kings and Magistrates*, his 1649 tract defending
the people's right to execute a king, Milton continues his pattern
of previous usage. As he argued that *Scripture and Reason* contra-
dicted Palmer's arguments against divorce, so he claims it justifies deposing the sovereign: "Of this faction diverse reverend and
lerned Divines, as they are stil'd in the Phylactery of thir own Title
page, pleading the lawfulnes of defensive Armes against this King,
in a Treatise call'd *Scripture and Reason*, seem in words to dis-
claime utterly the deposing of a King; but both the Scripture and
the reasons which they use, draw consequences after them, which
without their bidding, conclude it lawfull" (YP 3:252). Equating
their title page with a phylactery, Milton then dismantles that
title. When the words "Scripture" and "reason" are transformed

from empty titles to signifying, common words, they prove the opposite of what their authors claim. Similarly, simply by quoting the authorial epithet "diverse reverend and lerned Divines" from *Scripture and Reason*'s title page, Milton undermines its claims to authority; removed from their context of authoritative assertion, the words become merely "style." Rather than the personal, moral failing of hypocrisy, phylacteries represent the more sophisticated problem of meaningless language. More particularly, they name the danger that signifiers will be valued as having independent worth: that people will honor the letter rather than seeing through it to the spirit.

Milton's most interesting use of phylacteries occurs in the sonnet "On the New Forcers of Conscience under the Long Parliament." Written sometime in the mid-1640s, the sonnet scornfully addresses Presbyterians whom Milton had come to see as the enemies of reform, concluding with the hope that "the Parliament / May with their wholesome and preventive shears / Clip your Phylacteries, though balk your Ears" (15–17).[52] Janel Mueller connects the phylacteries in this passage to those in *Tenure*, arguing that Milton is advocating the excision of "(Presbyterian) title pages containing egregious misrepresentations" from printed books.[53] But this hyperliteral reading is peculiar: what would be gained by excising title pages?

In fact, I argue, questions of reading and interpretation are integral to the whole sonnet, which criticizes the Presbyterians in linguistic and textual terms. In that context, phylacteries signify an interpretive error rather than title pages to be censored. From the sonnet's first stanza, Milton presents the Presbyterians' betrayal as a linguistic trick:

> Because you have thrown off your prelate lord,
> And with stiff vows renounced his liturgy
> To seize the widowed whore Plurality
> From them whose sin ye envied, not abhorred.   (1–4)

The hypocrisy of the Presbyterians is intimately connected to language, both through the speech-acts of their "stiff vows" and the liturgical text those vows reject. The echo of "whore" in "abhorred," a word that reflects the Presbyterians' self-serving attack on such episcopal practices as holding multiple livings (pluralities), emphasizes the emptiness of such self-descriptions. The emphasis on text intensifies in the third stanza, which turns from speech to imagery of writing and printing. Because of the Presbyterians' attempted censorship, Milton fumes: "Men whose life, learning, faith and pure intent / Would have been held in high esteem with Paul / Must now be named and printed heretics" (9–11). The stanza struggles against the power of socially authorized language. Though he triumphantly cites Paul, he can do so only in the subjunctive. In contrast to the elaborate scriptural arguments of the prose tracts, "On the New Forcers" opposes its own, internally generated judgments to the unreliable explicit texts and words of others.

Given this theme, the conclusion offers not a practical incitement to censorship but a resolution of the gap between signifier and signified, between the nominal world in which the practice of pluralities has been abolished and the reality in which the Presbyterians have reinstated it. Here is the whole conclusion:

> the Parliament
> May with their wholesome and preventive shears
> Clip your phylacteries, though balk your Ears,[54]
> And succor our just fears
> When they shall read this clearly in your charge:
> New *Presbyter* is but old *Priest* writ large.   (15–20)

"Phylacteries" here mean what they do elsewhere in Milton: words treated as accepted or authoritative truths despite fundamental unsoundness on the level of their significance. Komorowski detects a central irony in what he reads as the poem's Erastian claims for both toleration and control of religious deviance, though the irony would simply make Milton an inconsistent thinker, who waffled on the question of religious coercion. Similarly, Mueller admits the call to censorship as a "rather minor proviso" to Milton's advocacy of "a free press for free English conscience."[55] But the simpler explanation is that Milton is calling on Parliament not to censor books but to critique ideology. The opposition between phylacteries and ears is not between books and bodies but, rather, between linguistic criticism and material coercion. Thus, Parliament's appropriate action is ultimately just to "read...clearly." The linguistic obfuscation of the Presbyterians is emphasized by the literal sense of "writ large"; "Presbyter" has more letters than "Priest." The Presbyterians are material readers, appealing to the physical letters on the page as they have to the text of their vows. To clip their phylacteries is simply to refuse to fall for their linguistic traps.

The Bible as Textual Idol?

What is implicitly radical in the usage of "phylactery" I have cited above is that Milton fuses the two Christian interpretations of phylacteries before him. On the one hand, traditional commentators on Matthew and general usage had seen phylacteries as basically negative. But, unlike Milton, they saw the sin as simply pride, moral hypocrisy, or pagan magic. On the other hand, Hebraists and their readers had unearthed a Jewish tradition, based in the Pentateuch, that read phylacteries as concerned with signification and adopted them as useful adjuncts of a new, text-centered Protestant culture. Milton, uniquely as far as I can tell, understands that very metatextuality as the sin of phylacteries. Though obviously an enthusiastic Reformer and Bible reader, Milton nonetheless suspects texts. Moreover, he suspects the possibility that interpretable signs will be converted into adored objects. Milton sees texts as potential idols.

It may seem strange to characterize Milton as worried about textual idolatry. After all, Milton's antilicensing tract, *Areopagitica*, is celebrated, albeit often imprecisely, for its vigorous, innovative defense of texts and their free circulation.[56] Further, the tract evokes the power and importance of books in language that is itself quasi-idolatrous:

> Books are not absolutely dead things, but doe contain a potencie of life in them to be as active as that soule was whose progeny they are; nay they do preserve as in a violl the purest efficacie and extraction of that living intellect that bred them....And

> yet on the other hand unlesse warinesse be us'd, as good almost kill a Man as kill a good Book; who kills a Man kills a reasonable creature, Gods Image; but hee who destroyes a good Booke, kills reason it selfe, kills the Image of God, as it were in the eye. (YP 2:492)

Milton, as Stanley Fish argues, seems here positively "to encourage idolatry" and a "'religion' of the book."[57] Because the passage "locates value and truth in a physical object," Fish thinks it "decidedly *un*Miltonic," and ultimately interprets it as a "false" preliminary step in a sequence that, in the end, demotes books to the status of "things indifferent," merely "the occasion for the trial and exercise that are necessary to the constituting of human virtue."[58]

Fish's reading accords with my claim that Milton fears bibliolatry, but reconciling my argument with the *Areopagitica* passage does not require such drastic measures. Rather, as David Ainsworth does, I would emphasize the "careful distinctions" Milton makes in this passage between real human beings and metaphorically living books.[59] The passage continues:

> Many a man lives a burden to the Earth; but a good Booke is the pretious life-blood of a master spirit, imbalm'd and treasur'd up on purpose to a life beyond life. 'Tis true, no age can restore a life, whereof perhaps there is no great losse; and revolutions of ages doe not oft recover the losse of a rejected truth, for the want of which whole Nations fare the worse. We should be wary therefore what persecution we raise against the living labours of publick men, how we spill that season'd life of man preserv'd and stor'd up in Books; since we see a kinde of homicide may be thus committed, sometimes a martyrdome, and if it extend to the whole impression, a kinde of massacre, whereof the execution ends not in the slaying of an elementall life, but strikes at that ethereall and fift essence, the breath of reason it selfe, slaies an immortality rather then a life. (YP 2:492–93)

Even as Milton calls the book the "eye" in the "Image of God," he inserts the cautionary "as it were." By making the metaphor explicit, he counters the threat of idolatry. The concrete vehicle of the eye, associated with the "Image of God" only through that image's human manifestation, underscores how books are merely images of images, which represent reason only indirectly, by representing people. Throughout the passage, he argues against destroying books because doing so threatens human thoughts. As his repeated images of containers and contents indicate, Milton cares about books because of the "potencie of life in them" and "the purest efficacie and extraction of that living intellect" preserved *in* them as "in a violl." The point is never the book, but the spirit inside. Finally, even in his hyperbolic comparisons between censorship and murder, Milton emphasizes the unimportance of the physical book by concluding, "and if it extend to the whole impression, a kinde of massacre" may result. This final metaphor distinguishes between each of many physical books, on the one hand, and the abstract text they collectively represent, on the other. But given that distinction, the former turns out to be trivial, retroactively undoing the seriousness of the destruction of a single, physical book. The *Areopagitica* passage thus exalts texts only and exactly when they offer access to human reason. Far from celebrating material books in themselves, Milton appreciates precisely their capacity to transcend their own letters and contain "an immortality rather then a life."[60]

If Milton's anxieties about textual idolatry are consistent with the *Areopagitica*, what about the possibility that they extend to the Bible? The possibility that the biblical text could become an idol is intrinsic in any account of phylacteries that is both metatextual and negative. Phylacteries, to state the obvious, are properly made from biblical text. To whatever extent they are cited as a critique of textuality, divinely revealed textuality cannot be logically exempted. Indeed, in a tantalizing moment in *De doctrina Christiana*, Milton hypothesizes that God "committed the contents of the New Testament to such wayward and uncertain guardians" to ensure its textual maculation specifically so that "this very fact might convince us that the Spirit which is given to us is a more certain guide than scripture, and that we ought to follow it" (YP 6:589). Though Milton is not unusual in prioritizing the Spirit over Scripture, his suggestion that God has intentionally made his word unreliable to avoid its being inappropriately revered betrays a fear of bibliolatry. The iconoclastic impulse here is very strong: in an intriguingly analogous ordinance, aniconic Jewish law requires that visual art, in order to avoid tempting the viewer to idolatry, contain a visible imperfection.[61] On the other hand, in our particular case, Milton does not use "phylactery" negatively to refer to a *biblical* text.[62] And the metaphor can easily become a dead one, as it is for the Smectymnuans, who refer to the pseudobiblical postscripts as "phylacteries." Then again, Milton's usage is consistent and theoretically careful; Smectymnuus's is not.

Two moments, admittedly without direct connection to phylacteries and chosen from a very large corpus, do suggest that Milton had a critical attitude toward the authority of the biblical text or subordinated it to natural reason.[63] First, in *The Tenure of Kings and Magistrates*, examining examples of regicide from the prose prophets, Milton writes, "And whereas *Jehu* had special command to slay *Jehoram* a successive and hereditarie Tyrant, it seems not the less imitable for that; for where a thing grounded so much on natural reason hath the addition of a command from God, what does it but establish the lawfulness of such an act" (YP 3:215–16). Milton here inverts the standard argument, that because Barak and others had special warrants to commit regicide, it is impossible to generalize from their acts. Milton subordinates divine order to natural reason. The divine command is an addition, and ultimately, the legitimacy of the act is founded in its generic attributes (*"such an* act") rather than the particular fact of God's having commanded it. In his 1651 tract *A Defense of the People of England*, he is even more explicit: "Jehu killed a king at the bidding of a prophet.... If [God] commanded it, it was surely permissible, praiseworthy, and noble. It was not however permissible and good to put a tyrant to death because God commanded it, but rather God commanded it because it was permissible and good" (YP 4:407). Just as "Presbyter" and "Prelate" turn out to require critical scrutiny, so too even God's command is only superadded to natural reason. The divine command may give evidence that Jehu acted rightly, but it did not authorize Jehu's deed.[64]

Indeed, in a truly remarkable moment in *Samson Agonistes*, Samson takes this principle even further, responding to Dalila's claim that she acted on divine command:

But zeal moved thee;
To please thy gods thou didst it; gods unable
To acquit themselves and prosecute their foes
But by ungodly deeds, the contradiction
Of their own deity, gods cannot be:
Less therefore to be pleased, obeyed, or feared,
These false pretexts and varnished colors failing,
Bare in thy guilt how foul must thou appear.   (895–902)

This is to take Socrates's argument in the *Euthyphro* very far, indeed, as far as Kant, who reasoned that since one could not be sure he was being addressed by God but could be sure of the moral law, Abraham ought to have disobeyed the command to sacrifice Isaac.[65] Nor should it be objected that these are only foreign gods, since, after all, the major development of Protestant idolatry discourse was to focus on Christian idolatry.[66] But what is most tantalizing is the hint buried in "pre*texts*," the suggestion that even religious texts can only be pretexts, ancillary to the true justifications of the human heart, that in the end, the entire Bible might be just a phylactery.

University of California, Berkeley

NOTES

1. I will use the Hebrew *tephillin* when talking about rabbinic conversation and "phylactery" when discussing Christian writers. This emphasizes the existence of a distinct Christian phylactery discourse with its own evolution and history. See below for the methodological justification for this distinction. I would like to thank Maya Rosen for her help, as well as Jason Rosenblatt and an anonymous reader for their generous and sharp critiques.

2. John Milton, *Political Writings*, ed. Martin Dzelzainis (New York, 2006), 43n. For the text of *Tenure of Kings and Magistrates*, I use *The Complete Prose Works of John Milton*, 8 vols., ed. Don M. Wolfe et al. (New Haven, Conn., 1953–82). All references to Milton's prose are to this edition, hereafter cited in the text as YP followed by volume and page number. A similar, and similarly structured, gloss on "phylactery" in *Tetrachordon* is given by William Kerrigan, John Rumrich, and Stephen Fallon in *The Complete Poetry and Essential Prose of John Milton* (New

York, 2007), 988n11: "Leather box containing excerpts of Deuteronomy and Exodus, worn by Jews during morning prayers as a sign of obedience to the law. Milton uses the term to figuratively mean ostentatious or hypocritical show of piety or rectitude." Hereafter, Milton's poetry is cited in the text by book and line to this edition.

3. Concerning Milton's iconoclasm generally, see, for instance, Barbara Lewalski, "Milton and Idolatry," *SEL* 43, no. 1 (Winter 2003): 213–32; and David Loewenstein, "'Casting Down Imaginations': Milton as Iconoclast," *Criticism* 31, no. 3 (Summer 1989): 253–70; but also Daniel Shore, "Why Milton Is Not an Iconoclast," *PMLA* 127, no. 1 (January 2012): 22–37. For the broader Puritan context, see James Simpson, *Under the Hammer: Iconoclasm in the Anglo-American Tradition* (Oxford, 2010); and Julie Spraggon, *Puritan Iconoclasm during the English Civil War* (Woodbridge, U.K., 2003).

4. Mathew Biberman, "Milton's Tephillin," *Milton Quarterly* 31, no. 4 (1997): 136–45. Biberman's argument is largely designed to defend Milton from charges of anti-Semitism (137). Biberman notes that his positive account of phylacteries as "your soul on display" faces the damning objection that "nowhere do we find [the word used] in a positive context" (139, 140). Biberman's apologetic agenda problematically leads him to place the phylactery-shearing of "On the New Forcers of Conscience under the Long Parliament" at the navel, imagining the victim mistakenly fearing imminent castration, and suggesting that Milton was following the Shulhan Arukh, an important sixteenth-century Jewish law code.

5. Most spectacularly, Denis Saurat traced Milton's various heresies to the Zohar, a medieval mystical text, in *Milton, Man and Thinker* (New York, 1925). But there are no grounds for thinking Milton had the specialized Aramaic skills to access the Zohar directly, and the supposed allusions are inconclusive. Similar problems plague Harris Fletcher's *Milton's Semitic Studies* (Chicago, 1926) and *Milton's Rabbinic Readings* (Urbana, Ill., 1930). A relatively more recent example is Golda Werman, *Milton and Midrash* (Washington, D.C., 1995).

6. Arnold's judgment can be extracted from "A French Critic on Milton," *London Quarterly Review* 143 (1877): 98–107, in conjunction with his remarks on "Hebraism and Hellenism" in Matthew Arnold, *Culture and Anarchy* (1869), in *Arnold: "Culture and Anarchy" and Other Writings,* ed. Stefan Collini (Cambridge, 1993), 126–38.

7. Jason Rosenblatt, *Renaissance England's Chief Rabbi: John Selden* (Oxford, 2006) and *Torah and Law in "Paradise Lost"* (Princeton, N.J., 1994), 3–12.

8. Jeffrey Shoulson, *Milton and the Rabbis: Hebraism, Hellenism, and Christianity* (New York, 2001), 3.

9. The literature on Hebraism is now quite large. An influential recent example is Eric Nelson, *The Hebrew Republic: Jewish Sources and the Transformation of European Political Thought* (Cambridge, Mass., 2010).

Other important programmatic articles include Alexander Altmann, "William Wollaston (1659–1724), English Deist and Rabbinic Scholar," *Transactions of the Jewish Historical Society of England* 16 (1945–51): 185–211; and Kalman Neuman, "Political Hebraism and the Early Modern 'Respublica Hebraeorum': On Defining the Field," *Hebraic Political Studies* 1, no. 1 (2005): 57–70. Notable examples of work that looks at Milton's Hebrew sources without presupposing sympathy or affinity include Mary Ann Radzinowicz, *Milton's Epics and the Book of Psalms* (Princeton, N.J., 1989). See also the essays collected in Douglas A. Brooks, ed., *Milton and the Jews* (Cambridge, 2012).

10. *Joseph Scaliger Epistolae* (Leiden, 1627), Letter 62, 193–97; cited in Rosenblatt, *Renaissance England's Chief Rabbi*, 79.

11. See, for instance, *Erubhin; or, Miscellanies Christian and Judaicall, and others Penned for recreation at vacant houres* (London, 1629), in which Lightfoot, to pick several examples at random, writes of the Jews' "abominable sacrifices" (41), calls the Talmud "the Jewes Councell of Trent" (21–22), discusses how the Jews "most wickedly fable" a particular midrash (14), asks seriously at one moment, "Could wee looke for a truth from a Jew?" (38), and introduces a Jewish prayer for the dead by promising, "Thus (courteous Reader) hast thou seene a Popish Jew interceding for the dead: have but the like patience a while, and thou shalt see how they are Popish almost entirely" (136).

12. Much work on the Reformation's transformation of literary signification has taken the eucharistic controversy as its catalyst. Malcolm Mackenzie Ross argues that "the dogmatic symbolism of the traditional Eucharistic rite had nourished the analogical mode of poetic symbol," such that the "Protestant revision of Eucharistic dogma" led to these symbols being "reduced to metaphor and below metaphor, finally to cliché." Malcolm Mackenzie Ross, *Poetry and Dogma: The Transfiguration of Eucharistic Symbols in Seventeenth Century English Poetry* (New York, 1969), vii. Ross's argument has, to put it mildly, proved controversial. Kimberly Johnson takes the opposite position in *Made Flesh: Sacrament and Poetics in Post-Reformation England* (Philadelphia, 2014), arguing that Protestant eucharistic theology led to "a poetics that foregrounds the ritual's inherent tensions between material surface and imperceptible substance, between sign and signified, between flesh and spirit" (27). See also Stephen Greenblatt's arguments about the transition from the altar to the theater in, for instance, "Remnants of the Sacred in Early Modern England," in *Subject and Object in Renaissance Culture*, ed. Margreta de Grazia, Maureen Quilligan, and Peter Stallybrass (Cambridge, 1996), 337–48.

13. Here and throughout, I have followed the 1611 King James Version but have modernized spelling.

14. For an account of these verses and their afterlife in antiquity, see Yehudah B. Cohn, *Tangled Up in Text: Tefillin and the Ancient World* (Providence, R.I., 2008).

15. Shanks Alexander, *Gender and Timebound Commandments in Judaism* (Cambridge, 2013), 152–54 and 172–75.

16. For the history of and alternatives to this choice, especially in the Second Temple period, see Cohen, *Tangled Up in Text*, 55–67, 75–77, 95–96.

17. Another plausible possibility was the Decalogue. See Moshe Weinfeld, *Deuteronomy 1–11: A New Translation with Introduction and Commentary* (New Haven, Conn., 1995), 340; Cohen, *Tangled Up in Text*, 42; and below.

18. There has been no comprehensive study of Karaite law after the discovery of the Dead Sea Scrolls. Bernard Revel, *The Karaite Halakah and Its Relation to Saduccean, Samaritan and Philonian Halakah* (Philadelphia, 1913), is badly outdated on questions of Karaite sources, but it contains good basic descriptions of early Karaite practices and polemics.

19. Rashbam separated the "plain sense" from the legally binding sense. See Martin Lockshin, "Tradition or Context: Two Exegetes Struggle with *Peshat*," in *From Ancient Judaism to Modern Israel*, vol. 3, ed. Jacob Neusner and Ernest S. Frerichs (Atlanta, 1989), 173–86.

20. Collected in *Torat Hayyim: Hamishah Humshei Torah*, vol. 3 (Jerusalem, 1993), 155. Translations of nonbiblical Hebrew are mine unless otherwise noted.

21. In both Proverbs verses, the preceding verse clarifies that the antecedent of "they" or "them" is "your parents' teaching."

22. *Torat Hayyim*, 155–56.

23. Israel Baroway, "The Bible as Poetry in the English Renaissance: An Introduction," *Journal of English and Germanic Philology* 32, no. 4 (1933): 447–80.

24. "Phylactery," n., *OED Online* (Oxford, June 2016), http://www.oed.com/view/Entry/143041?redirectedFrom=phylactery&.

25. *Westminster Colledge; or, Englands complaint against those that sit in the chamber cald Jerusalem, alias, Henry the Seventh Chapell: being a discourse in meeter, in behalfe of Saint Peter, concerning the power of the keyes* (London, 1647). "Alcoran" refers to the Quran, "Scottish" to the Scottish roots of Presbyterianism.

26. See Joseph E. Sanzo, *Scriptural Incipits on Amulets from Late Antique Egypt: Text, Typology, and Theory* (Tübingen, 2014), 161–63.

27. "Hoc Pharisaei male interpretantes, in membranulis decalogum (id est, decem verba) scribebant, & ligata in fronte portabant." *Bibliorum sacrorum cum glossa ordinaria*, vol. 1 (Venice, 1603), 1500. See also the *Glossa*'s anonymous note to Exodus 13:16 (607). Nicholas de Lyra does seem, in his gloss to Exodus 13:9, to have accurate knowledge of Jewish phylacteries: "On account of the opportunity of this, the Jews write *this* on leaves of paper and tie them on the left hand, similarly on the head" ("Iudaei occasione huius scribunt *hoc* in schedula, & ligant in manu sinistra, similiter in capite" [605]). But in his longer and more explicit gloss

to Matthew, he instead follows Jerome in misidentifying the Decalogue as the phylactery text ("charta in quibus scribebatur decalogus mandatorum"). *Bibliorum sacrorum cum glossa ordinaria*, 5:378–79.

28. "Huiusmodi faciunt hodie zelo Dei, sed non secundum scientiam, mulierculae in parvis evangeliis, & ligno crucis, & in huiusmodi rebus, quod superstitio est." *Bibliorum Sacrorum cum Glossa Ordinaria*, 5:378–79. See also the gloss to Deuteronomy 6:8, which retrojects Matthew's critique and links Jewish phylacteries to contemporary Eastern Christian protective amulets, underscoring its disinterest in the specifically textual questions: "Which until today the Babylonians do in order that they might be thought religious" ("Quod usque hodie faciunt Babylonii ut putentur religiosi").

29. J. B., *An English expositor: Teaching the interpretation of the hardest words in our language. With sundry explications, descriptions, and discourses* (London, 1621), M2.

30. John Gauden, *Hiera dakrya, Ecclesiae anglicanae suspiria: The tears, sighs, complaints, and prayers of the Church of England setting forth her former constitution, compared with her present condition: also the visible causes and probable cures of her distempers: in IV books* (London, 1659), 164.

31. See Michael H. Brown, ed., *The Geneva Bible: A Facsimile of the 1599 Edition with Undated Sternhold and Hopkins Psalms* (Ozark, Mo., 1991), on Matthew 23:5. Interestingly, the 1560 Geneva seems not to have conflated phylacteries and tzitzit, though it did continue the erroneous identification of the texts inside phylacteries with the Decalogue. See William Whittingham et al., *The Bible and Holy Scriptures Conteyned in the Olde and Newe Testament, translated according to the Ebrue and Greke, and conferred with the best translations in divers languages, with moste profitable annotations upon all the hard places, and other things of great importance as may appear in the epistle to the reader* (Geneva, 1560), Matthew 23:5n (13).

32. See Don C. Skemer, *Binding Words: Textual Amulets in the Middle Ages* (University Park, Pa., 2006), 87–89.

33. "When your head aches, we praise you if you place the gospel at your head, instead of having recourse to an amulet. For so far has human weakness proceeded, and so lamentable is the estate of those who have recourse to amulets, that we rejoice when we see a man who is upon his bed, and tossed about with fevers and pains, placing his hope on nothing else than that the gospel lies at his head; not because it is done for this purpose, but because the gospel is preferred to amulets." Augustine, *In Io. tre. 7:12*, in *A Select Library of the Nicene and Post-Nicene Fathers of the Christian Church*, ed. Philip Schaff, vol. 7, *Lectures or Tractates on the Gospel according to St. John*, trans. John Gibb and James Innes (Edinburgh, 1888), 52.

34. Johannes Buxtorf, *Synagoga Judaica: Das ist Jüden Schul* (Basel, 1603); *Synagoga judaica; hoc est, Schola judaeorum in qua nativitas, institutio, religio, vita, mors, sepulturaque ipsorum e libris eorundem* (Hanau, Germany, 1604); and *The Jewish Synagogue; or, An historical narration of the state of the Jews, at this day disperced over the face of the whole earth,* trans. Mr. A. of Queens College, Oxford (London, 1657); hereafter cited from this edition in the text.

35. "(El) Shaddai" is a name of God: see Exodus 6:2–3.

36. Indeed, John Lightfoot knew not only which verses were contained in phylacteries but also where they were discussed homiletically in the Talmud. John Lightfoot, *A Commentary on the New Testament from the Talmud and Hebraica* (Peabody, Mass., 1989).

37. See, for instance, Roland Bainton, "The Bible in the Reformation," in *The Cambridge History of the Bible,* vol. 3, *The West from the Reformation to the Present Day,* ed. S. L. Greenslade (Cambridge, 1975), 1–37.

38. Martin Luther, "Respecting the Reformation of the Christian Estate," in *Luther's Primary Works: Together with His Shorter and Larger Catechisms,* ed. Henry Wace (London, 1896), 233.

39. See Jonathan Sheehan, "Sacred and Profane: Idolatry, Antiquarianism, and the Polemics of Distinction in the Seventeenth Century," *Past and Present* 192 (August 2006): 37–66; and Simpson, *Under the Hammer,* 1–18.

40. Hugh Amory, "The Trout and the Milk: An Ethnobibliographical Talk," *Harvard Library Bulletin* 7 (1996): 50–65.

41. On May 12, 2015, I searched Early English Books Online for "phylactery" (EEBO controls for variant spellings, though because of the word's oddity, I checked myself as well) between 1473 and 1600 and then between 1620 (giving Buxtorf's book a decade and a half to circulate) and 1700.

42. Oliver Heywood, *A new creature; or, A short discourse, opening the nature, properties, and necessity of the great work of the new creation upon the souls of men* (London, 1695), 133.

43. William Smythies, *The spirit of meekness recommended for the reducing of the erroneous and such as have dissented from the Church of England* (London, 1684), 46.

44. John Johnson, *Balsamum Britannicum, Brittains balm; or, The means of recovery for a languishing kingdom* (York, 1648), 63.

45. *The spiritual bee; or, A miscellany of scriptural, historical, natural observations and occasional occurencyes applyed in divine meditations by an university pen* (Oxford, 1662), 76.

46. See, for instance, Blair Worden, "The Question of Secularization," in *A Nation Transformed: England after the Restoration,* ed. Alan Houston and Steven Pincus (Cambridge, 2001), 20–40.

47. David Nirenberg, *Anti-Judaism: The Western Tradition* (New York, 2013), 1–13, provocatively argues that this ossification is a recurrent

feature of Western philosophy, for which Jews have consistently proved a good figure.

48. Biberman, "Milton's Tephillin," 143n6, and see his "John Milton: The Triumph of Christian Hebraism in Verse" (PhD diss., Duke University, 1998).

49. See Ralph V. Turner, "William de Longchamp (d. 1197)," in *Oxford Dictionary of National Biography*. (Oxford, 2004), online ed., May 2007, http://www.oxforddnb.com/view/article/16980.

50. Michael Komorowski, "'On the New Forcers of Conscience' and Milton's Erastianism," in *Milton Studies*, vol. 55, ed. Laura L. Knoppers (Pittsburgh, 2014), 251.

51. Smectymnuus, *An Answer to a Booke Entituled An Humble Remonstrance* (London, 1641), 61, qtd. in Komorowski, "'On the New Forcers of Conscience' and Milton's Erastianism," 251.

52. On the dating of the term, in addition to Komorowski, "Milton's Erastianism," see also James Holly Hanford, "The Arrangement and Dates of Milton's Sonnets," *Modern Philology* 18, no. 9 (1921): 475–83; and John T. Shawcross, "Of Chronology and the Dates of Milton's Translation from Horace and the 'New Forcers of Conscience,'" *SEL* 3, no. 1 (1963): 77–84.

53. Janel Mueller, "The Mastery of Decorum: Politics as Poetry in Milton's Sonnets," *Critical Inquiry* 13, no. 3 (1987): 497.

54. In the manuscript, this line replaces the crossed out "Crop ye as close as marginal P—s ears," a reference to the pillorying and removal of William Prynne's ears for sedition.

55. Mueller, "Mastery of Decorum," 497.

56. For a critical discussion of this celebration, see William Kolbrener, "'Plainly Partial': The Liberal *Areopagitica*," *ELH* 60, no. 1 (1993): 57–78; as well as John Illo, "The Misreading of Milton," in *Radical Perspectives in the Arts*, ed. Lee Baxandall (Harmondsworth, U.K., 1972): 180–89; and Willmoore Kendall, "How to Read Milton's *Areopagitica*," *Journal of Politics* 22 (1960): 439–73.

57. Stanley Fish, "Driving from the Letter: Truth and Indeterminacy in Milton's *Areopagitica*," in *How Milton Works* (Cambridge, Mass., 2001), 190–91.

58. Ibid., 203.

59. David Ainsworth, *Milton and the Spiritual Reader: Reading and Religion in Seventeenth-Century England* (London, 2008), 20–21.

60. See also Jeffrey Masten's argument in *Textual Intercourse: Collaboration, Authorship, and Sexualities in Renaissance Drama* (Cambridge, U.K., 1997), that the *Areopagitica*, "even in its call for textual proliferation, generates an interest in a new textual and authorial identification" (144–45).

61. See, for instance, the discussion and sources quoted in R. Avraham Yitzchak HaCohen Kook's letter to the Betzalel Art School in *R. A. Y.*

Kook: Selected Letters, trans. Tzvi Feldman (Ma'aleh Adumim, Israel, 1986), 190–98.

62. I regret that I discovered Neil Forsyth's "Milton's Corrupt Bible" too late to incorporate it into this essay, as his argument strikingly parallels mine. In *The Oxford Handbook of the Bible in Early Modern England, c. 1530–1700*, ed. Kevin Killeen, Helen Smith, and Rachel Willie (Cambridge, 2015), www.oxfordhandbooks.com/view/10.1093/oxfordhb/9780199686971.001.0001/oxfordhb-9780199686971-e-13.

63. My argument, which traces the continuity between iconoclasm and secularization in Milton's thought, has affinities with the broader view of a secular Milton advanced by scholars such as David Quint and Victoria Kahn. See, for instance, David Quint, "The Disenchanted World of *Paradise Regained*," *Huntington Library Quarterly* 76, no. 1 (Spring 2013): 181–94; and Victoria Kahn, "Job's Complaint in *Paradise Regained*," *ELH* 76, no. 3 (Fall 2009): 625–60.

64. As Christopher Hill writes in *The World Turned Upside Down: Radical Ideas during the English Revolution* (London, 1991), "Milton was glad to find that ideas at which he arrived by searching his own conscience could be found in the Bible; but they had greater authority for him because they were found in his conscience than because they were found in the Bible" (264).

65. See Immanuel Kant, *The Conflict of the Faculties*, trans. Mary Gregor (New York, 1979), 115n. "We can use, as an example, the mythic sacrifice that Abraham was going to make by butchering and burning his only son at God's command.... Abraham should have replied to this supposedly divine voice: 'That I ought not to kill my good son is quite certain. But that you, this apparition, are God—of that I am not certain, and never can be, not even if this voice rings down to me from (visible) heaven.'" Sanford Budick argues for Milton's anticipation of and influence on Kant in *Kant and Milton* (Cambridge, Mass., 2010). But see Daniel Shore, "Milton and Kant?" *Milton Quarterly* 48, no. 1 (2014): 26–38.

66. See also William Empson, *Milton's God* (London, 1965), 215.

"The Minstrelsy of Heaven": Representation and the Politics of Lyric in *Paradise Lost*

Andrew S. Brown

In beginning *Paradise Lost* chronologically—though, crucially, not narratively—with the Father's exaltation of the Son in book 5, Milton founded his epic on a scene of representation that has proven endlessly vexing to later readers. The language of the Father's decree affords few details concerning the physical cause or theological reasoning behind the Son's newly elevated status, instead focusing on how it will transform the landscape of heaven. Beginning with an apparently exhaustive roll call of the angelic hierarchy of "Thrones, Dominations, Princedoms, Virtues, Powers," Milton's God makes a brilliant visual spectacle of his paternal approval by identifying the Son not yet by his "merit more than birthright" but merely as he "whom ye now behold / At my right hand."[1] Moreover, he goes on to choreograph the assembled host's response to his own originary speech-act with the claim that he "by myself have sworn to him shall bow / All knees in Heav'n, and shall confess him Lord" (5.607–08). William Empson observes of this moment that "to give no reason at all for the Exaltation

63

makes it appear a challenge," and some subsequent scholars similarly suggest that the deliberately unexplained, flagrantly ceremonial manner in which the Father enacts the Son's elevation appears to provide Satan with a defensible or at least plausible motive for his revolt.[2] Certainly, in the chiastic, sharp-edged turn of the lines that follow, as Raphael explains that "with his words / All seemed well pleased, all seemed, but were not all" (5.616–17), Milton's bare monosyllables keenly strip away any opportunity for readers to linger upon the splendorous scene without some degree of critical reflection.

Such readings have figured the portrayal of the Father in book 5 primarily as that of a political tyrant capriciously imposing "New laws" on the inhabitants of heaven and thereby licensing the emergence of "new minds" and "new counsels" among Satan and his followers (5.679–81). But through its depiction of the moment when the "only Son" (5.604) is first empowered to speak and act on his Father's behalf, *Paradise Lost* is also deeply implicated in contemporary debates surrounding the nature and purpose of representation more generally. In delineating the "theological contours" of Milton's account of the exaltation, John Rogers argues that this "seeming fiction" is rooted partly in the poet's engagement with the heretical doctrine of Socinianism, which grounded the liberty of Christ and indeed of all human beings in the actions of "a Father who punctuates Christian history with a series of arbitrary, voluntary, temporally specific decrees," thereby releasing them from any natural obligation to the deity and enabling them freely to express their obedience and devotion.[3] As Milton would have known, however, a related strain of Socinian theology asserted that the Son was an "image" or "person" of the Father, not in the conventional Trinitarian sense but, rather, in the same manner as human prophets such as Moses, serving as a representative of the deity in the physical world—a claim adopted by his contemporary, Thomas Hobbes, in chapter 16 of his *Leviathan*.[4]

In the comprehensive theory of representation outlined here, virtually any individual may covenant with another, establishing a contract in which an "Author" licenses an "Actor" to "beare his Person, or act in his name."[5] *Leviathan* follows this with the more radical claim, however, that both the "Son of man" and the "Holy Ghost" are also such actors or "personations" of the "true God" and bear an equally "Artificiall" relationship to the authoring deity.[6] In this way, Hobbes's capacious account juxtaposes the theological subtleties of Trinitarianism with the most basic processes whereby the "words and actions" of one person or thing can be made to represent another. As he insistently emphasizes, "There are few things, that are uncapable of being represented by Fiction," extending this model even to "Inanimate things, as a Church, an Hospital, a Bridge."[7] Such a concept of representation is not only theological or political but also in the most basic sense *poetic*, serving for Hobbes as a model for all subsequent forms of fictive and imaginative creation: from pagan rituals to contemporary statecraft and Christian covenant to literary expression.[8] Moreover, although the Hobbesian model of representation as a kind of poetic artifice is distinctive in addressing these contested theological questions, similarly expansive accounts of the intimate relationship between poetics and politics proliferated throughout the seventeenth century. As Victoria Kahn notes, even specific literary genres were frequently "construed as beneficial social contracts or coercive ideological fictions."[9]

Although neither Hobbes nor Milton can be said to adhere strictly to Socinian theology, the imaginative implications of such theories of representation crystallize a number of issues with which the exaltation scene of *Paradise Lost* is closely engaged. Even as the poem at once solicits and frustrates readers' attempts to understand the precise ontological relationship between these two persons of the deity, it also invites parallel reflections on the manifold senses in which the Son might be said to represent the Father in poetic terms. The chief rebel's immediate response to the event seethes with the conventional motives of pride and envy, available to Milton from earlier hexaemeral epics, but Raphael's claim that Satan could "not bear / Through pride that sight, and thought himself impaired" (5.664–65) suggests that his revolt is spurred by a perceived resemblance between himself and the Son, who has replaced him in his Father's favor.[10] Moreover, the subsequent address to his companions gathered at the "Mountain of the Congregation" emphasizes not just the ignominy of being "eclipsed under the name / Of King anointed" (5.776–77) but also the perversity of worshipping both the Father and the enigmatic reflection who sits visibly by his side: "Knee-tribute yet unpaid, prostration vile, / Too much to one, but double how endured / To one and to his image now proclaimed" (5.782–84). Here, it is the Son's status as a superfluous self-representation created by the Father that animates Satan's more rhetorically polished critique: God is not merely a tyrannical sovereign but a poor poet whose fictions of authentic rule, elaborate and brilliant as they may be, nonetheless fail to persuade his audience. If the "divine similitude" (3.384) that is the Son is not accepted as a legitimate agent of God, therefore, it is partly because his authority to speak and act on the Father's behalf is not fully endorsed by the heavenly multitude.

The fundamental challenge of representing the deity in verse was, of course, one with which Milton was acutely familiar, and the generic demands of epic (as distinct from those of systematic theologies like *De doctrina Christiana*) undoubtedly shaped his portrayal of the Son's elevation.[11] But Satan's own assessment of this scene as, above all, a failure of representation—as a failure to make the Son either identical to the Father or deserving of his own distinct praise—should remind us that the exaltation also functions as a radically poetic act within the fictive universe of *Paradise Lost*. Most obviously, the command with which the Father identifies the Son as his representative is literally comprised of poetry, weaving together widely dispersed scriptural sources into an authoritative utterance that is also, so far as readers are aware, the first appearance of the genre of the "decree" in the poem's history; in particular, the speech recalls several lines from Psalm 2, which Milton had translated into English verse in 1653.[12] In her classic study of the generic forms contained within *Paradise Lost*, Barbara Lewalski suggests that by assembling the Father's speech from this "mélange of psalmic and biblical echoes," Milton sought to exploit readers' visceral familiarity with his sources, thereby imbuing the deity's language with a tone that is immediately "majestic, awesome, unconditional—the voice of Omnipotence declaring the divine will."[13] However, the scene's thorough imbrication of the political, theological, and poetic aspects of representation also invites a more sustained consideration of not only why Milton adopted this form when scripting the exaltation for his contemporary audience but also of how such issues of generic choice and interpretation structure the internal action of the poem itself.

In their dizzyingly expansive portrayal of celestial strife, books 5 and 6 of *Paradise Lost* have long been identified as Milton's most explicit attempt to imitate and indeed to surpass the genre of classical epic. But attending more closely to the representational dimensions of moments like the Father's decree also reveals how these central books, often understood by early readers as aesthetically digressive, are in fact comprised of a rich panoply of more local though no less significant poetic gestures, in keeping with early modern theories that figured epic as an expansive superstructure capable of encompassing all other modes.[14] Reading these scenes simply as a heavenly allegory of Milton's own politics, that is, neglects the extent to which the specific qualities of their language are themselves subjected to intense scrutiny as part of the work's unfurling fabric of representation. After all, the entire episode is enclosed within the artificial frame of Raphael's narrative, only rendered legible through a necessarily imperfect process of "lik'ning spiritual to corporal forms" (5.573). To put the matter another way, what would it mean to consider figures such as the Father, the Son, and Satan not merely as theological or political actors but as creators and indeed critics of such constitutive fictions in their own right? And how might we better understand these roles—following Milton's insistence, in *The Reason of Church-Government*, that poetic "abilities...are of power beside the office of a pulpit, to imbreed and cherish in a great people the seeds of vertu, and publick civility"—not as distinct or only provisionally related, but as fundamentally intertwined?[15]

If the Father can be said to invent the genre of the decree in performing the Son's exaltation, so too do the other speakers of

Paradise Lost develop their own novel forms of expression in response to the ensuing crisis of heavenly representation. Studies of the poem's manifold generic elements have tended to figure it as a kind of museum for the exhibition of the classical and scriptural traditions Milton had inherited. In Rosalie Colie's phrase, the work "sums up its culture whole, in the language of forms that culture bequeathed," while Lewalski famously envisioned it as "an encyclopedia of literary forms which also affords a probing critique of the values those forms traditionally body forth."[16] Ultimately, however, the cosmogonic project at the core of the text also provides Milton with a forum for exploring the obscure origins of various modes of political and poetic representation, prompting readers to imagine them apart from their accreted history and significance even as such influences continue to bear on Milton's authorial practice. The juxtaposition of the Father's psalmic command with both the joyful collective hymning of Milton's angels and Satan's solitary dissent initiates a broader pattern of reflection on the capacity of these forms, and the closely related genre of the lyric, to serve political ends. Often conceived as a fixed or ideal mode within the work—an impression perhaps reinforced by the boldly vatic tone of the Miltonic "I" in the proem to book 1— the emergence of lyrical expressiveness within *Paradise Lost* is a vexed process that can only be fully understood alongside the matter of representation.

"Glittering Tissues": The Poetics of Exaltation

At the moment of the Son's exaltation, Milton's heaven is already defined by a series of densely nested representational practices. Raphael prefaces his account of the Father's decree by describing how

> th' empyreal host
> Of angels by imperial summons called,
> Innumerable before th' Almighty's throne
> Forthwith from all the ends of Heav'n appeared
> Under their hierarchs in orders bright;
> Ten thousand thousand ensigns high advanced,

Standards, and gonfalons twixt van and rear
Stream in the air, and for distinction serve
Of hierarchies, of orders, and degrees;
Or in their glittering tissues bear emblazed
Holy memorials, acts of zeal and love
Recorded eminent.   (5.583–94)

In response to the seeming superfluity of these displays, Empson
provides only the most incisive rendering of a longstanding critical
reaction: "Why do the angels have to be organized into an elaborate hierarchy at all? Are they organized to do something, or is it
merely what is called a 'pecking order' among hens?"[17]

It is true that Raphael's retelling seems to subordinate the narrowly practical significance of the angels' activities to what might
be called their social, or indeed their poetic, resonance. He slips
briefly but tellingly into the present tense in his account of how
the heavenly banners "Stream in the air / and for distinction
serve," spinning these introductory lines into a pearlescent reverie
that presents his auditor Adam with the brilliant visual immediacy of his peers' "Standards, and gonfalons." The politically representational function of these banners is not thereby obscured
but reinforced, however, as they are said to "bear emblazed / Holy
memorials" of each angel's prior actions—a process of quasi-
textualized record keeping that, through the infinitive mood of
Raphael's narration, can be imagined as stretching out indefinitely.
As David Quint notes, though these celestial standards appear at
first like the martial trappings of an epic army, they function, in
fact, as a pacific "series of merit badges, earned by their pious zeal
and love."[18] In this respect, they evoke Milton's account in book 3
of the Son's own meritorious decision to volunteer himself as
humankind's redeemer. But the deliberate artifice of the angels'
"glittering tissues" also allies them with the poem's other fictions
of representation, most potently exemplified by the Son himself.

Crucially, these banners are said to "for distinction serve / Of
hierarchies, of orders, and degrees" (5.590–91), and Milton emphasizes these cascading ranks of eminence with unusual persistence
throughout the following lines, culminating in the announcement
that the celestial hosts will under the Son's "great vicegerent reign

abide / United as one individual soul / Forever happy" (5.609–11).
The Father's careful use of the striking word "vicegerent" contrasts
with Raphael's later and more straightforward claim that the Son
was "proclaimed / Messiah King anointed" (5.663–64), as well as
the chief rebel's own rhetorically slippery reference to "our King /
The great Messiah" (5.690–91).[19] Although the term "vicegerent"
could be used to refer to earthly monarchs, most often in order to
reinforce their status as representatives of God, in Milton's time
it also bore connotations of other forms of subordinate authority, such as that of priests or magistrates. [20] The Son's mediatorial
role can thus be more fully understood as an extension of the angelic
modes of representation that Raphael so carefully delineates; while
even the loyal Abdiel will later assert that Satan and his followers
must "Confess him rightful King" (5.818), he also observes that the
angels will retain the "Essential powers" (5.841) of their heavenly
hierarchy.[21] In its attention to the fine gradations of politics, moreover, Milton's epic once again displays important affinities with
the thinking of Hobbes. As Katherine Attie notes, while the latter's
theory of representation was perceived by even his earliest critics
as emphasizing the sovereignty of the monarch, it also painstak-
ingly charts the labors of the manifold "agents and officers, who
perform, in the public view, scenes of the Leviathan's dynamic
power."[22] Indeed, Hobbes's list of the representatives responsible
for maintaining the fiction that is civil society—"a *Lieutenant*, a
Vicar, an *Attorney*, a *Deputy*, a *Procurator*"—resembles nothing
so much as a mundane version of the Father's summons of the
celestial host.[23]

Quint convincingly suggests that the skewed vision of heaven
concocted by Satan in book 5 is primarily a feudal or aristocratic
one in which the rebel angels chafe at their refiguration as a
"United" (5.610) mass and thus at the complete abolition of hierarchy that the Son's exaltation seems to imply.[24] But through the
latent connections between the lowliest cherub's "glittering tissues" and the Son's privileged place atop the "flaming mount,"
we might also see here something resembling a quasi-Hobbesian
commonwealth: a thickly populated political realm in which hierarchical relationships are neither hereditary nor inherent but are,

rather, fundamentally arbitrary and, as a direct consequence, poet-ically vibrant (5.592–98).[25] Critics have often asserted that these scenes invest a surplus of descriptive energy in the portrayal of heavenly kingship precisely in order to establish it as the only legit-imate form of monarchy. And indeed one would certainly go too far to claim that in Milton's celestial politics legitimate represen-tation originates naturally with "the people" more or less broadly conceived.[26] But the angels' ceaselessly streaming standards none-theless illustrate how the heaven of *Paradise Lost* is also founded on remarkably dispersed representational practices that frame the central act of the exaltation. *Pace* Empson, reading these heavenly forms of artifice not as ultimately superfluous "memorials" but as continually renewed fictions—that is, as the sustaining cause rather than merely the ornamental record of political life—helps to resituate the decree in a deeper poetic tissue.

"Frequent Songs": The Occasions of Lyric

This scene of celestial politics resumes in the wake of the Father's announcement, but as in Raphael's description of the ever waving banners, the celebration that attends on the Son's exalta-tion is remarkable chiefly for its seeming timelessness. Here, the angels' hymns are figured less as new melodic strains to accom-pany the heavenly command than as an unceasing *continuo* that courses beneath it:

> That day, as other solemn days, they spent
> In song and dance about the sacred hill,
> Mystical dance, which yonder starry sphere
> Of planets and of fixed in all her wheels
> Resembles nearest, mazes intricate,
> Eccentric, intervolved, yet regular
> Then most, when most irregular they seem.   (5.618–24)

Because Milton merely describes the angels' motions rather than directly reporting their words of admiration, it has often been assumed that this heavenly song and dance at least partially resembles the more fully developed hymn of admiration that erupts in the wake of the dialogue between the Father and Son in book 3.[27] Just as the Father's first decree is best understood not as a formulaic statement of rule but as a new genre of utterance, however, so too should the beguiling account of the angels' dances as more "regular / Then most, when most irregular they seem" give readers caution at too readily presuming the details of their representational form—especially given the explicit comparison here to the motions of the cosmos, which will later lead Raphael to chastise Adam for dreaming of how the "creatures there / Live, in what state, condition or degree" (8.175–76).

Unlike these dispersed "Melodious hymns" (5.656), the celestial song of praise in book 3 is deliberately, self-consciously lyrical in the most fundamental sense. With its bounded, tripartite structure and successive addresses to each person of the deity—hymning "Thee Father first" (3.372) before shifting its praise to "Thee next... of all creation first, / Begotten Son" (3.383–84)—this jubilant song borrows heavily from the classical "literary hymns" of Callimachus, a lyric form typically distinguished from congregational or public hymns by its narrower focalization on the relationship between the singer and the deity to which the gift is offered.[28] More pronounced, however, is the influence of the Psalms, which had by Milton's time become closely affiliated with other forms of religious and secular lyric through a long tradition of metrical verse translations.[29] Even in taking up their instruments and beginning to play, the angels enact a shift from classical praise for martial vigor to songs of Christian devotion through the imaginative supersession of readied "quivers" by the "golden harps" and crowns of the Davidic psalms:

> Then crowned again their golden harps they took,
> Harps ever tuned, that glittering by their side
> Like quivers hung, and with preamble sweet
> Of charming symphony they introduce
> Their sacred song, and waken raptures high.[30]   (3.365–69)

Mary Ann Radzinowicz identifies this song as both the angels' "first hymn and the first hymn in the poem," arguing that it serves as a reflective "lyrical" gloss on the tense action of the dialogue between Father and Son; she presumably excludes the earlier hymns in book 5 on the grounds that they do not explicitly announce themselves as songs of praise.[31] Francis Blessington likewise argues that such Miltonic "epic hymns" are designed primarily to furnish "relief from the inexorable action related in the narrative and dramatic structures," ultimately providing "the ideal toward which epic poetry should evolve."[32] However, such classifications of book 3's hymn within a relatively distinct category of "the lyric" belie the extent to which this concept was a vexed one in early modern theories of genre.

The apparently harmonious synthesis of classical and scriptural modes in this song possesses an instructive counterpoint in Milton's own more cautious discussion of lyric in *The Reason of Church-Government,* where he compares "those magnifick Odes and Hymns wherein *Pindarus* and *Callimachus* are in most things worthy" to the more righteous "matter" of biblical forms: "those frequent songs throughout the law and prophets beyond all these, not in their divine argument alone, but in the very critical art of composition may be easily made appear over all the kinds of Lyrick poesy, to be incomparable" (YP 1:815–16). Even as he is careful to distinguish between scriptural songs and secular poems, by presenting both of these genres as those best suited to celebrating "the deeds and triumphs of just and pious Nations doing valiantly through faith against the enemies of Christ," and to lamenting "the general relapses of Kingdoms and States from justice and Gods true worship," Milton attributed to them a shared political potency that had assumed new urgency in the mid-seventeenth century (YP 1:817).[33] Writing from exile in France, William Davenant claimed in the preface to his epic poem *Gondibert* that poetic *"Inspiration"* of the kind frequently claimed by Milton himself was "a spirituall Fit, deriv'd from the antient Ethnick Poets, who then, as they were Priests, were States-men too," though he also echoed Milton's implied criticism of those who "rather imitate the *Greek* Poets then the *Hebrew* Prophets, since the later were inspir'd for the use of others; and these, like the former, prophecy for themselves."[34]

Similarly, Hobbes argued in a response to Davenant that each of "the three Regions of Mankind, *Court, City,* and *Countrey*" possessed a corresponding and proper "manner of *Representation.*" This balance could be threatened by authors who claimed the mantles of "Prophets and Priests" and thereby encouraged "subversion or disturbance of the Commonwealths wherein they lived," as they had done among the Greeks "before the name of Poet was known."[35] Not only did hymn and lyric share a thoroughly entangled history, therefore, but the author who set out to emulate them also necessarily became a political actor, with the choice between genres potentially affecting the nation.

As such, especially when considered alongside Satan's critique of celestial representation—of which readers are reminded by the angels themselves, who recount how the Son "threw down / Th' aspiring Dominations" (3.392) that dared to scoff at the "divine similitude" (3.384)—the hymn of book 3 less resembles an assured act of lyric worship than it does yet another entry in a sustained political poetics. If we are to understand this hymn as a kind of lyric embedded within Milton's epic, it thus remains not only to ask which generic features distinguish this angelic song from its public, celebratory precedent in book 5, but also to chart how the perceived authority of these representations shifts from one scene of praise to the next.

In considering the relationship of each of these psalmic or hymnic utterances to the contested category of lyric, it may be helpful to seek a sort of guidance from the poet himself by examining the shift to a first-person perspective at the end of book 3's carefully structured song. This moment has been read as the almost unconscious intrusion of Milton's own voice into *Paradise Lost,* an instance where the taut fabric of epic narration is momentarily shot through with the bright lyrical praise that characterizes the proems:

> Hail Son of God, Savior of men, thy name
> Shall be the copious matter of my song
> Henceforth, and never shall my harp thy praise
> Forget, nor from thy Father's praise disjoin.[36]   (3.412–15)

As Samuel Fallon observes, the angels' insistence at the close that they will not "disjoin" their celebration of the Son from his "Father's praise" evinces the "tensions and rivalries" typical of the Callimachan hymn, which frequently registered the fact that "to praise one Olympian god was, inevitably, not to praise many others."[37] Indeed, it seems to be precisely these competing mandates to celebrate both the "author" and the "actor" that comprise the Christian deity, to use Hobbes's terms, which provoke the searching outburst of reflexivity and even possessiveness in the phrases "my song" and "my harp," part of an impassioned *envoi* that conveys these lines to God even as it binds them more firmly to their speaker. A hymn that begins by signaling its proximity to the object of praise—the angelic "shout" peals out "No sooner had th' Almighty ceased" (3.344–45)—is thus by its final lines pulled to the opposite pole in the relationship between singer and listener, made more immediate to readers by the bounded consciousness that has intervened in this sprawling epic.[38]

It is in these terms that book 3's song of praise has conventionally been understood as partaking of lyric expressiveness. Such an interpretation figures Milton's contribution to the genre as one that privileges interiorized subjectivity and thereby works to bridge what Joshua Scodel describes as the wide gulf between "the early seventeenth-century flowering of the 'metaphysical' lyric and the lyric resurgence of the late eighteenth century and Romanticism."[39] But just as Milton's chosen Callimachan form is defined by the vexed shifts among its various addressees, so too is the lyricism of these lines located in the fluid alterations in the identity and position of its speakers rather than in an unmediated authorial presence. As Heather Dubrow observes in *The Challenges of Orpheus*, the religious lyric of the period is largely defined by a complex play of "immediacy and distance" between the poet and the deity that is "repeatedly invoked, thematized, and questioned" by authors such as George Herbert and Henry Vaughan, as well as in works such as Milton's Nativity ode.[40] Read in this light, these lines are lyrical not only for the exuberant first-person voice with which they culminate, venturing briefly like a melody above the angels' ground, but also for their subtle shifts in perspective, which shade from the collective to the individual and, in the narrator's placid final comment that "they in Heav'n, above the starry sphere, / Their happy hours in joy and hymning spent" (3.416–17), back again.

Faced with the inherent ambiguity of "lyric" as a generic category, early modern authors and theorists thus increasingly came to identify the mode not with fixed structural qualities but with what Milton in *The Reason of Church-Government* describes as the demands of "occasion" required by "all the kinds of Lyric poesy": the manifold and variable connections between speakers, addressees, and listeners that shaped each work (YP 1:815–16).[41] In this context, we might reconsider the relationship between the ostensible lyric purity of the song in book 3 and the more mediated celebratory hymns of book 5. The fact that the angelic music for the Son's exaltation is reported rather than recited as verse might appear to minimize its effect as a lull in the narrative of *Paradise Lost*, an independently wrought poetic work to which the reader is called to attend. But Raphael also emphasizes its status as deliberate *artifice*, an activity that is akin to the erection of "Pavilions numberless" and "Celestial tabernacles" (5.653–54) and opposed to Satan's determination to "leave / Unworshipped, unobeyed the throne supreme" (5.669–70), which disrupts the celestial harmony much more completely than the weapons of war he and his compatriots will soon devise.

Where the praise of the deity in book 3 is immediately recognizable as a psalmodic hymn—a form well suited to addressing a being whose relationship to his creation appears, at least so far, to be relatively clear—the exaltation scene in book 5 thus reveals that such forms of celebration possess origins that are as contested as those of the Son, demanding a broader perspective that accounts for how lyrical praise could also interrogate "the relationship among presentness, representation, and distance" between speakers and addressees: precisely the theological and political issues raised by the Son's new role.[42] Milton's heaven may be, in Lewalski's phrase, "continually suffused with angelic harmonies and music, hymnic in purpose though not always in form," but the shift from these diffuse practices to the more narrowly political uses of genre within the poem deserves further attention.[43]

"A Kind of Psalmistry": The Critique of Lyric

These persistent tensions between hymn, lyric, and political rhetoric in *Paradise Lost* also inform several of Milton's other writings.[44] The *Apology against a Pamphlet* had presented readers with a largely conventional literary autobiography, tracing an ascent from Milton's juvenile admiration for "the smooth Elegiack Poets" to his preference for "the two famous renowners of *Beatrice* and *Laura*" and finally to an appreciation of the more sustained wisdom of classical epic and Christian philosophy—a narrative in keeping with his well-known claim that the author who hopes "to write well hereafter in laudable things, ought him selfe to bee a true Poem" (YP 1:889–90). Especially in his late sonnets, however, Milton also reveals his keen attunement to what Sharon Achinstein calls the "iconography of lyric poetry in social exchange."[45] By addressing these works directly to contemporary political figures such as Oliver Cromwell or Sir Henry Vane while also publishing them for a wider audience, he adapted the intimacy associated with earlier sonnets in order to articulate lyric's unique capacity both to represent and to enact the personal relationships that sustain the political life of the nation. Similarly, even as his most explicit account of genre in *The Reason of Church-Government* delineates the general power of scriptural "frequent songs" to instill "vertu" in "a great people," Milton here also invests his own identity in what is imagined as a deeply individual, if always flexible, contract between the poet and his audience: "Neither doe I think it shame to covnant with any knowing reader, that for some few yeers yet I may go on trust with him toward the payment of what I am now indebted" (YP 1:816, 820).[46]

But Milton's parenthetical comment in the same passage that "most abuse" their poetic abilities also evinces his recurrent anxiety with contemporary efforts to marshal lyric or hymnic forms of expression for political ends. Defending himself against the "Confuter" Bishop Hall's claim that his Smectymnuuan and animadversive polemic had degenerated into a *"theatricall"* and *"big-mouth'd"* performance of blasphemous worship, Milton argued in the *Apology against a Pamphlet* that his work was not "a prayer so much as a hymne in prose frequent both in the Prophets, and in humane authors," vehemently rejecting the implication that "no way should be left me to present my meaning but to make my selfe a canting Probationer of orisons...left so impoverisht of what to say, as to turne my Liturgy into my Ladies Psalter" (YP 1:930–31). In defining his political writing as a form of secular "Liturgy," Milton was compelled to distinguish his own genuine inspiration from the mindless, calcified repetitions of a papist prayer book as well as from sermonic or dramatic speeches. He had made just such a distinction in the astounding closing prayer from *Of Reformation,* in which the speaker's voice rises from "amidst the *Hymns,* and *Halleluiahs* of *Saints*" to utter "high *strains* in new and lofty *Measures*" (YP 1:616). This capacity of lyric and hymn to serve as potent political speech, even as they continually threaten to decay into hollow routines of worship, also marks their contested status in *Paradise Lost.*

The various pronouncements and debates that animate the angelic rebellion of books 5 and 6 have often been characterized as introducing explicitly partisan modes of rhetoric into the poem, but it is not immediately clear why such language should be set against the hymnic concord of the celestial assembly.[47] Satan is the first figure whose speech is reported after the Father's decree and, as already noted, he rejects the exaltation in large part as a failure of representation. Indeed, the "suggested cause" (5.702) he offers Beelzebub for the rebels' decampment to the "quarters of the north" (5.689) is that they must "prepare / Fit entertainment to receive our King" (5.689–90), presumably by augmenting the ceaseless angelic hymns with alternative forms of praise befitting the radical novelty of their political situation. Similarly, he later announces that his crew of angels has been assembled "only to consult how we may best / With what may be devised of honors new / Receive" (5.779–81) their new ruler, figuring their response as a benign revision of heavenly worship before launching into the more recognizably political claim that both Father and Son are tyrants who "look for adoration to th' abuse / Of those imperial titles which assert / Our being ordained to govern, not to serve" (5.800–02).

In her generic taxonomy of *Paradise Lost,* Lewalski argues that the "dominant speech forms" of the rebellious angels are "deliberative rhetoric and soliloquy," and she goes so far as to suggest that while "occasionally Satan inverts or parodies a strain or two of the songs which continually resound throughout heaven and Eden...he sings no hymns (the highest lyric genre)," for "true lyrics are outside their repertoire."[48] Just as Milton sought to assert the role of lyrical expression in political discourse even while cautioning against its frequent abuses, however, Satan repeatedly figures his own dissent as an effort to distinguish legitimate representations from the false hymnic concord peddled by heaven's king. Perhaps his most scathing charge is that the hosts marshaled by the Father in book 6 are "Minist'ring spirits, trained up in feast and song" (6.167): not potent, quasi-Hobbesian representatives or actors for the deity but, rather, the debased "minstrelsy of Heav'n" (6.168), warbling forth lyricized utterances that lack entirely the world-structuring capacity of true poetic and political works.[49] If, as Lewalski claims, the satanic discourse in books 5 and 6 encourages "the reader to make complex discriminations about the uses and perversions of language," it thus does so partly by recalling how, for Milton and his opponents alike, imagining new political circumstances also required attention to how the same means of representation could flourish or decay depending on their ends.[50]

Satan's assault on heavenly monarchy also derives much of its verbal potency from its echoes of Milton's regicide tracts, a likeness most clearly displayed in his attempt to raze the *Eikon Basilike*'s duplicitous representation of Charles I.[51] As in the rebel angel's critique, Milton attacked the highly popular "king's book" not merely as political fraud but as poetic imposture. Much of his response in *Eikonoklastes* is devoted to systematically cataloging and mocking the various generic influences on Charles's ostensibly intimate, individualized account of his sufferings, as in the derisive comment that "quaint Emblems and devices begg'd from the old Pageantry of some Twelf-nights entertainment at *Whitehall*, will doe but ill to make a Saint or Martyr (YP 3:343).[52] Most damning of all, however, was Milton's claim that Charles or his collaborators had lifted a prayer directly from Sidney's *New Arcadia*.[53] As a result of this controversy, *Eikonoklastes'* assault on the king's literary pretensions has often been linked to broader concerns surrounding the genre of romance, which Victoria Kahn observes had come to "connote not only errant passion but also imitation in the sense of fiction, deception, and paralogism."[54] Importantly, however, Milton also figures this borrowing as an indecorous attempt to adapt the heartfelt address of Sidney's work to a new occasion beyond its original context, and thereby to forge a counterfeit bond between the royal speaker and his faithful auditors. Having contemptuously noted that Charles had "as it were unhallow'd, and unchrist'nd the very duty of prayer it self," Milton goes on to denounce most fiercely how the king's book had already been adapted in explicitly lyric and melic modes, including psalms and hymns of praise: "I begun to think that the whole Book might perhaps be intended a peece of Poetrie. The words are good, the fiction smooth and cleanly; there wanted onely Rime, and that, they say, is bestow'd upon it lately" (YP 3:362, 406).[55] Indeed, in the same way that Charles had exploited the heightened emotions of romance for his own political purposes, the issuers of these psalmic offshoots of the *Eikon* suggested that the lyric expressiveness of the king's sentiments made them uniquely well suited for public emulation, as in Edward Reynolds's claim that they "like A *Diamond* cannot lose their *Luster* although they were mantled in *Cimmerian-Darkness*."[56]

By specifically objecting to the presentation of King Charles's experience in "the form of a privat Psalter... quilted out of Scripture phrase," Milton was thus also forced to confront attacks that had been leveled against his own writings: as "a kind of Psalmistry," this mode of expression hewed uncomfortably close to the expansive, slippery "kinds of Lyrick" for which he offered conditional praise in *The Reason of Church-Government*, as well as to the righteous polemical "Liturgy" he defended in the *Apology against a Pamphlet* (YP 3:360; 1:816, 931).[57] Elsewhere in *Paradise Lost*, Milton privileges spontaneous and lyrically ornate forms of worship over rote repetitions of the kind found in the king's book and its errant spawn, as when he insists that Adam and Eve's "orisons" (5.145) at the opening of book 5 are "Unmeditated" (5.149) as "such prompt eloquence / Flowed from their lips, in prose or numerous verse, / More tuneable than needed lute or harp" (5.149–51).[58] But at the moment of the heavenly revolt in books 5 and 6, the relationship between established and inventive forms of expression remains highly disputed, and it is through this very contestation that Milton advances a model for how lyric could serve as an authentic mode of political representation.

"Debate of Truth": The Politics of Lyric

Satan's newly incendiary rhetoric is soon interrupted by the faithful Abdiel's rousing dissent "in a flame of zeal severe" (5.807), a characterization that has traditionally prompted associations between his parrhesiastic language and that of contemporary Nonconformists like Milton.[59] Certainly, Raphael's account of Abdiel's first speech supports such an interpretation through its recursive embroidering of how he was "faithful found / Among the faithless, faithful only he; / Among innumerable false, unmoved, / Unshaken, unseduced, unterrified" (5.896–99). However, this striking image of "The flaming seraph fearless, though alone / Encompassed round with foes" (5.875–76)—though less obviously imitative of the Father's announcement from atop the "flaming mount" (5.598) than Satan's own darkly parodic reiteration, which begins by once again invoking the angelic "Thrones, Dominations, Princedoms, Virtues, Powers" (5.772)—also encourages readers to attend to the shifting significance of a single orator addressing an assembled audience.[60] In much the same way that the Father's decree reshapes the political landscape of heaven, Satan and Abdiel's emerging representational roles call attention to the new bonds that their own utterances establish between speakers, addressees, and listeners. Raphael's report of the debates between Satan and Abdiel repeatedly underscores not just what might be called the narrowly political theories that animate their speeches, but also how each articulates his own poetic authority to utter them at all. Abdiel's attack on Satan's "impious obloquy" (5.813) against the "just decree" (5.814) of the Father ultimately hinges on the gnomic question "Shalt thou give law to God, shalt thou dispute / With him the points of liberty, who made / Thee what thou art" (5.822–24), while among the rebels his own "zeal / None seconded, as out of season judged, / Or singular and rash" (5.849–51). In each case what is at stake is the question of *occasion*, in the sense articulated by Hobbes's response to Davenant's preface: to misjudge the type of "Representation" demanded by a situation is to gravely threaten the stability of the community.[61]

This emphasis on the relative position and perspective of each the poem's speakers is even more pronounced in the subsequent encounter between Satan and Abdiel in book 6. Where Raphael's account of the celestial displays that preceded the Son's exaltation emphasized their mutually reinforcing nature, with the scrupulous arrangement of the angels "Under their hierarchs in orders bright" (5.587) suggesting that their "Ten thousand thousand ensigns high advanced" (5.588) are intended to be visible to one another as well as to the Father himself, in these scenes political and poetic speech works largely to separate utterers from audiences. Although it was Satan's refusal to participate in the earlier celebrations that marked his original dissent from heavenly order, the righteous Abdiel now also sets himself apart from these martial demonstrations as he undertakes an exploration of "his own undaunted heart" (6.113), which weaves the interiority and spontaneity associated with Adam and Eve's hymns together with continued attention to the pragmatic dimensions of heavenly representation, directly linking poetic potency with political and martial power: "nor is it aught but just, / That he who in debate of truth hath won, / Should win in arms" (6.121–23).[62] Raphael's rapid narration all but collapses Abdiel's turn from this contemplative "pondering" (6.127) to his "Forth stepping" (6.128) from the angelic ranks, and the subsequent exchange of taunts between the opposing champions, while drawing heavily on classical epic convention, also stages a series of representational scenes in which the relationships between orators and auditors are centrally at issue. Abdiel now no longer celebrates his isolation among hostile ranks but explicitly references the public performance of fealty among his peers, as when he recalls to Satan how "I alone / Seemed in thy world erroneous to dissent / From all: my sect thou seest, now learn too late / How few sometimes may know, when thousands err" (6.145–48). By way of response, the chief rebel scornfully suggests that his adversary only appears "Before thy fellows, ambitious to win / From me some plume, that thy success may show / Destruction to the rest" (6.160–62). In the claim that Abdiel has constructed this artificial display of faith not to represent the deity but to glorify his own vatic power, Satan's critique also recalls Davenant's contemporary attack on authors who place the Greek poet-priests above the pious Hebrew prophets.[63]

Citing the similarities between the angelic strategies of self-presentation in this scene, both of which partake of the genre of political "debate" (5.681) originally initiated by the rebels, David Norbrook suggests that there is "no room in Heaven for deliberative rhetoric, for the arguments of the forum."[64] In this account, Abdiel's answers to Satan are an unfortunate exigency rather than a discursive triumph, and the hymnic "continual act of praise" offered by the angels after the exaltation remains the apex of heavenly representation in *Paradise Lost*.[65] In contrast, Radzinowicz demonstrates that Abdiel's utterances are closely modeled on the psalmic subgenre of the wisdom song, enabling the loyal angel to respond with speech that, like the Father's own command, fluently "interweaves scriptural and contemporary political language."[66] But in their relentlessly self-reflexive nature, the utterances of Satan and Abdiel also enact and comment upon the same labile alterations in the relationships among speakers, addressees, and auditors that characterized early modern lyric more broadly.[67] Moreover, it is precisely this new attention to such concerns of occasion that makes possible the poem's shift from the timeless song and dance of book 5 to the carefully constructed lyrical address that erupts in the hymn at the center of book 3. Not only the *content* but also the poetic *form* of this most extended and defining portrait of the deity is thus derived ultimately from these earlier struggles over the bounds of legitimate representation. Far from representing the debasement of lyrical expression in *Paradise Lost,* these scenes of political strife are its essential crucible.

It might be said that the much-contested politics of lyric that emerges over the course of books 5 and 6 is, despite its formative influence on the poem's treatment of genre, in the strictest sense superfluous. Even Abdiel's dissent can serve only as a token gesture of loyalty rather than as a strategic advantage, for upon his return to "the Mount of God" (6.05), he sees among the amassing armies "Already known what he for news had thought / To have reported" (6.20–21). As the Father notes in his praise of the faithful angel, however, Abdiel derives merit for this action precisely from his "care / To stand approved in sight of God, though worlds / Judged thee perverse" (6.35–37). Such a model of heavenly poetics deftly counters Satan's critique that the angels have slothfully abdicated their rightful place as "Minist'ring spirits" (6.166) and become the mere "minstrelsy of Heaven" (6.167). In the new representational scheme established after the Son's elevation, to be seen to speak, act, and even sing before God is to serve as a political agent in a narrower but more penetrating sense than that enacted by the angels' streaming banners, one that will also come to define the innovations undertaken by Adam and Eve in Eden.[68] By negotiating new roles as independent actors in the sight of an authoring deity, Satan and Abdiel are at once the first speakers of lyric in *Paradise Lost* and its first critics. They here pioneer what Dubrow describes as a "metalyrical" sense of its possibilities and limitations that also surfaces in the proems, as when at the opening of book 7 the Miltonic speaker calls out, "govern thou my song, / Urania, and fit audience find, though few" (7.30–31) and in the next anxious breath apotropaically wards off "that wild rout that tore the Thracian bard...till the savage clamor drowned / Both harp and voice" (7.35–37).[69]

But if the representational fissure opened by the exaltation makes possible such individualized expressiveness, books 5 and 6 of Milton's poem also contain a startling vision of its end. On one level, the Son's discourse to the Father before descending upon the rebel angels in his Chariot of Paternal Deity seems explicitly designed to resolve (from a satanic or Empsonian perspective, rather too belatedly) many of the issues resulting from his own appointment (6.750). He explains that he will "resign" the "Scepter and power" with which he has been invested as the Father's representative "when in the end / Thou shalt be all in all, and I in thee / Forever" (6.730–33). This apparent ontological shift is also linked, however, to an equally significant transformation of the poem's rituals of admiration:

> Then shall thy saints unmixed, and from th' impure
> Far separate, circling thy holy mount
> Unfeignèd hallelujahs to thee sing,
> Hymns of high praise, and I among them chief.[70]   (6.742–45)

In the syntactic ambiguity of this final line, the Son as an entity distinct from the Father is imagined as dissolving once more into a swell of undifferentiated celebration, becoming no longer a discrete subject for adoration but the "chief" strain in this ceaseless music. Songs or verses of praise for the deity are finally far from ideal modes in *Paradise Lost*: their emergence is as vexed as that of the Son himself, and their presence, like his, structures the epic not solely through moments of pacific worship but through the constantly shifting relationships between poetic speakers and the figures they strive, often unsuccessfully, to represent. Ultimately, the events of the poem — indeed, all of Milton's created history — are suspended in the charged span between such scenes of hymnic oblivion, in the contested space of lyric.

Yale University

Notes

1. John Milton, *Paradise Lost*, in *The Complete Poetry and Essential Prose of John Milton*, ed. William Kerrigan, John Rumrich, and Stephen M. Fallon (New York, 2007), 5.601, 3.309, 5.605–06; hereafter cited in the text by book and line number.

2. William Empson, *Milton's God* (London, 1961), 102. See also Neil Forsyth, *The Satanic Epic* (Princeton, N.J., 2003), 170–72; and Michael Bryson, *The Tyranny of Heaven: Milton's Rejection of God as King* (Newark, N.J., 2004), 92–93.

3. John Rogers, "The Political Theology of Milton's Heaven," in *The New Milton Criticism*, ed. Peter C. Herman and Elizabeth Sauer, 68–84 (Cambridge, 2012), 76.

4. On Hobbes's engagement with Socinianism, see Leo Strauss, *Hobbes's Critique of Religion and Related Writings* (Chicago, 2011), 69–72; Peter Geach, "The Religion of Thomas Hobbes," *Religious Studies* 17, no. 4 (1981): 549–58; and C. A. J. Coady, "The Socinian Connection: Further Thoughts on the Religion of Hobbes," *Religious Studies* 22, no. 2 (1986): 277–80. Sarah Mortimer, *Reason and Religion in the English Revolution: The Challenge of Socinianism* (Cambridge, 2010), provides a comprehensive account of Socinianism's influence in seventeenth century England; see especially chapters three and four on the Great Tew Circle, a group of philosophers with which Hobbes was affiliated.

5. Thomas Hobbes, *Leviathan; or, The Matter, Forme, and Power of a Common Wealth, Ecclesiastical and Civil* (London, 1651), 80.

6. Ibid., 81–83. Bryan Garsten, "Religion and Representation in Hobbes," in *Leviathan*, ed. Ian Shapiro, 519–46 (New Haven, Conn., 2010), 535–39, observes that Hobbes revised these claims in later editions in order to further emphasize the artificial relationship between God and his personations. On Hobbes and the idea of representation more generally, see Hanna Pitkin, *The Concept of Representation* (Berkeley, 1967), 14–37.

7. Hobbes, *Leviathan*, 81. For a comprehensive summary of Hobbes's Trinitarianism and its relationship to his political views, see Mónica Brito Vieira, *The Elements of Representation in Hobbes: Aesthetics, Theatre, Law, and Theology in the Construction of Hobbes's Theory of the State* (Boston, 2009), 209–33.

8. Recent accounts include Vieira, *Elements*, 15–74; Srinivas Aravamudan, "'The Unity of the Represical': Reading *Leviathan* against the Grain," *South Atlantic Quarterly* 104, no. 4 (2005): 631–53; and Paul Dumouchel, "Persona: Reason and Representation in Hobbes's Political Philosophy," *SubStance* 25, no. 2 (1996): 68–80.

9. Victoria Kahn, *Wayward Contracts: The Crisis of Political Obligation in England, 1640–1674* (Princeton, N.J., 2004), 18.

10. Stella Revard, *The War in Heaven: "Paradise Lost" and the Tradition of Satan's Rebellion* (Ithaca, N.Y., 1980), 10.

11. See, for instance, Maurice Kelley, *This Great Argument: A Study of Milton's "De Doctrina Christiana" as a Gloss upon "Paradise Lost"* (Princeton, N.J., 1941), 98–106; Phillip J. Donnelly, "The Teloi of Genres: *Paradise Lost* and *De Doctrina Christiana*," in *Milton Studies*, vol. 39, ed. Albert C. Labriola, 74–100 (Pittsburgh, 2000); and Samuel Fallon,

"Milton's Strange God: Theology and Narrative Form in *Paradise Lost*," *ELH* 79, no. 1 (2012): 33–57.

12. Milton, *Poems, &c. upon Several Occasions Both English and Latin* (London, 1673), 131. Revard, *War in Heaven*, 74–78, notes that Psalm 2 was also marshaled in seventeenth century arguments for distinguishing the Son's generation from his exaltation, including that of Milton's *De doctrina Christiana*.

13. Barbara Lewalski, *"Paradise Lost" and the Rhetoric of Literary Forms* (Princeton, N.J., 1985), 124.

14. On the early reception of books 5 and 6, see Revard, *War in Heaven*, 16–19, and Nicholas von Maltzahn, "The War in Heaven and the Miltonic Sublime," in *A Nation Transformed: England after the Restoration*, ed. Alan Houston and Steve Pincus, 154–79 (Cambridge, 2001). On the generic expansiveness of epic, see Rosalie L. Colie, *The Resources of Kind: Genre-Theory in the Renaissance* (Berkeley, 1973), 22–23. Ayesha Ramachandran, "Tasso's Petrarch: The Lyric Means to Epic Ends," *Modern Language Notes* 122, no. 1 (2007): 186–208, offers an account similar to my own of how lyric could serve not only as a constitutive part of epic but also could reshape it from within.

15. Milton, *The Reason of Church-Government*, in *The Complete Prose Works of John Milton*, 8 vols., ed. Don M. Wolfe et al. (New Haven, Conn., 1953–82), 1:816; hereafter cited as YP in the text.

16. Colie, *Resources of Kind*, 122; Lewalski, *Rhetoric of Literary Forms*, 23.

17. Empson, *Milton's God*, 103; see also Forsyth, *Satanic Epic*, 173–74.

18. David Quint, *Inside "Paradise Lost": Reading the Designs of Milton's Epic* (Princeton, N.J., 2014), 137.

19. This particular use of the term "vicegerent" is likely Milton's own, appearing in none of the sources for the decree noted by Lewalski, *Rhetoric of Literary Forms*, 323–24.

20. In addition to Milton's own acknowledgment, in *The Reason of Church-Government*, YP 1:771, "that the civill magistrate weares an autority of Gods giving, and ought to be obey'd as his vicegerent" (even as he firmly denies that an earthly king can serve as a "type" of Christ's role as the ruler of heaven), see Henry Parker, *The Case of Shipmony* (London, 1640), 45; and the anonymous *The priviledges and practice of parliaments in England* (London, 1640), both of which refer to such authorities in these terms.

21. Milton describes the Son's mediatorial function in theological terms in *De doctrina Christiana* (YP 6:214–19).

22. Katherine Attie, "Re-Membering the Body Politic: Hobbes and the Construction of Civic Immortality," *ELH: A Journal of English Literary History* 75, no. 3 (2008): 505.

23. Hobbes, *Leviathan*, 81–82.

24. Quint, *Inside "Paradise Lost,"* 132–44.

25. Laura L. Knoppers, *Historicizing Milton: Spectacle, Power, and Poetry in Restoration England* (Athens, Ga., 1994), 68–83, argues that Milton here envisions a heavenly "politics of joy" that could replace the venal forms of courtly celebration encouraged and indeed enforced after the Restoration. For a thorough discussion of contemporary angelologies and especially of the question of angelic hierarchy, see Feisal G. Mohamed, *In the Anteroom of Divinity: The Reformation of the Angels from Colet to Milton* (Toronto, 2008).

26. Quint, *Inside "Paradise Lost,"* 134–35; Roger Lejosne, "Milton, Satan, Salmasius and Abdiel," in *Milton and Republicanism*, ed. David Armitage, Armand Himy, and Quentin Skinner, 106–17 (Cambridge, 1995), 106. On seventeenth century cases for popular or parliamentary representation and the responses of both Hobbes and Milton to these arguments, see Mark Knights, *Representation and Misrepresentation in Later Stuart Britain: Partisanship and Political Culture* (Oxford, 2005), 30–40; Quentin Skinner, "Hobbes on Representation," *European Journal of Philosophy* 13, no. 2 (2005): 157–58; and Stephen M. Fallon, "Nascent Republican Theory in Milton's Regicide Prose," in *The Oxford Handbook of Literature and the English Revolution*, ed. Laura L. Knoppers, 309–26 (Oxford, 2013).

27. See, for instance, Lewalski, *Rhetoric of Literary Forms*, 162.

28. Ibid., 160–65; Samuel Fallon, "Milton's Strange God," 51. Paul H. Fry, *The Poet's Calling in the English Ode* (New Haven, Conn., 1980), discusses and ultimately collapses the distinction between these two forms in the work of Renaissance authors like Milton. On the manuscript evidence for Milton's careful reading and annotation of Callimachan hymns, see Nathan Dane II, "Milton's Callimachus," *Modern Language Notes* 56, no. 4 (1941): 278–79.

29. General summaries include Hannibal Hamlin, *Psalm Culture and Early Modern English Literature* (Cambridge, 2004); and Beth Quitslund, *The Reformation in Rhyme: Sternhold, Hopkins and the English Metrical Psalter, 1547–1603* (Aldershot, 2008).

30. John Crossett, "Milton and Pindar," *Notes and Queries* 9 (1962): 217–18, observes that in likening the angels' songs to shafts in these "Quivers," Milton may be referencing Pindar's comparison of his verses to arrows, extending the association between Pindar and Callimachus found in *The Reason of Church-Government* (discussed below).

31. Mary Ann Radzinowicz, *Milton's Epics and the Book of Psalms* (Princeton, N.J., 1989), 147–52.

32. Francis C. Blessington, "'That Undisturbed Song of Pure Conceit': *Paradise Lost* and the Epic-Hymn," in *Renaissance Genres: Essays on Theory, History, and Interpretation*, ed. Barbara Kiefer Lewalski, 468–95 (Cambridge, Mass., 1986), 472, 487.

33. Milton's idiosyncratic engagement with the genre of lyric was mirrored in the period by similar explorations among royalist authors, who

responded to the demise and subsequent rebirth of their cause with a wide range of experimental forms, such as Abraham Cowley's introduction of the Pindaric ode into English verse. On Milton's work within the ode form, see John K. Hale, "Milton Meditates the Ode," *Classical and Modern Literature* 16 (1996): 341–58. On the period's generic inventiveness more generally, see Ann Baynes Coiro, "The Personal Rule of Poets: Cavalier Poetry and the English Revolution," in Knoppers, *Oxford Handbook of Literature*, 206–37; Nigel Smith, "Lyric and the English Revolution," in *The Lyric Poem: Formations and Transformations*, ed. Marion Thain, 71–91 (Cambridge, 2013). Comprehensive accounts of the Pindaric ode's political function are offered in Stella Revard, *Pindar and the Renaissance Hymn-Ode, 1450–1700* (Tempe, Ariz., 2001), and *Politics, Poetics, and the Pindaric Ode, 1450–1700* (Tempe, Ariz., 2008).

34. *A Discourse upon Gondibert an Heroick Poem Written by Sr. William D'Avenant; With an Answer to It, by Mr. Hobbs* (Paris, 1650), 54. The circulation of this text independent of *Gondibert* indicates the extent to which debates over genre were understood to hold direct and potentially incendiary political relevance. On the relationship between Hobbes's comments here and *Leviathan*'s treatment of poetics, see Ted H. Miller, "The Uniqueness of *Leviathan*: Authorizing Poets, Philosophers, and Sovereigns," in *Leviathan after 350 Years*, ed. Tom Sorell and Luc Foisneau, 75–104 (Oxford, 2004).

35. Ibid., 120–29.

36. Radzinowicz, *Milton's Epics*, 147; Anne Ferry, *Milton's Epic Voice: The Narrator in "Paradise Lost"* (Cambridge, Mass., 1963), 49–55.

37. Samuel Fallon, "Milton's Strange God," 51.

38. On these issues of addressivity in lyric more generally, see Fry, *Poet's Calling*, 6–9, and William Waters, *Poetry's Touch: On Lyric Address* (Ithaca, N.Y., 2003).

39. Joshua Scodel, "Lyric Forms," in *The Cambridge Companion to English Literature, 1650–1740*, ed. Steven N. Zwicker (Cambridge, 1998), 120.

40. Heather Dubrow, *The Challenges of Orpheus: Lyric Poetry and Early Modern England* (Baltimore, 2007), 121, 145.

41. On lyric's strong association with occasionality more generally, see Arthur F. Marotti, *Manuscript, Print, and the English Renaissance Lyric* (Ithaca, N.Y., 1995); and Roland Greene, "Lyric," in *The Cambridge History of Literary Criticism*, vol. 3, *The Renaissance*, ed. Glyn P. Norton, 216–28 (Cambridge, 1999).

42. Dubrow, *Challenges of Orpheus*, 121.

43. Lewalski, *Rhetoric of Literary Forms*, 162.

44. Nigel Smith, *Literature and Revolution in England, 1640–1660* (New Haven, Conn., 1994), 6, argues that each of Milton's poems "remakes its genre as it is read," while Heather Dubrow, "The Masquing of Genre in *Comus*," in *Milton Studies*, vol. 44, ed. Albert C. Labriola, 62–83

(Pittsburgh, 2005), 79, suggests that they contain "apotropaic" gestures against the representational "perils associated with the literary types that they themselves variously test and attempt to discard." Other recent studies on Milton's engagement with both specific genres and the concept of generic distinction include Emily A. Ransom, "Digesting Job in *Paradise Lost*," *Studies in Philology* 111, no. 1 (2014): 110–31; and Emily Griffiths Jones, "Milton's Counter-Revision of Romantic Structure in *Paradise Regained*," *Huntington Library Quarterly* 76, no. 1 (2013): 59–81.

45. Sharon Achinstein, "Milton's Trifles: Lyric Disparagement in an Age of Walking Books," *Modern Language Quarterly* 73, no. 1 (2012): 17–19. Achinstein, *Literature and Dissent in Milton's England* (Cambridge, 2003), 118–19, also observes that the original publication of Milton's Sonnet 17 in a biography of its addressee, the disgraced Parliamentarian Henry Vane, was an explicitly political and radical act. See, too, Annabel Patterson, "Milton's Heroic Sonnets," in *A Concise Companion to Milton*, ed. Angelica Duran, 78–94 (Chichester, U.K., 2010); Anna K. Nardo, *Milton's Sonnets and the Ideal Community* (Lincoln, Neb., 1979); Brett A. Hudson, "Religious Dissent in John Milton's 1673 'Poems, &c. upon Several Occasions' and Nonconformist Speech-Acts in the Restoration" (diss., Middle Tennessee State University, 2012); and Patricia Joan Steenland, "Milton's Sonnets and the Lyric Response to History" (diss., Brown University, 1989).

46. On the imbrication of genre, identity, and politics in these tracts, see especially Stephen M. Fallon, *Milton's Peculiar Grace: Self-Representation and Authority* (Ithaca, N.Y., 2007), 88–109; and Thomas Kranidas, *Milton and the Rhetoric of Zeal* (Pittsburgh, 2005), 122–62.

47. Achinstein, *Literature and Dissent*, 118–26; David Norbrook, *Writing the English Republic: Poetry, Rhetoric, and Politics, 1627–1660* (Cambridge, 1999), 433–67; David Loewenstein, *Representing Revolution in Milton and His Contemporaries: Religion, Politics, and Polemics in Radical Puritanism* (Cambridge, 2001), 202–12; Blair Worden, "Milton's Republicanism and the Tyranny of Heaven," in *Machiavelli and Republicanism*, ed. Gisela Bock, Quentin Skinner, and Maurizio Viroli, 225–46 (Cambridge, 1991). For a recent reading of Satan's political rhetoric not as misguided sophistry but as a positive instance of republican discourse in Milton's work, see James Kuzner, *Open Subjects: English Renaissance Republicans, Modern Selfhoods, and the Virtue of Vulnerability* (Edinburgh, 2011), 165–98.

48. Lewalski, *Rhetoric of Literary Forms*, 80, 106.

49. As the virulently antiprelatical Milton would have been aware, the word "minister" referred most generally—like Hobbes's examples of "a *Lieutenant*, a *Vicar*, an *Attorney*, a *Deputy*, a *Procurator*"—to one who acts "under the authority of another; one who carries out executive duties as the agent or representative of a superior"; the term is also used in this

sense at 5.460. See "minister, n.", def. 1a., *OED Online*, Oxford University Press, June 2016, http://www.oed.com/view/Entry/118877.

50. Lewalski, *Rhetoric of Literary Forms*, 80.

51. Lejosne, "Milton, Satan, Salmasius, Abdiel," 107; Quint, *Inside "Paradise Lost*," 135.

52. Recent accounts include David Ainsworth, "Spiritual Reading in Milton's *Eikonoklastes*," *SEL* 45, no. 1 (2005): 171; and Steven N. Zwicker, *Lines of Authority: Politics and English Literary Culture, 1649–1689* (Ithaca, N.Y., 1993), 38–59. Knoppers, *Historicizing Milton*, 21–35, notes that Milton's reputation was closely linked to his attacks on the *Eikon Basilike* during this period, making these statements on genre particularly visible to his contemporaries.

53. On the "Pamela prayer" controversy, see Elizabeth A. Spiller, "Speaking for the Dead: King Charles, Anna Weamys, and the Commemorations of Sir Philip Sidney's *Arcadia*," *Criticism* 42, no. 2 (2000): 229–51; and Patterson, *Censorship and Interpretation*, 177–78. Dubrow, *Challenges of Orpheus*, 211–15, observes that the *New Arcadia* was mined for lyric fragments in this fashion with unusual regularity.

54. Kahn, *Wayward Contracts*, 140; see also Annabel Patterson, *Censorship and Interpretation: The Conditions of Writing and Reading in Early Modern England* (Madison, Wis., 1984), 172–78.

55. On the setting of the king's prayers to music, see Elizabeth Skerpan-Wheeler, "*Eikon Basilike* and the Rhetoric of Self-Representation," in *The Royal Image: Representations of Charles I*, ed. Thomas N. Corns, 122–40 (Cambridge, 1999), 134–35; and David Loewenstein, *Milton and the Drama of History: Historical Vision, Iconoclasm, and the Literary Imagination* (Cambridge, 1990), 67–68.

56. Edward Reynolds, *The Divine Penitential Meditations and Vowes of His Late Sacred Majesty* (London, 1649), A1r–v; compare Thomas Stanley, *Psalterium Carolinum* (London, 1660), A1r.

57. Clay Daniel, "*Eikonoklastes* and the Miltonic King," *South Central Review* 15, no. 2 (1998): 44, argues that the *Eikon Basilike* presented Milton with an unprecedented rhetorical challenge by forcing him to confront an "image of Miltonism" in the figure of the poet-king Charles; see also Stephen Fallon, *Milton's Peculiar Grace*, 155–57.

58. Lewalski, *Rhetoric of Literary Forms*, 203, characterizes this song as "the archetype of human hymnody, containing elements of all the sub-genres of hymn presumed to have evolved from it."

59. See, for instance, Achinstein, *Literature and Dissent*, 120. In contrast, Lejosne, "Milton, Satan, Salmasius, Abdiel," 109; and Norbrook, *Writing the English Republic*, 478, argue that Abdiel's royalism deliberately echoes that of Milton's erstwhile rival Claudius Salmasius.

60. Revard, *War in Heaven*, 163–67, observes that in most previous epic treatments of this subject, Satan's case for revolt is echoed by the

arguments of his supporters rather than immediately faced with such isolated opposition.

61. Davenant, *Discourse upon Gondibert,* 121.

62. Achinstein, *Literature and Dissent,* 142, observes that conscience was understood by seventeenth century radicals not merely as an interiorized state but as "a performance, a drama, because preserving the inner realm of conscience alone was not enough to define human freedom; the state's compulsory regime made actions matter."

63. Davenant, *Discourse upon Gondibert,* 54.

64. Norbrook, *Writing the English Republic,* 480.

65. Ibid.

66. Radzinowicz, *Milton's Epics,* 156; see also Allan H. Gilbert, "The Theological Basis of Satan's Rebellion and the Function of Abdiel in *Paradise Lost," Modern Philology* 40, no. 1 (1942): 19–42.

67. Dubrow, *Challenges of Orpheus,* 72–75.

68. On Adam and especially Eve as lyric speakers, see Lewalski, *Rhetoric of Literary Forms,* 173–219. Conversely, Eve's propensity for wandering has led some critics to associate her with the errant genre of romance; see Heather James, "Milton's Eve, the Romance Genre, and Ovid," *Comparative Literature* 45, no. 2 (1993): 121–45; and Kahn, *Wayward Contracts,* 207–22.

69. Dubrow, *Challenges of Orpheus,* 72.

70. Kimberly Johnson, "Raphael's 'Potent Tongue': Power and Spectacle in *Paradise Lost," Milton Quarterly* 46, no. 4 (2012): 212–16, argues that this speech positions lyrical parataxis and continuous hymnic worship against the unceasing forward motion of epic. Such a claim, however, relies upon a dichotomy between lyric and narrative that was not clearly defined in Milton's time; see Dubrow, *Challenges of Orpheus,* 189–227; and Barry Weller, "The Epic as Pastoral: Milton, Marvell, and the Plurality of Genre," *New Literary History* 30, no. 1 (1999): 143–57.

AFTER ARISTOTLE

Milton's Aristotelian *Now*

Ayelet Langer

O f all the markers that anchor the narrative of *Paradise Lost* in time, the "now," or putative present moment, is perhaps the most ambiguous. In Milton's epic the now ranges in function from designating the actual present moment in the narrative, referring to the time of narration or reading, and specifying a proleptic moment that anticipates future events in the history of humanity. In some of its occurrences in the poem, the now binds past and future events into one continuous whole. In others, the now serves as a boundary of time that disrupts the chronological time of the story. The diverse functions of the present moment in Milton's poem have fostered interpretations of the now as a distinct element that fails to adhere to any coherent order. As a marker of what Amy Boesky identifies as the multiplicity, mutability, and indeterminacy of time, the now has mostly been seen as a disruptive element that opens a gap in the temporal sequence of the poem.[1]

This essay proposes that underlying the various temporal functions of the Miltonic "now" is a concrete and intelligible structure that can only be fully revealed through an examination of the role of time in *Paradise Lost* in relation to the subject's developing consciousness of time. This structure, I propose, is modeled on Aristotle's notion of the now. Aristotle maintains that the mind recognizes the objective series of "before" and "after" in change by performing a mathematical act of counting these temporal markers as potential points of division, each of which takes place in a now.[2] By performing the act of counting, the mathematical mind transforms the kinetic relation of "before" and "after" into temporal order. In selecting mind and change as time's two preconditions, Aristotle renders time as a hybrid idea. At once objective and subjective, for Aristotle the now is the medium of interaction between mind and world through which the mathematical mind transforms kinetic into temporal order.[3]

Milton, I suggest, adopts this bivalency as the guiding principle of his representation of the subject's development of a concept of time. Yet whereas Aristotle provides us with a theory that explains the mathematical process by which the mind apprehends time, Milton offers us an insight into the powerful experience of the mind's transformation of the kinetic into the temporal in and through the representational dynamic of his poem. By following the narrative, then, readers experience the mind's interaction with the world in and through the now as a temporal scheme by which the subjective view of time is gradually formed. Yet Milton, I propose, goes beyond Aristotle, for he views the rational mind as totally dependent on the individual's moral stature. In *Paradise Lost* Milton uses Aristotle's theory of the now to represent the transformation of the kinetic into temporal order in the unfallen mind only. The fallen mind loses its capacity to interact with the world through the now, and as a result it fails to constitute a concept of time. Yet, contingent on free will, the now remains a potential of future interaction between mind and world. After postlapsarian Adam and Eve repent they recover a version of the prelapsarian concept of time through and in the now. Satan, who chooses not to repent, remains forever captured within the partial structure of the now, incapable of conceiving time. Though Milton's now functions primarily as a medium of interaction between mind and world, it also serves as a temporal element that unifies experience. In *Paradise Lost* Milton uses the same now to describe the development of time consciousness in Adam and Eve, thus unifying their pre- and postlapsarian identity in and through time. In his representation of the subject's development of a consciousness of time as a unified experience that takes place in the now, Milton, I suggest, joins the debate over the question of identity through time, which was central to moral and legal debates in the early modern period. For Milton time does not function as an element that disrupts the mind's experience; rather, time helps to unify the mind into one continuous whole. In order to explain how Milton uses Aristotle's definition of the now to distinguish between the mind's unfallen and fallen concepts of time, I follow the work of Ludwig Wittgenstein, who suggests that instead of asking Augustine's famous question, *what* then is time?, we should focus on the question, *how* is time used?[4] By analyzing the two distinct ways in which the now is used in the language of the unfallen and fallen mind I will show that sequentiality, that is, the continuous aspect of time that is reflected in Aristotle's series of "before" and "after," is indispensable for our understanding of morality in Milton's poem. In *Paradise Lost* the idea of sequence is not, as Boesky claims, "tested and exposed as flawed" but is, rather, the only medium in and through which the individual achieves a coherent sense of his or her self as a free moral agent who is capable of regeneration.[5]

The analysis of the now from the perspective of direct speech offers a way to view the representation of time in Milton's epic as a single coherent concept. What has often been interpreted as expressions of the multiplicity, mutability, and indeterminacy of time in *Paradise Lost* may be seen, I hope to show, as different variations of a single structure of time, which Milton models on Aristotle's description of the now. The discovery of a single structure of time, which represents both the unfallen and, with modifications, also the fallen mind, opens the way to an identification of a largely overlooked *tertium quid*: the regenerated mind. After Adam and Eve have repented, they recover a version of the unfallen concept of time. Yet in contrast to the unfallen structure, which is modeled exclusively on Aristotle's theory of the now, Milton's representation of the regenerated time consciousness of Adam and

Eve opens up the possibility of expectation and thus might be seen as a subjective, Augustinian construct. But, as we shall see, even when the future is built into the Miltonic now it never loses its Aristotelian structure. Aristotle's classical—indeed, pagan—idea of the now and Augustine's Christian notion of the present moment are strikingly intertwined in Milton, as in Renaissance poetry more broadly.

My exposition of Milton's representation of the concept of the now in *Paradise Lost* proceeds through the following steps: section 1 focuses attention on Aristotle's idea of the now. My analysis of *Paradise Lost* itself begins midpoem, looking first at the unfallen mind in Eden, before turning to the fallen mind of Satan with which the poem opens, compared with the fallen Adam. By discussing in detail the structure of the now in Edenic unfallen direct speech, section 2 concentrates on the first and second stages in the development of the concept of time in the human mind. The third section analyzes the structure of the now as it is found in the direct speech of both the fallen Satan (in books 1, 2, and 5) and fallen Adam (in books 9 and 10). Finally, I trace the recovery of the now as the medium of interaction between mind and world in the speech of repentant Adam and Eve (in books 10–12).

1

Aristotle first mentions the now in *Physics* 4.219a25–30a, in the transition from his discussion of change to his definition of time. This transition is grounded in one of the most important notions that Aristotle develops throughout his *Physics*: the relation of the before and the after. In a series of arguments, Aristotle shows that this relation exists on three different—yet related—levels: place, change, and time: "Therefore, the before and after is first of all in place. And there it is in position. But since the before and after is in magnitude, it is necessary that also the before and after is in change, by analogy with the things there. But the before and after is also in time, through the following always of the one upon the other of them."[6] The soul, or mind, enters the picture in the third and final level, when it recognizes the before and after in change and counts them as two different nows. Aristotle ultimately defines time as what is bounded within these two different, successive nows: "We mark off these [the before and after in change] by taking them to be different from each other and some third thing between them. For whenever we think of the extremes as different from the middle and the soul says that the nows are two, one before and one after, then it is and this it is that we say time is. For that which is marked off by the now is thought to be time. Let us take this as true."[7] Aristotle's understanding of time depends, then, on the mind's capacity to mark the two extremes of change. It is only when the mind counts two different nows that we apprehend time as a "third thing" that exists in between the nows. When the mind perceives only one single now instead of a series of two nows, no motion is perceived, and hence the mind is incapable of perceiving time: "When, therefore, we perceive the 'now' as one, and neither as 'before' and 'after' in a motion nor as the same element but in relation to a 'before' and an 'after,' no time is thought to have elapsed, because there has been no motion either. On the other hand, when we do perceive a 'before' and an 'after,' then we say that there is time. *For time is just this—number of motion in respect of 'before' and 'after.'*"[8] Whereas the before and after in change are given explicit expression in the definition of time that concludes this passage, the act of counting the nows is only indicated by the word "number."[9] Yet it remains clear that time comes into existence only when an act of measuring change in two different occurrences of now takes place.

For Aristotle, to measure change is to divide it into before and after nows. Yet it is important to bear in mind that the divisions that the mind makes in change are potential, not actual. When we count nows in change, we count potential divisions. In this respect the nows are all the same. A potential division is, in Ursula Coope's words, "a point at which a change *might* be interrupted."[10] Thus, the nows are different from one another because the changes that they interrupt are all different changes. Yet, at the same time, the nows are also the same, in that they are all potential divisions in change. This is why Aristotle argues that the now is always "different and different" and yet it is always the same.[11]

The prominent place that is given to measuring change in Aristotle's description of time raises the question of whether time for Aristotle is a subjective construct. This question will remain significant when we consider Milton's Aristotelian-derived concept of time in *Paradise Lost*. Aristotle explicitly discusses the dependence of time on the soul in *Physics* 4.14.223a16–28, where he says that if there were no soul there would be no time. In this essay I adopt the widely accepted view that although for Aristotle mind is indeed a necessary condition for the existence of time, it is not the only condition. In order for there to be time, there surely must be someone who counts—but what the mind counts is change. Thus, both mind, which is subjective, and change, which Aristotle defines earlier in the *Physics* as objective, are preconditions for time. As Aristotle argues in *Physics* 4.5.218b30, if there were no change, there would be no time. Thus, these passages from *Physics* make it clear that for Aristotle time is a hybrid concept, which is preconditioned by both objective and subjective elements. The intertwining of these two contrasting elements of world and mind in the now is grounded in Aristotle's notion of successiveness, which is reflected, first, in the series of before and after in change and, then, in the before and after in time. As we shall see in the following section, Aristotle's idea of successiveness is precisely what grounds Milton's distinction between the unfallen and fallen minds in *Paradise Lost*.

2

Similar in function to Aristotle's concept of the now, Milton's unfallen now is the moment at which mind and nature interact. The Miltonic now, like its Aristotelian prototype, is the medium within which the mind forms a concept of time by recognizing the pattern of regularity presented in changes and then transforming this pattern into temporal order.

In *Paradise Lost* Milton represents this process in two stages. In the first he forms a series of nows that divide, but only potentially, two cosmic changes: the first night and the first morning in Eden. In the second stage, opened with Raphael's instruction in book 5, the mind distances itself from natural change in order to form an independent series of inner, subjective nows. In his representation of the first stage of the unfallen now, Milton models each of the occurrences of the now in direct speech on Aristotle's definition of the now: the Miltonic nows form a series of before and after potential divisions in change, which the mind counts and, by counting, transforms the kinetic into temporal order.

The first series of *nows* in prelapsarian speech is contextualized within Milton's description of the first evening in paradise. Adam forms a series of two consecutive nows after he has recognized—and specified—cosmic change, that is, a change that is caused by the motion of the heavenly bodies:

> Fair consort, *the hour*
> *Of night,* and all things now retired to rest
> Mind us of like repose, since God hath set
> Labour and rest, as day and night to men
> Successive, and the timely dew of sleep
> *Now* falling with soft slumbrous weight inclines
> Our eyelids.[12]

The two nows that Adam forms potentially divide "the hour / Of night" in two places. The first is when "all things" "[retire] to rest," and the second is when sleep draws together Adam's and Eve's eyelids. Adam's series of two nows measures the change from day to night and makes this change accessible to the human mind. What seems to be an indefinite—or even infinite—change between day and night is made accessible to the mind only when it is divided—even if but potentially—and its (potential) parts counted. That "day and night to men / Successive" is further demonstrated by Adam's use of the temporal marker "tomorrow" as yet another potential divider by which the mind makes change divisible and hence accessible to the human mind:

> Tomorrow ere fresh morning streak the east
> With first approach of light, we must be risen.
> ....
> Meanwhile, as nature wills, night bids us rest.
> (PL 4.623–24; 4.633; emphases mine)

In this passage "Tomorrow" does not mark the last moment of night or the first moment of day but, rather, the moment that *precedes* the point at which night completes its change into day: "ere fresh morning streak the east." Adam's three dividers of change, then, function here as markers of pure becoming. By forming a series of dividers in change, the Miltonic nows capture change in its process of coming-into-being. In *Paradise Lost* the act of dividing change in and through the now is, as we shall see, a characteristic of the unfallen mind.

Adam's nows, therefore, do not coincide with the two extremes of change but, rather, divide the night at two different potential points in a way that enables the human mind to grasp what otherwise would have been seen as one, indivisible entity. There is no objective point at which we can say that night ceases to be and day comes into being. For Milton, as for Aristotle, change is a continuous process, which, in itself, is partless and indivisible. The series of two nows that Adam forms when he counts change is thus subjective. It divides change potentially at arbitrary points in order to transform indefinite continuity into a countable, temporal order that the human mind is capable of grasping.

Though both nows function as potential dividers in change, they also serve as connectors of time. The first now connects the long evening that the narrator describes in 4.352–602 with "the hour / Of night" that Adam notices in 4.610–11, whereas the second connects the "hour of night" with the dawn Adam expects to follow in lines 4.623–24. Thus, Adam's now functions as the principle of order that connects past and future events into one continuous whole.

In the prayer that follows, Adam, joined by Eve, forms a third and final now that completes this series of potential dividers in the change from night to day. Since some time must have elapsed since Adam had uttered the first now, when "all creatures" retired to sleep, and the second now, when he declared that it was "now" time for Eve and him to join nature in sleep, the third now is clearly not simultaneous with the other two but, rather, marks a third potential point of division on the indivisible continuity that stretches between night and day:

> Thou also mad'st the night,
> Maker omnipotent, and thou the day,
> Which we in our appointed work employed
> Have finished happy in our mutual help
> And mutual love,
> ....
> But thou hast promised from us two a race
> To fill the earth, who shall with us extol
> Thy goodness infinite, both *when* we wake,
> And *when* we seek, as *now*, thy gift of sleep.
> (*PL* 4.724–28, 732–35; emphases mine)

When Adam and Eve seek the Father's "gift of sleep" "now," they mark yet another possible division in the change between day and night. Together with the two preceding nows this third now makes change measurable and hence accessible to the unfallen mind, which at this point in the story has become mathematical, that is, capable of measuring change.

Milton situates the mind's further transformation of change into time in his description in book 5 of the interchange between darkness and night in paradise. After reassuring Eve that "evil into the mind of god or man / May come and go" (*PL* 5.117–18), Adam recognizes—and makes note of—the change from night to day: "Be not disheartened then, nor cloud those looks / That wont to be more cheerful and serene / Than *when fair morning first smiles on the world*" (*PL* 5.122–24; emphases mine). The transformation of this change into temporal order takes place in the lines that follow Adam's recognition of change, in which Adam forms a series of nows that function as potential divisions in the change he has identified. The first now occurs in Adam's direct speech immediately after he has noticed the coming-into-being of the morning, and this now is closely associated with nature:

And let us to our fresh employments rise
Among the groves, the fountains, *and the flowers*
That open now their choicest bosomed smells
Reserved from night, and kept for thee in store.

(*PL* 5.125–28; emphases mine)

Prompted again by the sunrise, which is still in the process of becoming, Adam divides the natural phenomenon of the coming-into-being of day at three potential additional points during his prayer to God. All three divisions are closely associated with natural phenomena. The first is linked to the cosmic motion of the "Moon, that *now* meetst the orient sun, *now* fly'st / With the fixed stars" (*PL* 5.175–76; emphases mine). The second is associated with the morning dew:

Ye mists and exhalations that *now* rise
From hill or steaming lake, dusky or grey,
Till the sun paint your fleecy skirts with gold,
In honour to the world's great author rise.

(*PL* 5.185–88; emphasis mine)

Concluding his prayer, Adam forms the final division in the change between darkness and light:

Hail universal Lord, be bounteous still
To give us only good; and if the night
Have gathered aught of evil or concealed,
Disperse it, as *now* light dispels the dark.   (*PL* 5.205–08)

Adam's transformation of the long coming-into-being of day, which the epic describes over more than 180 lines,[13] consists of five different potential divisions, all of which are marked by the now. These divisions define a series of measurable points in change, which, being countable, enable the mind to transform change into temporal order. At this stage of the development of the unfallen mind, the now is clearly a medium of interaction between nature and mind in which the mind develops a distinct sense of sequence parallel to the regularity presented in natural changes.

Formed within the temporal framework of the now that is opened up in the beginning of book 5 with noontime, the nows of the second stage are in no way related in unfallen direct speech to cosmic or earthly change. The dissociation of the unfallen now from cosmic change is evidence that the unfallen mind has formed an independent concept of time. The development of an inner form of time leads directly to self-consciousness. Accordingly, most of the changes that the unfallen mind now recognizes are changes in itself rather than changes in nature.

Adam forms the first now in dissociation with nature at the end of the meal that Eve and he share with Raphael, when it occurs to him that he could make the best of the occasion by asking the archangel about things "above his [Adam's] world":

> Inhabitant with God, *now* know I well
> Thy favour, in this honour done to man,
> Under whose lowly roof thou hast vouchsafed
> To enter, and these earthly fruits to taste,
> Food not of angels, yet accepted so,
> As that more willingly thou couldst not seem
> At heaven's high feasts to have fed: yet what compare?
> (*PL* 5.455, 461–67; emphasis mine)

For the first time in the development of the concept of time in the unfallen mind, the now is dissociated from cosmic change, which is specified earlier when the narrator describes Raphael making his way to the blissful bower:

> Him [Raphael] through the spicy forest onward come
> Adam discerned, as in the door he sat
> Of his cool bower, while *now the mounted sun*
> *Shot down direct his fervid rays* to warm
> Earth's inmost womb, more warmth than Adam needs.
> (*PL* 5.298–302; emphases mine)

It is not only the reader who is aware of the specific time of day at which Raphael chooses to visit the human pair. Adam, too, makes a clear reference to the time of day — mid-noon — when he informs Eve of the archangel's approach:

> Haste hither Eve, and worth thy sight behold
> Eastward among those trees, what glorious shape
> Comes this way moving; seems another morn
> Risen on *mid-noon*.   (*PL* 5.308–11; emphasis mine)

Yet though it is made clear that Adam is aware of the now of noon in which his conversation with the archangel takes place, Adam's use of the now at lines 5.461–62 above ("Inhabitant with God, *now* know I well / Thy favour"), points to an inner concept of time that is dissociated from this change in nature.

The now that marks the boundary between ignorance and knowledge in Adam's mind is at once the reference point to which the before and after in change are related and simultaneously a principle of order that unifies time. Adam's utterance "*now* know I well" implies a previous stage at which he was ignorant. By pointing to a previous stage of consciousness, this *now* thus shows that Adam has achieved a transformation of the relation before and after from change to a temporal plane. At the same time, Adam's acknowledgment of his past ignorance opens up the possibility of future instruction, which is initiated by his question "Yet what compare?" (*PL* 5.467). By unifying past and future events, the now in the phrase "now know I well" serves as a joining rather than a disruption of time.

In *Paradise Lost* the climactic point in the development of the concept of time in the unfallen mind is Adam's account of the creation of Eve. Similar in form to its unfallen predecessors, the now that Adam uses in his narration follows the two criteria that are indispensable for the formation of the unfallen now in its capacity as a connector of time. This now also fulfills the criterion of dissociation from the time of nature, yet it does so in a manner deserving of special attention.

The series of nows pronounced by Adam begins with Adam's request that Raphael now hear him relate his story. This now is uttered with the certainty of a mind that is capable of situating itself in a moment that links past and future events: "Thee I have heard relating what was done / Ere my remembrance: *now* hear me relate / My story" (*PL* 8.203–05; emphasis mine). When Adam asks Raphael to hear him "now," he marks the boundary between Raphael's account of what occurred prior to his remembrance and what will occur from this point onward (that is, Adam will relate his own story). More a principle of order than a marker of change, this now is essentially a link between cosmic and human history. Further, it is the point at which human history joins cosmic history to create one continuous sequence of events. Only after Adam has situated himself in relation to cosmic events before his "remembrance" is he capable of accounting for his own history. Adam's use of this now is also evidence that he has formed a concept of sequence: he recognizes this now as both the end point at which the process of Raphael's narration has been completed and the beginning of his future account.

As with the previous nows in the second stage of the development of the unfallen concept of time, this now, too, is dissociated from cosmic change. Though well aware of the time of day at which his narration takes place (it is still the same noon at which Raphael pays the human pair a visit), Adam's now is by no means initiated by this change in nature. Instead, it is a completely independent now, which functions as a link between past and future events that have nothing to do with the current position of the sun in the sky. Within this subjective moment, which is nonetheless created within the now of noon that measures cosmic change, Adam initiates a free movement between nature and mind by forming a series of two more nows, which together help to construct an inner time of consciousness.

At the center of these two moments is a formative event in Adam's life: the creation of Eve. Adam's account of this event begins immediately after his description of God's announcement that he is about to "bring" him "[his] likeness . . . exactly to [his] heart's desire":

> He ended, or I heard no more, for *now*
> My earthly by his heavenly overpowered,
> Which it had long stood under, strained to the height
> In that celestial colloquy sublime,

As with an object that excels the sense,
Dazzled and spent, sunk down, and sought repair
Of sleep, which instantly fell on me, called
By nature as in aid, and closed mine eyes.
Mine eyes he closed, but open left the cell
Of fancy my internal sight, by which
Abstract as in a trance methought I saw,
Though sleeping, where I lay, and saw the shape
Still glorious before whom awake I stood.

(PL 8.449–64; emphasis mine)

This "now" clearly marks the present moment in Adam's story, at which point his senses are dazzled to prepare him for the creation of Eve. Dissociated from natural change, this "now," too, is a subjective moment: rather than marking a change in nature it marks a change in Adam himself. Like all nows in this stage of the development of a concept of time in Adam's mind, this now, too, functions as a liminal moment that allows for a transition from world to mind, and vice versa. In this case the now is a liminal moment between wakefulness and sleep or consciousness and unconsciousness. With his senses dazzled and spent, Adam is no longer aware of the external world. Yet it is only his body that is "sunk down." "[His] cell / Of fancy, [his] internal sight" remains open. In the boundary domain that is created between being physically in the world yet with spent senses, Adam makes the transition between object and subject, world and mind.

The now in which Adam is forced into deep sleep is followed by another now, which marks Adam's recognition of the newly created Eve and, with it, the new experience of love:

Under his forming hands a creature grew,
Manlike, but different sex, so lovely fair,
That what seemed fair in all the world, seemed now
Mean, or in her summed up, in her contained
And in her looks, which from that time infused
Sweetness into my heart, unfelt before,
And into all things from her air inspired
The spirit of love and amorous delight.

(PL 8.470–77; emphasis mine)

This now, too, is a subjective moment, which helps complete the series of nows by which Adam transforms the process of Eve's coming-into-being into temporal order.

On waking from his trancelike sleep, Adam is overjoyed to discover that the creature seen in his dreams actually exists in reality. Turning to God in praise, Adam uses the now again as a boundary domain in which he makes a transition back from mind to world:

> This turn hath made amends; thou hast fulfilled
> Thy words, creator bounteous and benign,
> Giver of all things fair, but fairest this
> Of all thy gifts, nor enviest. I *now* see
> Bone of my bone, flesh of my flesh, myself
> Before me.   (*PL* 8.491–96; emphasis mine)

When Adam situates seeing "bone of [his] bone, flesh of [his] flesh, [himself] / Before [him]" in the now, he marks the achievement of a new stage of the development of his own mind, namely, the capacity to look at himself from the outside and, perhaps more important, to recognize the other in himself.

In *Paradise Lost* this recognition of the mind of an other requires, as we have seen, a succession of different nows that are opened up one within the other, and involves a process of, first, turning from world to mind, then returning from mind to world and, finally, forming the understanding of the other in inner time. This series of nows suggests that Adam's constitution of time is conditioned by a free movement between world and mind. Once the mind has achieved this free movement between itself and the world, it is capable of forming a concept of the process of creation itself. For Milton, the free movement between mind and world is a temporal process, which is at once subjective and objective.

3

That the mind continues to make use of the *now* even in its fallen condition is evidence that the Fall marks the beginning of a gradual degeneration of the mind rather than a sudden break with its unfallen condition. Yet the fallen *now* is but a fragmented version of its unfallen counterpart. In its fallen condition the *now* no longer defines a medium of interaction between mind and nature. Consequently, no transformation from the kinetic to the temporal order takes place, which means that the mind is incapable of developing a concept of time.

The series of failures that prevents the fallen Satan from developing a concept of time is evident in one of the most celebrated passages in *Paradise Lost,* the lament of Satan for the change in Beelzebub after the two have been "hurled" into hell:

> If thou beest he; but oh how fallen! how changed
> From him, who in the happy realms of light
> Clothed with transcendent brightness didst outshine
> Myriads though bright: if he whom mutual league,
> United thoughts and counsels, equal hope
> And hazard in the glorious enterprise,
> Joined with me once, *now* misery hath joined
> In equal ruin.   (*PL* 1.84–91; emphasis mine)

In contrast to the nows initially formed by innocent Adam, Satan's now does not define a medium of interaction between nature and mind. The now within which Satan frames the change in Beelzebub is restricted to Satan's own observation, an observation that he forms in the isolation of his own mind. In contrast to the nows found in the speech of prelapsarian Adam, the now recorded in this passage does not function as a potential divider in natural change. Instead, it marks a moment that is the end point of an already completed change that both Satan and Beelzebub have undergone, namely, from existing in heaven to dwelling in hell.[14]

That Satan uses one single now instead of two is further evidence that the fallen now is but a vestige of the unfallen one. According to Aristotle, the marking of a single now is an insufficient condition for the transformation of the kinetic into temporal order. By not forming a second now Satan fails to develop a concept of time, since it is only when the mind counts two different nows that it is capable of recognizing what is between the nows as time. For Satan, then, only change exists, but his mind lacks the tools for transforming change into a sequence of events.

What is most striking about Satan's fallen now is that in all of its occurrences it marks the final extreme of the same change: the fall from heaven to hell, from innocence to sin. On meeting Sin and Death on his way out of hell, for example, Satan uses the now to designate the present moment, which is situated at the final extreme of the change that he and Sin have undergone as a consequence of their fall:

> Dear Daughter, since thou claimst me for thy sire,
> And my fair son here showst me, the dear pledge
> Of dalliance had with thee in heaven, and joys
> Then sweet, *now* sad to mention, through dire change
> Befallen us unforeseen, unthought of, know
> I come no enemy, but to set free
> From out this dark and dismal house of pain
> Both him and thee.   (*PL* 2.817–24; emphasis mine)

For Satan, the "joys," which were "sweet" before his rebellion, are "now sad to mention." In contrast to the nows used by innocent Adam, which potentially divide a change that is still in the process of its coming-into-being, the now that Satan uses in this passage designates the extreme point of a change that has already been completed. Though the now that Satan forms in this passage marks a moment that is evidently later than his fall, it designates the same extreme of the change caused by that rebellion and fall. By returning to the end point of the "dire change," Satan collapses the present moment into the moment of his fall. Since Satan has lost his capacity to conceive time, his now is always the same fixed traumatic point at which he experienced his fall, the point at which his peers joined with him in misery and joys became permanently "sad to mention." In his reply to Abdiel, Satan makes it clear that the only time he recognizes is the present moment, the now:

> Who saw
> When this creation was? Rememberst thou
> Thy making, while the maker gave thee being?
> We know no time when we were not as now;
> Know none before us, self-begot, self-raised
> By our own quickening power.   (*PL* 5.856–61; emphasis mine)

The now Satan presents in this passage is profoundly different from the nows that Adam and Eve use in their unfallen direct speech. Rather than functioning as a principle of order that unifies the spectrum of time into one coherent whole, Satan's now is the moment into which all time has been collapsed.

After his fall Adam, too, uses a fragmented version of the now, which is but a shadow of his unfallen one. Similar in structure to Satan's now, Adam's fallen now no longer defines any medium of interaction between mind and nature. Formed in the isolation of Adam's mind, the fallen now is never a part of a series of nows, and it never functions as a potential divider in change. Rather, it designates the end extreme of a change, which is identical with the moment of Adam's fall.

Adam's loss of his capacity to transform change into time is reflected in all of the occurrences of the now in his direct speech immediately after his fall. Burning with lust after he has eaten "his fill," Adam incorporates four nows into his long speech to Eve:

> Eve, *now* I see thou art exact of taste,
> And elegant, of sapience no small part,
>
> ....
>
> Much pleasure we have lost, while we abstained
> From this delightful fruit, nor known till *now*
> True relish, tasting;
>
> ....
>
> But come, so well refreshed, *now* let us play,
> As meet is, after such delicious fare;
>
> ....
>
>   Fairer *now*
> Than ever, bounty of this virtuous tree.
>   (*PL* 9.1017–18, 1022–24, 1027–28, 1032–33; emphases mine)

Unlike Adam's prelapsarian nows, these nows do not function as four different potential divisions in one continuous natural change. Instead, they all mark different aspects of the fallen state of Adam's fixed mind, which now returns again and again to its moment of change. Having realized that by eating of the fruit he has crossed the boundary between ignorance and knowledge ("nor known till"), Adam situates in his moment of fall his newly formed admiration for Eve, whom he now sees as being "exact of taste, /

And elegant," wise, and fair. This opens the possibility for "play," which Adam continues to situate in the now, the same now that marks the moment at which his mind has changed. Though, like Satan before him, Adam does not mention his fall, it is clear that the moment in which his mind changed its structure from unfallen to fallen grounds all his references to the different changes he expresses in this passage.

4

Almost obsessively, Adam keeps returning to the moment of change between unfallen and fallen existence, even after he has realized the full consequences of the Fall.[15] Yet in contrast to Satan, who remains forever trapped within the fixed moment of his fall, Adam begins to regain his prelapsarian concept of time after he starts to contemplate repentance:

> How much more, if we pray him, will his ear
> Be open, and his heart to pity incline,
> And teach us further by what means to shun
> The inclement seasons, rain, ice, hail and snow,
> Which *now* the sky with various face begins
> To show us in this mountain.
>
> *(PL* 10.1060–65; emphasis mine)

Though in this passage Adam is concerned about the change he identifies in nature, his mind shows initial signs of regaining its prelapsarian condition. For the first time after the Fall, Adam's now marks a potential division in natural change: the "eternal spring" is gradually replaced with "inclement seasons" in a continuous process that Adam identifies and makes an attempt to measure with the now. It is true that Adam's now is not part of a series of two *nows* by which this change could be transformed into a temporal order. Yet, because it is coupled here with the word "begin," it may still be regarded as Adam's first step toward regaining his prelapsarian capacity to form a concept of time. What has hitherto been a fixed point into which all temporal layers collapse now opens up to the possibility of a sequence, with a definite point of beginning.

Perhaps the most significant feature of Adam's regenerated *now* is that it opens the possibility of the future. At 11.226, repentant

Adam, who discerns the approach of Michael in the garden, situates the "great tidings" he anticipates in the now: "Eve, *now* expect great tidings, which perhaps / Of us will soon determine, or impose / New laws to be observed" (*PL* 11.226–28; emphasis mine). What Adam asks Eve to do here is to open the now to expectation, which means building the possibility of the future into the present moment. Similar to the nows used in the first stage of the development of the prelapsarian concept of time, this now focuses on the near future. But the next nows in the series created by the repentant mind will graph an increasing understanding of the future as a stretch of time that extends toward—and perhaps even goes beyond—the end of time.

Similar to the nows that Adam forms in the second stage of his development of a concept of time, Adam's final nows in *Paradise Lost* are clearly dissociated from cosmic change. Yet rather than potentially dividing individual change, these nows mark potential division points in the future history of humankind. This history is represented in *Paradise Lost* in and through the series of nows that stretches from the now at which Adam first sees death as irreversible destruction (11.462) through the now when he rejoices at the vision of "[Christ's] day" ("but *now* I see / His day," 12.276–77) to finally achieving an understanding of the gamut of time, which includes the end of time and even the "abyss" of eternity that lies beyond it (12.553–56).[16] Rather than an "untransmuted lump of futurity," as C. S. Lewis termed them, books 11–12 are the context within which Adam completes his process of recovery from trauma by broadening his understanding of time in and through the present moment, the now, so that it includes not only his own future but the future history of humankind, too.[17]

Toward the end of *Paradise Lost*, Adam has acquired a full sense of time, from creation to salvation, which he is then capable of investing with moral meaning:

> *Henceforth* I learn that to obey is best,
> And love with fear the only God, to walk
> As in his presence, ever to observe
> His providence, and on him sole depend,

Merciful over all his works, with good
Still overcoming evil, and by small
Accomplishing great things, by things deemed weak
Subverting worldly strong, and worldly wise
By simply meek; that suffering for truth's sake
Is fortitude to highest victory,
And to the faithful death the gate of life;
Taught this by his example whom I *now*
Acknowledge my redeemer ever blest.   (*PL*, 12.561–73)

This moral understanding is achieved in between the two present moments that comprise Adam's last series of nows in *Paradise Lost*. The first moment, "henceforth"— from now on—is a Miltonic paraphrase on the Aristotelian now, which lexically epitomizes the process by which Adam has broadened the meaning of the now to include the future. The second, formed toward the end of this passage (12.572), coincides with the moment at which Michael urges Adam to descend from the hill of "speculation" to meet the *hour precise*, at which he and Eve are to be expelled from paradise (12.589).[18]

At this stage of the story, Milton's investment of the now with an expectation of the future is by no means Aristotelian. By building the future into the now, Milton seems to have shifted the focus from Aristotle's pagan idea of temporality to Augustine's Christian notion of time. In contrast to Aristotle's concept of the now as the medium of interaction between mind and world, for Augustine the now is a subjective, psychological moment, in which the mind retains the memory of the past and anticipates future events. At the end of this passage, when Adam concludes his moral understanding with an acknowledgment of his redeemer "ever blest," he does so in an Augustinian framework of time.

Yet even in this Christian moment Adam's understanding of time remains Aristotelian, for his moral understanding is achieved in and through the time that is bounded within the two different nows that Adam pronounces at the beginning and end of his statement of moral conduct (12.561, 572). Milton thus presents us with a liminal moment, which not only intertwines past and future events into one unit—the *now*—but also synthesizes Christian and pagan ideas of time to form a medium of interaction between mind and world that will help the human pair cope with their future life outside of paradise.

University of Haifa

NOTES

1. For an interpretation of the extended present in terms of genre and narrative deferral, see Patricia Parker, *Inescapable Romance: Studies in the Poetics of a Mode* (Princeton, N.J., 1979), 13–15; 114–58. Angela Esterhammer, *Creating States: Studies in the Performative Language of John Milton and William Blake* (Toronto, 1994), 69, sees the now as prophecy or "performative language." For a social interpretation of the now, see Blaine Greteman, "Milton and the Early Modern Social Network: The Case of the *Epitaphium Damonis,*" *Milton Quarterly* 49, no. 2 (2015): 79–95. The role of the now in Milton's personal transformation is analyzed in J. Martin Evans, *The Miltonic Moment* (Lexington, Ky., 1998). Time is interpreted as an element that disrupts the continuity of the narrative in Amy Boesky, "*Paradise Lost* and the Multiplicity of Time," in *A Companion to Milton,* ed. Thomas N. Corns, 380–92 (Oxford, 2001); Judith Scherer Herz, "Meanwhile: (Un)Making Time in *Paradise Lost,*" in *The New Milton Criticism,* ed. Peter C. Herman and Elizabeth Sauer, 85–101 (Cambridge, 2012); Blair Hoxby, "Milton's Steps in Time," *SEL* 38, no. 1 (1998): 149–72; Anthony Welch, "Reconsidering Chronology in *Paradise Lost,*" in *Milton Studies,* vol. 41, ed. Albert C. Labriola, 1–17 (Pittsburgh, 2002).

2. In this essay I use the term "series" to designate the order in which the nows are placed within the sequence of events.

3. For an interpretation of the Aristotelian now as the medium of interaction between mind and world, see Jonathan Lear, *Aristotle: The Desire to Understand* (Cambridge, 1988), 78. Ursula Coope explains the hybrid nature of the Aristotelian now in terms of the equal indispensability of both mind and world for Aristotle's theory of time. See Ursula Coope, *Time for Aristotle: Physics IV 10–14* (Oxford, 2005), 3–4.

4. Ludwig Wittgenstein, *Preliminary Studies for the "Philosophical Investigations" Generally Known as the Blue and Brown Books* (Oxford, 1958), 26.

5. Boesky, "Multiplicity of Time," 381.

6. *Physics* 4.11.219a14–19; Coope, *Time for Aristotle.*

7. Ibid., 4.11.219a25–30.

8. Jonathan Barnes, ed., *The Complete Works of Aristotle: The Revised Oxford Translation,* vol. 1 (Princeton, N.J., 1984), 4.219a.30–35; emphasis mine.

9. For the interpretation of "number" as the series of nows, see Sarah Waterlow, "Aristotle's Now," *Philosophical Quarterly* 34, no. 135 (1984): 104–28.

10. Coope, *Time for Aristotle,* 129; emphasis mine.

11. Aristotle, *Physics* 4.10.218a10.

12. John Milton, *Paradise Lost,* ed. Alastair Fowler, 2nd ed. (London, 1998), 4.610–16; emphases mine. All quotations from *Paradise Lost* are from this edition, hereafter cited in the text.

13. The description of the first sunrise in *Paradise Lost* extends over more than 140 lines, from 5.1 to 5.139–41.

14. To be sure, hell is situated beyond the scope of the heavenly bodies. Yet Satan's mind is incapable of recognizing the vicissitudes of day and night even when he has landed on earth. Though the approaching night is clearly specified in the lines immediately preceding Satan's monologue on recovering from his initial reaction to the sight of Adam and Eve in paradise (*PL* 4.352–55, 367–92), Satan shows no sign that he is aware of the interchange between day and night. That the mind is incapable of interacting with nature is thus a consequence of its fall, rather than of place.

15. In his words to Eve after they have had their fill of fallen love, Adam uses the word "now" in the sense of the moment of change between his unfallen and fallen life three times (9.1076, 1083, 1091). Similar uses of the now occur in Adam's direct speech in 9.1138; 10.722, 731, 822, 885, and 948.

16. The complete series of nows that Adam forms in the future history of humankind is as follows: 11.462, 766, 783, 874; 12.164, 273, 276, 376, 474, and 572.

17. C. S. Lewis, *A Preface to "Paradise Lost"* (1942; repr., Oxford, 1960), 129.

18. This is also the now in which Eve, who at this point of the story has also acquired an understanding of time as continuous, asks Adam to "lead on," while charging the moment with her strongest statement of love in the poem:

> but *now* lead on;
> In me is no delay; with thee to go,
> Is to stay here; without thee here to stay,
> Is to go hence unwilling; thou to me
> Art all things under heaven, all places thou,
> Who for my wilful crime art banished hence.   (*PL* 12.614–19)

As the poem draws to a close, Eve, like Adam before her, opens the now to the possibility of the future. Asking Adam, who has now become "all places" to her, to "lead on," Eve makes clear her wish to follow him in his future life outside Eden.

Body Out of Spirit: Medical Science and the Creation of Living Soul in *Paradise Lost*

Charlotte Nicholls

"It is not any more incredible that a bodily force should be able to issue from a spiritual substance, than that something spiritual should be able to arise from a body."

John Milton, *De doctrina Christiana*

In his defense of matter in *De doctrina Christiana*, Milton makes the curious assertion that body can emerge out of spirit; he states that it did so at the point of Creation, and he comments drily, "that is what we trust will happen to our own bodies at the resurrection."[1] This statement directly contradicts the orthodox Aristotelian theory of cause, which holds that any new form can be initiated only by the action of another form upon suitably receptive matter, a view that has often been attributed to Milton. This essay will argue, in contrast, that the emergence of body out of spirit, theorized in *De doctrina Christiana* and represented in the earliest parts of the Creation sequence of *Paradise Lost*, has no analogue as precise as that of the medical model of conception researched and developed by physicians of the early scientific revolution in a radical, experimental revision of Aristotelian medical theory.

119

Careful attention to the earliest parts of the Creation sequences in *Paradise Lost* reveals that it is the interaction of the Holy Spirit and originary matter that initiates the formation of the world, and that this interaction is presented in an extraordinarily biological way. Before the event of the first divine fiat, Raphael describes how the spirit of God touches the newly calmed circle of Chaos:

> Matter unformed and void: darkness profound
> Covered the abyss: but on the watery calm
> His brooding wings the spirit of God outspread,
> And vital virtue infused, and vital warmth
> Throughout the fluid mass, but downward purged
> The black tartareous cold infernal dregs
> Adverse to life: then founded, then conglobed
> Like things to like, the rest to several place
> Disparted, and between spun out the air,
> And earth self-balanced on her centre hung.[2]

This is the moment in *Paradise Lost* in which body (morphologically organized material being) emerges from the fluid embrace of spirit and matter. This passage echoes and elaborates the narrator's opening invocation to the Holy Spirit in book 1 in which the Spirit "Dovelike satst brooding on the vast abyss / And mad'st it pregnant" (*PL* 1.21–22). Just as contemporary medical evidence disrupted the tidy, algebraic Aristotelian theories of cause with evidence of the unformed, messy bodily fluids of conception and earliest fetal life, so this sequence disrupts the clean lines of ontological dualism with an infusing, purging, spinning mixture of spirit and matter that will become the "warm / Prolific humour" that "Fermented the great mother to conceive" (*PL* 7.279–81).

Critics who insist upon a version of Milton's natural philosophy that is conventionally dualist in terms of Aristotelian causality and the categories of form and matter have much to ignore in this early stage of Creation. Twentieth century voices such as William B. Hunter have insisted that Milton's Aristotelianism complies with the dualist organization in which the "power of matter" is almost an oxymoron, for this "power" is pure potentiality, the passive part of a system whereby "the formal element represents the activity or actuality of each entity; the material element is passive, with a characteristic capacity for being formed."[3] Noël Sugimura claims that "Aristotelian logic prompted [Milton] to admit the existence of a nonmaterial aspect to his philosophy."[4] These critics either precede or contest the significant body of critical work that has investigated in depth the shape and implications of Milton's animist materialism. This essay seeks to explore and develop the proposition made by John Rogers that the language of conception that characterizes Milton's Creation is much more than a rich seam of metaphor. It is, rather, part of a natural philosophy influenced by a radical strain of vitalism that emerged from the theory and practice of two scientists, William Harvey and Francis Glisson, whose medical research respectively implied and theorized vital matter.[5]

Harvey's *On Generation* (1651) offered scientific evidence about conception that demanded a revolution in theories of biological cause. Aristotelian causality precludes the activity or vitality of matter and the material cause. However, the emergence of body (that is, morphologically differentiated and functioning organic form) from the action of spirit is exactly what Harvey describes and attempts to retheorize in this work. This evidence is further explored by Francis Glisson, sometime president of the London College of Physicians, fellow of the Royal Society, and Regius Professor at the University of Cambridge, who had, in 1639, been among the first to accept and teach Harvey's research on the circulation of the blood. Teaching notes from Glisson's work at Cambridge in the 1650s give an intriguing account of the earliest life of the fetus.[6] In their careful studies of the emergence of the animal fetus, the two scientists found themselves in conflict with Aristotelian orthodoxy, since the earliest observable traces of life are active fluids, which gradually coalesce into structure. Harvey left many unanswered questions in the wake of his project; Glisson, unlike Harvey, engaged with the work of alchemical experimentalists. He used this new mode of investigation to build on the vitalist suggestions of Harvey's work, creating a system-atized vitalist natural philosophy.[7]

In his *Matter of Revolution*, John Rogers breaks new ground in arguing that primordial matter in *Paradise Lost* bears a striking resemblance to Harvey's *primordium*, or liquid matter of genera-tion. Rogers invokes Harvey's theory *ex ovo omnia* and links it loosely to the active, responsive matter of the Creation, which is self-forming, noting Harvey's use of the idea of fermentation to illustrate the pulsing, burgeoning activity of the bodily fluids.[8] In tracing the way that medical vitalism matches the vital matter of *Paradise Lost*, Rogers also sees a number of problems for Milton's theodicy. Rogers's first concern, in brief, is that the similarity to Harvey's work, because of which he was accused of proposing par-thenogenesis (or female-only generation), obviates the necessity of a divine impregnator. The second and third problems Rogers sees concern the presence of the "tartareous dregs" at this quite liter-ally seminal moment of Creation. The downward purge of "infer-nal" tartar at the Creation is read as evidence of the Son's failure to inseminate and divinize the matter of chaos. This leads Rogers to the conclusion that the presence and behavior of these dregs "adverse to life" "violently interrupts the gradualist monist con-tinuum of matter and spirit" that is critically agreed to character-ize Milton's natural philosophy.[9]

Rogers observes that the tartar at the Creation seems to be "an externally generated, precreative substance that must be purged from the original matter." Tartar, he notes, is identified by the con-temporary chemist J. B. Van Helmont as a fallen substance that causes illnesses and that issues "wholly from our errour, and the corruption of nature."[10] The logical conclusion is that "the radical moral power of Milton's animist materialism quite simply evapo-rates if even a portion of the material universe cannot be shown to have derived from the intrinsically good substance of an intrinsi-cally good God."[11] In this reading, either the infernal dregs origi-nate with God, or they signify an evil antecedent external to God. Intriguingly, there is an extraordinary symmetry between the out-line of these problems and the problems of ensoulment outlined by

Milton in *De doctrina Christiana*. There Milton declares that the orthodox position of God's infusion of the rational soul at some time during pregnancy and the Platonist view of preexistence both imply that since the Fall the soul that originates with God must either be created impure and thus fallen, or it must be created pure and then trapped in a fallen body. Milton argues with some passion that "this would argue injustice just as much as to have created them impure would argue [God's] impurity" (YP 6:321). The solution is traducianism, or the emergence of all grades of soul from the generation of the body. Repeatedly, Milton insists that "if sin is transmitted from the parents to the child in the act of generation, then the...original subject of sin, namely the rational soul, must also be propagated by the parents" (YP 6:321). The moment of conception, then, seems crucial for Milton's theodicy.

Rogers is surely right to comment that in this area of natural philosophy tartar reflects the problem of the origin of evil, but I suggest that encoded into the vitalist biology of Milton's Creation is a version of the free will defense. Rogers attributes to Harvey the same theory of fermentation as the (quite different) one held by iatrochemists such as Van Helmont, tending to gloss over differences and distinctions between these thinkers that can be usefully explored. I propose that the radical medical theory of Milton's contemporaries offers, in fact, a cogent solution to the problems of the tartareous dregs and to the related ones of theodicy.

A number of medical theories have been associated with Milton's natural philosophy. I propose to focus almost entirely on the work of Francis Glisson. Glisson was a leader in the field of nutrition, "one of the leading lights of the post-Harveian physiology...[who] wrote important works on the anatomy of the liver (*Anatomia hepatis*, 1654) and the abdominal organs (*De ventriculo*, 1677)."[12] Michael Schoenfeldt argues that early modern notions of digestion are fundamental to the natural philosophy of *Paradise Lost*, but digestion and nutrition were not—quite yet—seen as distinct from conception and fetal development. My thesis is that Glisson's work on nutrition and his associated research on the unformed fluids and matters of the body, dating from the 1650s and 1660s, are sources that can substantiate Milton's own, seemingly idiosyncratic, natural philosophy. In my reading, the tensions that Rogers finds between the literal medical vitalism of Milton's Creation and his overall theodicy can be resolved through Glisson's vitalism.[13]

Biographical Connections

Significantly, there were strong biographical links between Milton and Glisson: Glisson's colleague Nathan Paget was to become Milton's doctor and his close friend.[14] Professional connections between Paget and Glisson were noted by James Holly Hanford and, later, by Christopher Hill. In his study of the contents of Paget's library, Hill observes that numerous medical texts show him to be a "liberal, reforming, chemically minded doctor."[15] Rogers points to further biographical links between Milton and Paget (and thus Glisson), when in 1651 a brief note to the Examinations Committee of the Council of State recommends reprinting one of Milton's tracts (probably the *Defence of the English People*). The note refers to a complaint made by Milton that one Peter Cole had been printing an unauthorized English translation of Glisson's *De rachitude* [Of the rickets] (1650), the patent of which was owned by William Dugard, Milton's printer.[16] It is reasonable to speculate, as Rogers does, that Milton was protecting the interests of his friend Paget as well as those of his printer, given that Paget was one of eight members of the College of Physicians who contributed to *De rachitude*.[17] It is speculative (but tempting) to contemplate a possible shared experience between Paget and Glisson 15 years after their collaborative research project when, during the plague of 1665, they were among the few brave enough to remain in London to treat the ill and dying.[18] Less speculative is the fact that Paget owned a copy not only of Glisson's *Anatomia hepatis* (1654), but also of the revised version of 1657.[19] This demonstrates Paget's sustained and detailed interest in Glisson's work, and the significance of this study of the liver will become clear in my comparison of Milton's animist materialism with Glisson's theory of the vital, self-sustaining blood.

These points of confluence demonstrate that Glisson's ongoing work on vital bodily matter would have been readily available to Milton through Paget, but not why Milton would have had more than a general interest in it. However, a brief look at Milton's own medical history shows that he had every reason to research medical science, in particular the latest theories of active or vital bodily fluids being proposed by Glisson. His nephew, Edward Phillips, notes that during Milton's exchange with Salmasius, "his Sight, what with his continual Study, his being subject to the Head-ake, and his perpetual tampering with Physick to preserve it, had been decaying for above a dozen years before, and the sight of one for a long time clearly lost."[20]

While blindness has become a significant topos in Milton studies, less often commented on are Milton's years of suffering from gout. The definitive symptom of gout is intense and agonizing periods of pain in the joints (particularly those of the feet), and Milton's death in 1674 was probably caused by associated renal failure.[21] There is considerable contemporary evidence to support a diagnostic connection between the cause of "gutta serena" and the gout from which Milton was to suffer later in life. The disorders were thought to stem from the same problem: errant phlegmatic humors that, originating in poor digestion, rose upward as fumes through the body, were excreted out of the brain, and then collected in the wrong areas of the body.[22] The evidence indicates that, having struggled "perpetually" with painful treatments for more than a decade in an unsuccessful effort to save his sight, Milton would have been prescribed the same orthodox Galenic treatments for his gout. I suggest that Milton and his doctor would also have researched other possible theories of his illness and other, more effective, remedies.

The evidence that this did, in fact, occur, lies in a significant change of diagnosis after the loss of Milton's sight. An early anonymous biographer, while describing the struggle to treat Milton's blindness, remarks that "Issues or Seatons, made use of to save or retrieve that [first eye], were thought by drawing away the Spirits, which should have supply'd the Optic Vessels, to have hastn'd the loss of the other."[23] Here, the earlier course of treatment that Milton received is critiqued, even blamed for the loss of sight in his second eye. This is no small accusation. The initial treatments, issues and seatons, work by traumatizing the skin (of the head and neck in the treatment of blindness) in various ways, over an extended period of time, to encourage the production of pus, itself supposed in Galenic medicine to be the defluxion, or vile matter, causing the problem. The re-diagnosis indicated in the biography, I suggest, has moved away from the orthodox Galenic theory of humors toward the new medical theories of active, fermenting bodily substance.

Thomas Willis refers in 1659 to the decline of the Galenic system following advantages in anatomical knowledge. Defluxions are impossible, he argues, because a "passage from the Stomach into the Head, thorow so many Inwards, and bony Cloysters, like stops, seem impervious, or not passable for the sending up of fumes. Without doubt, much the greatest part of the Humor, with which the Brain is watered, and the Spirits inhabiting it ... is carried by the Arteries, and distilled in immediately from the Mass of Blood."[24] In other words, the only humors and spirits "watering" and "inhabiting" the brain are "distilled" out of the blood; fumes cannot possibly rise to the brain from the stomach because anatomical structure does not allow it. Willis was not, however, the earliest pioneer in this area of research, although his *On Fermentation* (1659) is counted as a foundational work in the development of ideas about active bodily substance: Francis Glisson in his *Anatomia hepatis* of 1654 was already developing a theory of the body in which the blood distills spirits out of itself.[25] Many previous physicians, including Harvey, had used figures of fermentation to explain processes like conception and nutrition, but these often referred to an airy vital spirit that created bubbles and related images of concoctive activity such as boiling milk or rising bread. These models of fermentation had not changed since antiquity; Aristotle himself used them.[26] Glisson's model, however, is the new fermentation belonging to what William Newman calls "chymistry," that is, a medical alchemy that is just developing the experimental rigor that will transform it into modern chemistry.[27] Glisson did not exclude Aristotelian elements or the Galenic humors from his model of the animate human body but, underlying them, he posited the five chymical elements (spirit, sulphur, water, salt, and earth) as the *minima naturalia* of life. This model was to be taken up and used through the later decades of the seventeenth century by figures such as Thomas Willis, Henry Power, Walter Charleton, and Robert Boyle, but it was already available to anyone who read *Anatomia hepatis* from 1654 onward.[28]

The Natural Philosophy of *Paradise Lost* and Glisson's Vital Matter

A connection between the vitalism of Francis Glisson and that of Milton has been suggested by a number of critics, but with reference to Glisson's early tract, *De rachitude*, the pirated edition referred to in Milton's complaint recorded in the note to the Council of State.[29] However, there are only traces of Glisson's mature vitalist philosophy in this text, in which his cornerstone theory (that of the active, self-producing blood) is still represented in anthropomorphic figures, and chymical theories of substance are only glanced at. The evolution of Glisson's theory of vital matter has been shown by Guido Giglioni to begin with an early classical medicine focusing on nutrition, which, over the course of three decades, becomes a late radicalism much influenced by chymical philosophers, J. B. Van Helmont in particular.[30] According to Giglioni, Glisson's notion of fermentation relied in particular upon the chymical work of Van Helmont, and he led the way in this field. In his work and the work of others, evidence of chymical substance transformation was applied to the body, both in experiments trying manually to distill the blood (such as those performed by Robert Boyle and other members of the Royal Society) and in the development of related theories to explain bodily functions, particularly those of the fluids.[31]

Glisson's system of vitalism culminated in his late tract *De natura substantiae energetica*, published in Latin in 1672. While this tract postdates the publication of *Paradise Lost*, its conclusions on natural philosophy correlate precisely with the radical materialism found in Milton's poetry and prose. Pagel catches the essence of this natural philosophy in his summary: "To Glisson, 'soul' is but one aspect, one grade of the living, i.e. of the 'energetic substance.' There is no difference in kind between these aspects and grades, from the lowest stage of matter endowed with the most 'dim perceptions' to the higher forms of consciousness in the living animal. In Glisson's philosophy, matter appears as much 'spiritualised' as soul is 'materialised,' so that the contrast between them is only artificial."[32] This matches precisely the matter/spirit relation in Milton's late work as critics such as Stephen Fallon, John Rumrich, and Michael Lieb have explained it.[33] However, Giglioni's paraphrasing and translations from the same tract add a significant new detail to this vision of materialized spirit and spiritualized matter. From the inner self-modification of vital matter emerges an upward flowering of self-formation: "Glisson regarded matter as an inherently living and perceptive substratum...as the organic efflorescence of forms is only a progressive and temporary superposition originating from matter itself, so the living modes ('*modes vitalis*'), the 'souls,' are the result of inner self-modification of life that 'does not live on a borrowed life but on itself.'"[34] In particular, then, Glisson's late work articulates a system that reflects most strikingly the natural philosophy of Milton's unfallen paradise, not just in the upward-moving continuum of matter and spirit, but, crucially, in the way that matter interacts with itself, blossoming into morphologically organized existence.

In an unforgettable teaching moment, Raphael explains how from the "one Almighty" comes

> one first matter all,
> Indued with various forms, various degrees
> Of substance, and in things that live, of life;
> But more refined, more spirituous, and pure,
> As nearer to him placed or nearer tending
> Each in their several active spheres assigned,
> Till body up to spirit work, in bounds

Proportioned to each kind. So from the root
Springs lighter the green stalk, from thence the leaves
More airy, last the bright consummate flower
Spirits odorous breathes.   (*PL* 5.472–82)

The correspondence between the two versions of active, self-
forming matter in Milton and Glisson is striking, but whether the
agency is that of God or of the matter itself has been a vexed question. The key verb here is "indue" (a variant of "endue"). This,
however, does not immediately clarify the source of agency in
the sequence since it is possible to read "indue" as either a tran-
sitive or an intransitive verb. Read with the "one Almighty" as
the subject, "indue" means to invest or endow, meaning that the
various forms and degrees of substance and the quality of life are
initiated by God. However, read as an intransitive verb, "indue"
seems to mean that matter here is clothing itself in, or taking on
the character of, the various forms and degrees of substance or,
indeed, the quality of life itself. It is significant that "indue" also
carries a sense of the Latin *induce*, to lead, which, like its English
relative "induce," implies relationship and mutual agency. This is
a deliberately rich constellation of meanings that implies mutual
agency between matter and its own divine origin — a constellation
that asks us to reconsider the seemingly typically Miltonic either/
or in which the various forms and degrees of substance are "nearer
to him placed or nearer tending." Rather than a simple refusal to
assign agency in one direction once and for all, the apparently non-
committal and frustrating "or" refers to the myriad of possible per-
mutations involving this mutual, interactive agency. By reading
Glisson alongside it, we find that Raphael's lesson reveals a subtle,
complex dance between the one Almighty and the infinite variations of form, degree, and life in the stuff of Creation.

Of course, the publication dates of *Paradise Lost* and *De natura
substantiae energetica* mean that direct influence is not possible,
and there is a danger of slipping into the vagaries of "circulations
of social energy." Nevertheless, the work of the two men may be
consciously linked. Glisson's earlier *Anatomia hepatis* (that same
publication owned in two editions by Milton's physician), with its

focus on the microcosm of the human body, shows us the roots of the final, vitalist theory in a model of self-vitalizing blood. Whereas Harvey had seen the blood as homogenous matter with an unexplained cargo of spirit, Glisson treats it as a mixed body with several different interacting chymical elements in it, some grosser and "natural," some more volatile and vital. Giglioni paraphrases and translates directly from Glisson's work: "Vital heat is caused and maintained by a chemical reaction occurring continuously in the blood through its circulation and volatilization. At each cardiac contraction, the blood in the heart is kindled as it were and becomes arterial and vital. The saline and sulphureous components of the blood are extremely active and they are the main responsible for its volatilization. 'When they [these components] rise to such a high rank, they gain the "honor" of being called vital spirits.'"[35] This is, explicitly, the sort of revolutionary body politic that has been read as implicit in Raphael's speech by Christopher Hill and many critics following him.[36] The elaboration of anatomy with chymical philosophy allows for an interaction between different grades of "spirituous" matter, which, for Glisson, creates the ceaseless pulse of life within the human body.

Glisson's version of vital spirit, as an intrinsic part of the blood, is a subtle, penetrating, volatile, highly exalted grade of matter. In *Anatomia hepatis* vital spirit is shown to create vital heat through its efforts to volatilize further and through its seductive and ferocious impulse to assimilate lower grades of matter and exalt them up to its own level of volatility. This process of increasing perfection and exaltation through chymical assimilation is summarized by Giglioni: "[Natural] spirits are initially fixed (when they are closely entangled with the other elements), then melted (through a process of ripening or fermentation) and, finally, they become volatile (when they are completely exalted) and transformed partly into the vital spirits of the blood and partly into the animal spirits of the nutritive juice."[37] In this biological process, the blood acts upon the food softened and processed into "chyle" by the stomach. Vital heat is both the cause and an effect of activity in this circular (and ascending) system in which the blood exalts and consumes its own spirit and matter, exalting itself into progressively more spirituous and pure versions of itself. There are clearly significant implications here for understanding the transformative, subliming unfallen body/soul described by Raphael.

In Raphael's natural philosophy, the ever more spirituous efflorescence of forms out of matter begins at the Creation and continues until these forms meet the human body, at which point there is a shift to the emergence of spirit out of matter. It is not just the organic form of the human body that is sustained by food; the animating spirits of the body *also* emerge from this process. The one first matter has become roots, stalks, and leaves, which give rise to

> flowers and their fruit
> Man's nourishment, by gradual scale sublimed
> To vital spirits aspire, to animal,
> To intellectual, give both life and sense,
> Fancy and understanding, whence the soul
> Reason receives, and reason is her being.   (*PL* 5.482–87)

In the work of both the poet and physician, the upward, transformative urge to ever more perfect formation and ever purer and more powerful spirit is part of a continuum linking the natural world and the human body. I suggest that the new chymical *anatomia animata* offers Milton a scientifically progressive version of transformative material spirit. Of course, he does with it almost exactly what conservative commentators such as Ralph Cudworth feared radical minds might do with such ideas. Vegetable food is sublimed into vital spirits that continue the process through into animal spirits and then burst through the traditional barrier between bodily ensoulment and rational soul, subliming out of themselves the novel category of intellectual spirits, the declared source of reason itself. While vegetation is present in the early stage of the process as Raphael describes it, human vegetative spirits are missing from Milton's schema. This, I believe, is because he is using the new model of the human body, in which the blood circulates and the liver is no longer the center of a lower order of venous blood, vegetative spirits, and concupiscent soul. This is the body whose fluids sublime, distill, and are no longer constrained by the tripartite systems of antiquity. This is the body in which the subvital order of the vegetative, normally ascribed to the female in classical theories of procreation, must be entirely reimagined, which we will see has significant consequences for ideas of biological cause and the generation of life. The interlocking tripartite systems of antiquity are now linked by bodily fluids that circulate and ferment.

Glisson explored in detail the "fermentation processes" through which the blood volatilizes the vital spirits, identifying different ways of separating the elements of the body. To clarify, a ferment, in the chymical medicine of Van Helmont, is a spiritual impulsion that adjoins a body; it works to make the object similar to itself, or to assimilate; it was thought to impregnate the body or substance seminally and multiply itself; it was thought to effervesce, expand, and be acidic in nature.[38] There are a number of chymical processes associated with this version of fermentation, in which lower grades of matter are sublimed into finer, more energetic and less earthy grades. One of these is *sublimatio*.[39] In chymical terms sublimation means a process of purifying a compound substance through heat, whereby the purest element is extracted in the change from a solid state to a vaporous state, with distillation the comparable process for liquids or solids dissolved in solvents; the various different sediments are collected from the lower and upper portions of an alembic, the vessel designed for precisely this use. Newman notes that while alchemists did make a distinction between distillation and sublimation, "they were not as fastidious as modern chemists...[and] frequently speak of liquids, such as mercury, subliming."[40] Indeed, in *Anatomia hepatis* Glisson indicates the fluid nature of the conceptual boundaries: "Separations of Elements are made by *distillation*, which may also be referred *sublimation*."[41]

Seventeenth century medicine appropriated chymical fermentation, and other chymical transformations, to give models both for the transformation of body into spirit and the corresponding emergence of body out of spirit. Harvey was not radical in his comment that "nutrition...indeed is a kind of generation," and Glisson's late work on acid digestion marked one of the first differentiations between the two processes.[42] The most immediately striking representation of actively subliming bodily matter/spirit in *Paradise Lost* is in the metabolic natural philosophy of Raphael's most famous speech. But the chymical theory of interacting bodily fluids also adds a new dimension to the contemporary theory of conception. This, again, offers a new perspective on the natural philosophy of *Paradise Lost,* this time on the emergence of the "embryon" earth at the beginning of Milton's Creation.

Revisions of Contemporary Theories of Conception

The chymical process that matches both Glisson's account of conception and Milton's of Creation most clearly is separation *per magisterium,* in which a volatile ingredient is added to a "mixt" or compound, causing the fermentation process. However, in order to read Creation and conception side by side it will be helpful first to pause for a moment and scan the contemporary theories of conception (both orthodox and heterodox) that were current in the years during which Glisson and Milton were writing. The model of conception inherited by the seventeenth century was neither singular nor uncontested. When Harvey made his discoveries, he was working in an area that had long been hotly debated by Galenic and Aristotelian authorities.[43] Galenic theory, which had great purchase on contemporary thought, contains a number of features that differentiate it both from Harvey and Glisson's Neoaristotelian model and from the representation of conception in *Paradise Lost*. Ambroise Paré, still a popular medical authority in the seventeenth century, describes a fermentation like boiling milk with a tripartite emergence of liver, heart, and brain emerging from the "bubbles"; also apparent are "cotyledons" or hairy strings that gather and feed the developing fetus in the womb.[44] More relevant to Milton's Creation is the Aristotelian model of the eduction of forms out of receptive matter. However, neither Milton nor the physicians use this dualist model without significant adjustment, and the adjustments they make are strikingly alike.

In Aristotelian terms, the organ, since it has form, may be animated, whereas matter, or substance without structure, may not be animated or have the quality of life. This was the prevalent paradigm inherited from Aristotle. The orthodox Aristotelian theory of generation required an originating form to generate further forms like, but separate from, itself out of receptive, but effectively lifeless, maternal menstrual matter. As Balme comments, "in arguing for teleology and for some other theories, he [Aristotle] does not speculate about how the theory works in physical terms...it is not a pictorial description, but a sort of algebraic analysis."[45] Therefore, the maternal is aligned with the material cause, the paternal with both the efficient cause and formal cause; final cause, or telos, is the new being generated.

The perceived necessity of form to support life and the corresponding exclusion of matter from ideas of life and value were fundamental to many schools of thought; the reconsideration of cause, prompted by medical research, created impassioned debate. John Henry quotes Cambridge Platonist Henry More, who, in his argument for an immaterial Spirit of Nature, claims that "particular Souls are, according to Aristotle, the Actings of an organical Body," and he adds, "the *Punctum saliens,* or Life point, discovers not any proper sense."[46] The *punctum saliens* is the first trace of a beating heart, the first flicker of pulsation in the bloody matter of the egg, which so fascinated both Harvey and Glisson. For More it does not constitute evidence of life, but Harvey's research indicated otherwise. Evidence from his studies of both chicken eggs and pregnant deer showed a "crystalline colliquament" from which emerges traces of blood, followed by the flickering *punctum saliens* of the fetus.[47]

Harvey was fully conscious of the philosophical challenge this evidence posed: "If the vital principle be the act of the organic body...it seems incredible that this principle can inhere in the chick before something in the shape of an organised body is extant."[48] Active and vital fluids were anathema to Aristotelian orthodoxy, but this was exactly what the empirical evidence showed. The fetus's "parts are not fashioned simultaneously, but emerge in their due succession and order: it appears, too, that its form proceeds simultaneously with its growth, and its growth with its form."[49] In an uncanny echo of this formulation, Milton, in the *Art of Logic,* theorizes a similar emergence of form: "*The form is generated within a thing simultaneously with the thing itself....* The rational soul is the form of man, because through it a man is a man and is distinguished from all other natures" (YP 8:234). Milton argues for traducianism (or ensoulment without the need for divine infusion of a rational soul) in detail and with conviction in *De doctrina Christiana*; this theory demands that the rational soul must emerge from the interaction of material and efficient causes.[50] In this instance Milton makes precisely the adjustments Harvey was forced to make to the theory of cause and employs the new theory to its most radical effect.

Harvey was accused of radicalism for eliding the categories of eggs, seeds, and matter in *On Generation,* with figures such as Alexander Ross reading his work as proposing parthenogenesis, or female-only generation.[51] This was not entirely fair, since, while he did theorize an extraordinarily vital and self-forming matter, he never understated the importance of seminal vital heat in conception. For Harvey, the efficient cause of the body's semen works just as the sunlight does on the muddiness of earthy matter, by exuding vital heat and fertilizing matter. However, he argues that the vital heat does not simply initiate informing movements within the semen. Rather, it adds a final stimulus to the already excessively vital matter of the entire womb: "The semen...produces an influence on *the whole of the uterus, and at the same time renders fruitful the whole of the yelks,* and finally of the perfect eggs which fall into it...and this the semen effects by its peculiar property or irradiative spirituous substance."[52] Here, an *almost* metaphysical vital heat is radiated from the semen, linking its power to the ethereal power of the stars and the sun as per Aristotle.[53] Harvey's irradiative spirituous substance, however, acts upon the entire matter of the uterus, not just the individual egg, "rendering fruitful" (that is, awakening vital fertility within the entirety of) the maternal interior.

This pattern of events in which vital spirit meets and initiates a perfecting animate vitality in an already excessively vital female matter is a particular model of generation that was at the forefront of medical science in the mid-seventeenth century. It diverges significantly from the Aristotelian and Galenic models of conception that preceded it. In a sentence that contradicts centuries of Aristotelian orthodoxy, Harvey concludes, "It is consequently manifest, in some animals at least, that nature has not, on account of the distinction into male and female, established it as law that the one, as agent, should confer form, the other, as passive, supply matter."[54] His alternative, the radiation of vital heat from the spirituous semen into a vitally responsive matter, is part of a reordered system of causality that emerges from and answers the experimental evidence against the eduction of forms. It also finds a striking echo in the order of events in the creation of the universe of *Paradise Lost*, in which Spirit adds a final perfecting impulse of formation to the entirety of an already excessively fertile "womb" that is simultaneously unformed, egglike, and containing seeds.[55]

There is further evidence that Milton was deeply involved in a peculiarly medical revision of the Aristotelian theory of cause. His comments on the material efficacy of God in *De doctrina Christiana* employ what Balme calls "the root of his [Aristotle's] theory of genesis: anything that is produced can only be produced by a similar thing previously existing."[56] This could be (and was) interpreted to support the position that form is a necessary precondition of the eduction of further forms, but for Milton it is the logical foundation of a radically materialist theology. In his discussion of the Creation, he concludes that "not even God's virtue and efficiency could have produced bodies out of nothing... unless there had been some bodily force in his own substance, for no one can give something he has not got" (YP 6:309).

In an intellectual shift that reflects Milton's assertion of God's bodily force, Glisson interprets exactly the same axiom to endow the matter of the blood with animating properties. Rather than being carried by the blood, vital spirit is part of the composition of the blood: "If the heart itself (which once was deemed to be the source of life) owes its life and vital heat to the vital blood (as is shown by the circuit of the blood), it will be very difficult to deny life to the blood. For a thing that communicates something to another thing must already have in itself what it is communicating."[57] The blood vitalizes; therefore, it must itself be intrinsically vital. The Aristotelian theory of generation is employed by both authors in the assertion of a heretical materialism. Just as the substance of God must have "some bodily force" in order to generate materiality, something within the very substance of the life-giving blood must have the power of animation.

John Rumrich maintains that we cannot underestimate the importance of this innovation. He quotes Aristotle's statement: "the begetter is of the same kind as the begotten...in form.... They are different in virtue of their matter (for that is different), but the same in form."[58] What Milton—and Glisson—have done is to reverse this so that "the begetter is of the same kind as the begotten not because they partake of the same *form*, but *because they share the same matter*."[59] Matter, vital matter, is what we share with the universe and, more particularly, with those who generate us; form (proper form rather than generic form) is what differentiates us into individual entities. The matter of generation is called by Harvey the "crystalline fluid" or "colliquament"; by Glisson it is called the "vital fluid" or "seminal matter"; by Milton it is termed "genial prolific fluid." For all three writers, body can emerge from the vital interactions of spirituous matter and material spirit.

Generation and Creation: Body Out of Spirit

Generation, the example par excellence of the emergence of form from unformed matter, relies in the body, and in the cosmos, upon the efficacy of spirit. Glisson's approach to spirit departs entirely from Aristotelian ideas of pneuma, from Galenic ideas of airy vital spirit, and from Helmontian notions of gas on the grounds of contrary anatomical evidence.[60] Spirit is, instead, like Milton's original light, liquid. It is not airy; it is a qualitatively different substance, fluid, volatile, and energetic, which calls forth a range of responses from other sorts of substance. Originally a classicist, Glisson is aware of the long and varied history of the notion, but he settles on chymical spirit as the most precise version of this slippery term. Giglioni translates and paraphrases from *Anatomia hepatis* (1654):

> "The word *spirit*," Glisson writes, "insofar as it is attributed to the bodies, has different meanings." It can generically refer to any kind of body which has been rarefied to the point of becoming volatile (in this respect "wind, air, breath and exhalations in general" were rightly viewed by the ancient authors as sorts of spirit). It can also mean "any body that is subtle, active, and very penetrating." Finally spirit can also mean "that element which, after a due process of fermentation, but not before, strives upwards spontaneously, and becomes volatile." This is "the most precise meaning of the word *spirit*, in that it is understood as an elementary part of a compound. The chemists call it *mercury*." [61]

This spirit is one of five chymical elements that, for Glisson, underlie the Aristotelian elements to make up the *minima naturalia* of all matter: "the elements of mixture, as they call them: spirit, oil, water, salt and dead earth." [62] We have already explored how the upward surge of spirit and matter in Milton's unfallen paradise can be substantiated by the interactions of these elements. Another process, separation *per magisterium*, I will argue, gives us a model for the emergence of form out of a fluid chaos of matter and spirit, thus illuminating the natural philosophy of Milton's Creation. This process, with its interactions of different grades of unformed substance in the body, relies upon Glisson's review of the notion of similary (sympathetic, elective, or even electric) attraction.

To understand the behavior of vital spirit and the matter of conception in Glisson's work, we must have a clear working model of similary attraction. The similary parts are the simple unformed substances of the body (as opposed to the formed organs): blood is a prime example, but sexual and generative bodily fluids are also included in the category. Each of these similary parts will be endowed by Glisson in his later work with a power of "natural perception" of that which is like itself; this similarity evokes a mutual attraction to and an appetite to conjoin with the other substance that is like (but not identical to) itself. Each substance also responds with a negative repulsion to that which is distinctly unlike itself.[63] Originally, the theory of attraction was Galenic and was not widely held to have any progressive medical significance. Indeed, mysterious forces of attraction between phenomena were often precisely the straw man theories to be overturned by the new impulsions of mechanism.[64] Sympathetic attraction was also associated with the mysterious excesses of hermetic alchemy as an "occult cause," emerging in disreputable arenas like that of the weapon salve debate.[65] There are, however, sound anatomical reasons for Glisson's proposal: the body's fluids or humors do move, collect, and congregate or excrete in different places. His longstanding interest in nutrition gave a wealth of physiological evidence upon which to rest theories of substance that must assimilate other substance, recognizing, in some primordial way, what is and what is not assimilable. Glisson modernizes this theory in the light of chymical substance transformation to account for a variety of responses of different grades of matter to one another. If "reason is but choosing," so is elective attraction. It orders the gathering of milk in the breast, the placing of acidic humors in the correct area of the stomach for digestion, and the nourishing and formation of the tiny fetus.[66]

Glisson's version of similar attraction is grounded in careful anatomy, unlike much hermetic alchemy, but it also differs from the preceding Galenic model, since different aspects of the five chymical elements may respond quite differently to an added ingredient or ferment. In separation *per magisterium,* the separation is effected through "similary attraction," in which different aspects of the "mixt" respond in various ways to the volatile new ingredient. In the prolegomena to *Anatomia hepatis,* Glisson notes that "Parts mixed are severed *per magisterium*: that is, by casting in another ingredient which hath more familiarity with one element of the mixture than the other, by means whereof the parts before mixed are separated.... Separations are made by congregation or attraction magnetical.... Thus parts of a like nature easily gather together leaving other parts with whom they had less affinity."[67]

This is a progressive, chymical theory of substance transformation. While it is not identical to the system of vitalist philosophy that was to come, Giglioni describes natural perception as present within *Anatomia hepatis* as a "tacit assumption to account for phenomena of similary attraction."[68]

With Glisson's theories of similary attraction and separation *per magisterium* in mind, let us turn again to that central moment of conception in the Miltonic Creation, in which we see the responses of various parts of the primal matter to the infusion of divine vital virtue and warmth:[69]

> His brooding wings the spirit of God outspread,
> And vital virtue infused, and vital warmth
> Throughout the fluid mass, but downward purged
> The black tartareous cold infernal dregs
> Adverse to life: then founded, then conglobed
> Like things to like, the rest to several place
> Disparted, and between spun out the air,
> And earth self-balanced on her centre hung.   (*PL* 7.235–42)

As with Raphael's depiction of the one first matter, the assignation of agency is equivocal; following the "but" we are not certain if it is the spirit of God that is purging, founding, conglobing, and spinning or the fluid mass itself. I suggest that, again, we are not meant to be certain, because once the vital virtue has been infused into the mass, the mixed mass itself is responding according to its own set of natures. The purge downward we will consider in detail shortly; like the earlier "fleeing" of the darkness and the other ergative verbs used throughout this sequence, purging indicates mutual agency between spirit and matter as one element of the "mixt" refuses assimilation and flees (or is excreted) downward. Still gross and less vital, but remaining at the basis of Creation, is a another solid part of this matter; this is "founding," creating the basis of the world, then "conglobing," a motion in which like things circle together in a curiously gravitational motion. Finally, the air may either be actively spinning in a circle as the other parts of the matter are or it is being spun like silk, or both. The paradox of the earth being independent ("self-balanced"), but also dependent (in that it is hanging), is reflected in the grammar that describes the double agency of Holy Spirit and vital matter.[70]

In medical science, similar separations occur as the vital heat and spirit meet in the vital fluid of the generative body. For Glisson, the emergence of the *punctum saliens* from seminal matter offered a prime example of "self-active and self-organizing matter," indicating without question the ability of living matter to form itself.[71] In the opening address of his *Six Anatomical Lectures* (published 1677, but written and presented in 1662), Glisson asks, "who will expound to me—without natural perception—how the plastic force forms the chick in the egg?"[72] His solution is innovative, theorizing the influence of vital spirit and vital heat on the colliquament of the egg, and this process corresponds precisely to the responsive whirling of various degrees of substance in Milton's Creation. The efficient cause of the attractions, separations, and effervescence of this original substance of the (soon to be) body is the vital spirit. The stimulating warmth of incubation activates the vital spirit and initiates a process of similary attraction:

> This vital fluid…begins to set itself apart from the other parts of the egg (with which it is promiscuously mingled) and to run through some rivulets or ramifications which afterwards become the veins. These rivulets come together and meet in one point which is afterward called the leaping point (*punctum saliens*) and heart.…As soon as these rivulets join together, the flow in them is restrained for a while and then it effervesces and needs a larger place. And since the flow cannot go back through the same path (because new streams are continually flowing), it necessarily has to return to the seminal matter from which it had flowed forth after having formed new channels. Hence a circumgyration arises, and finally the first channels become the veins, the second the arteries; and in the point of their confluence, the heart is born.[73]

The thicker fluid gathers together with that which is thick like itself, and is formed by the circular flowing movement of the more volatile component substance, which itself continues to effervesce and attempt to rarefy and expand: thus form emerges, spinning, from fluid and spirit. The movement that spirit sparks off in the "fluid mass" that has until now been "promiscuously mingled" is explicitly stated to be a separation of like substance to like substance. Thicker substances found the central structure through their tendency to unite, and the motion is circular. The movement of like substances to each other is a "conglobing," a circling together that we might imagine as a gravitational spinning. Just as the vital fluid and seminal matter of the egg has a "circumgyration" or circular movement, so is the prolific, genial fluid of the world embryo described as being on "circumfluous waters calm, in wide / Crystalline ocean" (*PL* 7.270–71).[74] Thus the fluid mass separates into a plurality of distinct interacting substances that will, together, create the beauty and order of form through the process that Glisson calls the *vitae chorea*, the dance of life.

By the second day of the Creation in *Paradise Lost*, shortly before the appearance of dry land, the earth is a fetus, enfolded within a fermenting ocean of generative bodily liquid:

> The earth was formed, but in the womb as yet
> Of waters, embryon immature involved,
> Appeared not: over all the face of earth
> Main ocean flowed, not idle, but with warm
> Prolific humour softening all her globe,
> Fermented the great mother to conceive.   (*PL*. 7.276–81)

This is a deeply bodily source of burgeoning vital fluids that will bring forth not only the formations of dry land that are the contours of the world but also all the different sorts of "soul living" from, explicitly, "her fertile womb" (*PL* 7.451–54).

Conclusions: Vitalism and Theodicy

John Rogers's thesis that the downward purge of "black tartareous cold infernal dregs" has "sabotaged" Milton's theodicy now needs to be revisited in the light of this more detailed model of the vital matter of conception. The concerns about parthenogenesis with which we began were quickly qualified by the attention paid by Harvey—and Milton—to the power of the inseminating spirit, be it holy or bodily, and the vital heat that it imparts to fertilize the entire womb. The problems implied by tartar are a little more complex. The presence of tartar, Rogers argues, "violently interrupts the gradualist monist continuum of matter and spirit"; it implies that a fallen, corrupted substance is present at the Creation and that God, in the form of the Son, is unable to transform this recalcitrant substance through the insemination of the Holy Spirit.[75] There is a grain of truth in this critique of the relationship between the natural philosophy of Milton's Creation and the theology that threads through it, and Rogers is right to link it to the problem of evil. However, Glisson's chymical model of perceptive, responsive matter neutralizes the poison of the dregs by offering a substantive system of natural philosophy that supports the profoundly libertarian nature of Milton's animist materialism. In short, it is the free will defense in biological form.

Traditional Galenic purgatives work through the older-style similary attraction, in which the purgative's acrid nature is similar to that of the bilious humor it seeks to remove and will draw it out as it passes through the body.[76] Glisson notes that for "regular physicians," this is sufficient theory "for the matter of purgations and other evacuations."[77] However, this comment is at the center of a detailed exploration of the various ways in which mixed bodies can be separated by chymical art. In Glisson's model of chymical fermentation as separation *per magisterium*, a plural set of matters, like all sentient beings, has a distinct set of responses to spiritual influence. This distinction is crucial to the expulsion sequences of *Paradise Lost*: Glisson's version elaborates the notion that purgation works through a simple identity between the purgative and the peccant matter that is purged. Rather than simply signifying the poisonous fallen matter of Van Helmont's Paracelsian tartar, Glisson's tartareous residues are stony elements within the "mixt" of the matter, which, through their natural perception of otherness, refuse assimilation with the spiritual impulsion of the ferment. Milton would have had every reason to be aware of the medical version of this process, and I suggest that, again, his source was a well-informed Glissonian view of tartar.

Gout, or tartar formation in the joints, was, like "gutta serena," originally thought to be the result of excessive, often phlegmatic, humors being produced in the stomach through bad digestion; they were then thought to exceed their bounds and flow out from their due places and collect, be it in the eyes or in the joints. (This explains the etymological link between "gutta serena" and "gout.") However, Glisson and other experimental physicians such as Willis developed another theory of tartar entirely based on the active, vital blood. Even the normal activity of the blood, in Glisson's schema, produces some waste matter. The mication of the blood, or the ceaseless production and consumption of spirit and vital heat, itself generates excrements of the body. Tellingly, they are "the salty and earthy parts which form the tartar."[78] Physicians investigating the body's substances found that those bodies, like the equivocal matter of Chaos, contained traces of elements that could not be volatilized by any spirit however powerful. Thomas Willis's tract on fermentation notes the remainder from a distillation of "a *Caput Mortuum*, or Dead Head; therefore it is called *Terra Damnata*, or damned Earth...nor capable of change, or exaltation."[79] The analogy made by Paracelsus between the dregs of sublimation and the damnation of the adversaries of God is retained as linguistic motif even by that most careful experimental iatrochemist, Thomas Willis.

These theories also cite a toxic fermentation in the blood rather than poor concoction and wandering humors; the production of vinous tartareous substance may lead to a number of health problems, in particular gout of the joints and gutta serena of the optic nerve.[80] Giglioni examines a teaching *determinatio* that can be dated to the early 1650s, in which:

> The real cause [of tartareous deposits in the body] is a process of fermentation occurring in the blood...which brings the mass of the blood to a "vinous condition."...The result of this fermentation is a tartareous residue which takes the form of a calculous sedimentation in the joints...chemistry gives the anatomist both explanatory and experimental resources. Gout, in Glisson's view, depends on the faulty disposition of the blood, which is caused by its "vinous" character, increase of tartar, and the specific nature of the humors running in the bloodstream.[81]

This fermentation is a malignant version of the normal activity of the blood, and I believe that this was the most current explanation for both Milton's almost complete blindness during the same period as well as for the gout that was to come. This theory makes possible a reading of the dregs as responsive matter that recognizes what is and is not assimilable to its own being, restating in biological form the problem of evil and the free will defense.

While the tartareous dregs may figure the problem of evil, they cannot figure *original* evil in *Paradise Lost* since by this time God has withdrawn his influence from Chaos; Satan and his legions have been seduced by Sin, fallen and fallen through it; hell has been created out of Chaos as a fit home for them; and allegorical figures, signifying the evil of ontological deprivation, have made homes in it.[82] *De doctrina Christiana* states that original matter is wholly good unless it "has become the property of another" and therefore vulnerable to infection and pollution, "since it is now in a mutable state, by the calculations of the devil or of man...which proceed from these creatures themselves" (YP 6:309). Therefore it is illogical that the dregs should be, as Rogers suggests, "an externally generated, precreative substance that must be purged from the original matter." Their darkness is, in this natural philosophy, utterly their own, inexplicable, but signifying the potential of the creations of God to reject divinity.

The notion of purgation at the Creation, and as Glisson conceives of it in terms of natural perception, provides a powerful set of analogies for Satan and his followers who, like the animated stuff of Creation, respond to the holy might of God by throwing themselves into the ordered place ordained for them. They are not, in the end, pushed, nor do they fall accidentally. Rather, like the inchoate substances of Creation and the animated substances of the body, they are in an endless interactive relationship with the Spirit. When faced with the burning vital heat of divinity, they recoil and leap to the place that suits them best, which is ultimately designated by the all-informing will of God. Without question, the apostate angels are driven out of heaven; "Pursue these sons of darkness, drive them out," God the Father commands at 6.715. Terrified of the Son's might, they look "into the wasteful deep" (6.862) through the gap in the crystal wall of heaven:

> the monstrous sight
> Strook them with horror backward, but far worse
> Urged them behind; headlong themselves they threw
> Down from the verge of heav'n, eternal wrath
> Burnt after them to the bottomless pit.   (*PL* 6.862–66)

It is not a pleasant or easy choice, but in the end it is their own. Like the naturally perceiving substances of Glisson's natural philosophy, they refuse assimilation and choose to leap downward. The Son has put on his face of terror and ridden toward them, his chariot flashing with lightning and "pernicious fire" (*PL* 6.849), but not a blow is struck. Unlike Adam and Eve, whose expulsion from paradise and (ultimately) back to the dust from whence they came might fruitfully be compared to this expulsion, the fallen angels are not conscious of remorse or guilt. Thus the material reality of the level to which they have fallen is infinitely worse. Like the tartareous dregs of *Paradise Lost* they have a divine origin, but like the vital chymical matter theorized by Glisson, they live by the same laws of radical liberty offered by Milton's God to the rest of Creation. The fallen, like the *minima naturalia* of life, are endowed with the choice to effervesce, expand, and rise up toward God or to become inert, cold, and pathologically opposed to their own living source. The denouement of *Paradise Lost* concludes with a prophecy in which the entire, cosmic scale conflict of good and evil is suddenly condensed within the mind of the human individual; likewise, the vital processes that created the world are drawn from the *vitae chorea* of the individual's burgeoning pulse of life.

University of Exeter

NOTES

An earlier version of this essay was presented at the Eleventh International Milton Symposium, July 23, 2015. I would like to thank Stephen Fallon and Karen Edwards in particular for reading earlier versions; their acute questions, their positive feedback, and their suggestions were most gratefully received.

1. *The Complete Prose Works of John Milton*, 8 vols., ed. Don M. Wolfe et al. (New Haven, Conn., 1953–82), 6:310; hereafter cited in the text as YP by volume and page number.

2. John Milton, *Paradise Lost*, ed. Alastair Fowler, 2nd ed. (London, 1998), 7.233–42. All further references to *Paradise Lost* will be to this edition, cited parenthetically in the text.

3. William B. Hunter, "Milton's Power of Matter," *Journal of the History of Ideas* 13, no. 4 (1952): 552.

4. N. K. Sugimura, *Matter of Glorious Trial: Spiritual and Material Substance in "Paradise Lost"* (New Haven, Conn., 2009), 17. Refreshingly, Sugimura recognizes the complexities of intellectual context that make it problematic to declare Milton an Aristotelian. Her argument that Milton's philosophy of substance bears the marks both of Aristotelianism and of Platonism is borne out by Milton's comment in the *Art of Logic* that his definition of form "combines the Platonic and the Aristotelian" (YP 8:232). While I agree that seventeenth century Aristotelianism is characterized by a distinct dualism of form and matter, this is, however, not true of contemporary medical revisions of Aristotelian cause.

5. John Rogers, *The Matter of Revolution: Science, Poetry, and Politics in the Age of Milton* (Ithaca, N.Y., 1996); see, in particular, "The Power of Matter in the English Revolution," 1–38; also, "Chaos, Creation and the Political Science of *Paradise Lost*," 103–43.

6. Guido Giglioni, "The Genesis of Francis Glisson's Philosophy of Life" (Ph.D. thesis, John Hopkins University, 2002). Giglioni notes that

> in Glisson's manuscript collection in the British Library there are more than 250 *determinationes* of medical disputations that Glisson wrote in his capacity as Regius Professor of Physic. If his medical, anatomical, and philosophical treatises...have drawn little attention from scholars, his archival papers have been almost completely ignored. In this dissertation, on the contrary, special emphasis will be laid upon Glisson's medical *determinationes* written between the late 1640s and the early 1660s. In my opinion, this is the period of incubation of Glisson's physiology of irritability and philosophy of hylozoism, and for this reason his *determinationes* are even more important as a document. (10)

I am greatly indebted to the scholarship and intellectual generosity of Guido Giglioni; his Ph.D. thesis has been fundamental to my own research. Because some works postdate Milton's *Paradise Lost*, while others would have been available to him, when using Giglioni's translations I note the source materials from which he was working.

7. Francis Glisson, *De natura substantiae energetica* (London, 1672).

8. Rogers, *Matter of Revolution*, 121.

9. Ibid., 119, 134–36.

10. Van Helmont is quoted in Rogers, *Matter of Revolution*, 136.

11. Rogers, *Matter of Revolution*, 137.

12. Giglioni, "Glisson's Philosophy," 2.

13. The most recent critic to comment on this central Creation passage (*PL* 7:233–42) is Stephen Fallon, who demonstrated a parity between Milton's view of matter in it and that of Newton, in "Living Matter in John Milton and Isaac Newton" (paper presented to the Eleventh International Milton Symposium, Exeter, July 2015). I suggest that one root of this connection is the vitalist medical theory of the 1650s and 1660s, which employed early chemistry as part of a new model of biological cause.

14. Barbara Lewalski, *The Life of John Milton* (Oxford, 2003), 409.

15. Christopher Hill, *Milton and the English Revolution* (London, 1977), 493–95. See also James H. Hanford, "Milton Forswears Physic," *Bulletin of the Medical Library Association* 32, no. 1 (1944): 23–34.

16. Rogers, *Matter of Revolution*, 105.

17. Francis Glisson, *A Treatise of the Rickets*, trans. Philip Armin (London, 1651). Those named in the preface are Francis Glisson, George Bate, Nathan Paget, Assuerus Regimorter, Thomas Sheaf, Edmund Trench, Robert Wright, and Jonathan Goddard. This connection has been noted by Hill, *Milton and the English Revolution*, 492, and also by William Riley Parker, *John Milton: A Biography*, 2 vols. (Oxford, 1968), 2:979.

18. For this information Giglioni cites Nathanial Hodges, *Loimologia sive pestis nuperae apud populum Londinensem grassantis narratio historica* (London, 1672), 18–19.

19. *Bibliotheca medica, viri clarissimi Nathanis Paget, M.D.* (London, 1681). Francis Glisson, *Anatomia hepatis*, in *English Manuscripts of Francis Glisson: 1. From "Anatomia hepatis" (The Anatomy of the Liver), 1654*, ed. Andrew Cunningham (Cambridge, 1993). Only the early sections are available in English. Page references are to this edition. Giglioni's study of Glisson's work provides a number of detailed translations of the Latin sections using *Anatomia Hepatis*. (Amsterdam, 1659).

20. *The Early Lives of Milton*, ed. Helen Darbishire (London, 1932), 72.

21. Lewalski, *Life of John Milton*, 36. For a detailed account of the changing reputation and theories of gout, see Roy Porter and G. S. Rousseau, *Gout: The Patrician Malady* (New Haven, Conn., 2000).

22. In 1649 Culpeper prescribed hot, dry remedies for gout, but these were also given as remedies for defluxions of "peccant matter" in the eye. For "Gout and other cold afflictions of the joints," he prescribed "*Herba Campborata*," noting that it "is of a drying faculty, and therefore stops defluxions either in the eyes or upon the lungues, the gout, cramps, palsies, aches, strengthens the nerves." Nicholas Culpeper, *A physicall directory; or, A translation of the London dispensatory made by the Colledge of Physicians in London* (London, 1649), 136.

23. Darbishire, *Early Lives of Milton*, 28. For details of issues and seatons, see Ambroise Paré, *The workes of that famous chirurgion*

Ambrose Parey translated out of Latine and compared with the French (London, 1634), 645. See also Walter Baley, *Two treatises concerning the preseruation of eie-sight. The first written by Doctor Baily sometimes of Oxford: the other collected out of those two famous phisicions Fernelius and Riolanus* (London, 1616), 44. John Kirkup, *The Evolution of Surgical Instruments* (San Francisco, 2006), 403.

24. Thomas Willis, *Dr. Willis's practice of physick being the whole works of that renowned and famous physician*, trans. Samuel Pordage (London, 1684), 91.

25. Walter Charleton, *Natural History of Nutrition, Life, and Voluntary Motion, methodically delivered in exercitations physicoanatomical* (London, 1659), borrows wholesale from Glisson's work.

26. Gad Freudenthal, *Aristotle's Theory of Material Substance: Heat and Pneuma, Form and Soul* (Oxford, 1999), 122.

27. William R. Newman notes that the contemporary term "chymistry" marks the crossover process from medieval alchemical practice into protomodern concerns with interacting substances, stating, "Lawrence Principe and I have been using this archaic word for nearly a decade to refer to early modern alchemy-chemistry, a discipline that still viewed the transformation of base metals into gold (*chrysopoeia*) as viable and yet contained much in addition that is identifiable to us moderns as chemistry." William R. Newman, *Atoms and Alchemy: Chymistry and the Experimental Origins of the Scientific Revolution* (London, 2006), xi. For reasons of clarity, I will also adopt this term since the stage of development of alchemy/chemistry in the medical works I deal with is precisely within the epistemological shift that Newman describes.

28. Antonio Clericuzio notes in *Elements, Principles and Corpuscles: A Study of Atomism and Chemistry in the Seventeenth Century* (Dordrecht, 2000), that Power, Charleton, and Willis all based their views of spirit "on the teachings of Francis Glisson" (97).

29. Most recently see Leah S. Marcus, "Ecocriticism and Vitalism in *Paradise Lost*," *Milton Quarterly* 49, no. 2 (2015): 103.

30. Giglioni describes Glisson's work as "chymical Galenism" in order to "distinguish his position—a critical and creative reconciliation of tradition and innovation—from both reactionary Galenism and radical Paracelsianism" ("Glisson's Philosophy," 10).

31. For example, Boyle's character Carneades notes of the artificial distillation of human blood that different strengths of fire cause differing separations. Robert Boyle, *The Sceptical Chymist: The Classic 1661 Text* (Mineola, N.Y., 2003), 53–55.

32. Walter Pagel, "The Reaction to Aristotle in Seventeenth-Century Biological Thought: Campanella, Van Helmont, Glanvill, Charleton, Harvey, Glisson, Descartes," in *Science, Medicine and History: Essays on the Evolution of Scientific Thought and Medical Practice Written in Honour of Charles Singer*, 2 vols., ed. E. A. Underwood (London, 1953), 1:507.

33. Stephen Fallon, *Milton among the Philosophers: Poetry and Materialism in Seventeenth-Century England* (Ithaca, N.Y., 1991); John Rumrich, *The Matter of Glory: A New Preface to "Paradise Lost"* (London, 1987); Michael Lieb, *The Sinews of Ulysses: Form and Convention in Milton's Works* (Pittsburgh, 1989); *Dialectics of Creation: Patterns of Birth and Regeneration in "Paradise Lost"* (Amherst, Mass., 1970).

34. Glisson is quoted in Guido Giglioni, "Anatomist Atheist?: The Hylozoistic Foundations of Francis Glisson's Anatomical Research," in *Religio Medici: Medicine and Religion in Seventeenth-Century England,* ed. Ole Peter Grell and Andrew Cunningham (Aldershot, 1996), 126.

35. Glisson is quoted in Giglioni, "Glisson's Philosophy," 78. Giglioni cites *Anatomia hepatis,* 325, 340–41; also MS Sloane 3309, ff. 370r–v.

36. Christopher Hill, "William Harvey and the Idea of Monarchy," *Past and Present* 27, no. 1 (1964): 54–72. Most relevant to this study is Rogers's exploration of the body and the body politic in his first chapter, "The Power of Matter in the English Revolution," *Matter of Revolution,* 1–38. My own study of this material focuses upon the parities among anatomy, poetry, and theodicy; however, there are adjustments that could be made to the political readings from my findings.

37. Giglioni, "Glisson's Philosophy," 126. Giglioni cites *Anatomia hepatis,* 322–26, 339–41; also Francis Glisson, *Tractatus de Ventriculo et Intestinis. Cui Praemittitur Alius, De Partibus Continentibus in Genere; & in Specie de Iis Abdominis* (Amsterdam, 1677), 233.

38. Walter Pagel, *Joan Baptista Van Helmont: Reformer of Science and Medicine* (Cambridge, 2002), 87.

39. The complete list is *"colatura, subsidentia, magisterium, distillatio, sublimatio, extractio and fermentatio"* (Glisson, *Anatomia hepatis,* 26–27).

. 40. Newman, *Atoms and Alchemy,* xiii.

41. Glisson, *Anatomia hepatis,* 69.

42. William Harvey, *The Works of William Harvey: Physician to the King, Professor of Anatomy and Surgery to the College of Physicians* (1847), ed. R. Willis (Whitefish, Mont., 2009), 509.

43. See Vivian Nutton, "The Anatomy of the Soul in Early Renaissance Medicine," in *The Human Embryo: Aristotle and the Arabic and European Traditions,* ed. G. R. Dunstan (Exeter, 1990), 136–57.

44. Paré, *Works,* 893. These cotyledons had long been shown by Vesalius to be features of animal, rather than human, anatomy.

45. D. M. Balme, "Human Is Generated by Human," in *The Human Embryo: Aristotle and the Arabic and European Traditions,* ed. G. R. Dunstan (Exeter, 1990), 24.

46. Henry More is quoted in John Henry, "Medicine and Pneumatology: Henry More, Richard Baxter and Francis Glisson's *Treatise on the Energetic Nature of Substance,*" *Medical History* 31 (1987): 25. The scale

of dualism ran from the extreme versions of Hobbes and Descartes through to the less predictable dualism of J. B. Van Helmont, who designated all matter water with spiritual animating force working through it. See Pagel, *Van Helmont*, 98.

47. Harvey also calls this the "primigenial moisture" (*Works*, 509–13).

48. All living beings are generated from eggs. Harvey argues "that which is called primordium among things arising spontaneously, and seed among plants, is an egg among oviparous animals, i.e. a certain corporeal substance, from which, through the motions and efficacy of an internal principle, a plant or animal of one description or another is produced; but the prime conception in viviparous animals is of the same precise nature"; he describes the interaction of male and female efficient causes as "a kind of contagion." See his "Exercise the 26th On the Nature of the egg" (*Works*, 278).

49. Harvey, *Works*, 336.

50. The discussion in *De doctrina Christiana* details the theodical importance of traducianism (see YP 6:318–24); the comments in the *Art of Logic* exploring how traducianism could function have not received nearly as much critical attention.

51. Alexander Ross, *Arcana microcosmi* (London, 1652).

52. Harvey, *Works*, 191.

53. Sugimura is right, I think, to read this as potentially dualistic in the Aristotelian sources. I argue that the seventeenth century medical interpretation of this formulation is, however, materialistic and vitalistic, as is Milton's own (*Matter of Glorious Trial*, 131).

54. Harvey, *Works*, 300.

55. Chaos, of course, is characterized by its unformed quality, but it is also divided into a circle and "brooded" on by the Holy Spirit; the original matter also contains "the seeds of all subsequent good" (YP 6:308).

56. Balme, "Human Is Generated," 23.

57. Glisson is quoted in Giglioni, "Glisson's Philosophy," 85. Giglioni cites MS Sloane 3310 ("Sanguis est summa et principalis pars corporis"), f. 228r.

58. Aristotle, quoted in Rumrich, *Matter of Glory*, 65.

59. Rumrich, *Matter of Glory*, 65.

60. Giglioni notes that in *De ventriculo* Glisson rejects Helmont's association of vital spirit with his notion of Gas, arguing that vital spirit is "intimately intermingled with the blood and does not produce bubbles or foam; rather, it blends the other elements of the blood in a homogeneous mixture, enlivens, expands, and contracts them uniformly in the course of its palpitating motion (*micatio*)" (Giglioni, "Glisson's Philosophy," 132).

61. Glisson is quoted in ibid., 124. Giglioni cites Glisson, *Anatomia hepatis*, 322.

62. Glisson, *Anatomia hepatis*, 19.

63. Giglioni, "Glisson's Philosophy," 63. Giglioni cites Glisson, *Anatomia hepatis*, 190, 363.

64. Roger French notes that "where attraction was denied in the body and in machines, it was replaced by impulsion." Roger French, *William Harvey's Natural Philosophy* (Cambridge, 1994), 108, 356.

65. For an account of the weapon salve debates, see Allen G. Debus, *The Chemical Philosophy: Paracelsian Science and Medicine in the Sixteenth and Seventeenth Centuries*, 2 vols. (New York 2002), 1:246–48; 2:303–07. For the weapon salve debate in *Paradise Lost*, see Charlotte Nicholls, "Your bodies may at last turn all to spirit": Medical Science and the *Anatomia Animata* in Milton's *Paradise Lost* (Ph.D. thesis, University of Exeter, 2010), 210–11.

66. Giglioni, "Glisson's Philosophy," 65.

67. Glisson, *Anatomia hepatis*, 69–71.

68. Giglioni, "Glisson's Philosophy," 120.

69. This connection between alchemical separation and the Creation has a Paracelsian background: "The alchemical *scheidung* also assumes a religious significance: the doctor...simply re-enacts, in an earthly dimension, the original *scheidung* of beings according to Genesis." M. L. Bianchi, "The Visible and the Invisible: From Alchemy to Paracelsus," in *Alchemy and Chemistry in the Sixteenth and Seventeenth Centuries*, ed. Piyo Rattansi and Antonio Clercuzio (London, 1994), 21.

70. Stephen Fallon made precisely this point about this sequence of verse in his presentation, "Living Matter."

71. Giglioni, "Glisson's Philosophy," 93.

72. Glisson, *Six Anatomical Lectures*, in *English Manuscripts of Francis Glisson 2. Lectures and Other Papers*, ed. Andrew Cunningham (Cambridge, 1998), 41.

73. Glisson is quoted in Giglioni, "Glisson's Philosophy," 83. Giglioni translates from Glisson's *Anatomia hepatis*, 310–11; he also cites MS Sloane 3308, ff. 226r–28r. Five years after the publication of *Anatomia hepatis*, Walter Charleton had obviously been influenced by Glisson's work; he almost replicates this passage in his *Natural History of Nutrition*, 42–43.

74. It is tempting to correlate this crystalline ocean (which is clearly not the crystalline sphere above) with Harvey's liquid colliquament, repeatedly described as crystalline in his *On Generation*.

75. Rogers, *Matter of Revolution*, 119, 134–36.

76. Glisson's development of the old idea is explored in Giglioni, "Glisson's Philosophy," 63–67.

77. Glisson, *Anatomia hepatis*, 75.

78. Giglioni, "Glisson's Philosophy," 124. Giglioni cites MS Sloane 3309, f. 95r; also 3309, f. 99r, and MS Sloane 3309 ("Sanguis est fons catarrhorum"), ff. 360r–61r for the sources of his translation and paraphrase.

79. Thomas Willis, *Of Fermentation*, in *Dr. Willis's practice of physick being the whole works of that renowned and famous physician*, trans. Samuel Pordage (London, 1684), 6.

80. Willis, *Of Feavers*, in ibid., 103.

81. Glisson is quoted in Giglioni, "Glisson's Philosophy," 149. Giglioni cites MS Sloane 3310 ("Arthritidis causa non est necessario frigida"), ff. 45r–50r; also MS Sloane 3310 ("Podagra est curabilis"), ff. 123r–24v, 127r–28v.

82. Here I must pay my respects to Fallon's *Milton among the Philosophers* for the understanding of evil as ontological deprivation in *Paradise Lost*.

Solitude and Difference in Books 8 and 9 of *Paradise Lost*

Christopher Koester

From the melancholic speaker of *Il Penseroso* to the solitary narrator of *Paradise Lost*, John Milton's literary personas frequently emphasize their own physical, mental, and spiritual apartness. Nor is this solitary condition limited to his poetic voices; the same can be said about most of Milton's major characters. Beginning with his God, who describes himself as "alone / From all eternity" (*PL* 8:405–06), solitude is the modus operandi of characters as diverse as the Son, Samson, Satan, and the Lady of *Comus*, as well as the subject of the present discussion, Adam and Eve.[1] Despite its nearly ubiquitous presence in his poetry, though, the solitary is often overlooked among critics who identify Milton as a man more committed to religious and political *solidarity* than individual *solitude*. As I argue, however, Milton's notion of solidarity, including marital solidarity, actually depends on his concept of solitude. Without solitude, solidarity risks turning into conformity, as the search for unity erases the individualities of those seeking it. Aware of this dilemma, yet still an avid supporter of unity, Milton attempts to solve the problem in his epic by depicting Adam and Eve as simultaneously committed to unity and individuality, marital society and personal solitude. Focused primarily on Adam, my essay investigates the way he responds to this dual commitment during moments of critical decision, beginning with his original solitude and subsequent request for a mate in book 8, followed by his conversation with Eve in book 9 about the function of solitude in marriage. I conclude that solitude in Milton's first humans should not be regarded simply as a passing condition or imbalance of bodily humors but instead as an ongoing orientation predicated on the idea that their differences from each other protect them from conformity.

The better to understand the connection between solitude and difference, I begin with an analysis of Adam's origin story in book 8. Through a vividly conceptualized account of Adam's solitude, Milton depicts the first man's growing awareness of his differences from beast and God, differences that ultimately prompt him to decline both the surrounding creatures and the deity as potential companions.[2] By gradually asserting his difference from the beasts and God, Adam embodies the early modern belief that, as Erica Fudge writes, "humans are created and not simply born."[3] Though equipped with certain innate human faculties, including the capacity to speak and think rationally, Adam does not become a fully realized human until after he gains self-knowledge, a progression that shows Milton adhering to the early modern belief that humanness depends to some degree on education and a creation of self through processes of development and discovery. With this acquisition of self-knowledge through education, however, comes the possibility of losing it. According to Fudge, early moderns well understood "the risk that humans may cease to be human, may stop acting according to their education, and may revert back to their natural sensuality."[4] Such a loss occurs in the wake of Adam's decision to eat the fruit, which sees him momentarily regressing from a fully realized human to a more animalistic state, as indicated by his lust-filled sex with Eve, as well as his desire to "In solitude live savage, in some glade / Obscured" (9.1085–86). If humanness, for Milton, entails knowing oneself aright, an education that occurs through a sincere commitment to contemplative solitude, then refusing—or, in the case of an indissoluble marriage, being forbidden—to act on that self-knowledge can result in a loss of humanity and a return to the much more "savage" solitude that Milton repeatedly denounces throughout his divorce tracts.

As these last comments about marriage make clear, Adam's struggle to know himself and to recognize his difference from the creatures around him does not end with the creation of Eve. Instead, Adam brings the lessons he learns in solitude concerning difference with him into marriage, a marriage based, at least in part, on Milton's belief, stated in *Tetrachordon*, that the soul "cannot well doe without company, so in no company so well as where the different sexe in most resembling unlikenes, and most unlike resemblance cannot but please best and be pleas'd in the aptitude of that variety" (YP 2:597). These companionate differences enable the experience of solitude, which Milton conceives as an epiphenomenon of material/spiritual individuation and hierarchical separation, to persist even within marriage, lending some credence to the idea, recently proposed by R. V. Young, that by the time Milton wrote *Paradise Lost*, "solitude has become the essential condition of man and devil."[5] Literary scholars whose work engages book 8 tend to focus on how God consents to Adam's request, claiming that he "Knew it not good for man to be alone" and admitting that the preceding solitude was a "trial" that tested Adam's capacity to "judge of fit and meet" (8.445–48). Reason dictates that Adam's reward for passing such a test would be commensurate with the trial he endured to receive it, and thus would involve the introduction of still more difference, that is, a mate "most resembling unlikenes, and [of] most unlike resemblance." Instead, God announces his plan to provide Adam "Thy likeness, thy fit help, thy other self, / Thy wish, exactly to thy heart's desire" (8.450–51). Rather than more difference, God ostensibly supplies Adam a mate of "likeness," suggesting Milton's notion of marriage owed much to Aristotle's definition of friendship, founded on the idea that friends represent "equality and likeness" to each other.[6]

So it would seem, anyway. Undeniable as it is that Aristotle influenced Milton's thinking on marriage and friendship, another strand of thought emerges the more we examine the poet's words, one that takes into account the notion of spousal difference Milton promulgates in *Tetrachordon*. My reading attends to this alternate understanding of marriage by reevaluating Milton's use of the word "likeness," which departs from an Aristotelian definition of friendship that foregrounds the self-sameness of the partners.[7] Rather than similitude, Milton more often depicts likeness based on shared dissimilarities, or a "vision of equality-in-difference," in the words of James Grantham Turner.[8] Different from beast and God, Adam is also different from Eve, whose God-decreed "likeness" to him consists, first and foremost, in the fact that, like Adam, she too is born alone, and she too must establish her subjectivity *via negativa*. Even this likeness, however, contains a difference since, in contrast to her male counterpart, who differentiates himself from beast and God, Eve is made to choose between different versions of herself, one which appears as a "shape within the watery gleam," and another in the form of godly Adam, her "other half" (*PL* 4.461, 488). In reaction to Aristotle's philosophy concerning friendship, then, and his more rigid distinction between society and solitude, Milton offers a complex approach to marriage in which hierarchically separated partners are presented as both together and alone, alike and not.[9] This dual commitment begins to falter, however, during the separation scene. There, Adam errs when attempting to reconcile his difference from Eve by way of sameness. Whereas good marital conversation depends on the interplay of similarity and difference, Adam turns an otherwise productive conversation about the role of solitude in marriage into a self-jeopardizing debate the moment he reduces love to conformity and sameness.

Discussing their solitary beginnings, Mary Beth Long notes how the different origin stories of Adam and Eve negatively impact their conversation in book 9, at which time "Adam considers solitude a test he has already endured, while Eve thinks of it as a privilege she has yet to attain."[10] Ultimately, my reading extends Long's admirable work by examining how Adam's solitude better prepares him for that conversation by providing him a more rigorous introduction to difference, a concept inextricably linked to solitude in

Milton's texts. Born into different solitudes, Adam and Eve recognize and respond to different differences. As a result, they bring to marriage different understandings of difference itself.[11] Whereas God is so radically different that his difference cannot be thought (he truly is, in his own words, "alone / From all eternity"), Eve represents difference within reason, a recognizable difference, and a difference that Adam (unlike Eve) is better prepared to interpret. Perhaps to be made in God's image, "Inward and outward both, his image fair" (8.221), is to be made alone and different from all other creations; our "likeness" involves our shared ability to recognize and communicate those differences to one another. Indeed, the final lines of the poem attest to that version of likeness-in-difference in a fallen world, as Adam and Eve "hand in hand with wandering steps and slow, / Through Eden took their solitary way" (12.648–49).

I

In a compelling account of Adam's solitude, Timothy Harrison finds Adam "possessed of an immediately clear awareness of himself," believing his "capacity to speak and employ his reason separates him from the other animals."[12] Similarly, Thomas Luxon believes Adam "comes into being with language and his subjectivity hard-wired."[13] Yet, rational speech is not always a guarantor of humanness in the early modern world. As Fudge observes, "being born with a rational soul is not enough," insofar as "there is something more required than the mere possession of this essence of the human."[14] Fudge locates two conflicting views of humanness in early modern society. The first, which underlies the work of Harrison, Luxon, and others, rests on the "comforting notion of the human as a given status; as a being born and not made." The second view is that humans are "constructed by education, custom, and culture, and this human is, inevitably, reliant on the existence of education, custom, and culture."[15] Milton's description of Adam's solitude proves especially interesting for the way it holds in tension *both* views of the human. While some traits associated with humanness appear innate to Adam, others seem to develop through a process of education, as the first man slowly discovers things about himself and his surroundings.[16] Precisely how slowly is not known, since Adam's retelling condenses real time into narrative time, possibly reducing the duration of some events, while expanding others. Known for certain, though, is that Adam struggled to figure out, in his own words, "who I was" (8.270). Harrison and Luxon's readings, then, offer only a partial explanation of Adam's beginning. To understand his humanness in its entirety, we must also investigate Adam's solitude from the perspective of an emergent self whose realization depends on his ability to step outside of the animal-human continuum in order to recognize it *as* a continuum. If he wants to reject the animal world as inadequate for companionship, he must first reject the animal within himself.

"The difference between the human and the animal," Fudge writes of the early modern world, "is the difference between ignorance and self-knowledge."[17] While Adam eventually gains the self-knowledge demanded by the Roman injunction, *nosce te ipsum,* that knowledge is not present the moment he awakes on earth. Rather, it takes time to acquire. Instead of acting on an inborn self-knowledge, Adam admits to not knowing "who I was, or where, or from what cause" (8.270). Even *that* realization, however, seems to have taken a while to register with the first man. Assuming the sequence of narrative events corresponds to events as they actually happened, then Adam's not knowing "who [he] was" follows an even more primitive stage of his development in which he does not know what he does not know. Adam remembers how in this state of extreme ignorance he relies on instinct rather than education, explaining to Raphael that the first use of his limbs is powered "By quick instinctive motion" (8.259). While the upward leap lands him on his feet, a human stance, the fact that it is powered by instinct, a lower faculty, and one more often associated with beasts than humans in the early modern world, suggests his first movements are involuntary and thus more closely linked to the impulsive motility of animals. Before he comes to realize what he does not know, a realization that sets him on the path toward self-knowledge and a fully realized human status, Adam exists in a state of blissful ignorance, in which he acts on human instinct rather than human education.

Adam quickly evolves from these instinctual movements to more quintessentially human activities, such as bodily exploration ("Myself I then perused" [8.267]) and exercise of speech ("to speak I tried, and forthwith spake" [8.271]), both of which affirm his possession of the reason-based faculties necessary to cultivate his inchoate humanness. However, the appearance of these skills does not a human make. Despite their existence in Adam, neither his ability to examine his body nor his ability to speak can ensure the development of inward self-knowledge, a defining feature of the human in the early modern period. Nor can these traits, by themselves, guarantee that Adam will pass God's trial, which intends to test the first man's ability to "judge of fit and meet." If the mere presence of speech and reason were enough, then the test itself would be somewhat pointless, functioning more like a quality control inspection that Adam succeeds in passing without participating. To pass the test, Adam must first learn how to employ his reason properly, toward the acquisition of self-knowledge. While his bodily self-exploration shows Adam admiring his physical form ("Myself I then perused, and limb by limb / Surveyed" [8.267–68]), it is not until he questions the creatures around him that Adam begins to exhibit an interest in learning "who [he] was, or where, or from what cause" (8.270). Not surprisingly, that attempt rather quickly fails. His efforts at interpellation ("Tell, if ye saw, how came I thus, how here?" [8.277]) fall apart the moment the creatures "answer none returned," at which point he retires, "pensive," to an embankment (8.285–87). Use of the word "pensive" reveals a lot about Adam's condition. Failing to discover anything about himself from the flora and fauna, the sky and the earth, Adam begins to look inward, in a moment of profound introspection. Whereas his earliest encounters with the animal world are governed by a logic of sameness, as he tries and fails to communicate with creatures that he falsely identifies as equals, this more pensive Adam has learned to recognize difference, a critically important step in the development of self-knowledge. When the creatures "answer none returned," Adam is forced to confront for the first time the somewhat disconcerting fact that he is not like them.

Exhausted from the work of trying to solve "who [he] was," Adam next relates how his pensive thoughts lead to an unexpected nap. During this sleep, Adam thinks he is slipping back into a preconscious existence, believing himself "passing to [his] former state / Insensible" (8.290–91). God intervenes, however, in the form of an "inward apparition" that "gently moved / [his] fancy to believe [he] yet had being" (8.293–94). If Adam falls asleep with only a nascent awareness of his difference from the creatures around him, that situation certainly has changed by the time God intervenes, calling out, "Thy mansion wants thee, Adam, rise, / First man, of men innumerable ordained / First father" (8.296–98). The perfect pedagogue, God instructs Adam in some of the answers he so desperately sought from the creatures around him, as he learns his name ("Adam"), his title ("First man"), his job description ("First father"), as well as, a little later, the source of his being ("Whom thou soughtst I am" [8.316]). Upon gaining this information, Adam progresses from an unknowing human with animal inclinations to a newly educated human aware not only of himself and his purpose, but also his maker. Describing how he "fell / Submiss" at God's feet, Adam claims he is "reared" by God (8.315–16). The primary definition of "reared" suggests that God helps Adam back to his feet. Its secondary definition, though, meaning to bring up morally or intellectually, could also apply. Contrast this moment of divine rearing by God with Adam's previous instance of rearing to his feet "by quick instinctive motion," and his gradual development as a human becomes all the more apparent. While Milton depicts Adam as manifesting certain innate human characteristics, he also shows his commitment to humanness as a process of personal and spiritual growth that occurs over time and with the help of the master educator, God.

Interestingly, Eve does not receive the same sort of solitary education as Adam.[18] Whereas Adam's solitude culminates in a trial that assesses the self-knowledge he has gained up to that point

("Thus far to try thee, Adam, I was pleased, / And find thee knowing not of beasts alone, / Which thou hast rightly named, but of
thyself" [8.347–49]), Eve encounters no such test. God "took"
Adam "by the hand" (8.300) in an effort to educate him about
Eden's landscape, the "rigid interdiction" (8.334) and the animals he names, eventually engaging in debate with Adam about
his self-declared "single imperfection" (8.423). By contrast, Eve
relates how Adam "seized" her hand in order to put an end to her
narcissistic obsession with her own image in "the watery gleam"
(4.489, 461). In brief, solitary Adam receives a much more rigorous lesson in difference, one that sees him develop from a human
operating on instinct to a fully realized and self-knowledgeable
human capable of well-reasoned arguments about "disparity" and
"proportion due" (8.386, 385). Insofar as education forms one axis
by which Milton evaluates humanness, Eve seems endowed with
slightly less humanity than Adam, a fact scholars have long noted
by calling attention to the line, "He for God only, she for God in
him" (4.299). Unlike Adam, who gains a deep knowledge of himself and his difference from the animals, Eve receives an education
in the much more superficial task of discerning which appearances
are real and which illusory, an education that occurs almost by
accident during an interruption in which Adam grabs her hand.
Reading Eve's solitary scene, some scholars have claimed she does
not appear to experience the same "single imperfection" as Adam,
which is true.[19] Yet, Adam's understanding of his imperfection is
the result of the self-knowledge he acquires through a prolonged,
rigorous, and solitary introduction to the concept of difference.
Were Eve permitted that same level of solitary education, perhaps
she too would have arrived at the same conclusion.

Milton's belief in a humanness realized through a process of
education brings with it the possibility that humans can also fail to
maintain their humanness, thus reverting back to a more beastly
state. We witness that reversal after Adam and Eve eat the forbidden
fruit, a time when they feel "As with new wine intoxicated both"
(9.1008). "Getting drunk," writes Fudge, "is a failure to assign due
place to the beasts of one's mind."[20] In calling attention to their

inebriated state, the narrator shows how their failure causes Adam and Eve to release an inner beastliness, ultimately engaging in a lust-filled ("in lust they burn") act of sex (9.1015). The possibility of reverting back to a beast also helps to explain the many negative representations of solitude in Milton's divorce tracts. By a "desire and longing" emplaced within him by God, Adam "put off an unkindly solitarines" through "the cheerfull society of wedlock," Milton writes in *The Doctrine and Discipline of Divorce*, in one of many such instances in which he criticizes solitude as a negative condition (YP 2:251). Close scrutiny of Milton's language here and elsewhere in the divorce tracts, however, reveals the likely reason behind his seemingly antisolitary stance. The word "unkindly," evocative of the nonhuman, establishes a link between the animal and the unhappy spouse, who will return to this "unkindly solitarines" without the ability to divorce.[21] Meanwhile, positive formulations of solitude in the divorce tracts, though fewer in number, praise the *vita contemplativa* and the solitude of God, "sufficiently possessed / Of happiness," despite the fact that he is "alone / From all eternity" (*PL* 8.403–06). In *Tetrachordon*, for instance, Milton describes the solitary labors of the mind as the primary occupation of a Christian, relegating marital conversation to that which occurs only because "No mortall nature can endure either in the actions of Religion, or study of wisdome, without somtime slackning the cords of intense thought and labour" (YP 2:596). In other words, the solitude that Milton condemns in the divorce tracts resembles the solitude that Adam experiences during his primitively human state. At no point, though, does Milton condemn contemplative solitude. Rather, he openly praises the solitary life in poems such as *Il Penseroso* and in his personal letters, while also presenting the Son of *Paradise Regained* as entering the wilderness, "the better to converse / With solitude" (1.190–91).

Complicating matters somewhat is the fact that Adam denounces his beastly solitude during a moment of contemplative solitude with God. In other words, Adam needs the good version of solitude to recognize that the bad version, the beastly version, is not for him. Not only does this good version of solitude serve as

the newly enlightened place from which Adam denounces the bad
version, it also marks the closest Adam comes to understanding
the contemplative solitude of his God, whose solitude represents a
perfected version of Adam's own. With divine aid, Adam has lifted
himself from the solitude of the beasts to the perch of a contemplative solitude that elevates him just barely enough to carry on a
conversation with his maker, though not enough to secure a lasting friendship with him. Here, Luxon's reading of the scene proves
especially insightful. As he observes, "Conversation with God
could make Adam even more godlike, but in the end friendship
with God the Father is out of the question, even though Milton
fancies that Adam conversed at length with God and together they
made a new being, a woman to be Adam's proper friend. God does
not need a friend, so the two cannot get the same things from each
other as friendship requires; they are hopelessly unequal. Until
Adam lives in heaven, he cannot live with God; besides, carrying
on a conversation with God appears to overwhelm Adam."[22] Luxon
is right to point out that God and Adam are "hopelessly unequal."
At the same time, I question what it means to be Adam's "proper
friend." According to Luxon, who locates Aristotle in Milton's
thinking on friendship, a proper friend is a friend of similitude, and
God cannot be a proper friend because he is so different. Though I
agree about God's radical difference, I hesitate to say that the ideal
friendship for Milton depends on equality and exact likeness. If Eve
makes an ideal companion, it is because she is hope*fully* unequal
to Adam, in contrast to God and Adam, who, as Luxon writes, are
"hope*lessly* unequal." The problem for Adam is not difference
itself, but that God is too different, his alterity too great for Adam
to comprehend. Meanwhile, Eve is perfectly different. Their basic
dissimilitude suggests that Milton's understanding of friendship is
not based in likeness, but likeness-through-difference.[23] God's difference is extrarational; the creatures' difference is irrational; Adam
and Eve's difference, meanwhile, is perfectly rational, insofar as
it is "most resembling unlikenes, and most unlike resemblance,"
to invoke the phrase Milton uses in *Tetrachordon*. Adam himself
indicates as much when comparing proper friendship to the right

"proportion" (8.385) of an instrument's strings. He believes ideal partnership is one that produces harmony through (in keeping with the metaphor) differences of pitch, intensity, and timbre, which correspond to differences in a given string's thickness, tension, and material composition.

II

Milton carefully extends the Genesis story in ways that allow for solitude to persist even within marriage. Eve's creation does not eliminate Adam's solitude. Rather, it shifts its direction from the ground to the sky, from the solitude of the animals to the solitude of two individual humans striving, and helping each other strive, toward a solitary God. For all of Milton's talk in the divorce tracts about marriage as a union of like minds—and there is a lot of such talk—he ultimately conceives this union not as conformity, but as a peaceful opportunity to manifest individual difference and solitude. Milton's emphasis in *Tetrachordon* and elsewhere on the "different sexe" and the "unlikenes" of the partners suggests he was as much or more influenced by a Greek pederastic model of male-male relations than an Aristotelian model of friendship based on the likeness of male-male friends. Adapting the pederastic model to suit a heterosexual union, Milton replaces the hierarchy of man/boy found in the works of Plato and other Greek texts with the hierarchy of husband/wife, as reified in the much-discussed description of Adam and Eve as "he for God only, she for God in him" (4.299). While Eve is created in Adam's "likeness," nevertheless, likeness is not sameness, and differences abound even between the partners of an ideal marriage. True as it might be that husband and wife offer "mutual help / And mutual love" to each other, the help and love they bring to marriage necessarily differs depending on the individuals involved (4.727–28). So committed is Milton to this idea of individual difference in marriage that he chooses to endorse it even when that endorsement means disrupting the gendering of the aforementioned hierarchy. In the event that a woman should "exceed her husband in prudence and dexterity," Milton writes, "the wiser should govern the lesse wise, whether male or female" (YP 2:589). His willingness to support this sort of gender inversion demonstrates the importance of hierarchy to Milton's conception of marriage, a marriage that promotes difference and (if the match is a good one) the contemplative variety of solitude, no matter which gender takes the lead.

Milton returns to the discussion of individuation only a few paragraphs later in *Tetrachordon*. To the extent that "the unity of minde is neerer and greater then the union of bodies," he argues, "so doubtles, is the dissimilitude greater, and more dividuall, as that which makes between bodies all difference and distinction. Especially when as besides the singular and substantial differences of every Soul, there is an intimat quality of good or evil, through the whol progeny of *Adam*, which like a radical heat, or mortal chilnes joyns them, or disjoyns them irresistibly" (YP 2:606). Though written in the service of defending divorce on the grounds of incompatibility, this passage also reveals a lot about Milton's understanding of marital unity, which must account for the "difference and distinction" of "every Soul." Nor is this the only passage in which unity involves degrees of difference, both of mind and body. In the same way that "the unity of minde is *neerer* and greater then the union of bodies" in marriage, so too is marriage "the *neerest* resemblance of our union with Christ," a passage that itself recalls Abdiel's claim in *Paradise Lost* that God intends "to exalt / Our happy state under one head more *near* / United" and Raphael's description of spirits "*nearer* to [God] placed or *nearer* tending" (YP 2:606; *PL* 5.829–31, 476; my italics). Similarly, Milton writes in *Of Education* that "The end then of learning is to repair the ruins of our first parents by regaining to know God aright, and out of that knowledge to love him, to imitate him, to be like him, as we may the *neerest* by possessing our souls of true vertue, which being united to the heavenly grace of faith makes up the highest perfection" (YP 2:366–67; my italics). The "neerest" we come in our endeavors to "imitate" and be "like" God still involves individuation, according to Milton, resulting in a community founded on a basic and enduring sense of difference.

In all of these cases, unity of both mind and body consists in nearness, not sameness, suggesting permanent difference rather than complete ontic merger.[24] This stands in contrast to Pico della Mirandola's influential *Orations on the Dignity of Man*, which outlines a Neoplatonic process by which a person "gathers himself into the centre of his own unity, thus becoming a single spirit with God [unus Deo spiritus factus] in the solitary darkness of the Father, he, who had been placed above all things, will become superior to all things."[25] Whether in marriage in particular or his theology more broadly, Milton strategically avoids defining unity as consisting in what Pico calls a "single spirit." Instead, unity involves a version of likeness that must always take into consideration the "singular and substantial differences of every Soul," enabling solitude and difference to persist within godly society, whether in marriage or among the angels, whose community also consists of a "constant mind / Though single" (5.902–03).[26] Such a stance remains consistent with Milton's Antitrinitarianism, which denies the coessentiality and coequality of the Father and Son. Milton writes in *De doctrina Christiana* that even though "the Father dwells in [the Son]…[that] does not mean that their essence is one, only that their communion is extremely close" (YP 6:220). Lacking this permanent ontic division, God could not be "alone / From all eternity." His solitude depends on his enduring, essential difference from all creation, including his own Son.

Returning to *Paradise Lost*, Eve's difference from Adam means that his solitude does not end with her creation, but continues to serve a function in their marriage. Unlike Aristotle's notion of friendship based in likeness, Milton conceives of friendship, for which Puritan marriage serves as the ideal, as involving two people alike in their "most resembling unlikenes, and most unlike resemblance." Milton's God seemingly endorses a more conventional understanding of likeness when he tells Adam that he:

> Knew it not good for man to be alone,
> And no such company as then thou sawst
> Intended thee, for trial only brought,
> To see how thou couldst judge of fit and meet:

What next I bring shall please thee, be assured,
Thy likeness, thy fit help, thy other self,
Thy wish, exactly to thy heart's desire.   (8.445–51)

Yet we must read these lines within a general understanding of Milton's notion of friendship as difference. Eve's "likeness" to Adam consists, paradoxically, in her "most resembling unlikenes," which has the effect of perpetuating difference. To rephrase God's edict, then, it is "not good for man to be alone" *by himself*, that is, numerically singular, without mate, a "single imperfection" (8.423). Here, Milton interprets God's pronouncement against aloneness in Genesis 2:18 as an indictment not of solitude itself, but of the particularly radical version of solitude that would persist in the absence of a mate.[27] Adam is not capable of living like God, whose ontic superiority means he is truly "alone / From all eternity." Adam needs a mate whose difference from him resembles (is "like") his difference from her, and in that way they are alike through their very difference from each other. The "single imperfection" that Adam laments is not solitude per se, but a solitude so radically different from the solitudes of beast and God that it cannot produce happiness unless experienced alongside another solitary human.

Initially, Adam seems to mistake Eve for another version of himself, leaving the reader to wonder whether their relationship is one founded in self-sameness.[28] Enthralled by her presence, in a moment that nearly sees him relapsing into a more animalistic state, Adam declares, "I now see / Bone of my bone, flesh of my flesh, myself / Before me" (8.494–96). As we saw, however, Adam is able to "judge of fit and meet," and eventually he revises this assessment when acknowledging Eve to be "the inferior, in the mind / And inward faculties, which most excel, / In outward also her resembling less / His image who made both" (8.541–44). "Resembling less," the phrase Adam uses to qualify Eve's likeness to God, confirms that the Milton of *Paradise Lost* has not abandoned the language of nearness and "unlike resemblance" initially found in *Tetrachordon*. Nor are the gender differences Adam notices, outward and inward, faults of nature. "Accuse not nature," Raphael admonishes Adam, advising him to "weigh with her thyself," and also that love "hath his seat / In reason, and is judicious, [and] is the scale / By which to heavenly love thou mayst ascend" (8.561, 570, 590–92). Using metaphors of weight and scale, Raphael has to remind Adam that Eve is different. But this difference is entirely necessary, lest he return to an irrationally beastlike state, "sunk in carnal pleasure," the very sort of pleasure against which Milton rails in his divorce tracts as the sign of a bad and bestial marriage (8.593). Were Adam to surrender to these base desires, he would likely experience something akin to his first and more animalistic moment in Eden, a testament to a vestigial animality still within him.

In his original solitude, Adam learns to recognize difference and, through that difference, to declare his "single imperfection" (8.423) as well as his desire for a mate. Rather than "Like of his like" (8.424), however, this mate registers even more difference, both physically and intellectually. Similar to his earlier defense of schism within church and state, Milton seems to promote a version of marriage in *Paradise Lost* in which intellectual difference has a place, and solitude a permanent platform. Alluding to God's spiritual church, Milton writes in *Areopagitica* that:

> There must be many schisms and many dissections made in the quarry and in the timber, ere the house of God can be built. And when every stone is laid artfully together, it cannot be united into a continuity, it can but be contiguous in this world; neither can every peece of the building be of one form; nay rather the perfection consists in this, that out of the many moderat varieties and brotherly dissimilitudes that are not vastly disproportionall arises the goodly and the gracefull symmetry that commends the whole pile and structure. (YP 2:555)

In this life, at least, there can be no consensus among believers, much the same way that the architecture of a church consists not in a "continuous" and unified structure, but rather "contiguous" subdivisions that "commend" the whole. As Balachandra Rajan contends, Milton identifies himself as among those Puritans committed to "multiplying dissensions as a creative ferment within which the collective search was to be launched and out of which the redeemed consensus would emerge."[29] While the teleological end still remains the "gracefull symmetry" of the redeemed church, it is a goal best achieved through "brotherly dissimilitudes" and the solitudes that co-occur with them.

III

The greatest test of Adam's ability to identify and manage difference occurs during the separation conversation, in which the first couple negotiates the questions of solitude and difference raised here. In *Milton's Eve*, Diane McColley argues that Adam's "final speech changes direction" because he "finds in his own word 'obedience' illumination for his rapidly working mind and comprehends what true obedience is."[30] The obedience to which McColley refers here is the obedience of Eve. *She* must prove her constancy to God while away from Adam, and, finally realizing this fact, Adam suddenly insists that she go. McColley contends that Adam's "rapidly working mind" "incorporates" Eve's logic into his own argument, and this "integration" shows his acumen as a critical thinker.[31] To incorporate Eve's logic into Adam's own, however, diametrically opposes the Miltonic philosophy of "nearness." It behooves us, then, to reconsider not only McColley's claim, but also John Rumrich's assertion that "One of them must get his or her way—they cannot both stay together and be apart."[32] Perhaps Adam and Eve *can* "stay together and be apart," much the same way they remain "hand in hand" while taking their "solitary way" through paradise. This latter possibility is indirectly registered in Stanley Fish's reading of the separation scene. Fish remarks in *How Milton Works* that "In the course of answering the question of what it means to garden, they garden themselves—that is, they encourage and/or retard the growth of the thoughts by which their situation in all of its aspects is conceived."[33] For Fish, this means "to grow in the exercise of obedience by discerning its imperatives in a number of situations," the present one included.[34] I, too, find the separation scene to be one of self-cultivation. In the scene, Milton relies on a model of growth previously supplied by Raphael, whose description of spiritual growth explains how "from the root / Springs lighter the green stalk, from thence the leaves / More airy, last the bright consummate flower / Spirits odorous breathes" (5.479–82). Phrased with similarly ramose imagery in *Areopagitica,* the metaphor designates the "firm root, out of which we all grow, though into branches" (YP 2:556). In other words, spiritual growth entails a process of diversification, as each branch grows up next to and apart from those around it, creating unity of the whole plant through division of its branches.

Though not at first, Adam learns to recognize this fact. Despite his earlier admission that "solitude sometimes is best society," he quickly proposes a solution whose underlying logic argues the exact opposite: that *society* still involves solitude, and that Eve can test herself alone while in his presence (9.249). He attempts to shift the locus of Eve's desired trial from further afield to right next to him, inviting her to "trial choose / With me, best witness of thy virtue tried" (9.316–17). A cursory glance at Milton's other uses of the word "trial" confirms that he has a solitary test in mind. In *Areopagitica,* for instance, Milton's defense of the right to read texts alone, without the stamp of the imprimatur, and to decide, solitarily, the merits of a given work, leads him to claim that what "purifies us is triall, and triall is by what is contrary" (YP 2:515). Upon the Son's entrance into the desert in *Paradise Regained,* "the better to converse / With solitude," Satan appears in order "to try" him (*PR* 1.190–91, 123). "Alone and helpless," the Lady of *Comus* will "in the happy trial prove most glory" (582, 591). Samson's solitude at the mill also ends in a singular "trial" of "strength" (*Samson Agonistes* 1643–44). Finally, as already seen, Adam's original solitude culminates in a trial, in which God tests his ability to "judge of fit and meet." More than coincidental, Milton describes these characters as experiencing solitude during times of trial that nonetheless occur in the presence of others. Whatever the situation, and more could be named, mention of the solitary invariably precedes moments of trial in Milton's texts, suggesting solitude's indispensability to his conception of Christian virtue and human freedom.[35] Unlike Adam, however, whose solitude was tested in God's presence, Eve seeks her solitary trial away from him. This desired relocation effectively sidesteps Adam, her differential ideal, and, in theory, the perfect witness of her solitude, a movement that also disrupts the Miltonic logic of "He for God only, she for God in him." Much as his solitary conversation with God found Adam "expressing well the spirit within [him] free" (8.440), Adam expects Eve to express a similarly self-assertive attitude in *his* presence. Less experienced than Adam, though, for reasons already discussed, Eve desires to test her solitude at a distance.

At issue, then, is how Adam can persuade Eve to test herself in his presence and do so without coercion. To force Eve to test herself in his presence—thereby integrating *her* logic into *his*—would constitute an infringement on her free will. Adam must convince Eve to test her solitude in his presence in such a way that her free will is not compromised in the process. Milton himself was familiar with the rhetorical dilemma surrounding this type of persuasion. In his prose tracts, he seeks an audience at once skeptical and persuadable. Lacking skepticism, his readers might accept his arguments unquestioningly, as unthinking conformists. If his readers prove too intransigent, then he lacks a reason to write altogether. Rhetorically, then, Milton's aim must be to convince his prose readers to convince themselves of the veracity of his claims. His "fit audience" is one receptive to his arguments, though still discriminating. In other words, he seeks solitary readers capable of independent decision. While he supplies the argument, his readers must decide *on their own* the truthfulness of his words or risk believing him for the wrong reason, turning polemic into propaganda, persuasion into mere conformity. This rhetorical setup is grounded in difference and the idea that consensus need not end in conformity.[36] In the context of Milton's epic, that puts Adam in a tough situation. He must try to convince Eve to convince herself to stay with him, or, failing at that, let her go in such a way that he does not compromise his own sense of selfhood.

An evaluation of Adam's performance finds him starting off well, stumbling in the middle, and ending even worse. The problems begin the moment Adam admits that "other doubt" prevents him from supporting Eve's decision to depart from his side (9.251). Until then, Adam has opposed Eve's desire based on practical grounds, pointing out that the stated goal of her departure — to maximize productivity — is not necessary, since "not so strictly hath our Lord imposed / Labour" (9.235–36). As soon as Adam mentions Satan, though, the cause behind his "other doubt," the conversation shifts from productivity to questions of moral integrity. With that conversational turn comes an urge to compare themselves to one another. Initially, Adam resists that urge, claiming his love for Eve is "beyond / Compare" (9.227–28). Following his comment about Satan, however, that hesitancy to compare seems to disappear, as Adam increasingly understands his love for Eve by way of parallels that emphasize their self-similitude. Adam admits that "in [her] sight" he becomes "More wise, more watchful, stronger," while "shame" encourages him to try harder, "unit[ing]" his vigor with virtue (9.310–14). The difference that Adam implicitly acknowledges by his use of the word "more" is immediately undercut by an assumed likeness as he wonders aloud, "Why shouldst not thou *like* sense within thee feel / When I am present" (9.315–16; my italics). In other words, Adam tries (and fails) to understand difference in terms of a likeness that tends toward sameness. Though not yet sameness, his language is slowly shifting in that direction. Rather than likeness through difference, Adam engages a comparison that occludes meaningful difference by an imagined likeness in feeling. The prescriptive tone of Adam's question ("Why shouldst not thou") suggests that he wishes Eve to feel "More wise, more watchful, stronger" when around him, just as he feels when around her. Adam wants her to be more like him, but also *by* him, wrongly associating nearness with sameness. While Adam seems to want Eve to "trial choose / With" him, inviting her to test her solitude in his presence, a closer look at the line about "like sense" complicates that request by revealing that the solitary trial Adam intends is really an attempt to become more like each other.

Eve immediately picks up on the implications behind Adam's comparison, questioning why they cannot also be equally alike while apart, "endued / Single with like defence" (9.324–25). In her response, Eve implies she already *does* feel as confident as Adam, claiming ownership over "like defence." Indeed, she must feel that way, or so her logic has her believe. Otherwise, they might find out that their "happy state" was "Left so imperfect by the maker wise, / As not secure to single or combined" (9.337–39). Facing a slighted Eve, "who thought / Less attribúted to her faith sincere" (9.319–20), Adam listens intently as she leverages his own words against him, turning a desired likeness into a likeness of necessity. The problem, though, is that Adam never actually says Eve was like him; he only wonders why she did not also feel "More wise, more watchful, stronger" while around him. Taking advantage of Adam's wishful thinking, Eve uses it to advance her case for departure. After she finishes, Adam "fervently replie[s]" (9.342) to Eve in language that indicates their conversation has changed from mild disagreement to full-on debate. As the argument intensifies, Adam moves from desiring a likeness that could still allow for some difference to demanding exact sameness. Frustrated by Eve's having used his own words against him, Adam doubles down, exchanging likeness for sameness while reducing love to conformity: "Not then mistrust, but tender love enjoins, / That I should mind thee oft, and mind thou me" (9.357–58). A few lines later, Adam exhorts Eve to "approve thy constancy" by "approv[ing] / First thy obedience" (9.367–68). In other words, the conversation no longer involves marshaling evidence for or against Eve's departure. Rather, it becomes a contest of wills, which assumes in advance that one of them must ultimately comply with the other, ending in complete conformity.

As Adam shifts the terms of the debate, it comes down to a question of who will capitulate first, him or her. Though Adam insists that Eve comply with his will, in reality, he assents to her reasoning. Exasperated, he finally directs her to leave:

> But if thou think, trial unsought may find
> Us both securer than thus warned thou seemst,
> Go; for thy stay, not free, absents thee more;
> Go in thy native innocence, rely

> On what thou hast of virtue, summon all,
> For God towards thee hath done his part, do thine.   (9.370–75)

Employing imperatives, Adam commands Eve to leave him, telling her to "Go," to "rely," to "summon," and, finally, to "do" her part in protecting herself against potential threats. These imperatives give the illusion that Adam has retained power over the situation, and in some ways he still maintains control. Yet, in a larger sense, Adam loses power at this argumentative juncture. His belief that involuntary companionship ("thy stay, not free, absents thee more") will create *more* solitude between them, and, correspondingly, that Eve's departure will render them *less* alone, and thus more like each other, falsely assumes that conformity should be the end goal of marriage, that togetherness necessarily involves compliance. If compliance is the objective, however, then it only remains to be seen which side will comply with the other, and, in this case, that person is Adam. Though he frames it as a directive, Adam's final argument is derivative of Eve's, as he tries to pass off (or integrate, to use McColley's word) as his own idea the very argument that he receives from her.

Adam's conformist rhetoric redoubles upon seeing fallen Eve. Encountering his wife for the first time after she has eaten the fruit, he experiences an existential crisis. "How can I live without thee," he exclaims, "how forgo / Thy sweet converse and love so dearly joined, / To live again in these wild woods forlorn?" (9.908–10). Adam feels that Eve's fall and subsequent transformation have rendered her too different, too knowledgeable, and thus too much like God, whose solitude overwhelmed him. He believes—perhaps correctly—that he must now give up their "sweet converse," the same way he had to end his converse with God, whose difference completely overpowered him. This is a real and pressing concern, though one that Adam will rather quickly move past. Worried about Eve's difference from him, and whether or not it is now too great for him to continue their "sweet converse," Adam unexpectedly reverses his position and begins emphasizing her sameness. No sooner has he raised the issue of her difference than he returns to the idea of exact equivalence when designating her "flesh of flesh, / Bone of my bone," adding that "from thy state / Mine never shall be parted, bliss or woe" (9.914–16). In other words, fallen Eve is simultaneously too different from Adam and too similar. Ultimately, however, his belief in their sameness wins out, as he claims to feel:

> The bond of nature draw me to my own,
> My own in thee, for what thou art is mine;
> Our state cannot be severed, we are one,
> One flesh; to lose thee were to lose myself. (9.956–59)

In the space of four lines, Adam manages entirely to disavow the very basis of Miltonic marriage, which involves likeness-through-difference. Though he claims that "to lose thee were to lose myself," it is clear that Adam has already lost his own sense of identity. His sense of self now appears entirely subsumed within Eve's, despite the fact that, only a moment earlier, he claimed she newly represented a difference so profound it would necessarily foreclose their "sweet converse." His passion for Eve at this moment overrides his more rational faculties. Inebriated, Eve fully supports his decision, encouraging him to indulge in the fruit. Adam eats, and she immediately celebrates this "glorious trial of exceeding love," praising him for "Engaging me to emulate" (9.961, 963). Eve's characterization of this dramatic moment as a "trial of exceeding love" attempts to transform Miltonic trial from a solitary expression of individual will into an instance of emulation and self-negation.

Not long after ingesting the fruit, Adam will realize the error of his ways, and, fittingly, he seeks a return to solitude, though not the positive variety of contemplative solitude associated with his God. Regaining his composure after a lust-filled act of sex, the very kind of animal sex Milton warns that a bad marriage will occasion, Adam exclaims, "Oh might I here / In solitude live savage, in some glade / Obscured" (9.1084–86). Remembering, but all too late, that Miltonic humanness demands solitude, and that solitary relationships consist of some level of disunion, the bringing together of minds "most resembling unlikenes," Adam succumbs to despair, wishing to "in solitude live savage" rather than maintain a human solitude that sees them solitarily striving together toward their solitary God. Instead of "brotherly dissimilitudes," Milton's social ideal, the two spend the next few hours in "mutual accusation"

(9.1187). When the Son appears to pass judgment on the couple, he states in no uncertain terms that Adam's failure has to do with his disregard of difference. He has failed to protect his solitude by heeding the dissimilitude between him and Eve:

> Was she thy God, that her thou didst obey
> Before his voice, or was she made thy guide,
> Superior, or but equal, that to her
> Thou didst resign thy manhood, and the place
> Wherein God set thee above her made of thee,
> And for thee, whose perfection far excelled
> Hers in all real dignity[?]   (10.145–51)

Adam has "resign[ed]" his "manhood," a manhood that consists in the hierarchical "place / Wherein God set thee above her." Had Adam "known [himself] aright," the Son goes on to say, he would have known it was his prerogative to "bear rule" over Eve, not she over him (10.155–56). The Son's emphasis on "know[ing] aright" takes us back to Adam's description of his original solitude, the Latin injunction, *nosce te ipsum* (to know thyself), and God's assertion that Adam "couldst judge of fit and meet." Adam's initial solitude prepared him to distinguish between himself and others, especially Eve, his "other self" (8.450). Adam's solitude—the sign of his alterity from beast and God—provided him the education necessary to recognize differences great and small, an education that tragically fails him at the most crucial moment.

IV

Adam and Eve exit Eden both alone and together, a befitting (but still hopeful) conclusion to a tragedy initiated by a failure to manage solitude and difference within marriage:

> The world was all before them, where to choose
> Their place of rest, and providence their guide:
> They hand in hand with wandering steps and slow,
> Through Eden took their solitary way.   (12.646–49)

This image of a couple "hand in hand" and yet "solitary" flummoxed eighteenth century literary critic Richard Bentley. Never of the mind to tolerate literary blunders, Bentley was not about to let his 1732 edition of John Milton's *Paradise Lost* end with, of all things, a contradiction, and he famously emended the final lines to read: "Then hand in hand with *social* steps their way / Through Eden took, with heav'nly comfort cheer'd."[37] While Bentley defended his emendation as a necessary corrective against the faulty hand of an unreliable amanuensis, his reason for changing the lines might have been as much personal as academic. In a sermon preached years earlier, Bentley expressed his belief that humans cannot be alone, since: "Our Creator has implanted in mankind such appetites and inclinations, such as natural wants and exigencies, that they lead him spontaneously to the love of society and friendship, to the desire of government and community. Without society and government, man would be found in a worse condition than the very beasts of the field."[38] The final two lines of *Paradise Lost*, then, directly conflicted with Bentley's ideological investment in a society without solitude, where humans "spontaneously" love the company of one another. Channeling Aristotle, Bentley suggests that without society "man would be found in a worse condition than the very beasts of the field," emphasizing the beast side of Aristotle's famous beast-or-God formulation. Nor is Bentley the only critic to find the final lines of the poem troublesome. Joseph Addison, another eighteenth century critic, recommended that the final two lines of the poem be expurgated entirely.

The critical legacies of Bentley and Addison survive among scholars who assume Milton's notion of human society is one based exclusively, if not also unsuccessfully, on Aristotelian friendship, in which solitude represents a condition to be condemned categorically. While Milton clearly adopts much of Aristotle's terminology concerning friendship, he also revises that terminology in ways that better suit his own understanding of marriage, and in so doing he anticipates the poet Rainer Maria Rilke, who writes:

> It is a question in marriage, to my feeling, not of creating a quick community of spirit by tearing down and destroying all boundaries, but rather a good marriage is that in which each appoints the other guardian of his solitude, and shows him this confidence, the greatest in his power to bestow. A *togetherness*

between two people is an impossibility, and where it seems, nevertheless, to exist, it is a narrowing, a reciprocal agreement which robs either one party or both of his fullest freedom and development. But, once the realization is accepted that even between the *closest* human beings infinite distances continue to exist, a wonderful living side by side can grow up, if they succeed in loving the distance between them which makes it possible for each to see the other whole and against a wide sky![39]

Certainly, the more Adam learns about God, the more he realizes that "infinite distances continue to exist" between him and his maker; the nearer he approaches God's glory, the better he is able to understand that, as he puts it, "To attain / The height and depth of thy eternal ways / All human thoughts come short" (8.412–14). Insofar as Adam is "for God only, [Eve] for God in him," this same law of inscrutability applies on a much smaller scale to marriage, a bond that Milton calls the "mystery of joy and union" in the divorce tracts and the "mysterious law" of "wedded love" in *Paradise Lost* (YP 2:258; *PL* 4.750). It is a mystery in which both parties remain at least partially obscured from the other, and sometimes *by* the other, as Adam implies when imploring Eve to "leave not the faithful side / That gave thee being, *still shades thee* and protects" (9.265–66; my italics). In casting a protective shade on Eve, Adam must himself appear at least partially obnubilated to her, and thus he is not unlike Milton's chiaroscuro God, "throned inaccessible," except "when [he] shad'st / The full blaze of [his] beams" (3.377–78), suggesting we can only see him faintly, through a mantle of darkness. As this interplay of light and shadow serves to demonstrate, Milton's notion of marriage — like marriage itself — is complicated, involving partners equally unequal, alike in that they are so different from one another. For Milton, the mystery of "one flesh" is the mystery of a couple whose complex relationship makes them both more illumined and more obscured, more together and more alone, each of them a guardian of the other's solitude, and of the freedom to make independent choices, even if, in the case of Eve, that choice involves seeking solitude somewhere else.

Indiana University

NOTES

1. I would like to thank the anonymous readers for *Milton Studies*, whose helpful and attentive feedback greatly improved this essay's overall argument and structure. Milton's poetry is cited from Alastair Fowler, ed., *John Milton, Paradise Lost*, 2nd ed. (London, 2007), and John Carey, ed., *Milton: Complete Short Poems*, 2nd ed. (London, 2007). All prose citations are from the *Complete Prose Works of John Milton*, 8 vols., ed. Don M. Wolfe et al. (New Haven, Conn., 1953–82); hereafter cited parenthetically in the text as YP.

2. It is worth noting some of the superficial differences between Adam's solitude—an involuntary solitude—and the solitude that Aristotle discusses in *Politics*, which concerns a misanthropic person voluntarily leaving society. Whereas Aristotle writes that a human in solitude loses his or her humanity, becoming either a beast or a god, Milton demonstrates how Adam's humanness actually depends on a solitude in which he succeeds in identifying his radical difference from animals and the deity before entering human society. Instead of becoming a beast or God in solitude, as Aristotle writes of the misanthrope *exiting* society, Adam does quite the opposite, *entering* a love-filled human society through a solitary trial that finds him rejecting both beast and God as too different for companionship. See Aristotle, "Politics," in *The Basic Works of Aristotle*, ed. Richard McKeon (New York, 1941), 1130.

3. Erica Fudge, *Brutal Reasoning: Animals, Rationality, and Humanity in Early Modern England* (Ithaca, N.Y., 2006), 60.

4. Ibid., 60.

5. R. V. Young, "Milton and Solitude," *Ben Jonson Journal* 21, no. 1 (2014): 98. My emphasis on Miltonic difference and solitude resists the recent critical attempts to downplay the role of dissent and disunity in his works. For instance, Joanna Picciotto, *Labors of Innocence* (Cambridge, Mass., 2010), argues that Milton regarded truth as an "ongoing collaborative construction," and that, for him, as for many in his cohort, "diversity of opinion was only tolerable to the extent that it offered a means toward ultimate consensus" (5, 8–9). For an account of difference and unity more consistent with my own, see N. K. Sugimura, *"Matter of Glorious Trial": Spiritual and Material Substance in "Paradise Lost"* (New Haven, Conn., 2009), who describes Milton's angelic world as a "totality of oneness in which differences nonetheless abound," as Milton (perhaps unsuccessfully) tries to reconcile "the Many and the one," "difference with unity" while not "compromising the idea of the individual, the union, or the theodicy in the process" (159, 195).

6. Aristotle, "Nicomachean Ethics," in *The Basic Works of Aristotle*, ed. Richard McKeon (New York, 1941), 1067. Aristotle adds on the same page that those not already equal "can be equalized."

7. For a well-argued (though very different) interpretation of Adam's solitude, see Thomas H. Luxon, *Single Imperfection: Milton, Marriage, and Friendship* (Pittsburgh, 2005). In Luxon's reading, Milton attempts to apply an Aristotelian model of friendship-based-on-likeness to seventeenth century marriage as a way of avoiding difference, which Luxon considers anathema to Milton's notion of unity. See also Luxon's "'How Life Began': Sexual Reproduction in Book 8 of *Paradise Lost*," in *Sex before Sex: Figuring the Act in Early Modern England*, ed. James M. Bromley and Will Stockton (Minneapolis, 2013), 263–90. There, Luxon acknowledges the importance of difference in Milton's ontogeny, though he still subordinates that difference to likeness, writing that "When Adam first expresses desire for a mate, the difference on which he focuses, the difference that gives rise to his desire, is of a kind far less remarkable than sexual difference—it is numerical difference. What is more, it appears to be a numerical difference grounded in the likeness of one individual to another" (267).

8. James Grantham Turner, *One Flesh: Paradisal Marriage and Sexual Relations in the Age of Milton* (Oxford, 1987), 280.

9. On Milton's willingness to reconceive the meaning of words, see again Sugimura, "*Matter of Glorious Trial*," esp. 78–79.

10. Mary Beth Long, "Contextualizing Eve's and Adam's Solitudes in Book 9 of *Paradise Lost*," *Milton Quarterly* 37, no. 2 (2003): 106.

11. For more on the interplay of likeness and difference, see Ronald Levao, "'Among Unequals What Society': *Paradise Lost* and the Forms of Intimacy," *Modern Language Quarterly* 61, no. 1 (2000): 90.

12. Timothy M. Harrison, "Adamic Awakening and the Feeling of Being Alive in *Paradise Lost*," in *Milton Studies*, vol. 54, ed. Laura L. Knoppers, 29–58 (Pittsburgh, 2013), 32, 44.

13. Luxon, *Single Imperfection*, 102.

14. Fudge, *Brutal Reasoning*, 49.

15. Ibid., 50.

16. See also Mandy Green, *Milton's Ovidian Eve* (Burlington, Vt., 2009), wherein she claims that Adam is "endowed with an immediate sense of selfhood though not identity" (41).

17. Fudge, *Brutal Reasoning*, 28.

18. See also William Poole, *Milton and the Idea of the Fall* (Cambridge, 2005) on Adam and Eve's creation and education (168–81, esp. 171–73).

19. See, for instance, Barbara Lewalski's assertion in *The Life of John Milton* (Oxford, 2000), that Adam's discussion with God in book 8 "testifies to a psychological and emotional neediness that in some ways undercuts gender hierarchy" (483). Following Lewalski, Green observes that "Unlike Eve, Adam finds the weight of his solitude oppressive" (*Milton's Ovidian Eve*, 42).

20. Fudge, *Brutal Reasoning*, 62.

21. See also Bruce Boehrer, who argues that the "lower creation" serves in Milton's divorce tracts as "a master trope, both of likeness and of difference, of homogeneity and of discrimination, figuring the concurrent—and sometimes contradictory—importance of both these principles for Milton's understanding of human intimacy." Bruce Boehrer, "Animal Love in Milton: The Case of 'Epitaphium Damonis,'" *English Literary History* 70, no. 3 (2003): 805.

22. Luxon, *Single Imperfection*, 103.

23. Turner, *One Flesh*, 285, asserts that "Milton has succeeded in bringing to life, in the *praxis* of his art, two quite different models of the politics of love: one is drawn from the experience of being in love with an equal, and the mutual surrender of 'due benevolence,' the other from the hierarchical arrangement of the universe, and the craving for male supremacy. His treatment of Genesis stands out from all others because his imagination responds generously to both of these, to the ecstatic egalitarian love of 'one flesh' as well as to the patriarchal love of superior and inferior; he has hatched the contradictions in the text and the tradition that elsewhere lie dormant" (285).

24. See also Sugimura, "*Matter of Glorious Trial*," 195.

25. Pico della Mirandola, *Oration on the Dignity of Man: A New Translation and Commentary*, ed. Francesco Borghesi, Michael Papio, and Massimo Riva (Cambridge, 2012), 121.

26. For this reason, I am inclined to qualify Stephen Fallon's monistic interpretation that in Miltonic marriage "union of minds is more than metaphorical." Stephen Fallon, *Milton among the Philosophers: Poetry and Materialism in Seventeenth-Century England* (Ithaca, N.Y., 1991), 76.

27. Glossing God's Genesis edict against aloneness in *Tetrachordon*, Milton does not denounce solitude categorically. Rather, he comments that "And heer *alone* is meant alone without woman; otherwise *Adam* had the company of God himself, and Angels to convers with; all creatures to delight him seriously, or to make him sport.... Yet for all this till *Eve* was giv'n him, God reckn'd him to be alone" (YP 2:595).

28. Green notes a tendency among scholars to read the "potential for narcissism in Adam's attitude toward Eve." Green herself argues that the "terms used by God to describe Adam's prospective consort help to condition Adam's response to Eve and blur the boundaries between self and other" (*Milton's Ovidian Eve*, 42).

29. Balachandra Rajan, *The Form of the Unfinished: English Poetics from Spenser to Pound* (Princeton, N.J., 1985), 11. Contrasting Thomas Hobbes and Milton, Victoria Kahn finds that "Hobbes's eloquence was almost always in the service of absolute obedience," while "Milton's imaginative energies were far more often engaged by breach of contract and dissent." Victoria Kahn, *Wayward Contracts: The Crisis of Political Obligation in England, 1640–1674* (Princeton, N.J., 2004), 222.

30. Diane McColley, *Milton's Eve* (Urbana, Ill., 1983), 181.

31. Ibid., 180–81.

32. John Rumrich, *Matter of Glory: A New Preface to "Paradise Lost"* (Pittsburgh, 1987), 124.

33. Stanley Fish, *How Milton Works* (Cambridge, Mass., 2001), 530.

34. Ibid., 532.

35. That such trials, while solitary, can still occur in the company of others, shows Milton building on the work of a diverse range of early modern writers, including Michel de Montaigne, who writes in "Of Solitude," in *The Complete Essays of Montaigne,* trans. Donald M. Frame (Stanford, Calif., 1958), that "real solitude...may be enjoyed in the midst of cities and the courts of kings," even if it "is best enjoyed alone" (176); and Francis Bacon, who in "Of Friendship," in *The Essays of Francis Bacon* (Blacksburg, Va., 2001) observes that "little do men perceive what solitude is, and how far it extendeth[,] for a crowd is not company" (37).

36. For more on Milton's rhetorical strategy in the prose tracts, see Daniel Shore, *Milton and the Art of Rhetoric* (Cambridge, 2012), esp. 21–26.

37. Richard Bentley, *Milton's Paradise Lost: A New Edition, by Richard Bentley, D.D.* (London, 1732), 106.

38. Richard Bentley, "A Sermon preach'd before King George I," in *The Works of Richard Bentley, D.D.,* vol. 3, ed. Rev. Alexander Dyce (London, 1838), 267. See also Robert E. Bourdette Jr., who similarly remarks that the optimism of Bentley's sermon "requires [his] explicit emphasis in the final lines of *Paradise Lost* and man's naturally *social* state." Robert E. Bourdette Jr., "'To Milton Lending Sense': Richard Bentley and *Paradise Lost,*" *Milton Quarterly* 14, no. 2 (1980): 37–49, 46.

39. Rainer Maria Rilke, "To Emanuel von Bodman," *Letters of Rainer Maria Rilke, 1892–1910,* trans. Jane Bannard Greene and M. D. Herter Norton (New York, 1945), 57–58.

LANGUAGE AND SOUND

A Study of Milton's Greek

John K. Hale

If Shakespeare had small Latin and less Greek, Milton had much Latin but even more Greek. The Greek that he quotes in his voluminous Latin prose would amaze us, for variety and depth alike, if it were not so scattered. Translations further disadvantage the Greek whenever one of Milton's Latin texts appears solely in English translation, homogenizing the Greek that they include and losing its interplay with the Latin in the English: this practice forfeits the code-switch and obscures the purpose it had for Milton. Editors too belittle the Greek, being occupationally likelier to gloss Milton's contextual thrust than to dwell on the flavor of each Greek original and Milton's understanding of it. Instead, to bring out features of that understanding that have been obscured or forgotten, the present study gathers his most substantial or significant Greek quotations in order to examine how he appreciates and exploits them.[1]

By "substantial or significant" passages, two emphases are intended. First, the longer a quotation, the more opportunity to assess it; yet equal length does not mean equal significance. Contrariwise, quality, in a short stabbing thrust, may outweigh quantity. Second, the criterion points us to the Greek of poets. Milton's Latin prose tends to cite less from Greek prose writers than from Greek poets. When it does cite Greek prose, in the *Defences* for instance, he routinely quotes only a few words of it, like a caption or lemma, before beginning again and continuing with the full passage quoted in a literal Latin translation. Now contrast how he cites Greek poets: only the full actual words will do, whether or not he then renders them into a literal Latin. To put the point with its full proper strength, Milton quotes Greek poets in their own, Greek words, since these are what make (say) Homer Homer. These hold the authority he finds, persistently, in Greek poets.

That authority contains two main elements — the pleasurable and the useful, mixed, in Horace's formulation.[2] Each quotation supports Milton's local, rhetorical purpose. That purpose is aided by what his choice of resource antecedently shows, namely, his delight in its qualities or beauty. The proportioning varies, but both aspects deserve scrutiny here. If anything, since Greek is no longer at the fingertips of Milton's readership, I shall favor the pleasurable over the useful, since translations and editions favor the useful.

That is why my study dwells on the outstanding specimens, and arranges them more by Greek origins than by the chronology or genre of Milton's works. Greek poets come first, and are taken by priority of date and also genre. I begin with Homer, as used for the *Second Defence* and *De doctrina Christiana,* because for the Greeks and their reception history, Homer is first and foundational — for poetry, epic, and poetic diction; for myths of gods and social identity; and for festivals, cults, and culture. The trajectory continues into later poets who emulated Homer, writing the secondary (non-oral) epics that Milton valued for his entire life: these are viewed in the *Second Defence* again, and in the letter to Philaras. They are followed by the dramatists: the three tragedians and Aristophanes in the *First Defence,* where Milton crosses swords with Salmasius about drama itself. Greek prose authors are not considered except for the New Testament. Finally, Greek criticism (Aristotle and Longinus) is applied to the extracts and to Milton's extracting.[3]

Homer in the *Second Defence*

Although their occasion and tenor overlap, the *Defences* vary in scope and address, and so they do in their way with Greek authors. The *First Defence* aspires to be a comprehensive rebuttal, chapter by chapter, of Salmasius's defense of the king. Accordingly, its Greek helps to answer the notable humanist scholar, and this need controls Milton's choice of authors. Homer, however, figures so little, and the dramatists so prominently, that we postpone consideration of the *First Defence*. By contrast, the *Second Defence* serves two new purposes: it rebuts the accusations of the presumed new opponent, Morus, and it attacks Morus. The rebuttal is achieved by a self-praising autobiography, and the attack is by sharp critique. The former enlists Homer; Milton quotes the Greek in full, then adds a word-for-word Latin version.[4]

In its context, as M. M. Willcock writes, Achilles's reply to Odysseus is "the most powerful speech in the *Iliad*. Achilleus has been a simple hero, embodying the perfection of the qualities of the heroic age. In other words, he has lived for 'honor,' his standing in the eyes of other people. . . . Now, in the bitterness of the public insult he has received from Agamemnon, he questions the whole basis of his life."[5] Milton's situation corresponds only in two broad respects: he too claims honor, and he justifies a decisive life-choice. He appropriates the famous words, in pride not bitterness, and proceeds to distinguish himself from Achilles:

> occurrebántque animo bina illa fata, quae retulisse Delphis consulentem de se matrem, narrat Thetidis filius.

> Διχθαδίας κῆρας φέρεμεν θανάτοιο τέλοσδε.
> Εἰ μέν κ'αὖθι μένων Τρώων πόλιν ἀμφιμάχωμαι
> Ὤλετο μέν μοι νόστος, ἀτὰρ κλέος ἄφθιτον ἔσται.
> Εἰ δέ κεν οἴκαδ' ἵκωμι φίλην ἐς πατρίδα γαῖαν
> Ὤλετο μοι κλέος ἐσθλὸν, ἐπὶ δηρὸν δέ μοι αἰὼν
> Ἔσσεται. Iliad. 9.[6]

Milton translates the Greek in full:

> *Duplicia fata ducere ad mortis finem:*
> *Si hic manens circa Troum urbem pugnavero,*

Amittitur mihi reditus; sed Gloria immortalis erit,
Si domum revertor dulce ad Patrium solum,
Amittitur mihi Gloria pulcra, sed diuturna vita
Erit.

Nor did I fail to recollect the two-fold destiny, which the son of Thetis reports that his mother brought back concerning himself, when she went to consult the oracle at Delphi:

Two fates conduct me to the realms of night:
If staying here around Troy-town I fight,
I return no more; but my glory fair
Shall shine immortal, and my deeds declare:
If to my dear and native land I'm led,
Long is my life; but my glory is fled. Iliad 9.[411–16][7]

Milton appropriates the passage by ignoring one alternative, the safe nameless life offered to Achilles, in order to distinguish his own path. Milton chose the path of glory with a blindness brought on by doing his duty. (And blindness is only "a little suffering," as if he got a better bargain than Achilles did.) "On the contrary I proposed to purchase a greater good with a less evil" (69 and 71): not "glory with death," but "at the price of blindness only, to perform one of the noblest acts of duty"; and duty [*officii munus*] "being a thing in its own nature more substantial even than glory." Thus, while gaining a boost from Homer's Achilles, Milton makes his own heroic gesture different.

This glory will make Milton's *name* live. He has already contrasted himself with "unnamed" opponents, twisting the neutral epithet "anonymous" (ἀνώνυμοι) "into "nameless ones" or nobodies.[8] Besides showing a high opinion of his own choices, and insisting he made a choice of blindness, he is harnessing Greek heroic verse to a heroic view of the mid-seventeenth-century crisis, complete with a role for himself. Milton achieves his glory for a higher purpose, an *even* higher purpose — duty. Homer's Achilles does not feel any duty except to himself, his social heroic-age self, and to his choice of fate, which has now turned sour. But Milton annexes as much as he can of the impassioned power of Achilles's words at a crisis in order to define his own self by contrasts. He is having it both ways: he wants maximal endorsement from the Greek, but reinterprets it so as to corroborate a Christian duty.

Homer in *De Doctrina Christiana*

My second major quotation from Homer comes in *De doctrina Christiana* (1.4) as the finale of Milton's chapter on predestination. The structuring of the allusion is much the same as for Achilles: Greek verses, followed up by a word-for-word Latin construe. This time, the text and a literal English translation come from the new Oxford edition, by Donald Cullington and myself.[9] Milton's chapter concludes (YP 6:202, OM 8:116–9):

> Haec qui attenderit, facile perspiciet, in hac potissimum doctrina esse toties offensum, dum poena obdurationis à decreto reprobationis non distinguitur. iuxta illud Prov. 19. 3:. *stultitia hominis pervertit viam ipsius, et adversus Iehovam indignatur animus eius.* Accusant enim[10] revera Deum, tametsi id vehementer negant: et ab **Homero** etiam ethnico egregiè redarguuntur, Odyss. I. 7.:

> Αὐτῶν γὰρ σφετέρῃσιν ἀτασθαλίῃσιν ὄλοντο.

> Suis enim ipsorum flagitiis perierunt.
> Et rursus, inducta Iovis persona:

> Ὦ πόποι, οἷον δή νυ θεοὺς βροτοὶ αἰτιόωνται!
> Ἐξ ἡμέων γάρ φασι κάκ' ἔμμεναι. Οἱ δὲ καὶ αὐτοὶ
> Σφῇσιν ἀτασθαλίῃσιν ὑπὲρ μόρον ἄλγε' ἔχουσιν.

> Papae, ut scilicet Deos, mortales accusant!
> Ex nobis enim dicunt mala esse: illi vero ipsi
> Suismet flagitiis, praeter fatum, dolores patiuntur.

A person who heeds these things will easily discern that in this doctrine in particular offence has so often been caused when the punishment of hardening is not distinguished from a decree of reprobation. According to that verse, Prov. 19: 3: *man's folly twists his way, and against Jehovah his spirit protests.* For they actually accuse God, although they strenuously deny it; and they are superbly confuted even by pagan Homer, *Odyssey*, I.7:

For by their own personal outrages they perished.

And again, when the character of Jupiter has been brought in:

Oh dear! how indeed mortals reproach gods!
For they say that evils come out of us, yet they themselves
By their own outrages suffer sorrows beyond fate.

Homer contributes an official disclosure by Zeus to the chapter on predestination. For this subject, dear to his heart and central to politics as well as religion in his day, Milton hands over the entire climax to Homer; to a more rhetorical and more literary clausula than in any other chapter of *De doctrina*. Note, too, that this time he does not distance himself from the pagan Homer. We should look for reasons, in Homer or the chapter. He can do it because the passages quoted from the *Odyssey* themselves guide that whole poem, and convey Milton's final point with resounding — Greek, indeed Homeric — authority. Human sinners blame divinity for their destruction, though it is really self-destruction. The emphasis falls on the pronouns, "themselves": *auton, autoi, sphesin*. Zeus speaks from Olympus to a council of the gods much as the Father speaks to the council of heaven in book 3 of *Paradise Lost*. Curiously enough, both lay down the law to a conclave at which the most obstructive celestial is absent: Poseidon, visiting the Aethiopes, and Satan already flung out of heaven.

The reliance on Homer at such a climax is the single most striking pagan allusion in *De doctrina*. The *Odyssey* is corroborating by an *a fortiori*: Homer the pagan vindicates Milton because his point is clear *etiam Homero ethnico* ("even to the pagan Homer"). Milton means his view is correct because it is evident "even" or possibly "also" to pagan Homer.[11] Whether "even" or "also," the greatest Greek poet gave a more disinterested, less defensive corroboration, from the mouth of Zeus *ex cathedra*.

As we move past Homer, to post-Homeric epic, the relations perceived between quotation and comment become modified. For example, Milton takes only what he wants from the figure of the blind seer Phineus, explicitly disallowing the rest; but then (in a letter) he quotes some more about Phineus without any overt comment. The Greek dramatists then make Milton address this problem of adjustment more directly, for (drama being conflict, and authorial comment being withheld) how can one know what a drama advocates? Because Milton does it a great deal, exploiting his long immersion in Euripides, the question needs an answer.

Phineus, Part 1

Deity looms larger in the next allusion, the first of several where Milton compares himself as blind seer with Phineus in the *Argonautica*. Two such allusions in the same year, one in the *Second Defence* and one in the letter to Philaras, taken together with the more prominent linkage in the invocation to book 3 of *Paradise Lost*, invite us to examine their quoted Greek, to establish Milton's identification with Phineus, its kind and degree.

> De augure Tiresia quod traditur, vulgò notum. De Phineo sic cecinit Apollius in Argonauticis:
>
> Οὐδ' ὅσσον ὀπίζετο καὶ Διὸς αὐτοῦ
> Χρείων ἀτρεκέως ἱερὸν νόον ἀνθρώποισιν·
> Τῷ καί οἱ γῆρας μὲν ἐπὶ δηναιὸν ἴαλλεν,
> Εκ δ' ἕλετο ὀφθαλμῶν γλυκερὸν φάος.
>
> — neque est veritus Iovem ipsum
> Edens veraciter mentem divinam hominibus:
> Quare & senectam ei diuturnam dedit,
> Eripuit autem oculorum dulce lumen.   [CM 8:62–65]

> What is handed down of the augur Tiresias is well known. Of Phineus thus sang Apollonius in his Argonautics:

> For he showed not the slightest reverence even for Zeus himself by accurately prophesying his sacred intentions to men. Therefore Zeus sent upon him a prolonged old age, and took sweet light from his eyes.[12]

Apollonius goes on to present Phineus's old age as utter misery, for Zeus ensures he is not only blind but also famished. In his own continuation, Milton ignores both old age and hunger to dwell on his blindness, a blindness not to punish any evil-doing but more like a blessing to others, as it is in the roll call that follows — Timo-leon, Appius Claudius, and (so he argues) Isaac and Jacob, as both beloved of God.

The original four lines affirm that Phineus defied Zeus's will and was punished for it. Punished, moreover, doubly, with blind-ness *and* longevity; also that Phineus told divine intention fear-lessly. Milton needs to deny the punishment while keeping the fearless prophesying. He does so straightaway by insisting that "God himself is truth" (*deus & ipse veritas est*), and that to believe otherwise is impious. Accordingly, his own blindness is not punishment for any crime: *Ob nullam igitur noxam, divinus vir [Phineus] . . . caruisse luminibus videtur* ("it does not appear, therefore, that it was for any crime that this ancient sage [was] deprived of light"). So Milton quotes the Greek poem to prove it had *mis*judged, and so — by lengthy reasoning and more pages about blind deliverers from history — Milton's own blindness is not a punishment.

Why did Milton need Phineus at all if the quotation needed such reinterpretation? I suggest (1) that Phineus as blind seer was still a better exemplar for his argument than Tiresias, who briefly pre-cedes him in his catalog of blind heroes. In myth, Phineus adhered more boldly to the seer's occupational principle of proclaiming the truth.[13] (2) Phineus better suited Milton's roll of honor of histori-cal blind deliverers, since his place in the record is that he truth-fully showed the Argonauts the way into uncharted waters. (Not so unlike the English ship of state in the 1650s.) (3) To generalize, Phineus told the truth as a seer should, at cost to himself, for the greater good of a people. But last, in the present enquiry, (4) Milton simply enjoyed the *Argonautica*, and the passage came to mind for the same reason that he quoted it again a few months later: it filled out his idea of the benevolent blind seer.

That last point is not the least. Milton was passionate about Greek poetry in general. Homer in particular was his favorite.[14] And as for Homer's Hellenistic and Alexandrian imitators, he knew and appreciated them. The record of his reading, the exu-berant thoroughness of his practice of scholarship, and what we know of his teaching practice, all demonstrate this. Respectively: we know how long he toiled through Greek historians, into church historians, until he finally gave up. But it was Greek *poets* whom he annotated so intelligently, and in Euripides's case not once but twice. His copy of Euripides, and also of the dimmer talent of Aratus, shows his diligence and occasional flashes of irritated brilliance.[15] Similarly in his teaching, as John Aubrey records from Milton's nephew Edward Phillips that "within 3 years they went through ye best of Latin & Greec Poetts Lucretius & Manilius of ye Latins; & with him the use of the Globes; Hesiod, Aratus, Dionysius Afer, Oppian Apollonii Argonautica & Quintus Calaber."[16] Several of these poets are alluded to in the *Defences*, but allusions to the *Argonautica* occur most often and are the longest. Milton's habit of mind and preferences help to guide the alluding. He seems to enjoy alluding to Greek poets, or to this one, as our next instance shows.

Phineus, Part 2

In September 1654, Milton wrote the letter to Philaras in which he describes the onset and symptoms of his blindness. The account is factual until mention of the accompanying mists and heaviness reminds him ("not seldom") of Phineus. He quotes the passage that follows close to our preceding one. This one tells how Phineus meets the Argonauts. He crumples up on the threshold as he goes out to meet them. By a mixture of hearing and divination, he knows of their arrival and knows who they are — his deliverers, as he is theirs:

> frontem totam atque tempora inveterati quidam vapores videntur insedisse; qui somnolentâ quadam gravitate oculos, a cibò praesertim usque ad vesperam, plerunque urgent atque deprimunt; ut mihi haud raro veniat in mentem Salmydessii Vatis Phinei in *Argonauticis*:
>
> Κάρος δέ μιν ἀμφεκάλυψεν
> Πορφύρεος, γαῖαν δὲ πέριξ ἐδόκησε φέρεσθαι
> Νείοθεν ἀβληχρῷ δ'ἐπὶ κώματι κέκλιτ'ἄναυδος

Inveterate mists now seem to have settled in my forehead and temples, which weigh me down and depress me with a kind of sleepy heaviness, especially from meal-time to evening; so that not seldom there comes into my mind the description of the Salmydessian seer Phineus in the *Argonautics*:

All round him then there grew
A purple thickness; and he thought the Earth
Whirling beneath his feet, and so he sank,
Speechless at length, into a feeble sleep.[17]

I must note that Milton does not translate this Greek, since in his private letters he knows he does not need to translate the Greek for certain readers. What is more, this particular letter is being written to a Greek — Greek to a Greek — just as to his Grecian friend Diodati he lards his letters with more Greek than others.[18] Moreover, this quotation contributes to no surrounding argument.

If we move on to *Paradise Lost*, to the sonorous and endorsing wish to equal "Blind Thamyris and blind Maeonides / And Tiresias and Phineus prophets old" (3.35–36), we might speculate that the repeated attention to Phineus points toward an identification. Fearless declaring of the truth as revealed to the solitary victim of blindness, for duty and conscience' sake — this sounds like Milton's self-image. I risk the speculation because the Greek allusions differ greatly from one another. The first gives Milton, after differentiation, a heroic self-image. The second has no usefulness that I can see: it seems closer to intrinsic self-expression. And if so, it stands out among the other allusions so far examined. Those served some local purpose for Milton. Apt or polemical, taken straight like Zeus or modified like Achilles, they relied on Milton's understanding of Greek poets, and only secondarily showed his delight in them. Is this always true in his political works? Likely enough, yet it will emerge that the forms of the instrumentality vary, as does the proportioning of useful to delightful.

Tragedians

Our transition from epic to drama gives me an opportunity to comment on the Greek dimension within the whole of the exchange. How did Salmasius in *Defensio regia* wield Greek to defend the king? Does Milton's *First Defence* refute the Greek of Salmasius or is the Greek a voluntary of his own? Did the attack on Milton in *Regii sanguinis clamor* adduce fresh Greek or in turn refute Milton's? And similarly with Milton's reply in the *Second Defence* to that, and so on, until Salmasius's anticlimactic last word, posthumous and unfinished, by which time Milton had been silenced by the Restoration of Charles II. Of all these, only the exchange in chapter 6 regarding the use of drama for evidence needs attention here, because Milton challenges Salmasius outright on this question of literary interpretation.[19]

This question is: How do we know what a Greek author thinks when we quote one of his *characters*, who is perhaps a faulty being at a moment of extreme emotion? This problem could have been asked of epic with Achilles or Phineus. It becomes pressing when a dramatist is quoted, because there the author does not speak in his own voice at all: it is the characters who speak, or a chorus figure of limited, reactive vision. It is not that Greek drama causes doubts uniquely. Why would anyone quote Iago's pithy words about Honor, for he says the exact opposite to Roderigo and to Cassio, in entire dependence on the needs of his manipulations at the time?[20] And, for example, why do people like to quote Polonius: "To thine own self be true"? Or, "By indirections find directions out"? They are the tedious apothegms of a "wretched rash intruding fool."[21] Yet we do quote them. Quotations from drama — most of all when they take the form of a *sententia* — have their uses, and their moments. It may be for their wording or their thought or wit. They may also be reinforced, or undercut, by reflecting on the speaker or the stage situation; and these modifications may be legitimate or defeat the point of quoting. Cases vary.

Milton addresses the problem itself in chapter 5 of the *First Defence*. The quoting from Greek tragedy originated in Salmasius. A block of quotations by Milton comes halfway through book 5, after Greek historians and philosophers, because that is where Salmasius chose to place them. "'Aeschylus by himself is enough to inform us,' you say, 'that kings in Greece held a power not liable to any laws or any judicature; for in the tragedy of *The Suppliants*

he calls the king of the Argives 'a ruler not subject to judgment'"
(CM 7:307). The Argive king is indeed called Πρύτανις ἄκριτος
("non-iudicabilem rectorem," "a ruler not subject to judgement")
(CM 7:306–09). Nonetheless, retorts Milton, "we must not regard
the poet's words as his own, but consider who it is that speaks in
the play, and what that person says" (ibid.). Different characters
speak, some good, some not, some foolish, and so forth: "and they
speak not always what is the poet's opinion, but what is most fit-
ting to each character" (ibid.). In the particular instance, the speakers are the eponymous suppliant women, flattering the Argive king
(blandius, "coaxing," in Gruzelier's excellent version).²² And still
the king replies, "I would not do this [protect the women against
the pursuing Egyptian fleet] without the people's consent, not even
if I could" (CM 7:370–71). He brings the matter to the people, who
decree them aid. So the king says, "Be of good cheer, daughters,"
for the "absolute votes of the people have decreed well." Δήμου
δέδοκται παντελῆ ψηφίσματα (601): a more decisive authority,
jeers Milton, than women who are foreigners and suppliants. He
dubs Salmasius sciolus, a "smatterer."²³

Milton rubs it in by quoting lines to similar effect from another
Suppliants, that of Euripides, and two more plays of that writer,
and then two of Sophocles, to show that Salmasius has shot himself in the foot. For Milton, arguing, all three dramatists agree with
him.²⁴ The passages as quoted and translated by Milton follow.

(1) "This city is not ruled by one man, but is free, and the people
reign" (Οὐ γὰρ ἄρχεται / ἑνὸς πρὸς ἀνδρὸς, ἀλλ᾽ἐλευθέρα πόλις /
Δῆμος δ᾽ἀνάσσει) — thus Euripides, Supplices 404–05.²⁵

(2) Another king of Athens, Demophoon, says, "For I do not
rule over them in a tyrannical way as if they were barbarians, but
if I do things that are just, justice is done to me in return" (Οὐ
γὰρ τυραννίδ᾽ὥστε βαρβάρων ἔχω, / Ἀλλ᾽ ἢν δίκαια δρῶ, δίκαια
πείσομαι). This uses the same contractual syntax as his father,
Theseus.²⁶

(3) In Sophocles's Oedipus tyrannus two characters tell Oedipus, "I am not your slave" (Οὐ γάρ τι σοὶ ζῶ δοῦλος) and "I have
right in this city too, not you alone" (Κἀμοὶ πόλεως μέτεστι τῆσδ᾽
οὐ σοὶ μόνῳ).²⁷

(4) Lastly, in the *Antigone* Haemon tells Creon, now king in place of Oedipus, "That is no state which belongs to one man" (Πόλις γὰρ οὐκ ἔσθ'ἥτις ἀνδρὸς ἔσθ' ἑνός).²⁸ Different rulers and subjects, including one subject who becomes ruler: same maxim.

These are quoted for their thought, mostly disregarding the passages' contexts and whole actions. This procedure could be challenged, but nobody has, since only a pedant would object. The *Greek* is a pleasure to savor: recognition concedes authority. Most of all it does this because the six passages come in a fusillade, which continues past the drama into other authors. Take the first of them, Homer. Milton cites Achilles again:

> Δημοβόρος βασιλεὺς, ἐπεὶ οὐτιδανοῖσιν ἀνάσσεις.
> Ἦ γὰρ ἂν Ἀτρείδη νῦν ὕστατα λωβήσαιο.   (*Iliad* 1.231–32)

> populi vorator rex, quoniam hominibus nihili imperas,
> Alioqui enim Atrida, nunc postremum iniuriam faceres.

> King who devours the people, since you rule over men of no substance, for otherwise, son of Atreus, you would be doing wrong now for the last time.²⁹

Its opening epithet makes Milton's point: a king must not exploit his people. More strongly, Milton understands Achilles (a king himself) to "submit a king to his own people to be judged" (*rex ipse regem suo populo judicandum his verbis submittere*). Homer's authority is being invoked, yet again, to drive home Milton's rival reading of Greek tragedy. Homer is being *pressed* into service because although Achilles's speech has a quite different intention, such is Homer's stature and authority that Milton can generalize its contrast and apply it to Charles I. He has been Δημοβόρος ("devouring his own people"). The sting is in the epithet because, as everywhere in Homer or for that matter succeeding epic, epithets carry the weight of a judgment.

Any misgivings about Milton's preference for rhetorical victories, and for hasty excerpting, pale by comparison with the aptness of his quotation, what with his knowledge and appreciation of all three dramatists and his sheer delight in the congenial Euripides. He fishes up three apposite apothegms from three different plays.³⁰

Likewise, in his prose works as a whole, Milton dwells on the *Supplices*, as a play whose action turns on kingship. That is, Theseus, good ruler of beloved Athens, takes advice, consults, and then acts to uphold a fundamental piety — to honor the dead, not humiliate them even after death. He does things that, in Milton's view, a good king should.

One might still question Milton's reliance on the play on several grounds. First, it did not earn particular commendation from Aristotle in the *Poetics*. It has a linear, not complex, plot. It is not remarkable for tragic effect, *catharsis*. Still, it typifies the many Greek tragedies which do *not* work in Aristotle's preferred way. Second, the play is not as didactic as Milton makes it seem because it concentrates on two matters that have no place in Milton's argument. The Greeks disagreed about most things but agreed on the taboo against dishonoring the dead: witness the *Supplices* and *Antigone*.[31] Theseus is indeed upholding a *nomos*, law or custom, yet not one that matters to Milton. Third, Theseus is a rather particular king: young, untried, plunged into a crisis of judgment by the suppliants' appeal, and quite unusually ready to listen.[32] He even changes his mind upon persuasion. Not many monarchies operated like this. Fourth, the entire action, though political because it concerns conflicts between and within states, is about family (in fact, several families), about family obligations. The suppliants, complete with children, supplicate for their dead husbands. Theseus must hear reasons from his own mother, Aethra, who indeed changes his mind. At the end, there are the delayed last rites for husbands, and one widow jumps to her death, an act of suttee that her father's dissuasion cannot avert. In this respect, like so many Greek tragedies, *Oedipus* or the *Bacchae* or the *Oresteia*, the political is subsumed by the familial.

Milton's liking for the play is directed by the concerns of his own time and place. He appropriates the characters' words to his own purposes. So did Salmasius, so perhaps do we all. It is only the degree of the absorption, and of awareness of doing so, which differentiates users. I claim some such awareness for Milton on three main grounds. We know he knew the whole of Euripides exceptionally well; he states the difficulty clearly in refuting Salmasius; and no one, least of all Salmasius in his posthumous *Responsio*, impugns his usage. This attests better than anything else to the authority of Greek tragedy, not for Milton alone but for his age and culture. Milton delights in Euripides elsewhere, but his usefulness sometimes outweighs delight.

Old Comedy

The Greek excerpts considered so far have tended to exalt, or to penetrate. But the staple meter of tragedy, the iambic trimeter, was equally suited to mockery and denigration; *iambizein* means "to lampoon." The element shared by the preceding argumentative iambics concerning right polity with personal lampooning is critique. So in the *Frogs* of Aristophanes the central agon or contest is between two characters named "Aeschylus" and "Euripides." They test each other's verses for value by weight when dropped onto a scale. The pontifical thunderous "Aeschylus" wins one round, hands down, over the lightweight rhetorician "Euripides." He mocks Euripides for the fact that his portentous narrative summaries can be deflated by the paltry final half-line — the metrical pay-off — "he lost his little oil-bottle." Aeschylus interrupts several passages spoken by his rival, to demonstrate that they can be completed with this insignificant main clause: Ληκύθιον ἀπώλεσε. And even though his own favorite tragedian is being deflated, Milton enjoyed the joke enough to use it against Salmasius — to tell him, "*You* have lost your little oil-bottle."

What did Milton mean? It can hardly be a jibe about Greek meter in the new context. What the Greek tag attacked more generally, since it parodies an inept Greek clausula in Euripides's verse, was bathos and tedium.[33] And though Aristophanes certainly meant some sexual innuendo too, what with the phallic shape of an oil-bottle, and adjacent jokes about male "oil," and even though Milton busies himself elsewhere to impugn Salmasius's sexuality, the present thrust seems to mean only that Salmasius has been wasting his energy, by misinterpreting what Paul said about "the powers that be," de facto, since these are now Cromwell not Charles. A chance missed? But the reductive allusion delights in Aristophanes, in his running gag, and in the brilliant ambience of old comedy, where a public audience at an open-air festival took their pleasure by enjoying a metrical put-down.

Such sallies belong in the entertainment aspect of the *Defences*. They include some inventive ones, but on the whole are one-sided and predictable. Let us move to a much more palpable hit that Milton makes, by using Greek, against Morus. It is not an insult, but a brilliant rebuke. He tells him, suddenly bursting out into Greek, φιμώθητι.

The New Testament

Milton has been rebutting Morus's slanders against his life by narrating it, up to the point when he wrote *Eikonoklastes* to refute the *Eikon Basilike*.[34] He writes it in plain style. Now he pauses and changes register, to face Morus down.

> Hactenus ad obturandum os tuum, More, & mendacia redarguenda bonorum maximè virorum in gratiam, qui me aliàs non norint, mei rationem reddidi. Tu igitur, More, tibi dico immunde, φιμώθητι, obmutesce inquam; quo enim magis mihi maledixeris, eo me rationes meas uberiùs explicare coegeris.

> (It is chiefly, More, for the sake of those good men [the members of the Council of State who on January 8 1650 ordered Milton to answer Salmasius], who have otherwise no knowledge of me, that, to stop your mouth and confound your lies, I have so far given an account of myself. I tell you, then, foul priest, *hold your peace*, I say: for the more you revile me, the more fully will you compel me to explain my own conduct.) (CM 8:138–39)

Burnett-Hadas in Columbia here renders the Latin too flatly, and North in Yale is not much better: "Do you then, I bid you, unclean More, be silent. Hold your tongue, I say!" (YP 4.1:629).[35] The real force is felt when speaking the rebuke aloud (as this command by Jesus originally was), to stress *immunde*, φιμώθητι, *obmutesce inquam*. Of the three words, one comes from the Gospel source, Mark 1:23–25: "a man with an *unclean* spirit" (ἀκαθάρτῳ). The second speaks Jesus's twofold command itself: φιμώθητι καὶ ἔξελθε ἐξ αὐτοῦ. And third, *obmutesce* finds a mouth-filling Latin translation of the Greek imperative: it comes from Beza's Latin version. But current English translations obscure the quoting, and mute the climax. *Immunde* ("unclean"), brings in biblical authority. And then the sudden switch into Greek, that Greek, rubs Morus's nose in the Gospel. *Obmutesce* explains and reiterates. *Inquam* ("I declare"), enforces it. But it is the sudden swoop into one-word rebuke that packs the punch. We were not expecting an exorcism.

However, to explore Milton's ways with New Testament Greek deserves a separate study, with a more theological focus, and in a similar way with his scattered usage of postbiblical Greek. I forego consideration, too, of Milton's own Greek, both his early poems and his titles or other paratexts: they sit more loosely to their local purpose, and have been examined elsewhere.[36] Instead, returning to Horace's praise of the poet who mingles usefulness with delight, since the examples have confirmed the usefulness to Milton of his love of Greek, let me conclude by suggesting some of the general ways by which Greek allusions express the delight Milton found in Greek.

Delight

First, Greek opens Milton outwards, to a relish for difference and otherness. By the time he finished the *Defences*, Milton was a man who knew his own mind on public matters, and knew how to win — or at least not lose — every argument. Greek, however, modified this oversupply of rhetorical and polemic fluency in the way Milton appreciates difference. He respects Homer, and carefully differentiates his own fate from that of Achilles or Phineus. Homer opens him up, repeatedly, to difference. This line of thought could be carried forward into the Greek presence in *Paradise Lost*. The poem begins by establishing a host of epic credentials: it plunges *in medias res*, it invokes Homer ("Aonian mount"), and its profusion of similes appropriates Homeric similes (shield, fallen leaves, bees). Other Greeks infuse book 2, in the Empedoclean strife of "Hot, Cold, Moist, and Dry, four champions fierce" (*PL* 2.898).

The ekphrasis exhilaratingly annexes early Greek cosmogony. In a swift aside, Satan is likened to "the Arimaspian" from Herodotus, the one-eyed thief of gold (*PL* 2.945; Herodotus *Histories,* 3.116): it just allows time to register how many points of connection are offered with Satan's journey of one-eyed theft into Eden. Herodotus epitomizes Greek curiosity, wonder, and delight in looking across the boundaries of the known, Greek world into northern Europe. Milton continues the theme when he links Satan's first view of the universe to a "scout's" of some foreign land or metropolis (*PL* 3.549). In *Marvelous Possessions,* Stephen Greenblatt links Herodotus to the Conquistadores, and adduces Milton.[37] Rightly so, for Milton thrills to the same idea of value in otherness with a mixture of wonder and skepticism, whose prophet is Herodotus.

Next, I speculate that something Greek and especially Homeric lies at the root of Milton's sense of what poetry is. The 1668 note on "The Verse" of *Paradise Lost* speaks of "true musical delight," which "consists only in apt numbers, fit quantity [notional vowel length] of syllables, and the sense variously drawn out from one verse into another." Though the last of these causes of delight relates most to "our best *English* tragedies," the other two use terms that are musical before they are mathematical, and derive from Greek verse. The terms suggest Greek metrics and, above all, those of the Homeric hexameter.[38] They move more freely than Latin ones, and allow more exceptions to the rules as taught by humanist practice. Despite the different principles of English, which are accentual not quantitative and are based on spoken accent not vowel-length, Milton's absorption of Homer was shown early on when he set Psalm 114 into these hexameters. We must forget the galloping accentual dactylic of English poets like Tennyson or Browning, "Into the valley of death . . .," because Homer's rhythm is musical and duple, like Milton's, not triple, Μῆνιν ἄειδε θεά Πηληιάδεω Ἀχιλῆος (*Menin aeide thea Pelëiadeo Achillêos*). Without claiming that Milton mimics this, I do think he heard it. I speculate that it explains the weight that he gives to his consonants and pauses: "O'er bog or steep, through straight, rough, dense or rare / With head, hands, wings or feet pursues his way, / And swims or sinks, or wades, or creeps, or flies" (2.948–50).

All in all, Milton's delight in Greek theory and practice alike is seen in his lifelong adherence to Aristotle's thinking in the *Poetics*. He thinks *about* his plays or epics through Greek because epic and tragedy together were Aristotle's highest forms of serious mimesis. Milton himself hesitated between the two forms for *Adam Unparadized*, while *Samson* is "that sort of dramatic poem which is called tragedy." He ponders Greek practice in order to decide his own, and Greek theory as well as practice comes into it. Nothing is more plainly Aristotelian than his preface to *Samson*: tragedy is "said by Aristotle to be of power" by "raising pity and fear, or terror." "Power" acknowledges the psychotherapeutic basis of Aristotle's ideas. It is the power "to purge the mind of those and such-like passions," where "purge" enlists the medical sense. But then Milton moves further, to explain in words more his own: "that is[,] to temper and reduce them to just measure with a kind of delight, stirred up by reading or seeing[39] those passions well imitated." To moderate or control them, and to "lead them back to exact proportioning" — this echoes Aristotle's mean or median state, *to meson*, but now, too, "measure" makes one think of musical measure. So does "with a kind of delight," if we recall the 1668 note on "The Verse," which speaks of "true musical delight." Though the two delights are not the same, I suggest they overlap. For the present discussion, too, they overlap with his delight in Greek poetry.

One last way to appreciate it is by enlisting the other great Greek theorist, whom we know as "Longinus." The local impact of Milton's Greek, be it quotation or allusion or imitation, is that of *hupsos* ("height" or "sublimity"), which Longinus analyzes and explains. Whether it comes from nature or art or both, it "sweeps away resistance." The hearer neglects to niggle or stand back or rely on stock response. Something "irresistible" sidelines all those obstacles to persuasion. Longinus instances the narrative by Demosthenes of the evening when news came of the decisive defeat of Athens by Philip of Macedon: *hespera men gar en* ("For it was evening").[40] Longinus gives as another example the opening of Genesis, "by the lawgiver of the Jews": "God said . . . Let there be light, and there was light; let there be land, and there was land" (*PL* 9.9).[41]

In *Paradise Lost,* Milton exhibits this power in an abundance that itself sweeps away doubt, which is why Addison used Longinus so much to develop his own response to the poem. And as for Milton's Greek, the switches into Greek partake of the same effect, by jolting or bouncing attention into the language of this great originary literature, whereupon its local magic takes over continued attention. He has thereby seized attention, maybe distracting it from awkward facts or prejudices of his own, but compelling a renewed and enlivened attention. Φιμώθητι!; or Achilles's destined choice: Διχθαδίας κῆρας φέρεμεν θανάτοιο τέλοσδε; or, as John Aubrey remarked concerning Milton's politically suspect sonnets to Cromwell or Vane, "He [Milton] hath hung back these two years as to imparting copies to me for the Collection of mine. Were they made in commendation of the Devill, 'twere all one to me; 'tis the ὕψος [*hupsos*] that I looke after."[42] Aubrey's enthusiasm captures Milton's own passionate lifelong delight in Greek. Not, of course, to claim that Milton's sublimity owes anything to reading and heeding Longinus, for he mentions Longinus only within a plain listing of ancient critics: "Cicero, Hermogenes, Longinus" (*Of Education,* YP 2:403). I contend, rather, that Milton and Longinus had been thrilled to the core by the same *hupsos* they found within Greek poetry. Longinus responded by a theory, Milton in his practice — both the allusions we have been charting and his own epic sublimity.

University of Otago

NOTES

1. Since writing *Milton's Languages: The Impact of Multilingualism on Style* (Cambridge, 1997), I have written mostly about his voluminous Latin prose works. It is timely to be gathering the Greek within those works, and to be supplementing my earlier concentration on Milton's verse. I gratefully acknowledge help with the essay from J. Donald Cullington and Robin Hankey.

2. *Omne tulit punctum qui miscuit utile dulci* ("The writer who both profits and delights the audience deservedly wins all the prizes") (*Ars Poetica,* 343).

3. For the most part, a few longer specimens are analyzed closely, with their Greek in Greek script given before the translation. If Milton translates into Latin, that version is given between the Greek and the English. Unless otherwise noted, texts are from *The Works of John Milton*, 18 vols., gen. ed. Frank Allen Patterson (New York, 1931–38); hereafter cited as CM. The translations vary, however, because Columbia's choice of versions includes some archaic or insufficient ones. Instead, I choose for each work the version that I think best catches its general spirit or local meaning, ideally but seldom both.

4. The Greek of the *Third Defence, Pro se defensio,* is sparser and mundane: four different single words, none in quotation.

5. *The Iliad of Homer, Books I–XII,* ed. M. M. Willcock (London, 1978), 276, note to *Iliad* 9.308–429.

6. John Milton, *Defensio Secunda,* ed. Eugene J. Strittmatter, trans. George Burnet (London, 1808), revised by Moses Hadas (CM 8).

7. "It has generally been assumed (*e.g.,* Columbia, XVIII, 606) that this translation was by Milton, but it bears many striking resemblances to a bilingual edition of Homer published in 1606 at Aurelia Allobrogum [Geneva]," says the Yale editor. This would be worth checking for all Milton's Latin prose renderings of Homer. *Complete Prose Works of John Milton,* 8 vols., ed. Don M. Wolfe et al. (New Haven, Conn., 1953–82), 4.1:1650–55, part 1, preface and notes by Donald A. Roberts, trans. Helen North (588n180). Hereafter, this edition will be cited as YP followed by volume, part (if applicable), and page number.

8. CM 8:22; see also YP 4:560n56: "The Greek expression is a parody of the form of address employed as the formal opening of many Greek orations. Normally used with great dignity it is here a gibe."

9. *De doctrina Christiana,* in *The Complete Works of John Milton,* vol. 8, ed. John K. Hale and J. Donald Cullington (Oxford, 2012), 116–19; hereafter cited as OM.

10. *Enim* ("for") is mirrored in the γαρ of both the passages of Homer that follow. It returns in several more passages quoted from Greek tragedy. Authors naturally quote to enlist authority and give reasons, and Greek ones correctly and aptly quoted have extra clout for humanists. Beyond that, I suggest that Milton shows a special flair and affinity in his use of Greek poets in his argumentative prose.

11. The first translator, Charles Sumner, left the word out of his version. Carey in YP has "even," as does OM.

12. English version from the Loeb edition: Apollonius Rhodius, *Argonautica,* ed. and trans. William H. Race (Cambridge, Mass., 2008), 129. I avoid Columbia's verse rendering of the Greek lines because its sub-Popean heroic couplets distort the agency of Zeus:

> Not Jove himself he feared; his daring ken
> With truth disclosed the will of fate to men;
> With length of years did Jove him hence requite,
> But his eyes bereft of the days' sweet light. (2.236–37)

The Yale translator has "a prolonged old age, / But deprived him," etc., as if old age was a blessing. Not so! Zeus sends a double *punishment*. The Greek has *men . . . de . . .* , where *de* may often mean a mild "but." Here, however, Milton's Latin version, which seems to be his own, renders *de* as *autem*, which is often not adversative but adds a new, connected point.

13. One might doubt this statement since Tiresias was the better-known seer. But when Tiresias tells the momentous truth to Oedipus in Sophocles's *Oedipus*, it is only with great reluctance. Contrast Phineus, in reputation: "he showed not the slightest reverence even for Zeus" when prophesying the truth. And Tiresias is known for several more things, such as his sex change, which would make a more diffused impact, whereas Phineus makes all his impact at the moment when he enters the *Argonautica*.

14. Among several testimonies, Milton's daughter Deborah said that Isaiah, Homer, and Ovid's *Metamorphoses* were books she and her sisters were often called upon to read to their father. See *The Early Lives of Milton*, ed. Helen Darbishire (London, 1932), 343, note supporting 179.

15. See my *Milton's Languages*, 74–80, and more fully, "Milton's Euripides Marginalia: Their Significance for Milton Studies," in *Milton Studies*, vol. 27, ed. James D. Simmonds, 23–35 (Pittsburgh, 1991).

16. Most of the entry appears in the actual hand of Phillips. Aubrey adds / Apollonii Argonautica/ superscript. Darbishire, *Early Lives of Milton*, 12, has a photograph of the page in MS.

17. CM 12:68–69, Masson's translation. My own version is found in *John Milton, Latin Writings: A Selection*, ed. John K. Hale (Assen, Netherlands, 1998): "And a dark stupor covered him, it seemed that the earth whirled under his feet; he lay in a trance without strength, unspeaking" (201).

18. The two letters from Diodati to Milton are written in Greek. See also *Milton's Languages*, 208n7.

19. Salmasius favors Greek witness from the New Testament, the Septuagint, and the church fathers. Interlardings from pagan poets are few: Homer (3), Tyrtaeus, Euripides, and Aeschylus. By contrast, Milton does not quote much biblical Greek, and does no more than his duty by the church fathers. Both Salmasius and Milton address themselves most earnestly to the *Politics* of Aristotle. I have not found substantial or significant Greek material in subsequent contributions to the exchange, except Milton's in his *Second Defence*.

20. *Othello* 2.3.256–61 versus 3.3.159–65, in William Shakespeare, *The Complete Works*, ed. Peter Alexander (London, 1951).

21. *Hamlet*, 1.2.78–79 versus 2.1.66; then 3.4.31 (Hamlet's words, but fair comment).

22. John Milton, *Political Writings*, ed. Martin Dzelzainis, trans. Claire Gruzelier, (Cambridge, 1991), 163.

23. Is this a fair comment, on a distinguished classical scholar? Salmasius had edited Greek texts but not dramas. His allusions hereabouts do seem hasty, nor could I find that he went deeper into the whole matter in his posthumous *Responsio*.

24. "Creon" appears to figure on both sides of the argument, bullied in *Oedipus*, himself bullying in *Antigone*. But he is a different character in each play, doing what the plot requires. The interpretative principle is the same in both.

25. Gruzelier, in Dzelzainis, *Political Writings*, 164.

26. See Euripides's *Heraclidae*, 423–24, in Dzelzainis, *Political Writings*, 165, used by Milton already in the English of *Tenure of Kings and Magistrates* (12).

27. Sophocles's *Oedipus tyrannus*, in Dzelzainis, *Political Writings*, 165, lines 410 and 630.

28. Ibid., line 737.

29. Text from CM 7:312; trans. Gruzelier, in Dzelzainis, *Political Writings*, 165.

30. The *Orestes* is the third play of Euripides, referred to but not quoted between the two *Supplices*: trans. Gruzelier, in Dzelzainis, *Political Writings*, 164.

31. Similarly, again, in the *Iliad*, with the dead body of Patroclus.

32. Oedipus in the *Oedipus tyrannus*, and his successor Creon in *Antigone* are more typical stage kings, forceful and touchy.

33. Translations show the uncertainty: "Your pitcher has gone once too often to the well" (CM 7:173); "Your purple patch has faded" (YP 4.1:385); and Gruzelier resorts to a vague literalism without point, "you have destroyed your own pitcher" (Dzelzainis, *Political Writings*, 115). A range of feasible indecencies is offered by Kenneth Dover in his entertaining note to *Frogs*, lines 1200 and following: Aristophanes, *Frogs*, ed. Kenneth Dover (Oxford, 1993), 338.

34. Greek titles, both, to elevate propagandas. Both writers keep the Greek /k/, for greater Greek authority than the English /c/.

35. The Yale editor's note is much better than its translation (4.1:629n343): "Some of Milton's name-calling is very general and therefore somewhat dull. Here, however, he shoots a very sharp barb. . . . Milton made certain that his Biblical source would not be overlooked by quoting St. Mark's Greek. . . . Finally, he addresses More as *immunde*, thou unclean one," again quoting Mark.

36. Milton's Greek poems are discussed in Hale, *Milton's Languages*. His titles and paratexts are sampled in *A Companion to Milton*, ed. Thomas N. Corns (Oxford, 2016); see Hale, "Classical Literary Tradition," 29–30.

37. Stephen Greenblatt, *Marvelous Possessions: The Wonder of the New World* (Oxford, 1991), esp. 156n30.

38. Technically, the meter of Euripides, though iambic like Milton's English, is trimeters, three long "feet" of four syllables each; thus made up of twelve syllables, not the Italian or English ten, nor five "feet." Though Milton adored Euripides in other ways, like his love of *sententiae* or back-answering stichomythia, he did not emulate the actual sound or length of his line.

39. The alternatives, "reading or seeing," remind us that *Samson* was "never intended" for the stage. Yet again, Milton's choice recalls Aristotle's, who found contemporary stagings repugnant.

40. "It was evening" quoted from *Classical Literary Criticism*, ed. and trans. T. S. Dorsch (Harmondsworth, 1964), Longinus, chap. 10, 116. Longinus is commending Demosthenes's speech, *De Corona*.

41. Ibid., chap. 9, 111.

42. In a letter to Anthony Wood, May 1684, incorporated into the composite narrative of Oliver Lawson Dick, ed., *Aubrey's Brief Lives* (1949; repr., New York, 1962), cited in the *Life of Milton*, 274–75.

"Bless Us! What a Word on a Title Page Is This!": Linguistic Purism and Milton's English Verse

Alexandra Reider

We have long known that there are many moments in *Paradise Lost* when non-English languages influence the diction and syntax of Milton's English verse. In 1712, Joseph Addison counted them among the "Defects of the Poem": "If, in the last Place, we consider the *Language* of this great Poet, we must allow what I have hinted at in a former Paper, that it is often too much labored, and sometimes obscured by old Words, Transpositions, and Foreign Idioms."[1] Thomas Newton was more even-handed in his 1749 annotated edition of the poem when he noted that Milton, "in conformity with the practice of the ancient poets, and with Aristotle's rule, has infused a great many Latinisms as well as Graecisms, and sometimes Hebraisms, into the language of his poem."[2] In his 1997 *Milton's Languages: The Impact of Multilingualism on Style*, John K. Hale applies the question of foreign influence to a larger set of works, seeking out instances of the influence of Latin, Greek, Hebrew, and Italian diction and syntax primarily on Milton's

English poetry, but also on some of the Latin prose.[3] Hale carefully and abundantly documents points of influence and connections between individual languages, and his conclusion brooks no dissent by the work's end: yes, Milton's non-English languages absolutely shaped his writings, broadly considered. This conclusion makes a wider swathe of Milton's corpus available to the kind of observation, seen just now in Addison and Newton, most often made about *Paradise Lost*. Mining Milton's texts for subterranean signs of foreign-language influence has reaped considerable dividends for our understanding of the writer and will certainly continue to do so.

It is precisely because Milton drew on foreign languages more than most writers that he must have known he was inviting charges of "adulterating" English.[4] And, I would suggest, he did know: at least one poem, Sonnet 11, discloses an awareness of linguistic purism, the belief that the best English, or the best form of any language, is one free from foreign influence.[5] Then, subsequent poems that span Milton's career include scenes in which the "purity" of language features prominently—or in which such "purity" has conspicuously fallen away. I use "purity" to mean insulation from change and foreign influence, well aware that such insulation is more idealized than realized. The linguist Endre Brunstad puts it plainly: "From a linguistic point of view, there is no such thing as a 'pure' language."[6]

This essay articulates Milton's ongoing concern with the relationship of his work to the intellectual problem of the purity of language. It begins with a major revision of our understanding of Sonnet 11. I want to argue that this poem, far from being an exercise in nostalgia for classical learning, stages Milton's recognition of the pervasiveness of linguistic purism and of the role it may have played in the reception of *Tetrachordon*. This reading lays the foundation for a consideration of three moments in Milton's verse that bear on either the purity or the foreignness of language, on scales both large (discrete languages in contact) and small (one primary language). In other words, the concerns that Milton signals by giving voice to linguistic purists in Sonnet 11 haunt him long after the poem's close. In Sonnet 12 and the Tower of Babel scene in book 12 of *Paradise Lost*, the collision of foreign languages poses seemingly insurmountable hurdles.[7] Then, in book 4 of *Paradise Regained*, we learn that Jesus most values Hebrew and the culture that it preserves in its purity. In these episodes, linguistic purity proves the best and, in some instances, only engine of cultural achievement; conversely, the presence of more than one language is shown to impede human progress and triumph. Each scene differs in its particulars, but the underlying message is clear: Milton sees a benefit to purity of language. This is perhaps surprising, given that he so often chooses to inflect his English with foreign elements. This stylistic choice, I argue, amounts to a direct response to Quintilian, Sir John Cheke, and Milton's audience manqué in Sonnet 11.

In that sonnet, Milton implies that *Tetrachordon*, a follow-up to his poorly received *The Doctrine and Discipline of Divorce*, was itself poorly received because of its Greek title. Passersby at the bookstall act out different reasons readers may not have made it past the title page. Those who stand "spelling false" likely do not understand the Greek term; more provocatively, the reaction of another browser signals distress and displeasure: "Bless us! What a word on / A title page is this!"[8] The specification that the shocking word is on a "title page" suggests discontent at seeing one particular word featured so prominently. The most obvious candidate is the Greek word *tetrachordon*, which stands at the head of the page on a line of its own.[9] This reaction raises the possibility that the word's foreignness is itself the deterrent, a possibility borne out and amplified by a fuller understanding of the ensuing references to Quintilian and Sir John Cheke.

Our understanding of Sonnet 11 changes radically depending on how we understand the references to Quintilian and Cheke. In one reading, easily the standard, Quintilian and Cheke represent respective "golden ages" of learning against which Milton ruefully contrasts his own age. One might understandably construe Quintilian and Cheke as outstanding versions of the "good intellects" (Sonnet 11, 4) who are receptive to ("numb'r[ed]" by) Milton's tract: they both promoted education in the Greek language. In his *Institutio oratoria*, Quintilian writes, "A sermone Graeco puerum incipere malo, quia Latinum, qui pluribus in usu est, vel nobis nolentibus perbibet, simul quia disciplinis quoque Graecis prius instituendus est, unde et nostrae fluxerunt" ("I prefer a boy to begin by speaking Greek, because he will imbibe Latin, which more people speak, whether we will or no; and also because he will need to be taught Greek learning first, it being the source of ours too").[10] Quintilian's sense of the value in this training comes, at least in part, from the benefits for Latin: "Nam et rerum copia Graeci auctores abundant et plurimum artis in eloquentiam intulerunt et hos transferentibus verbis uti optimis licet: omnibus enim utimur nostris" ("The Greek authors are full of varied matter, and they introduced a great deal of art into the practice of eloquence; when we translate them, we are free to use the best possible words, for the words we use will all be our own").[11] Sir John Cheke was the first Regius professor of Greek at Cambridge between 1540 and 1551 and, as Sonnet 11 mentions, was tutor to Prince Edward. Cheke was, by all accounts, a learned and respected English humanist. There is more to this nostalgia than meets the eye, however. I would argue that Milton uses Quintilian and Sir John Cheke not as counterpoints to the bookstall goers, but as something closer to a precedent for them.

Milton could imagine that, much like the shocked bookstall browser, Quintilian would respond negatively to the use of "barbarisms," words foreign to their respective native tongues. In *Institutio oratoria*, Quintilian explains,

> Barbarum pluribus modis accipimus. Unum gente, quale sit si quis Afrum vel Hispanum Latinae orationi nomen inserat: ut ferrum quo rotae vinciuntur dici solet 'cantus', quamquam eo tamquam recepto utitur Persius, sicut Catullus 'ploxenum' circa Padum invenit, et in oratione Labieni (sive illa Corneli Galli est) in Pollionem 'casamo' [adsectator] e Gallia ductum est: nam 'mastrucam', quod est Sardum, inridens Cicero ex industria dixit.[12]

> [We understand Barbarism in several senses. One type is the ethnic word, as when an African or Spanish expression is used

in a Latin text: for example, the iron tyre of a wheel is called *cantus*, though Persius actually uses it as a received term; similarly, Catullus found *ploxenum* in the Po valley, and in Labienus' (or is it Cornelius Gallus'?) speech against Pollio, the word *casamo* [("follower")] comes from Gaul, while Cicero used the Sardinian *mastruca* deliberately, simply to ridicule it.]

The poem states only that Scottish surnames ("Gordon, / Colkitto, or Macdonnel, or Galasp" [8–9]) "would have made Quintilian stare and gasp" (11). Yet Quintilian's writings give every indication that he also would disapprove of giving an English-language tract a Greek title. Directly after suggesting that boys begin their education with Greek as a means to improve their Latin, Quintilian warns against following this protocol too long:

> Non tamen hoc adeo superstitiose fieri velim ut diu tantum Graece loquatur aut discat, sicut plerisque moris est. Hoc enim accidunt et oris plurima vitia in peregrinum sonum corrupti et sermonis, cui cum Graecae figurae adsidua consuetudine haeserunt, in diversa quoque loquendi ratione pertinacissime durant. Non longe itaque Latina subsequi debent et cito pariter ire. Ita fiet ut, cum aequali cura linguam utramque tueri coeperimus, neutra alteri officiat.[13]

> [However, I do not want a fetish to be made of this, so that he spends a long time speaking and learning nothing but Greek, as is commonly done. This gives rise to many faults both of pronunciation (owing to the distortion of the mouth produced by forming foreign sounds) and of language, because the Greek idioms stick in the mind through continual usage and persist obstinately even in speaking the other tongue. So Latin ought to follow not far behind, and soon proceed side by side with Greek. The result will be that, once we begin to pay equal attention to both languages, neither will get in the way of the other.]

According to Quintilian, education in Greek is only beneficial as long as it remains clearly distinct from Latin. Overindulgence in Greek is a rhetorical vice.[14] Milton, then, is guilty of a linguistic move of which Quintilian would have disapproved.[15] Quintilian, who first seemed to be Milton's ally, now appears more allied with his would-be audience.

Ironically, John Cheke, who devoted himself to furthering classical education in England, was also a devout linguistic purist. Cheke writes in a 1557 letter to Sir Thomas Hoby: "I am of this opinion that our own tung shold be written cleane and pure, unmixt and unmangeled with borowing of other tunges, wherin if we take not heed bi tijm, ever borowing and never payeng, she shall be fain to keep her house as bankrupt."[16] Cheke's conviction that English should be "written cleane and pure" was so strong that he even undertook to translate the Bible anew because he disapproved of the Latinate English of the available versions.[17] Sir John Cheke would have been eminently familiar with a term such as *tetrachordon*, and he would likely not have approved of it as the title of an English-language pamphlet.

The work of Sonnet 11, then, is not to bemoan the ignorance of Milton's (non)readers but instead to trace a longstanding concern for the purity of language that now leaves his works unread. By depicting a would-be audience and reputed scholars who alike adhere to linguistic purism, Milton portrays his writing as vulnerable to long-standing (he may also be suggesting "old-fashioned") concerns over the adoption of foreign words. The references to Quintilian and Cheke work first for Milton and then against him, appearing to summon up wistfulness for classical learning and scorn at latter-day ignorance before joining Milton's would-be audience in disapproval of his Greek title.[18] The parallel is not exact; at least some of Milton's nonreaders puzzle over the foreign title that Quintilian and Cheke would have readily understood. Even so, the sentiment of "Bless us! What a word on / A title page is this!" (Sonnet 11, 5–6) pervades the poem more than has been previously understood.[19] Deeply familiar with these earlier scholars and citing them in other works, Milton would have known that they were both linguistic purists.[20] My reading of the poem, which collapses the distance between Quintilian, Cheke, and Milton's would-be audience, thus complicates its apparent point that the publishing of *Tetrachordon* made visible an easy division between the "numbered" and the "unnumbered," the good intellects and the bad.

The recognition of Quintilian and Cheke as themselves linguistic purists sheds further light on one of Sonnet 11's more difficult interpretive cruces. The apostrophe to "O soul of Sir John Cheke" laments, "Thy age, like ours...Hated not learning worse than toad or asp" (12–13). The question of which sentiment it is, exactly, that unites the two ages still puzzles critics. As Edward Le Comte puts it, "Take your pick of opposite paraphrases."[21] Three have been offered: that Milton's age hated learning more than Cheke's; that Cheke's age actually did hate learning (with no measure of this hatred in relation to that of Milton's age); and that the two ages were equal in their hatred (or lack thereof) of learning. J. Milton French most influentially articulated the first view, grounded in foreign language stylistics: "Milton, saturated as he was by Latin style, merely transposed the 'like ours' from the spot where a modern writer would naturally put it to one where its reference is somewhat ambiguous. He (or we) might probably have said in simpler prose, 'Thy age hated not learning, like ours [i.e. as ours does], worse than toad or asp.' In other words, 'Your age did not hate learning as ours does.'"[22] J. S. Smart raised the second view as a historicist counterpoint: "Many men in that age, which has been thought so propitious to such studies, *hated not learning worse than toad or asp,* —but as much as they hated either. [Roger] Ascham speaks of 'blind buzzards, who in late years, of wilful maliciousness, would neither learn themselves nor could teach others anything at all.'"[23] E. A. J. Honigmann elaborates: "In the Preface to Cheke's *True Subiect to the Rebell* (1641), it was stressed that his age *hated learning*—there was 'an universall stupor & lethargy.'"[24] The third view, parity of hatred, comes in two opposed forms, both dependent on taking the syntax as naturally English. On the one hand, Howard Schultz argues that Milton's wording suggests that "both generations hated learning."[25] Patrick J. Cook, on the other, reasons that "we put the least strain on Milton's syntax if we find both ages free from hating learning worse than toad or asp. The apparently unlike stall-readers are in fact most resembling—resembling both Milton and the earlier age he praises in both the poem and the treatise. They are assuredly slow-witted, but they show no signs of hating learning."[26] I dwell somewhat on these differing opinions to emphasize how vexing these lines have been: Annabel Patterson has called them "an epitome of Milton's troublemaking for his readers."[27] My own suspicion is that through his unusual syntax, Milton hoped to inspire this very debate, which has no one obvious resolution based on syntax alone.

Because the references to Quintilian and Sir John Cheke also inspire radically different readings, our interpretation of those figures does much to determine our reading of whose age hated learning worse. If we recognize that the references to Quintilian and Cheke work against a purely nostalgic view of classical learning, we can see a critique of intolerance and linguistic purism in both ages. Whose age hated learning worse? The third view, parity of hatred, is the best response (albeit the one with the least critical momentum behind it): the two ages were as bad as each other, at least in their linguistic purism. Yet faced with Milton's admiration of Quintilian and Cheke, we cannot say that disapproval of foreign words in a language's lexicon was enough for Milton to flag someone as unlearned. The line between the numbered and the unnumbered, so clear at the start of the poem, is blurred to the point of disappearing by the poem's end. The division is unrestored as Milton's tract, we are left to presume, remains unread, his ideas unentertained. Milton wonders if, in this instance, his Greek title was to blame.

In Milton's Sonnet 12, his opponents respond to his proposed reforms once more—not with mere dismissal, but with a "barbarous noise" (3) that deliberately evokes the biblical scene at the Tower of Babel. Critics have largely overlooked the poem's preoccupation with the state of language, carried over from its companion poem.[28] In this sonnet, Milton suggests a level of primal chaos by making reference to foreignness of language on a larger scale. His opponents cannot accept the offered freedom and instead engage in animalistic cacophony:

> I did but prompt the age to quit their clogs
> By the known rules of ancient liberty,
> When straight a barbarous noise environs me
> Of owls and cuckoos, asses, apes and dogs.   (Sonnet 12, 1–4)

The "barbarous" sound of Milton's opponents recalls Quintilian's disapproval of *barbarismus*, the "barbarism," one type of which is foreign terms. In Sonnet 11, Milton implicitly acknowledges the "charge" of foreignness put to him by the constellation of Quintilian, Cheke, and his (non)readers, but in echoing Quintilian here, Milton himself takes on the role of arbiter of language. A few lines later, he returns to the political consequences of such foreignness when he reminds his audience once again of the larger goal they fail to attain: "But this is got by casting pearl to hogs; / That bawl for freedom in their senseless mood, / And still revolt when truth would set them free" (8–10).

Milton has turned the audience who, in Sonnet 11, wishes him to use a purer English into a throng of creatures that not only does not use English at all but also uses many varieties of not-English. An owl, one might imagine, "speaks" a different "language" than a dog.[29] Honigmann explains that this noise is a direct and targeted response to Milton's Presbyterian critics who disapproved of his radical position on divorce: "The Presbyterians pointed to the extraordinary multiplication of sects...the 'sectaries,' they held, were light-headed innovators whose clamouring had brought about a second Babel.... Writing of the *barbarous noise* of his 'verminous' opponents...Milton therefore turned the Presbyterians' jargon against themselves."[30] Milton thus caricatures his would-be audience and his critics in a single stroke.

The "second Babel" of Sonnet 12 is not Milton's only rendition of the story. He also gives us an account of the episode as part of the human history Michael forecasts at the end of *Paradise Lost*. A tyrant, implicitly Nimrod, upends a time of peace and "paternal rule" (*PL* 12.24).[31] Together with "a crew, whom like ambition joins / With him or under him to tyrannize" (38–39), Nimrod plots to build "A city and tow'r, whose top may reach to Heav'n" (44). Their goal is enduring fame and repute that would outlast diaspora and death: to "get themselves a name, lest far dispersed / In foreign lands their memory be lost, / Regardless whether good or evil fame" (45–47). God, however, sees and intervenes:

> But God who oft descends to visit men
> Unseen, and through their habitations walks

> To mark their doings, them beholding soon,
> Comes down to see their city, ere the tower
> Obstruct Heav'n tow'rs, and in derision sets
> Upon their tongues a various spirit to raze
> Quite out their native language, and instead
> To sow a jangling noise of words unknown:
> Forthwith a hideous gabble rises loud
> Among the builders; each to other calls
> Not understood, till hoarse, and all in rage,
> As mocked they storm; great laughter was in Heav'n
> And looking down, to see the hubbub strange
> And hear the din; thus was the building left
> Ridiculous, and the work Confusion named.   (*PL* 12.48–62)

There is a linguistic angle to the irony that building, and then failing to build, the tower is what creates insurmountable division among the people, considering that the landmark was originally conceived as a testament to human prowess and a bulwark against division. Linguistic division ends up replacing geographic division and, Milton suggests, proves far more alienating—and lastingly so. The human history that Milton, through Michael, gives us does not reach Pentecost, at which the gift of tongues from the Holy Spirit was commonly understood to reverse the fracture wreaked at Babel.[32] In Milton's biblical diegesis, foreignness persists.

The Babel narrative establishes an origin story for the idea that purity of language paves the way for cultural achievement as well as the corollary that foreignness of language obstructs such progress. The tower the ambitious men are building to "get themselves a name" (*PL* 12.45) seems to stand a real chance of achieving heavenly heights: the conjunction "ere" (51) projects forward with a certitude that is lacking in, for example, "lest," another monosyllable that anticipates a subjunctive verb. God sees to it that such potential is not realized, although what is "raze[d]" (53) is not the building, as the verb might lead one to expect, but the builders' "native language" (54).[33] The anticipated presence of the physical structure created by the enjambment with "raze" is replaced by a linguistic structure in the following line. The fungibility of the tower and the multiplicity of languages continue as the foreignness is sown, implying that it, like seeds, can grow. And it does: "a hideous gabble rises loud" (56)—again, instead of a tower. Foreignness of language, the "jangling noise of words unknown" (55), not only halts the growth of the tower; it soars in its place.

This episode presents foreignness of language as a means to an end, and a laughable one. The descriptor "jangling" recalls the derogative description of rhyme as "the jingling sound of like endings" in Milton's note on *Paradise Lost*'s verse style, "a fault avoided by the learned ancients both in poetry and all good oratory."[34] The alliterative and near-homophonic compounded dismissal of "jangling" and "jingling" admonishes the reader to avoid tintinnabulation at all costs. That this profusion of languages is aurally offensive is even more evident in the phrase "a hideous gabble rises" (*PL* 12.56). The mixture of language is disgusting, deformed, and thus dismissible. It is certainly dismissed in heaven where, once the "gabble" arrives, "great laughter" arises (59). God has already acted "in derision" (52) when he instituted foreignness of language; that derision is now spread more widely among several actors.[35] Linguistic purity, because it was the agent of the proud and overambitious, comes out of this episode tainted; any "progress" that was halted and glory that was frustrated was that of tyrants, those "not content / With fair equality, fraternal state" (25–26). In this scene, large-scale foreignness of language may be aesthetically objectionable, but it is ultimately ordained by God and deployed to curtail despotism and pride, by far the greater evils.

If such foreignness worked against Milton in Sonnet 11 and against his detractors in Sonnet 12, in *Paradise Regained* it is linguistic purity that again finds favor. This favor arises from the potential of a single language to safeguard a people and preserve their culture. In book 4 of *Paradise Regained*, the pure language is Hebrew, and Jesus asserts that knowledge of it and of the culture to which it grants access renders other knowledge and culture superfluous. When Satan offers Jesus access to all knowledge, including the knowledge of the Greeks and Romans, Jesus dismisses the proposal as unnecessary: "Think not but that I know these things, or think / I know them not; not therefore am I short / Of knowing what I ought" (*PR* 4.286–88). A few lines later, Jesus explains that he most values that which is preserved in his "native language":

> Or if I would delight my private hours
> With music or with poem, where so soon
> As in our native language can I find
> That solace? All our law and story strewed
> With hymns, our psalms with artful terms inscribed,
> Our Hebrew songs and harps in Babylon,
> That pleased so well our victors' ear, declare
> That rather Greece from us these arts derived;
> Ill imitated, while they loudest sing
> The vices of their deities, and their own
> In fable, hymn, or song, so personating
> Their gods ridiculous, and themselves past shame.   (4.331–42)

Here we see Jesus place Hebrew above the common concerns of life, citing its heritage as a source of "solace" (334) to "delight [his] private hours" (331)—not as his sole means of communication. And indeed, it would not have been: Jesus likely spoke Aramaic in his day-to-day life.[36] Yet Hebrew is the only language deified, discussed, or even mentioned in this passage. In line 336, "Hebrew" could be an adjective for either the language or the people, but the mention of a "native language" suggests the former; no language is named in association with "Greece" (338). The ambiguity is functional as the language becomes metonymic for a people and their cultural history. Witness the sense of exclusive possession that surrounds it, line after line: "*our* native language" (333), "*our* law and story" (334), "*our* psalms" (335), "*Our* Hebrew songs and harps" (336; emphases mine). When the "our" shifts from signaling participation in cultural heritage to recognizing historical oppression with "*our* victors' ear" (337), the sense of persecution is softened somewhat by the suggestion that the victors are "ours," not that the Jews are "theirs." This Hebrew, then, is a somewhat singular construction that elides many centuries and two Testaments: purity is at a remove from the quotidian. Reliance upon this one language over a period of time becomes a way for Jesus and the rest of his "we" to assert a continual Jewish identity and to claim affiliation with the vastness of the language's holdings.

Small but striking instances of diction and syntax shared across this moment and the earlier Babel episode reveal the consistency of the linguistic principles underpinning both scenes. The Tower of Babel is left unfinished and "Ridiculous" (*PL* 12.62); the Greek gods are "ridiculous" (*PR* 4.342) because they were plagiarized from the Hebrew culture. In both scenes, "ridiculous" describes the result of a move away from linguistic purity: when a culture overreaches, other languages — "a jangling noise of words unknown" (*PL* 12.55) and Greek — try to provide the same benefits as the purer languages and fail. Then, after Jesus's defense of the Hebrew language, its holdings, and its heritage, Satan proves "Quite at a loss, for all his darts were spent" (*PR* 4.366). The diction and syntax of this line, which starts with "Quite," recall the moment at Babel at which God sets a spirit to "raze / Quite out" the builders' native language (*PL* 12.53–54). "Quite" appears at the beginning of both lines to anticipate and heighten moments of linguistic dysfunction and paralysis that contrast with the achievements available to humanity when everyone speaks a pure language. Milton's shared language across these two episodes emphasizes the consistency of his views on linguistic purity and its perceived advantages.

Use of a single, pure language in Milton's biblical verse helps a community cohere around a larger cultural project. In the Babel episode, the building project halts and the builders' ambitions fail when their ability to work together vanishes along with their one, pure language. But in *Paradise Regained*, a pure language binds a people to their culture, to their past, and to one another, even in times of captivity. In both instances, practicing such purity can lead or provide access to remarkable human achievements. Its obverse is described at various points as animalistic and ridiculous. Yet linguistic purity is also the first thing cast aside at Babel when the enterprise angers God. That purity may be valuable for people, but it is valued by God only as much as it facilitates obedience and worship. This is perhaps why Milton grants Hebrew a special status across biblical time: from the captivity in Babylon to the showdown with Satan in the desert, the Jewish people present the Hebrew language to their enemies as a united front in order to persevere and maintain their faith.

In his English verse, Milton assembles two timelines: linguistic purism in the classical tradition and linguistic purity in the biblical tradition. By uniting Quintilian and Cheke in Sonnet 11, Milton gives us some sense of the historical depth of the ideology of linguistic purism: it reaches back over 1,500 years.[37] Quintilian and Cheke can be construed as representing the Latin and Greek traditions, respectively, from which Milton draws, even as in Sonnet 11 he imagines that these same representatives might chide him for doing so. Milton's second timeline, linguistic purity in the biblical tradition, extends from Babel to Jesus's temptation in the desert, from one "Ridiculous" and first-word "Quite" to another. It reveals that Milton attributes to the power of a single, pure language the ability to unite a community. The tyrannical impulse to reach heaven can only be disrupted by foreignness of language in *Paradise Lost*, and Hebrew unites the Jewish community against all those who would do them harm in *Paradise Regained*. Milton delivers no judgment of his own on these communities, leaving that to God and those who might laugh in heaven. His judgment is instead reserved for the English audience who does not buy his books.

Given Milton's consistent association of linguistic purity with cultural achievement, one wonders what Milton envisioned for his own legacy when his verse was so often noticeably foreign, both in its English and its non-English. If his response to the reaction to *Tetrachordon* is any indication, Milton recognized that a large part of his potential audience would not understand, or quite possibly would not approve of, such foreign inflection. Milton would also have known that his English poetry would probably find a very small audience, at best, elsewhere in Europe. According to Thomas N. Corns, as a "well-travelled humanist intellectual, Milton knew how peripheral English life and culture were to the mainstream of continental European thought and art, how dependent on continental Europe the English intelligentsia were, and how the English were perceived and represented in continental Europe."[38] Corns goes on to observe that "in the seventeenth century England was positioned on the edge of European consciousness, its language rarely understood outside mercantile ports with direct links to England, its towering literary achievements unconsidered by the French or Spanish or German or Italians."[39]   .

Fittingly enough, time abroad may have changed Milton's perspective and allowed him to realize that he could approach his English differently. Hale ascribes to Milton, either during his time in Italy in 1638–39 or upon his return, a "firmer grasp" of the realization that not only had English "absorbed much from Latin and from other tongues, but that—in syntax as well as words—it could absorb more."[40] The impact would be most felt several decades later in the heavily Latinate style of *Paradise Lost*, first published in 1667. Hale goes so far as to term that work evidence of "an experimentalism of bilingual engagement, Milton using his entire intellectual—which means, multilingual—armoury in his best poem."[41] But not every Miltonic poem evinces "bilingual engagement." *Paradise Regained*, for one, has a markedly plainer style, one in which Margaret Kean finds "many echoes of Milton's early poems."[42] Thus, while we may broadly observe an increase in foreign-language influence on Milton's poetry as he advanced in his career, the style was by no means a given for his later work.

Milton's investment in the literary status of a foreign English emerges over the course of his career. In his early "At a Vacation Exercise," Milton voices the desire to one day "at Heav'n's door / Look in" in his native language (34–35). Roughly 15 years later, he attributes the failure of one of his divorce pamphlets to, in part, its not being *prima facie* English enough. Decades later again, when *Paradise Lost* appears, it stands confidently as a miniature site of Babel itself by virtue of the Latin undercurrent of Milton's English, his "bilingual engagement."[43] In 1724, Leonard Welsted commented on the skill needed to "improve a Language by introducing foreign Treasures into it; the Words, so introduced, ought to be such, as, in a manner, naturalize Themselves; that is, they ought to fall into the Idiom, and suit with the Genius of the Tongue, they are brought into, so luckily, as almost to seem, originally, of its own Growth."[44] For Wested, Milton was a prime example of the failure to naturalize foreign words into his English: "otherwise, the Attempt will end in nothing but an uncouth unnatural Jargon, like the Phrase and Stile of *Milton*, which is a second *Babel*, or Confusion of all Languages; a Fault, that can never be enough regretted in that immortal Poet."[45]

Milton's language may be a "second *Babel*," but why should this be so regrettable? At Babel, the "hideous gabble rises" into heaven when the tower could not; it is stronger and can soar higher. A more foreign English is the kind of language with which Milton finally looks in "at Heav'n's door," in this scene and throughout *Paradise Lost*. The English language that initially gave voice to Milton's concerns ultimately becomes, with some supplement, the means by which he might supersede them. His success in this endeavor is his reply to Quintilian, Cheke, and those bygone bookstall browsers, all of whom would wish his English to be different.

Yale University

NOTES

I am grateful to John Rogers for his encouragement and his many helpful comments, as well as to Daniel Cowling and the two anonymous readers at *Milton Studies* for theirs.

1. Joseph Addison, "Defects of the Poem," *Spectator*, no. 297 (Feb. 9, 1712). Cited from the collected edition reprinted in 1712–15, vol. 4, 266. Quotation from John Leonard, *Faithful Labourers: A Reception History of "Paradise Lost," 1667–1970*, vol. 1, *Style and Genre* (Oxford, 2013), 19.

2. Thomas Newton, ed., *Paradise Lost: A Poem in Twelve Books*, 2 vols. (London, 1749), 1:10.

3. John K. Hale, *Milton's Languages: The Impact of Multilingualism on Style* (Cambridge, 1997).

4. Hale writes that Milton "stands out less in any one language-art than for the number of them and for the standard he maintained" (*Milton's Languages*, 16). Milton knew English, Latin, Greek, Hebrew, Aramaic, Syriac, Italian, French, Spanish, and quite possibly Dutch (8). Milton composed verse in Latin, Greek, Italian, and, of course, English.

5. The definition in George Thomas, *Linguistic Purism* (New York, 1992), is particularly thorough: "Purism is the manifestation of a desire on

the part of a speech community (or some section of it) to preserve a language from, or rid it of, putative foreign elements or other elements held to be undesirable (including those originating in dialects, sociolects and styles of the same language). It may be directed at all linguistic levels but primarily the lexicon. Above all, purism is an aspect of the codification, cultivation and planning of standard languages" (12). Recent scholarship on language purism focuses on contemporary or near-contemporary issues. See, for example, Endre Brunstad, "Standard Language and Linguistic Purism," *Sociolinguistica* 17, no. 1 (2003): 52–70; Nancy C. Dorian, "Purism vs. Compromise in Language Revitalization and Language Revival," *Language in Society* 23, no. 4 (1994): 479–94; Christiane Fäcke, "Language and Dialect between Linguistic Purism and Plurilingualism," in *New Theoretical Perspectives in Multilingualism Research*, ed. Werner Wiater and Gerda Videsott (Frankfurt am Main, 2011), 171–84; and *The Politics of Language Purism*, ed. Björn H. Jernudd and Michael J. Shapiro (Berlin, 1989). In early modern England, the debate over foreign influence on the English lexis was known as the "inkhorn debate." See Alvin Vos, "Humanistic Standards of Diction in the Inkhorn Controversy," *Studies in Philology* 73, no. 4 (1976): 376–96. I use "linguistic purism" here because I think it the more capacious term: it pertains to syntax as well as diction, in addition to foreign words not intended to be borrowings but that are nevertheless present in a language, such as *tetrachordon*.

6. Brunstad, "Standard Language," 52. In this essay, I will not continue to place "purity" and "pure" in quotation marks, though I use the terms with the underlying linguistic reality in mind.

7. In calling these respective poems Sonnets 11 and 12, I follow the 1673 printed edition of the poems.

8. John Milton, Sonnet 11, lines 7, 5–6. Unless otherwise noted, all Milton quotations come from *The Complete Poetry and Essential Prose of John Milton*, ed. William Kerrigan, John Rumrich, and Stephen M. Fallon (New York, 2007).

9. The title page of Milton's pamphlet reads, *Tetrachordon*: Expositions Upon *The foure chief places in Scripture, which treat of Mariage, or nullities in Mariage.*

10. Quintilian, *Institutio oratoria*, 1.1.12, in *The Orator's Education, Volume I: Books 1–2*, ed. and trans. Donald A. Russell, (Cambridge, Mass., 2002), 70–71.

11. Ibid., 10.5.3, in *Orator's Education*, 4:356–57.

12. Ibid., 1.5.8, in *Orator's Education*, 1:124–27.

13. Ibid., 1.1.13, in *Orator's Education*, 1:70–71.

14. At one point Quintilian does admit that "confessis quoque Graecis utimur verbis ubi nostra desunt, sicut illi a nobis nonnumquam mutuantur" ("we also openly use Greek words where we have none of our own, just as they sometimes borrow from us") (Ibid., 1.5.58). The key stipulation

for Quintilian is that such foreignness must be a last resort; a title that is at least as much about the author's intelligence as about the work probably would not clear Quintilian's high bar of necessity.

15. Not only that: Milton's Quintilian is also guilty of a linguistic move of which the historical Quintilian would have disapproved. The stall-reader who cries, "Bless us! What a word on / A title page is this!" vocalizes dismay (Sonnet 11, 5–6); Quintilian is left to "stare and gasp" (11) at the names Gordon, Colkitto, Macdonnel, and Galasp. Quintilian, though a famed classical rhetorician, is at a loss for words; it is the less revered stall-reader who voices an opinion. The chiastic nature of the two lines emphasizes their inverse relation: "Cries the stall-reader" (5) mirrors "Quintilian stare and gasp." This behavior is comically out of character for Quintilian: as E. A. J. Honigmann points out, Quintilian "repeatedly rebuked orators who proceeded by fits and starts, or pant, or have a halting delivery, and also disapproved of 'rigid and distended' eyes." *Milton's Sonnets,* ed. E. A. J. Honigmann (New York, 1966), 124–25. Honigmann does not supply examples, although Quintilian does indeed provide several choice quotations on these points in *Institutio oratoria* at, for instance, 1.11.4, 1.11.8, 11.3.19–20, and 11.3.75–76.

16. "A Letter of Syr J. Cheekes To his loving frind Mayster Thomas Hoby," in Baldassarre Castiglione, *The courtyer of Count Baldessar Castilio,* trans. Thomas Hoby (London, 1561), [3A]1 (the final leaf) recto. This quotation makes it into Thomas's general introduction to *Linguistic Purism,* 85. I silently modernize i/j and v/u throughout this essay.

17. David Norton, *A History of the English Bible as Literature* (Cambridge, 2000), describes Cheke resolutely trying to remedy the fault he perceived in English Bible translations:

> he translated Matthew and the beginning of Mark, avoiding words of Latin origin (and attempting also to reform spelling). This incomplete and rough work was not published until 1843. It can hardly have been of influence in its time, but it helps to show both the difficulties of language facing the early translators, and the difficulties of comprehension facing those of their readers who lacked Latin and biblical scholarship. Among his choices of words are "mooned" for "lunatic," "tollers" for "publicans," "hundreder" for "centurion," "bywords" for "parables," "orders" for "traditions," "freshman" for "proselyte," and "crossed" for "crucified." For him, rain does not descend but fall: "and there fell a great shower, and the rivers came down, and the winds blew and beat upon that house, and it fell not for it was ground-wrought on a rock" (p. 40; Matt. 7:25). Throughout the century there was a sharp consciousness of the distinction between vocabulary of Anglo-Saxon origin and vocabulary of Latin origin. The significance of Cheke is that he underlines the

difficulties there could be at this time even with what seem to be thoroughly ordinary words of Latin origin. (26–27)

Cheke's translation was published as *The Gospel according to Saint Matthew* (Cambridge, 1843).

18. If Milton had wished solely to imply that everyone should master Greek, he could have substituted, for example, Cicero for Quintilian and Sir Thomas More for Sir John Cheke. Cicero artfully sprinkled his Latin with Greek, and with the name "Utopia," More went one further than Milton: he invented his Greek word. On Cicero and Greek, see *The Cambridge Companion to Cicero*, ed. Catherine Steel (Cambridge, 2013), 57 and 205. More's pun (the neologism "utopia" suggests both "no-place" and "good place" in the Greek) is introduced in the first and last lines of the Latin prefatory hexastich: "Utopia priscis dicta, ob infrequentiam...Eutopia merito sum vocanda nomine." Thomas More, *Libellus vere aureus nec minus salutaris quam festivus de optimo rei publicae statu deque nova insula Utopia* (Louvain, 1516), 4.

19. Kerrigan et al. note Quintilian's disapproval of foreign words without commenting on the consequent irony of his appearance here (*Complete Poetry*, 147–48). More often, modern editions of Milton gloss Quintilian and Cheke as learned scholars who contrast with the ignorance of Milton's own time.

20. In *Of Education,* Milton describes the first three books of Quintilian's *Institutio oratoria* as possessing "classic authority," and in *Tetrachordon* he writes that Cheke was "a man at that time counted the learnedest of Englishmen." *Of Education*, in Kerrigan et al., *Complete Poetry*, 974, and *Tetrachordon*, in *The Divorce Tracts of John Milton: Texts and Contexts*, ed. Sara J. van den Berg and W. Scott Howard (Pittsburgh, 2010), 359, respectively. Further to the point that Cheke's view on unmixed English would have been available to Milton: the Castiglione translation in question dates to the mid-sixteenth century, and Cheke's stance appears to have stayed in circulation in learned circles thereafter, featuring in John Strype's 1705 biography: "that indeed was Cheke's Conceit, that in writing *English,* none but *English* Words should be used, thinking it a Dishonour to our Mother Tongue, to be beholden to other Nations for their Words and Phrases to express our Minds." John Strype, *The Life of the Learned Sir John Cheke, Kt* (London, 1705), 213.

21. Edward Le Comte, *Milton Re-viewed: Ten Essays* (New York, 1991), 88.

22. J. Milton French, "A Comment," *Modern Language Notes* 70, no. 6 (1955): 404.

23. John S. Smart, *The Sonnets of Milton* (Glasgow, 1921), 73.

24. Honigmann, *Milton's Sonnets*, 125.

25. Howard Schultz, "A Book Was Writ of Late," *Modern Language Notes* 69, no. 7 (1954): 495.

26. Patrick J. Cook, "Resembling Unlikeness: A Reading of Milton's *Tetrachordon* Sonnet," *Milton Quarterly* 26, no. 4 (1992): 123.

27. Annabel Patterson, *Early Modern Liberalism* (Cambridge, 1997), 75.

28. I say "largely" because Richard J. Du Rocher is an exception: on his way to a broader and unrelated point, he mentions in passing that "Milton is outraged by his detractors' impurity—linguistically and ideologically." Richard J. Du Rocher, "The Wealth and Blood of Milton's Sonnet XI," *Milton Quarterly* 17, no. 1 (1983): 16. For more recent critical studies of the sonnet, see John Leonard, "Revolting as Backsliding in Milton's Sonnet XII," *Notes and Queries* 43, no. 3 (1996): 269–73; and Elizabeth Sauer, "Radical Politics and Milton's Civil War Verse: 'License' and 'Libertie,'" in *Approaches to Teaching Milton's Shorter Poetry and Prose*, ed. Peter C. Herman (New York, 2007), 97–102.

29. Ludwig Wittgenstein's famous aphorism "If a lion could talk, we could not understand him" comes to mind. Wittgenstein, *Philosophical Investigations*, trans. G. E. M. Anscombe (New York, 1953), 223.

30. Honigmann, *Milton's Sonnets*, 116–17. Honigmann supplies two key Presbyterian quotations in this regard: "They [the sectaries] all pretend to set the right bound, build the Lords house; but it is *Babel*, not *Bethel*, if we may guesse by the division of their languages," from Nathaniel Hardy, *The Arraignment of Licentious Liberty* (London, 1647), 14; and "all manner Sectaries creepe forth, and multiplie, as frogs, and flies, and vermine in the Spring; and there is *variance, hatred, emulation, wrath, strife, sedition, heresies, envyings, revilings, and the like*," from John Ward, *God Judging among the Gods* (London, 1645), 31.

31. John Leonard wonders if Nimrod's name was razed along with his language. See John Leonard, *Naming in Paradise: Milton and the Language of Adam and Eve* (Oxford, 1990), 54.

32. For the contemporary understanding of this typological connection, see David Cram, "Linguistic Eschatology: Babel and Pentecost in Seventeenth-Century Thought," *Language and History* 56, no. 1 (2013): 44–56.

33. *Oxford English Dictionary Online*, 3rd ed. (2008), s.v. "raze," def. 6.

34. "The Verse," *Paradise Lost*, 290.

35. Milton may have even hoped readers would share in that derision. Thomas Newton remarked upon the unusual diction at this moment: "As the poet represents this confusion among the builders as an object of ridicule, so he makes use of some ridiculous words, such as are not very usual in poetry, to heighten that ridicule, as *jangling noise, hideous gabble, strange hubbub*." See Newton's edition of *Paradise Lost*, 2:385. Quotation from Leonard, *Naming in Paradise*, 55; I have incorporated Newton's italics.

36. Angel Sáenz-Badillos, *A History of the Hebrew Language,* trans. John Elwolde (Cambridge, 1993), 167–71, esp. 170. Cited in Hale, *Milton's Languages,* 208–09. John Leonard elaborates: "The term 'Hebrew' can mislead, for it was applied to the language of the Jews both before and after the Babylonian captivity.... The 'Hebrew' spoken by Jesus was Aramaic— a different language from the Hebrew spoken by Samson.... The language properly called 'Hebrew' is known only from the Old Testament" (*Naming in Paradise,* 16).

37. Quintilian was born around 35 AD and was known as a skilled rhetorician in Rome by 85–86. Cheke became the first Regius Professor of Greek in 1540. See Russell, "General Introduction" to *Orator's Education,* 1–2, and Alan Bryson, "John Cheke," in the *Oxford Dictionary of National Biography Online* (2008).

38. Thomas N. Corns, "Milton and the Limitations of Englishness," in *Early Modern Nationalism and Milton's England,* ed. David Loewenstein and Paul Stevens (Toronto, 2008), 213.

39. Ibid.

40. Hale, *Milton's Languages,* 64–65.

41. Ibid., 107. Milton may have been encouraged by the success of (or perhaps he hoped to outdo) earlier English writers such as John Lyly and Edmund Spenser, who fought for the status of English as a literary vernacular. See Catherine Nicholson, *Uncommon Tongues: Eloquence and Eccentricity in the English Renaissance* (Philadelphia, 2014). Yet Hale contends that "every generation of the Renaissance had to think the *Questione* [*della Lingua*] through, so gravitational did the pull of Latin remain till after Milton" (*Milton's Languages,* 3).

42. Margaret Kean, "*Paradise Regained,*" in *A Companion to Milton,* ed. Thomas N. Corns (Oxford, 2001), 430.

43. Hale, *Milton's Languages,* 107.

44. Leonard Welsted, "A Dissertation concerning the Perfection of the *English* Language, the State of Poetry," prefixed to *Epistles, Odes, &c. Written on Several Subjects* (London, 1724), ix. Quotation from Leonard, *Faithful Labourers,* 1:21.

45. Ibid.

"How cam'st thou speakable of mute": Satanic Acoustics in *Paradise Lost*

Katherine Cox

In his 1936 essay, "A Note on the Verse of John Milton," T. S. Eliot claims that Milton's blindness "helped him to concentrate on what he could do best." This was, in Eliot's opinion, Milton's ability to write superbly musical poetry.[1] But for Eliot the genius of his sound is also the sign of his poetic limitation. In his zeal for the aural, Milton neglects the other senses, producing imbalanced poetry in which "the inner meaning is separated from the surface."[2] Eliot's backhanded praise of Milton's "auditory imagination" thus begins by echoing traditional acclaim for the "organ music" of Milton's blank verse before joining in the complaint of F. R. Leavis and Ezra Pound, who equated Milton's "orotundity" with mediocre poetry.[3]

Controversy over Milton's imposing sound effects has abated since Eliot's time. But we can still learn from his contention that Milton's blindness and musical inclination produced poetry that is, above all, acoustically imaginative. Scholars have often noted the play of sounds in Milton's lines—their syntactical arrangement, rhythm, alliteration, repetition, and so on—but comparatively few have sought evidence of Milton's aural imagination in the figuration, characters, and larger narrative structures of *Paradise Lost*, which, along with his style of versification, reflect the poet's distinctive aural concerns. The studies that do cover this terrain tend to look at the political or cultural meanings of Milton's music in early modern England.[4] As Matthew Steggle and Beverley Sherry suggest, the acoustical as well as semantic and musical qualities of Miltonic sounds warrant further critical attention.[5] Milton's wariness of sensuous sound, often attributed to a Puritan bias against polyphony or verbally impoverished forms of music, may be more definitely explained by Milton's metaphysical understanding of the fallen atmosphere and its satanic acoustics.[6]

Of all the notable acoustical features of Milton's epic, satanic aurality stands apart for its centrality in the episode on which the narrative crisis depends. For the Fall to occur, the serpent must speak. Before Eve eats the forbidden fruit, her innocence is threatened by the sound of the serpent's speech, which "into her heart too easy entrance won."[7] The penetrating character of this acoustical attack can be attributed to the fact that "sound...for Milton...is unmistakably corporeal."[8] Satan's identity as an aerial being who has a powerful sway over the atmosphere is certainly also at play. I argue elsewhere that Milton associates Satan with the "prince of the power of the aire" mentioned in Ephesians 2:2 and uses this doctrinal point and its traditional elaborations to characterize the fallen angels throughout his epic poetry as powers of air and weather.[9] Milton's depiction of the devils in *Paradise Lost* as elementally similar to, and manipulators of, the atmosphere anticipates their role in *Paradise Regained* as rulers of the postlapsarian middle air.[10]

Despite the basic physical connection between sound and atmosphere, scholars have failed to recognize the co-dependence in Milton's poetry of acoustical and meteorological representation.[11] The paradisal airs that carry endlessly mutable praise to the Creator and move tunefully through the garden's leaves illustrate the fundamentally acoustical condition of the atmosphere (*PL* 5.180–84 and 4.264–66). Satan, the prospective "Prince of the air" (10.185), radically exploits this atmospheric condition. His success with Eve and, indeed, his whole office in the fallen world as man's deceiver, may be attributed to the cultivation of a studied acoustics that capitalizes on his pneumatic being. I will argue that the mechanical and magical instruments Satan uses to produce deadly sounds prior to the temptation prefigure the method he employs to produce the serpent's voice and that these technologies arise directly from his meteorological agency.

Several insights emerge from a reading of the technical means of production and material basis of satanic sound in *Paradise Lost.* Taking a global view of diabolical acoustics, rather than focusing on the devils' fallen music, allows for comparison of diverse aural phenomena—instrumental symphonies, the discharge of cannons, cries of anguish, even musically unaccompanied speech. It also reveals that, in *Paradise Lost,* the conditions of sonic production and the integrity of acoustical material define the potential of sound to corrupt more than, for example, its balance of semantic intelligibility and harmony. I differ, therefore, with Erin Minear's suggestion that wordless satanic "music proves more powerful than the hollow rhetoric" because it implies that Satan used a less than optimal weapon to tempt Eve, and also misunderstands the technically similar production and identical substance of both satanic music and the serpent's speech.[12] Hell's music and the serpent's rhetoric are made of the same stuff—satanically compromised air—and are manufactured in the same way—instrumentally; they only *seem* different because Satan has switched instruments. Hence, aural contamination may occur in *Paradise Lost* more insidiously than previously supposed at a physical, nonrational level, not simply at the level of words or discernable harmonies, but rather on an elemental scale, where the actual material of sound and its physical disposition are embodied. Finally, that satanic sound is simultaneously highly artificial and environmental powerfully illustrates how Milton's vitalist universe accommodates and adapts aspects of mechanical materialism.

The episodes in books 4 and 9 wherein Satan causes Eve to dream and the serpent to speak contain clues as to how Satan uses his meteorological power to produce acoustical deceptions. When Satan is discovered at Eve's ear, "assaying by his devilish art to reach / The *organs* of her fancy" (4.801–02; italics mine), the narrator uses an acoustical pun to depict one of the possible routes into her mind. Eve's fancy is an organ being played by Satan. Arguing that the "possibility of sin" enters the world through a voice that cannot be assigned singly to Satan, Stephen Hequembourg finds "no ground for asserting that Satan spoke, scripted, or serenaded" when he attempted to suborn Eve.[13] True, the text provides no evidence that Satan transfers verbal matter into Eve's mind, but there are compelling reasons to think that Satan subjects her to noxious sound when he manipulates the organs of her fancy to "forge / Illusions as he list, phantasms and dreams" (4.802–03). Milton places the devil at Eve's ear (what other kind of sensation passes through the ear but sound?), and the forgery he applies to her imaginative "organs" suggests the forge bellows used to power such instruments.[14]

Anticipating the smithing diction of forgery, the verb "assay," which describes Satan's trial of Eve's faculties, evokes the process of testing the composition or purity of metals.[15] This metallurgical meaning converges with yet another sense of "assay," first recorded in 1665 — to sound the depth of something.[16] These definitions subtly recall the acoustical method Satan employs to determine Eve's moral corruptibility. As navigators plumbed the depths of the sea, Satan's aim is to *sound* Eve's mind, and his evaluation of her as if she were precious ore corresponds to his reliance on, as we shall see, the metallic properties of instruments. The presence of organ terminology suggests that Satan's sounding of Eve is productive in addition to probing. The emanative and affective nature of his acoustics is evident in the text's other possible explanation of how Satan manipulates Eve: by "inspiring venom" (4.804). This inbreathed venom aims to taint Eve's animal spirits and inflate her desires (4.808–09). The word "inspire" is used again in book 9 to characterize Satan's transformation of the serpent's "brutal sense" into intelligent faculties (188–89). That Milton in each episode uses this verb, which denotes blowing or breathing into, to depict potential moments of contamination stresses the distinctly aerial conveyances through which Satan accesses and influences God's creatures.

The connection between Satan's meteorological identity and the serpent's acoustical animation is perhaps most manifest when Satan approaches the serpent as "a black mist" (9.180) and enters "at his mouth" (9.187). But the production of the serpent's speech is not simply a matter of possession. As with Eve's dream, which is engendered either by the organlike action of the fancy *or* by the more direct influx of "inspiring venom," the manufacture of the snake's speech, with "serpent tongue / Organic, *or* impulse of vocal air" (9.529–30; italics mine), hinges on two alternative explanations. In Eve's case, the options given for Satan's operation have been treated as identifying the different inferior faculties susceptible to demonic influence.[17] Taken alongside the description of the serpent's animation, however, the account of the dream's inception fits a pattern of alternation that points to different aspects of satanic instrumentation. By offering these alternatives, Milton implies that Satan has the ability to affect sounds via both the movement of *organs*, the actual apparatuses of sense and speech and, more mysteriously, through the spiritual transference or pulsation of air. Milton's refusal to identify which method—mechanical or spiritual—Satan employs is indicative of a representational strategy used throughout the epic that does not privilege one or the other side of the rebel angel's being.

Organs had a deep personal significance for Milton. John Aubrey records that he "had an organ in his house; he played on that most."[18] Outside of his home, Milton might have heard the music of John Tomkins, organist at St. Paul's and likely an associate of the elder John Milton, or that of the famous organist Frescobaldi, whom he could have heard while in Rome, mixing in the society of Cardinal Francesco Barberini.[19] Growing up the son of a composer no doubt afforded him ample exposure to the instrument. Milton seems to have taken some interest in the organ's history, noting in his Commonplace Book when it was first brought to France.[20] Not surprisingly, then, in *Of Education* the organ is twice recommended as an instrument that should be played after dinner for "recreating" the spirits (YP 2:410).

That the poet grew up around organ music and was himself an organist goes a long way toward explaining why the instrument is a recurring figure in *Paradise Lost*; but another rationale lies in the word's multiplicity of meanings, which include musical, biological, and mechanical senses. In Milton's time the word "organ" might denote a pipe, a specific body part, or any kind of mechanical instrument, such as a piece of artillery.[21] All of these senses are at play in Milton's descriptions of the bodily mechanisms through which Satan manipulates Eve and the serpent. The phrases "organs of her fancy" (4.801) and "serpent tongue / Organic" (9.529–30), which clearly designate the bodily sensitive faculties that receive Satan's attempts, also represent Eve and the serpent as Satan's musical instruments and machines. As we shall see, the organ is a leitmotif that connects the musical, mechanical, and bodily apparatuses through which Satan tempts and deceives.

Early in book 1 the fallen angels exhibit their command over both instruments and the atmosphere. Hell's "dusky air" (*PL* 1.226) attracts and disburdens them. It bears Satan's "unusual weight" (1.227) when he rises out of the flaming lake, and it is later pumped through flutes and recorders "blowing martial sounds" (1.540). "Breathing united force with fixèd thought" (1.560), the angels march silently along to piped music that "charmed / Their painful steps o'er the burnt soil" (1.561–62). They are revived not only by air and music but also by metals. Instrumental metal described as "sonorous" (1.540) rouses the martial spirits of the angelic hosts, and they lift their glinting weapons on high:

> Ten thousand banners rise into the air
> With orient colours waving: with them rose
> A forest huge of spears: and thronging helms
> Appeared, and serried shields in thick array
> Of depth immeasurable.   (1.545–49)

Finally, when they raise their imperial ensign, the "warlike sound / Of trumpets loud and clarions" rings out (1.531–32).

The striking prevalence of metals in this scene and the emphasis on their contact with air is intriguing. Why does Milton go to such lengths to enumerate the devils' weapons and surround them with sonorous music, breath, and the billowing wind overhead? The musical breezes that surround and permeate the defeated rebel angels portend their future status as rulers of the postlapsarian air. But the question of the metals remains. Aristotle attributes the generation of metals to the submersion in the ground and the condensation of certain vapors that he calls exhalations. He conjectures that moist exhalation turns to metal through cooling and by coming into contact with rocks.[22] By Aristotle's logic, then, metal should emerge from the devils' contact with hell's rocky surface, since, as spirits of air, the fallen angels resemble exhalations trapped beneath the ground.[23] They are likened to dense vapor when Satan, summoning them from off the burning lake and onto "firm brimstone" (1.350), is compared with Moses calling up the locusts over Egypt in a "pitchy cloud" (1.340). The demons are surrounded by metal instruments as a consequence of their moving like a front of vaporous air through hell's atmosphere.

The comparison of the devils' ensign with "a meteor streaming to the wind" (1.537) prefigures their meteorological potential and plans for atmospheric domination. The image puns on the definition of the word μετέωρον, of which "meteor" is a transliteration: "something raised up."[24] The account of the streaming ensign thus symbolically corresponds to the defiant hell-rending shout "upsent" (1.541) by the devils and the rising motion of their weapons. In the Renaissance the term "meteor" "covered all atmospheric processes and anomalies," including the weather itself as well as comets, stones, and metals.[25] The rising motion of exhalation underlies all of these phenomena and characterizes the devil's acoustics.[26] This crucial description of the fallen angels raising their imperial banner elucidates the moment when Satan raises passions in Eve, "*blown up* with high conceits" (4.809; my italics) from the vapors of her animal spirits. Meteorlike, these prideful notions are the remnant or "flag" that Satan leaves behind in her mind. By mixing with her spirits, Satan's venomous inspiration establishes the internal physio-meteorological climate that renders her a fit instrument of his purpose.

The potential movement of satanic breath through the veins of Eve's body parallels the action of "liquid fire" (1.701) and molten ore through the venous matrix of Pandaemonium. The conceits used to describe how the devils construct their great capitol by preparing and recasting liquid gold imply their material presence in the structure of Pandaemonium, which as they build they infuse with their spirituous being:

> As in an organ from one blast of wind
> To many a row of pipes the sound-board breathes.
> Anon out of the earth a fabric huge
> Rose like an exhalation.   (1.708–11)

The first simile links the fallen spirits with organ-blowers who pump the "blast of wind" through the organlike mold. But as flexible powers of air, the spirits are also materially associated with the fluid substance that passes like wind through its pipes and hardens into the golden walls of the palace. The second simile solidifies this connection. The meteorological image of "exhalation" explicitly identifies the demons with their edifice. The golden, metallic fabric of Pandaemonium is *like an exhalation* because it was made by exhalationlike beings and is affiliated with their substance.

By implying a physical relationship among air, gold, and the pipe organ's music, Milton elaborates an ancient theory that attributed the sonority of metals to their porous and aerated internal structures.[27] Albertus Magnus believed that gold, silver, and copper were more resonant than other metals because they contain a superior balance of "subtle water and subtle earth," and also a substantial amount of vapor.[28] Albertus writes, "for this reason these metals are strongly resonant and retain the sound for a long time, because they are full of air, and, when vibrating as a result of a strong blow, they continuously expel air from themselves."[29] By alluding to the airy, exhalationlike properties of the gold used to construct Pandaemonium, Milton underscores its function as an acoustical space, producing sweet music and the charming sound of the devils' political rhetoric.

That pipes, recorders, trumpets, and clarions are intimately connected with the demonic in *Paradise Lost* is not wholly surprising;

according to an ancient tradition, wind instruments were considered less noble than strings and were thought to promote the passions.[30] Yet wind instruments also appear in heaven's symphonies, so Milton's treatment of pipes and horns appears to complicate this classical prejudice.[31] Milton's use of the pipe organ—his favorite instrument—to characterize the construction of Pandaemonium where Satan and his followers plot the Fall is similarly perplexing. His closeness to the instrument may have uniquely positioned him to appreciate what might be characterized as its central subterfuge, that a single operator may, with relative ease, create and control a massive, almost unearthly sound. While susceptible to the sublime power of the organ's sound, the organist is always perfectly aware of its cause: an elaborate network of bellows, tanks, stops, and pipes that transform and amplify the machine's initial source of air. Because the organ's miraculous-seeming sound is actually highly engineered—Marin Mersenne called the instrument "one of the most admirable pneumatic machines ever invented"—it aptly symbolizes the artifice of satanic acoustics.[32] The organ simile implies, then, that Satan achieves his impressive-sounding transformation of hell's soil through mere artifice or workmanship. This may have aroused disdain from some of Milton's early readers, for whom the study of mechanics would not have qualified as a liberal art. When John Wilkins published *Mathematical Magick* in 1648, he lamented the persistent bias against practical or artificial (as opposed to divine or natural) investigations in philosophy and declared they should be treated "with greater industry and respect, than they commonly meet with in these times."[33] As late as the nineteenth century, Leigh Hunt hesitated to call the organ a "machine," although a more suitable term than "instrument," because of the lasting stigma: machinery brings "the mechanism itself, however fine and skillful, somewhat too strongly before us."[34] Milton's simile *deliberately* brings the mechanism before us, inviting us to inspect the organ's sound board and many rows of pipes and imagine the passages, like those of the building's "various mould" (*PL* 1.706), that carry air to each row. While contemplating this fascinating description involves a great degree of pleasure, the association of fallen angels with organ builders, nevertheless, reflects their demoted metaphysical status. That Milton has Mammon, "the least erected spirit that fell" (1.679), lead the excavations for the building project expresses the low standing of the mechanical arts in hell.

In addition to disparaging the devils' accomplishment, the analogy of Pandaemonium to a mechanical pipe organ associates their work with magic. Wilkins references the commonplace confusion of mechanical operation with magic when he writes of his book's title, "This whole Discourse I call *Mathematical Magick,* because the art of such Mechanical inventions as are here chiefly insisted upon, hath been formerly so styled; and in allusion to vulgar opinion, which doth commonly attribute all such strange operations unto the power of Magick."[35] His point is that geometry or applied mathematics, rather than magic, lies behind the marvels that philosophers of old veiled under "mystical expressions, as might excite the peoples wonder and reverence, fearing lest a more easie and familiar discovery, might expose them to contempt."[36] Magic, whether genuine or purported, is employed in the construction of Pandaemonium. Its indoor lamps are suspended by "subtle magic" (1.727), and its foundations are laid with "wondrous art" (1.703) and "strange conveyance" (1.707). Such language obscures the devils' actual means of accomplishing their engineering feats, just as the ancient philosophers in Wilkins's account veiled their arts in secrecy. But the organ simile, by openly depicting the instrument's mechanism, discloses the constructedness of hell's temple.

Milton's use of the alternate strategies of veiling and revealing to describe the devils' assembly of their capitol building is calculated. By integrating simile with direct representation and layering allusions to magic with detailed accounts of the demons' engineering techniques, he keeps the precise nature of satanic industry ambiguous. The devils' powers are magical in that they utterly excel the industry of human beings, and yet their reliance on artifice or craft reminds us that their abilities are less than divine and undeserving of admiration.[37]

If the entanglement of magic and mechanism in Milton's description of Pandaemonium betrays something like Wilkins's skepticism of the occult, it also paints an unflattering picture of the acoustical machines that interest Wilkins. Milton's idea of hell's instruments as responsive to environmental forces is neither original nor purely fictional for his time. In *Mathematical Magick* Wilkins mentions an automatic virginal, a type of harpsichord that, much like Satan's instruments, generates sound through its clever engineering and the application of meteorological power. This device, attributed to the inventor Cornelius Drebbel (1572–1633), allegedly played music when placed in the sun and would cease to play when removed from sunlight. "The warmth of the sun," Wilkins explains, "working upon some moisture within it, and rarifying the inward air unto so great an extension, that it must needs seek for a vent or issue, did thereby give several motions unto the instrument."[38] Wilkins's empirically exact account of this remarkable instrument explains how a simple movement of air, or pneumatics, can propel a mechanism that produces what seems to be a magical, self-generating sound. By allowing readers to "see"—at least partially—both the mechanism of hell's organ and the airy spirits that pneumatically bring it to life, Milton similarly exposes Pandaemonium's apparently magical acoustics as the product of artful engineering. Milton and Wilkins part ways, however, in their regard for mechanical genius; for Wilkins it opens up wonderful possibilities, while in Milton's description of hell, it is the devil's handiwork.

We have seen from Aristotle's theory of metals, which remained part of the meteorological tradition through the Renaissance, that the aerial bodies of Milton's devils are implicated in the very material of their instruments. Likewise, the natural philosophy of Albertus Magnus—which suggests that the more air contained in the metal instrument, the better the sound—implies that the quality of satanic acoustics depends on their direct involvement in the fabrication of their instruments. This explains in part why wind and metal instruments that appear in heaven become weapons in the hands of the devils. The narrator does not describe the creation or mechanical workings of heaven's pipes, organs, or golden harps. They appear complete, "ever tuned" (*PL* 3.366) and organismlike in their labor to please God with song (7.594–97). In contrast, the poem emphasizes the making and mechanisms of the instruments of hell, thereby disclosing the corporeal yet perversely artificial relation between the demons and their sound makers.

The corporeality of satanic instrumentation in *Paradise Lost* may also evoke and satirize Catholic ceremonies meant to protect consecrated metal from demonic spirits. The Catholic ceremony of "baptizing" church bells, a practice that was formalized in the tenth century, was thought to imbue them with sounds capable of repelling Satan and his agents of weather.[39] According to the service for the benediction of bells in the 1595 Roman Pontifical of Clement VIII, after bathing and anointing the bells with the sign of the cross, the bishop would give the following blessing:

> And when its (*their*) melody shall fall upon the ears of the people, may they receive an increase of Faith; may all the snares of the enemy, the crash of hail-storms, hurricanes, the violence of tempests be driven far away; may the deadly thunder be weakened, may the winds become salubrious, and be kept in check; may the right hand of Thy strength overcome the powers of the air, so that hearing this bell (*these bells*) they may tremble and flee before the standard of the holy cross of Thy Son depicted upon it (*them*).[40]

Medieval and early modern church bells across Europe bore inscriptions that echo this challenge to the "powers of air."[41]

Verses from the late fifteenth century bell tower at Gulval Church, Cornwall, for instance, declared that its pealing bells had the power to banish whatever forces—banal, meteorological, or demoniacal—might impede one from attending church:

> Who hears the bell, appears betime,
> And in his seat against we chime.
> Therefore I'd have you not to vapour,
> Nor blame yᵉ lads that use the Clapper,
> By which are scared the fiends of hell,
> And all by virtue of a bell.[42]

Belief in the efficacy of church bells encouraged many parishes to ring them during thunderstorms.[43] Well into the nineteenth century, Longfellow dramatized this custom in the prologue to *The*

Golden Legend, which depicts the bells of Strasbourg Cathedral defending the church against Lucifer who attacks in the form of a storm. His thwarted "Powers of the Air" complain,

> All thy thunders
> Here are harmless!
> For these bells have been anointed,
> And baptized with holy water!
> They defy our utmost power.[44]

The structure of Pandaemonium resembles these parish bells materially and symbolically. Made with the resonant material of gold and compared with an exhaling pipe organ, the "archèd roof" (*PL* 1.726) of Satan's temple is designed to reverberate like a bell. The freshly christened appearance of Satan's temple, "new rubbed with balm" (1.774), corresponds with the custom of applying holy water and oil to the consecrated bells.[45] Similarly, the palace's pneumatic origins, in a hill that emanated "fire and rolling smoke" (1.671), recall the ceremonial practice of fumigating *campanae* with incense.[46] Like the "thick" and "airy crowd" (1.775) of spirits who fill the palace as if they are fairies making "jocund music" (1.787), fumes of incense flow into the bell during *its* inaugural ceremony, and invest it with talismanic, acoustical power.

And yet, the moral function of the bells of Christendom is diametrically opposed to that of Pandaemonium, however structurally similar Satan's palace may be. The acoustical properties of Satan's temple consolidate and reinforce his power over the air, rather than dispersing it as the bells were supposed to do. Acting as a literal sounding board for the devils' machinations, the acoustics of Pandaemonium invert the apotropaic effects ascribed to pealing church bells or similar metal instruments like the ancient Roman *tintinnabulum* (demon-repelling wind chimes).[47] This key difference gives Milton's invention satirical energy. Without denying that "sonorous metal" can influence atmospheric phenomena, Milton uses Pandaemonium to critique those who employ musical instruments to subdue or control the spirit world.

Besides the Catholic clergy, other potential targets of this satire include Paracelsian alchemists like Heinrich Khunrath (1560–1605), whose major treatise, *Amphitheatrum sapientiae aeternae*, was published posthumously in 1609. Penelope Gouk argues that Khunrath and his circle regarded instrumental music as essential to alchemical practice because it enabled the philosopher to improve his spiritual health and more successfully commune with God.[48] "Particular musical instruments were thought to provide access to the human *spiritus* through their harmony, a process that made it possible to restore balance between body and soul, and especially to alleviate melancholy."[49] Not only can music refresh the alchemist, whose soul was particularly susceptible to melancholia, it also protects him from evil spirits.[50] The enthusiasm for instrumental music that obtained in Paracelsian alchemical circles around 1600 sheds light on the Miltonic phrase "sounding alchemy" (*PL* 2.517). This obscure phrase is usually interpreted as a synecdoche for hell's trumpets, but it also likely alludes to the mystical belief that music and alchemy are mutually necessary for achieving good health and spiritual understanding.[51] Milton's usage does not reflect positively on the aims or efficacy of this type of alchemy. Surrounded by rousing music issuing from alchemically and meteorologically forged instruments, Satan is analogized to the magus who uses music to rejuvenate his melancholic soul and increase his spiritual prowess. Because hell's music emboldens rather than impedes Satan and his followers, Milton implies the hubris and futility of attempting to ward off evil with musical instruments. This is not to say that Milton denied music's rejuvenating properties; he recommends the prophylactic use of organ music in *Of Education*. More disturbing than a humanistic practice that incorporates musical performance, however, is an alchemical one because of its dubious association with metals.

Part demonology, part satire, the description of the demons' acoustical activities in book 1 of *Paradise Lost* reveals vital information about the satanic production of sounds, often through ironic allusion to human-made acoustics. We are shown that the devils' meteorological power and mechanical skill are physically realized in their instruments, while subtly reminded that there are people who also use instruments devilishly, with spiritual pretensions or technological hubris. In addition to parodying those who make idols of their instruments, the passages from book 1 shed light on the ontology of satanic acoustics. Readers learn that satanic sounds are instrumental—they pass through and are transfigured by some kind of device—and that metal instruments in particular, whose very fabric and resonating cavity were each thought to contain air, are prone to satanic appropriation. The devils make the counterfeiting of sweet, sublime, and, finally, human sounds into a mainstay of their ongoing rebellion. Instruments or instrumentlike mechanisms enable the demons to convert meteorological resources into deceptive sounds like the "dulcet symphonies and voices sweet" that waft out of the pipe organ-like structure of Pandaemonium and, as we shall see, the words that mysteriously emerge from the serpent's "organic" tongue (*PL* 1.712).

Marin Mersenne's encyclopedic *Harmonie universelle* (1636–37) discusses the receptivity of wind instruments to all sorts of in-blown air: "it is certain that the instruments (of which we are speaking) are able to sound with every sort of wind, whether it comes in as the simple motion of air, as that of the bellows which serve organs and musettes, or whether it is mixed of vapors and water, like that of the mouth, which is so full of moisture that the reeds and tubes of the instrument become all damp and wet."[52] The final image of moisture from the musician's body commingling with the instrument recalls the confusion of the fallen angels' breath with their martial instruments as well as their exhalationlike bodies with the animating wind inside Pandaemonium. Raphael's description in book 6 of the rebel angels being crushed by heaven's uprooted mountains illustrates even more plainly how their substance may be transformed into the very medium of sound. The pun on the word "wind" in Raphael's remark that Satan's troops took a long time to *"wind* / Out of" their suits of armor (*PL* 6.659–60; my italics), compares the crushed spirits to the meteorological forces they will control in the fallen world. The play on words also suggests that the spirits resemble the "wind" inside of instruments.[53] As in hell their exhalationlike bodies supply the wind and music emanating from its grand pipe organ, so in heaven do they expel sounds from pipelike chambers:

"Their armour helped their harm, crushed in and bruised / Into their substance pent, which wrought them pain / Implacable, and many a dolorous groan" (6.656–58). The word "pent" used to describe the rebel angels' confinement within their metal armor evokes Francis Bacon's characterization of the disposition of the air inside of wind instruments and pipe organs. Bacon uses this term repeatedly to describe the necessary physical conditions for propagating sound: "where the air is pent and straitened, there breath or other blowing, (which carry but a gentle percussion) suffice to create sound; as in pipes and wind-instruments."[54] The acoustical diction Milton uses to describe the constriction or penning in of the angels' vaporous bodies analogizes them to the air within musical instruments and represents their groans as the notes emitted by flutes or a pipe organ.

Early readers would be especially apt to visualize the demons as embodying instruments because of familiar representations in the visual arts. Two artworks inspired by Athanasius's *Life of St. Anthony*, for instance, depict demons playing or carrying instruments and with pipe or horn appendages.[55] Jacques Callot's 1635 etching, *The Temptation of St. Anthony*, is particularly creative and grotesque in the ways it imagines devils using their bodies instrumentally. One demon strums the lute and another plays a horn protruding from his anus. In the foreground, a large scaly creature—wheeled and fired like a cannon—blasts smoke, ammunition, and presumably a terrible noise into the fray. Another devil, from the prospect of a cloud, spews out toxic sounds and gasses from his buttocks. Callot's image thus graphically captures the early modern conception of the demonic body. Its organs, artificial rather than biological, are incorporated musical instruments, engines, and implements that enable the demon to harass humans. Satan risks becoming like these musical cyborgs as he increasingly embodies his status as prince of the air and uses it as a platform for acoustical warfare. In the mountain-throwing episode, his troops fall victim to their own violent acoustical methods when crushed by their armor and unwillingly transformed into instruments. Their pitiful concert of groans darkly doubles hell's "dulcet symphonies." It also anticipates Satan's instrumentation of Eve and the serpent, and finally, the moment in book 10 when the devils are reduced to hissing serpents. Trapped in their suits of armor, their sounds are involuntary—a condition of their bodily imprisonment and punishment.[56]

Raphael's account of the war in heaven reveals the rebel angels' meteorological procedure for lacing sounds with fraud. Satan's "hollowed" (*PL* 6.574) engines—"deep-throated" (6.586) instruments with "mouths" (6.587) that roar, belch, and exhale smoke—illustrate the duplicitous and destructive aspects of his acoustics. The artillery causes havoc for the good angels in the usual way, by scattering their ranks with "balls / Of missive ruin" (6.518–19). But it also serves up a different kind of ammunition in the form of a piercingly loud and deceptive blast. By siphoning "sulphurous and nitrous" (6.512) meteorological materials into their cannons, Satan and his crew attempt to make a weapon that sounds as terrifying as thunder, the coveted armament of God.[57] They succeed at least in producing an exceedingly violent and startling sound, "embowell[ing] with outrageous noise the air" (6.588). In one respect, this language creates the impression that ethereal air is corporeal and endowed with viscera vulnerable to the mangling force of demoniac sound. But the word "embowel" may also suggest the animal bladders used as the bagpipe's wind reservoir, implying that the heavenly air undergoes a kind of violence associated with satanic instrumentation.[58] Much as heaven's "materials dark and crude" (6.478) become the explosive charges for the rebels' outrageous artillery, so the air is crudely "convey[ed] into the bowels" of the instrument the devils aim to make of the entire atmosphere: a resonator of false thunder.[59] The opposing senses of the word "embowel," which can denote both the loss of and the filling up of guts, paradoxically render the air an eviscerated yet acoustically repurposed space.

If the blast of Satan's engines is meant to simulate the intimidating sound of thunder, then the initial appearance of the cannons augurs an altogether different kind of sound. To the puzzled or "amused" (*PL* 6.581) faithful angels, their shape expresses vocality: "their mouths / With hideous orifice gaped on us wide, / Portending hollow truce" (6.576–78). As the novel appearance of the cannons momentarily diverts the heavenly soldiers, early modern readers may have connected their arresting appearance with that of the basilisk, an imposing-looking medieval cannon that was aptly named after a mythical serpent who kills its prey with a glance. Thus, while Adam and Eve could not have intuited the serpentine associations of the weapons in Raphael's tale, early audiences likely understood the cannons as a direct type of the serpent in the garden, attributing their disarming appearance, shrewd mechanism, and violent acoustics to the latter satanic instrument.

Each of the episodes discussed thus far shows Satan making and using different kinds of organs. The grand organ blast of the infernal council, the demons' embodiment of instruments in their metal garments of war, and their fabrication of military engines that are as brutally violent as they are loud, illustrate the rich interplay between the musical, corporeal, and technological senses of organ. The demons' ability to fashion these organs and make each of them sound depends on their meteorological bodies, that is, their similarity to wind and the pneumatic ingredient in metals. Satan clearly draws on his embodied experience with organic devices when he inspires Eve's dream and animates the snake. But how does he counterfeit human speech in the body of an animal?

Satan's acoustical career may be said to culminate in his vocalization of the serpent, which under his influence becomes yet another sort of instrument. For early modern readers of *Paradise Lost*, this transformation would have required no stretch of the imagination. As early as the sixteenth century, a wind instrument called the serpent was being used in France to accompany church choirs.[60] This impressive horn—some were eight feet long—takes its name from the snaky shape of its tube, whose initial *S* curve repeats itself in a wider loop at the bottom of the instrument.[61] That Milton was aware of this instrument is evident from its resemblance to Eden's serpent. Brass or other kinds of metal were sometimes used to make serpents; but they were typically constructed of wood and wrapped with leather.[62] Often they were fitted with a brass crook, a piece of tube inserted between the mouthpiece and the body of the instrument in order to change its tone.[63] A flash of metal appears on Milton's serpent in the same place. We are told that he has a "burnished neck of verdant gold" (*PL* 9.501). More significantly, the snake's erect stature as it approaches Eve "on his rear, / Circular base of rising folds, that towered / Fold above fold a surging maze" (9.497–99) mirrors the ascending, folded appearance of the horn. It too has a "circular base"; the lowermost coil curls around until it almost closes. Furthermore the word "base," in Milton's description, may allude to the low register of the serpent whose deep tones were especially valued for filling out the bass parts in choral music.[64] According to Mersenne's account, the serpent is "capable of supporting twenty very strong voices," and its tone may be easily modulated, "so that it will be suitable to join with the soft voices of chamber music, whose graces and diminutions it imitates."[65] The versatility of the musical serpent matches the subtlety of Milton's snake, who shifts his tone mid-argument in response to Eve (9.664–68). If he had not witnessed a serpent being performed himself, then Milton could have seen striking illustrations of them in Mersenne's *Harmonie universelle* and Athanasius Kircher's *Musurgia universalis*.[66]

Milton's characterization of Satan as an operator and maker of instruments appears all the more strategic in that, in his day, serpents were actual instruments used in concert music to augment and imitate the human voice. In the late Renaissance, large organs began to be built with pipes that were designed to sound like the human voice.[67] Controlled with an organ stop called the vox *humana*, this feature is still used in theater organs today.[68] The two-pronged account of Satan's method of inspiring the serpent ("with serpent tongue / Organic, or impulse of vocal air") leads Hequembourg to the forked question: "Is the serpent more like a singer or more like a trumpet?"[69] Drawing such a dichotomy on the basis of these phrases, however, misinterprets the word "tongue" and ignores the polysemy of the word "organic" and its allusion to Satan's history of using, making, or embodying instruments. The narrator's interjection after the serpent tries his wiles on Eve, "so glozed the tempter, and his proem *tuned*" (*PL* 9.549; italics mine), continues the idea that the serpent is being used instrumentally. Indeed, that instrumental serpents were a feature of the Renaissance musical world suggests that Satan speaks to Eve in the language of instruments—in a "tongue / Organic."

Some pipe organ terminology is necessary to decipher this phrase. Organ pipes come in two different types—flues and reeds; the former kind emits air through a simple slit in the side of the pipe called a "mouth"; the latter type incorporates a metal reed called the "tongue."[70] The *OED* gives 1551 as the earliest date "tongue" was used in this precise context.[71] The positioning of the tongue is essential for the tuning of the organ pipe: "the choice of the sounding frequency is basically made by the reed, and the air column must follow."[72] Thus, the text's equivocation about how Satan manages what we might call "the serpent trick" is not about whether the snake is a complicit singer or a passive trumpet. The serpent undoubtedly serves as an instrument. The textual vacillation refers to, rather, the tempter's acoustical technique. We must keep in mind two conceptions of Satan. The first is of a mechanical genius who uses the tuning mechanism of the tongue to determine the frequency of each note. The second conception (foregrounding "impulse of vocal air") is of Satan as a spiritual and aerial being; enclosed in the serpent, possibly even in its windpipe, Satan vibrates with sound, his aerial body serving as the column of moving air within an instrument.[73]

In the early modern period, the word "impulse" might denote the "[f]orce or influence exerted on the mind" by a good or evil spirit.[74] The serpent's artificial language immediately impresses Satan's spiritual influence on Eve's mind. Its impulse of air travels into Eve's ear and then her mind and heart, causing her to marvel greatly at the voice and provoking this demand: "redouble then this miracle, and say, / How cam'st thou speakable of mute" (*PL* 9.562–63). Just four lines later, Eve redoubles her own speech, still uttered in the imperative mood: "say, for such wonder claims attention due" (9.566). Her rhythmic repetition of this monosyllabic word, "say / ... / Say," echoes the serpent's acoustical impulse in her mind. She resonates to his sounds. Keeping these reverberations alive in Eve's organs—indeed, inspiring her to continue them vocally in the highly echoic language she uses to ponder the interdicted fruit—is crucial to Satan's success (9.745–79). Even after he ends his argument, "in her ears the sound / Yet rung of his persuasive words" (9.736–37), its aural power over Eve's mind undampened. These lines bear an unsettling likeness to the description of Adam, added to the poem in 1674, listening to Raphael's magnificent account of the world's creation, and before that, of the war in heaven. After Raphael ends his narration, Adam thinks mistakenly that the angel is still speaking, for "in Adam's ear / So charming left his voice" (8.1–2). Raphael's voice seems to dilate like the serpent's speech in the listener's ear, even after the words are uttered, raising doubts about how safely *any* sound can be conveyed in the organs of its auditors.

Such a doubt may also underlie Milton's anxious desire to find a "fit audience" (*PL* 7.31) for his poem. The perils of communication lie not only in human organs, but also in the passage of sound into written and then printed form. Bruce Smith, a scholar keenly attuned to the embodiment of sound in early modernity, notes that "at every step in the process that transforms a manuscript into a printed text, a body of some sort interposes itself between the act of speaking and the act of reading."[75] On its way to publication, Milton's poem passed through the bodies of the amanuenses who heard and transcribed its words, as well as the various, often metal, apparatuses of the printing house, whose components bore the names of body parts.[76] The "evil tongues" (7.26), then, of book 7 may be interpreted both as a synecdoche of Milton's corrupt political environment and a suitably organic figure for the satanic acoustics of the fallen atmosphere. In commenting on the composition of his epic, Milton acknowledges that evil "dissonance" (7.32) threatens to invade the sound of his song as it passes through bodies and instruments. What I have been calling satanic acoustics, the artificial animation of organs by corrupt meteorological materials, therefore, is a potential outcome of reading or hearing *Paradise Lost*, an outcome of which the poem is aware. Milton's wish, implicit in the lines he added to the epic in the final year of his life, is that readers too will be recreated by its sound as Adam emerges from Raphael's tale "as new waked" (8.4).

University of Texas, Austin

Notes

I am grateful to attendees of the "Soundscapes in *Paradise Lost*" panel at the Eleventh International Milton Symposium, the *Milton Studies* anonymous readers, Laura Knoppers, and, in particular, John Rumrich, for their valuable insights, feedback, and support, all of which enriched and strengthened this essay.

1. On the basis of "the single effect of grandeur of sound," Eliot finds that there is "nothing finer in poetry" than what Milton's achieves. T. S. Eliot, "Milton I," in *On Poetry and Poets* (New York, 1957), 158, 164; originally printed in *Essays and Studies of the English Association* as "A Note on the Verse of John Milton" (Oxford, 1936). Eliot means "best" in a both a personal and a relative sense (i.e., compared to other poets).

2. The downside of what Eliot dubs Milton's "rhetorical style" is "that a dislocation takes place, through the hypertrophy of the auditory imagination at the expense of the visual and tactile, so that the inner meaning is separated from the surface, and tends to become something occult, or at least without effect upon the reader until fully understood" (ibid., 162).

3. John Leonard's ample account of the "Milton controversy" of the twentieth century and its roots in early Milton criticism traces, among other things, fluctuating opinions of Milton's sonorous style. Leonard identifies Daniel Webb's *Remarks on the Beauties of Poetry* (1762) as the first work of criticism to connect the sound of Milton's blank verse to organ music. In the nineteenth century, Leigh Hunt, Tennyson, and James Russell Lowell used an organ metaphor to discuss Milton's musical virtuosity. However, Leonard explains that, subsequent to Ezra Pound's critique of Milton's highly Latinized language, "the 'sonority' that had hitherto been seen as a virtue will be seen as a vice, and eulogies of Milton's 'organ music' will only harden the opposition." John Leonard, *Style and Genre*, vol. 1 of *Faithful Labourers: A Reception History of "Paradise Lost," 1667–1970* (Oxford, 2013), 59–265, 174. For Leavis's disparagement of the pompous sound of Milton's poetry, see "Milton's Verse," *Scrutiny* 2 (1933): 126.

4. Marc Berley, *After the Heavenly Tune: English Poetry and the Aspiration to Song* (Pittsburgh, 2000), 180–205, reads *Paradise Lost*

as deeply influenced by speculative music in its cultivation of a poetic of striving for heavenly song. Stephen M. Buhler, "Counterpoint and Controversy: Milton and the Critiques of Polyphonic Music," in *Milton Studies*, vol. 36, ed. Albert C. Labriola (Pittsburgh, 1998), 18–40, argues that Milton's depiction of polyphonic music reinforces arguments made by reformers against contrapuntal music. Erin Minear's analysis of *Paradise Lost in Reverberating Song in Shakespeare and Milton: Language, Memory, and Musical Representation* (Surrey, England, 2011), 227–56, explores the poem's evaluation of verbal and nonverbal forms of music and its self-representation by these standards. Joseph M. Ortiz, *Shakespeare and the Politics of Music* (Ithaca, N.Y., 2011), 213–42, contends that in *A Maske* Milton employs music in protest of Reformist strictures that would eliminate figuration.

5. "The tendency has been to think in 'logocentric' terms, as if there were language, and then as a separate and unrelated category, non-linguistic sound.... What an 'acoustic approach' can bring to this discussion, though, is the observation that *Paradise Lost* confounds language and music with all other sorts of noise into a continuum." Matthew Steggle, "*Paradise Lost* and the Acoustics of Hell," *Early Modern Literary Studies* 7, no. 1 (2001): 12. Beverley Sherry argues in "Milton, Materialism, and the Sound of *Paradise Lost*," *Essays in Criticism* 60, no. 3 (2010): 220–41, that the sound of the epic is "material and animate" (220), like every other part of Milton's cosmos, and that its substance is endued with spirit, or animated, by the poet's creative process.

6. For example, Bulher connects "an alertness toward music's affective powers" in Milton's poetry to the prevalent notion among reformers that "polyphony's appeal to the senses cannot be balanced by language's appeal to the rational soul" ("Counterpoint and Controversy," 19–20).

7. John Milton, *Paradise Lost*, ed. Alastair Fowler, 2nd ed. (Harlow, England, 1998), book 9, line 734, p. 513. All quotations of *Paradise Lost* are from this edition and hereafter will be cited in the text by book and line number.

8. Sherry, "Milton, Materialism, Sound," 224.

9. Katherine Cox, "The Power of the Air in Milton's Epic Poetry," *SEL* 56, no. 1 (2016), 149–70. The quotation is from the King James Version of the Bible.

10. Satan's "place" in the latter epic, for example, is described as the "mid air." *Milton: The Complete Shorter Poems*, 2nd ed., ed. John Carey (Harlow, England, 2007), line 39, p. 426.

11. In a rare analysis of the air in *Paradise Lost*, Jayne Elizabeth Lewis connects its fall with the rise of what she calls "literary atmosphere" in the long eighteenth century. For Lewis, Satan's influence on the atmosphere of paradise renders it analogous to the literary medium of Milton's poem: the fallen air becomes visible, material, and limitedly expressive.

This reading, though valuable for its appreciation of literary atmospheric resonance, discounts the consistently acoustical nature of Satan's pneumatic incursions and ignores their meteorological genesis. Jayne Elizabeth Lewis, *Air's Appearance: Literary Atmosphere in British Fiction, 1660–1794* (Chicago, 2012), 36–40, 53–54.

12. Minear, *Reverberating Song,* 234.

13. Stephen Hequembourg, "Milton's 'Unoriginal' Voice: Quotation Marks in *Paradise Lost,*" *Modern Philology* 112, no. 1 (2014): 159.

14. Forge bellows were used to supply air to pipe organs, replacing more fragile animal bladders with a technology originally intended for stoking fires; see Douglas Earl Bush and Richard Kassel, *The Organ: An Encyclopedia* (New York, 2006), 63.

15. *Oxford English Dictionary Online,* June 2016, s.v. "assay," v., 4.

16. Ibid., s.v. "assay," v., 6.

17. "Satan attempts in *Paradise Lost* to reach either directly to the organ of fancy, highest of the powers which he could subject to his rule, or alternatively (IV, 804) to the animal spirits which were the source of sense data and which would retain somewhat past experiences which he could mold to his own purposes." William B. Hunter, "Eve's Demonic Dream," *ELH* 13 (1946): 263.

18. John Aubrey, "Minutes of the Life of Mr. John Milton," in *The Complete Poetry and Essential Prose of John Milton,* ed. William Kerrigan, John Rumrich, and Stephen M. Fallon (New York, 2007), xxvii.

19. Sigmund Spaeth, *Milton's Knowledge of Music* (Ann Arbor, Mich., 1963), 16, 16n4, 22.

20. "Organs first in France. The ambassadors of the Greek Emperor Constantine brought King Pepin some organs, which had never before been seen in France." John Milton, *The Complete Prose Works of John Milton,* ed. Don M. Wolfe et al. (New Haven, Conn., 1953–82), 1:383; hereafter cited in the text as YP, followed by volume and page number.

21. *OED Online,* s.v. "organ," n., 1.

22. "The moist exhalation, then, is the material of the metals. Along with portions of the dry exhalation it is trapped underground, where it condenses, particularly if it comes into contact with rocks, and then hardens, probably through cold....Because the metals contain earthy matter, they cannot revert to water, and for the same reason they are, with the exception of pure gold, affected by fire"; paraphrase of Aristotle's theory from *Meteorologica,* in D. E. Eichholz, "Aristotle's Theory of the Formation of Metals and Minerals," *Classical Quarterly* 43 (1949): 143.

23. There was some disagreement about how metals came to be. While many Renaissance theorists thought that metals were derived from some combination of mercury, sulphur, and nitre, others identified exhalation as their primary ingredient. Harinder Marjara explains that the main ingredients thought to be involved in generating metals changed over time.

In the early Renaissance, alchemists believed that sulphur and mercury were responsible for the formation of metals; later, in the seventeenth century, sulphur and nitre were the preferred combination. Harinder Marjara, *The Contemplation of Created Things: Science in "Paradise Lost"* (Toronto, 1992), 172–78.

24. S. K. Heninger, *A Handbook of Renaissance Meteorology with Particular Reference to Elizabethan and Jacobean Literature* (Durham, N.C., 1960), 3.

25. Ibid., 4, 147–48.

26. Heninger gives a concise explanation of Aristotelian exhalation theory, the predominant meteorological model in the Renaissance (ibid., 9).

27. Pietro d'Abano links sonority to the inward structure of metal. Similar discussions appear in the pseudo-Aristotelian *Problemata* and the *Quaestiones* of Nicolaus Peripateticus; see Charles Burnett, "Sound and Its Perception in the Middle Ages," in *Studies in Hearing and Musical Judgement from Antiquity to the Seventeenth Century*, ed. Charles Burnett, Michael Fend, and Penelope Gouk (London, 1991), 51n70.

28. Ibid., 51.

29. "Et ideo ista sonora sunt vehementer et dui retinent sonum, eo quod aëre plena sunt, quae trementia ex ictu forti continue a se expellunt." Albertus Magnus, *Opera omnia*, vol. 7, *De anima*, ed. Clemens Stroick (Münster, Germany, 1955), 2.3.17.27–29, p. 124; translation by Burnett, "Sound and Its Perception," 51.

30. This opposition derives from the antagonism between the *kithara* and the *aulos* in the mythological contests between Apollo and Marsyas and Apollo and Pan, in which Phoebus's string music always triumphs over the satyrs' pipes. Plato denounces the playing of *aulos* as devoted only to pleasure in *Republic*, book 3. For the classical background and further discussion of historical symbolism of string and wind instruments, see Emanuel Winternitz, *Musical Instruments and Their Symbolism in Western Art* (New Haven, Conn., 1979), 150–65.

31. For instance, on the first Sabbath, "the solemn pipe, / And dulcimer, all organs of sweet stop" (*PL* 7.595–96) join the voices of heaven in a hymn of Creation.

32. Marin Mersenne, *The Books on Instruments*, trans. Roger E. Chapman (The Hague, 1957), book 6, p. 391. These books are part of the larger work, *Harmonie Universelle* (1636–37).

33. John Wilkins, *Mathematical Magick; or, the Wonders That May Be Performed by Mechanichal Geometry. In Two Books* (London, 1680), 10. For the distinction between divine, natural, and artificial sciences, see 1–2.

34. Leigh Hunt, "An Organ in the House (Introductory Article)," *The Musical Times and Singing Class Circular* 6, no. 130 (September 1, 1854): 159.

35. Wilkins, "To the Reader," in *Mathematical Magick*.

36. Ibid., 3–4.

37. The inconceivably swift construction of Pandaemonium outpaces humanity's greatest building feats (*PL* 1.692–99).

38. Wilkins, *Mathematical Magick*, 149. See also Penelope Gouk, *Music, Science and Natural Magic in Seventeenth-Century England* (New Haven, Conn., 1999), 168.

39. H. B. Walters, *Church Bells of England* (London, 1912), 256–57.

40. "Et cum melodia illius auribus insonuerit populorum, crescat in eis devotio fidei; procul pelantur omnes insidiæ inimici, fragor grandinum, procella turbinum, impetus tempestatum; temperentur infesta tonitrua; ventorum flabra fiant salubriter, ac moderate suspensa; prosternat aëreas potestates dextera tuæ virtutis; ut hoc audietes tintinnabulum contremiscant, & fugiant ante sanctæ crucis Filij tui in eo depictum vexillum." *Pontificale Romanum Clementis VIII* (Paris, 1615), 299. Translation by J. S. M. Lynch, *Right of the Blessing of a Bell, or of Several Bells, according to the Roman Pontifical* (New York, 1912), 23.

41. White, *History of the Warfare*, 345.

42. Walters, *Church Bells of England*, 263; see also the entry on the parish of Gulval in Joseph Polsue, *A Complete Parochial History of the County of Cornwall*, vol. 2 (Truro, England, 1868), 115–17. For the dates of the bell tower construction, see J. Charles Cox, *Cornwall* (London, 1912), 118.

43. Walters cites several church records that provide for bell ringing in the time of dangerous storms (*Church Bells of England*, 262).

44. Henry Wadsworth Longfellow, *The Golden Legend* (London, 1854), 1–2.

45. Lynch, *Blessing of a Bell*, 22.

46. William Smith and Samuel Cheetham, eds., *Dictionary of Christian Antiquities*, vol. 1 (London, 1876), 185.

47. In ancient Rome and Greece, livestock, warriors, and the deceased were all adorned with bells to ward off predators and evil spirits. Satis N. Coleman, *Bells: Their History, Legends, Making, and Uses* (Chicago, 1928), 26–28. On *tintinnulabum*, the protective symbol of the phallus was often displayed along with bells. An example of these protective chimes appears in Patricia Simons, *The Sex of Men in Premodern Europe: A Cultural History* (Cambridge, 2011), 55–56.

48. Penelope Gouk, "Transforming Matter, Refining the Spirit: Alchemy, Music and Experimental Philosophy around 1600," *European Review* 21, no. 2 (2013): 147–49, 155–56.

49. Ibid., 155.

50. Gouk observes that Khunrath and Agrippa both held sacred harmony as a deterrent to evil. She translates the inscription in an engraving entitled "Lab-Oratorium," from Khunrath's *Amphitheatrum sapientiae aeternae* (1595), depicting an assortment of stringed instruments in the

middle of an alchemist's laboratory, as follows: "Sacred Music is the dispeller of sadness and evil spirits, because the Spirit [Spiritus] of Jehovah gladly sings in a heart filled with pious joy" (ibid., 151).

51. Ibid., 146–47, 149, 155–56.

52. Mersenne, *Books on Instruments*, book 5, p. 294.

53. Milton uses "wind" in a similarly witty vein to characterize the pneumatic conveyance of sound in *L'Allegro* ("Lap me in soft *Lydian Aires,...*/ In notes, with many a winding bout" [136–39]) and in *A Maske* ("Wind me into the easie-hearted man" [163]). The word evokes the airy quality of sound that enables it to wiggle into physically and psychologically confined spaces. See *Poems of Mr. John Milton* (London, 1645).

54. Francis Bacon, *Sylva sylvarum*, in *The Works of Francis Bacon*, ed. James Spedding, Robert Ellis, and Douglas Heath, vol. 2 of 14 (London, 1857), 391, §116. See also, for example, 404, §164 and 422, §232.

55. A demon in the interior of Hieronymous Bosch's triptych of *The Temptations of St. Anthony* (c. 1500, Museu Nacional de Arte Antiga, Lisbon) is shown with a pommer (shawm) nose pipe. Others carry a harp, lute, and an organistrum. Nose pipes appear in at least four other scenes of hell by Bosch and his followers, and anus pipes in at least one; see John H. Planer, "Damned Music: The Symbolism of the Bagpipes in the Art of Hieronymus Bosch and His Followers," in *Music from the Middle Ages through the Twentieth Century: Essays in Honor of Gwynn McPeek*, ed. Carmelo P. Comberiati and Matthew C. Steel (New York, 1998), 340–41, tables 2 and 3. See also Jacques Callot, *The Temptation of St. Anthony*, c. 1635, Spencer Museum of Art, University of Kansas, discussed above.

56. Some of the embodied instruments in Bosch's works have been interpreted as symbols of punishment: "the instruments torment the damned directly by imprisoning them...; penetrating their orifices; or ensnaring them" (Planer, "Damned Music," 343).

57. Satan predicts that on hearing (and feeling) the effect of his cannons, the angels will "fear we have disarmed / The thunderer of his only dreaded bolt" (*PL* 6.490–91).

58. The sack of the bagpipe is typically "made of the skin or bladder of an animal, usually a goat or a sheep" (Winternitz, *Musical Instruments*, 67).

59. *OED Online*, s.v. "embowel," v., 3.a.

60. Murray Campbell, Clive Greated, and Arnold Myers, eds., *Musical Instruments: History, Technology, and Performance of Instruments of Western Music* (Oxford, 2004), 160. Traditionally, the inventor is given as Edmé Guillaume of Auxerre, France, and the date of invention, 1590.

61. "Appendix 3: Brass Instrument Sizes," in ibid., 478. The size of a typical serpent with a nominal pitch of C is eight feet.

62. Mersenne, *Books on Instruments*, book 5, p. 350. See also Campbell, Greated, and Myers, *Musical Instruments*, 159–60.

63. Campbell, Greated, and Myers, *Musical Instruments*, 160. Mersenne indicates that the crook, which he calls a tube, may be "ivory, horn, silver, or tin" (*Books on Instruments*, book 5, p. 353).

64. Mersenne, *Books on Instruments*, book 5, p. 353.

65. Ibid.

66. Athanasius Kircher, *Musurgia universalis* (Rome, 1650), 6.4.505.

67. Campbell, Greated, and Myers, *Musical Instruments*, 393.

68. S.v. "Vox Humana/Voix Humaine/Voce Umana," in Bush and Kassel, *The Organ*, 612.

69. Hequembourg, "Milton's 'Unoriginal' Voice," 173.

70. Campbell, Greated, and Myers, *Musical Instruments*, 387, 389.

71. *OED Online*, s.v. "tongue," n., 14.c.

72. Campbell, Greated, and Myers, *Musical Instruments*, 390.

73. Helkiah Crooke, in *A Description of the Body of Man* (1616), includes the windpipe or "weazon" in his account of the organs that produce the human voice. In the *The French Academie* (1618), Pierre de La Primaudaye refers to the human vocal apparatus as a portative organ. See Bruce Smith, *The Acoustic World of Early Modern England: Attending to the O-Factor* (Chicago, 1999), 4.

74. *OED Online*, s.v. "impulse," n., 3.a.

75. Smith, *Acoustic World*, 125.

76. See ibid., 125, on the organic names of early modern printing house technology.

Readers in (Literary) History

The Genius of Every Age: Milton and Dryden

Diana Treviño Benet

According to an old story, John Dryden asked John Milton for permission to "tag" *Paradise Lost,* and Milton granted it.[1] But after reading *The State of Innocence,* we may wonder how Milton would have responded if Dryden had explained that he meant to treat *Paradise Lost* as a builder might use an ancient structure, breaking it down to its smallest components and recycling some of the materials to erect a building with little resemblance to the first. Dryden omits the narrator and most of the heavenly characters from *Paradise Lost;* chops up many of its speeches, reassigning the bits and pieces to different characters; condenses the epic radically in the process of converting it into heroic drama, a genre with its own ethos; and tosses out Milton's theology. He cannibalizes the great Christian epic to create a work radically incompatible with Milton's aims and vision.

The result is so strange that scholars reading *The State of Innocence* have wildly differing views of it. Louis Martz considers it "basically serious...a religious poem," but Steven Zwicker dismisses it as a "ridiculous adaptation of *Paradise Lost.*"[2] Sharon Achinstein opines that Dryden's work is "not just a tagging of

Milton's lines but rather a thoughtful condensation and tightening of his language and structure," while Nicholas von Maltzahn argues that *State of Innocence* is an "outstanding contribution to English libertine literature" as well as "a Hobbesian recension of its more godly original."[3] In a different vein, Anthony Welch suggests that Dryden's opera was an "intervention in the reception history of *Paradise Lost*."[4] Barbara K. Lewalski proposes that Dryden's "opera-drama" is a challenge to the "essential substance as well as [the] style" of Milton's epic.[5] And recently, Joad Raymond calls it "a translation that discloses the shift in Restoration literary modes."[6] The work's hybrid nature accounts for the differing interpretations. *The State of Innocence* is Dryden's effort to supersede Milton's recently published epic with his own sexy, condensed, sometimes ridiculous dramatization of Milton's version of the Genesis story, tailored to his idea of the perspective and taste of the "modern" audience.

The State of Innocence represents a departure from the practice of poetic (as opposed to dramatic) literary appropriation that had been developing in England since Wyatt and Surrey translated Petrarch's sonnets.[7] Foreign works such as those Italian poems and the classics — the products of a different tongue or a distant time — were usually considered to be available for the taking. There were also some adaptations of contemporary English poetry that did not raise issues of property or literary honesty: answer poems; extensions of existing texts; parodies of amorous, topical, or political verses; and recastings of religious texts were unexceptionable.

In the context of the appropriation of English writers by other English writers, however, Dryden's 1677 publication of *The State of Innocence* is extraordinary. Although the first English author to be adapted was Shakespeare, Milton is the first poet whose published work was openly arrogated by a contemporary. As Marcie Frank exclaims, "Milton only died in 1674, the same year Dryden finished *The State of Innocence!*"[8] Dryden may have thought his appropriation was justified because some authors approved rewriting that involved generic as well as linguistic translation. "'Tis true," he wrote, "that where ever I have lik'd any story in a

Romance, Novel, or forreign Play, I have made no difficulty, nor
ever shall, to take the foundation of it, to build it up, and to make
it proper for the *English* Stage."[9] Since *Paradise Lost* was neither
ancient nor foreign, reasons of cultural or linguistic accessibility
that might have been supposed to make its rewriting desirable
were irrelevant; but Dryden might be said to "take the foundation"
of the epic to "make it proper for the *English* stage." And, indeed,
Lara Dodds has shown how well he "translated" some aspects of
"Milton's verse into theatrical effect."[10] However, Dryden's play
is not a straightforward adaptation of *Paradise Lost*. The fact that
The State of Innocence was written for the stage cannot account for
the drastic changes Dryden makes to the poem's character, meaning, and theology. This essay details the alterations that make
Dryden's appropriation an anomaly raising questions of motive
and intention.

Frank proposes that Dryden "makes discursively available
Milton's work, divorced from his political beliefs, recasting it as
a literary contribution to a native tradition." Similarly, Welch
argues that, in part, the "drastic rewriting of *Paradise Lost* was
meant to smooth out its political unorthodoxies." And Gordon
Campbell and Thomas Corns suggest that the opera "marks a stage
in Milton's rehabilitation with a wider reading public unsympathetic to his political beliefs."[11] But I disagree with suggestions
that the epic needed "rescuing" because it was read in a political
context. Von Maltzahn has shown that three contemporary readers were untroubled: Thomas Tomkins, the Episcopal licenser;
Sir John Hobart, the Parliamentarian; and John Beale, a minister
and fellow of the Royal Society, failed to see political implications
in Milton's epic.[12] As Joseph Wittreich concludes, "*Paradise Lost*
is obviously implanted with various interpretive codes, but in the
early receptions, even when the prevailing concerns suggest otherwise, it is the aesthetic code that predominates, and predominates
so completely, that the political code, when not fully silenced, is
sealed within insinuations."[13]

Dryden was preoccupied with the English literary past and with
securing his place within a tradition that he was himself in the

process of defining. He was the first author who struggled publicly with the national literary past, partly because his ambition perceived that past as burden or threat. And though Milton was Dryden's contemporary, he is, along with Shakespeare, in the first small group of authors whose genius makes them figures to reckon with. As Dustin Griffin points out, Milton and Dryden's "lives overlap by forty-three years, and [their] writing careers by twenty-five (1649 to 1674)."[14] Dryden boldly appropriated the work of a contemporary because Milton's accomplishment challenged him, and because Milton's "self-professed antiquity supplie[d] Dryden with the leverage he need[ed] to place him in the past."[15]

The State of Innocence was Dryden's effort to throw Milton, prematurely, into the new mausoleum of literary history—of which Dryden himself was architect-builder—and to relegate *Paradise Lost* to the heap of dead works superseded by progress and taste. By treating Milton's epic (before it was widely known) as the old-fashioned work of a bygone era, Dryden attempted to prevent it and Milton from occupying the cultural space that he aspired to occupy with his own oeuvre. To impose the principle of succession between himself and a contemporary, Dryden had to establish *Paradise Lost* as part of the literary past that he could "translate" for his own age. He had to produce a line of demarcation that would function as decisively as a temporal separation. The rewriting—the process and its product, *The State of Innocence*—was the concrete, literary barrier that Dryden erected to separate the Age of Milton from the Age of Dryden.

Literary History and Rewriting: From Disinheritance to Empowerment

The growing perception in England of a national literary identity stimulated a great deal of thought. As Gerald MacLean declares, "Before 1660, there had been little general concern over questions of the national literature as such. But by the time Dryden died at the end of the century, literary history had become a key component of a nationalist cultural enterprise."[16] A key feature of this enterprise was that it "could look backward into its own past in order to trace its origins and progress,"[17] and a key figure in its emergence was Dryden. Everything for this author was filtered through a need to negotiate his own artistic identity and achievement in relation to the past. Though Dryden struggled with the literary past and his predecessors, ultimately, the results of his contention transcended the personal sphere: "it is to Dryden that England owes its very concept of a literary period and of literary succession."[18]

An important factor in the growing awareness of an English tradition was the London stage. As Cedric D. Reverand II shows, during 1660–65, before plague closed the theaters, the plays of Shakespeare, Francis Beaumont and John Fletcher, and Ben Jonson dominated the stage.[19] Since Dryden's plays competed with these, he felt the encroachment of the past most keenly as a play-wright. A glimpse into his response to the past is afforded by his metaphor for literary succession. It originates with Neander, the "new man" usually assumed to speak for Dryden in *An Essay of Dramatick Poesie* (1667), and he is referring to Jonson, Fletcher, and Shakespeare:

> We acknowledge them our Fathers in wit, but they have ruin'd their Estates themselves before they came to their childrens hands. There is scarce an Humour, a Character, or any kind of Plot, which they have not us'd. All comes sullied or wasted to us: and were they to entertain this Age, they could not now make so plenteous treatments out of such decay'd Fortunes. This there-fore will be a good Argument to us either not to write at all, or to attempt some other way. There is no bayes to be expected in their Walks: *Tentanda via est, qua me quoque possum tollere humo.*
>
> This way of writing in Verse they have onely left free to us; our age is arriv'd to a perfection in it, which they never knew; and which (if we may guess by what of theirs we have seen in Verse, as *The Faithful Shepherdess*, and *Sad Shepherd*) 'tis prob-able they never could have reach'd. For the Genius of every age is different. (*Works* 17:73)

Richard Terry points out that this parental metaphor, which becomes the main figure for a theory of literary tradition, expresses the "sensitivity to being a latecomer [that] made Dryden prey to a particular set of anxieties," a major one being "that there was nothing left to say since everything had already been said by earlier writers."[20] Thinking of literature as a quantifiable inheritance and judging his powers of invention as weak, Neander feels a sense of scarcity and virtual disinheritance. He expresses the anxiety of impoverished belatedness.

Some two years after calling Jonson, Fletcher, and Shakespeare "our fathers in wit," Dryden found a way whereby he might prosper. In 1670, he collaborated with Sir William Davenant in adapting Shakespeare's *The Tempest*. The experience was crucial. It showed Dryden that there was scope for "our age" in improving the "imperfect" work of predecessors. Enthusiastically, he points to the defects of Shakespeare and Fletcher: "in every page [there is] either some Solecism of Speech, or some notorious flaw in Sence" (*Works* 11:205). "Witness the lameness of their Plots," he advises the reader (11:206). It is hardly necessary to argue that Dryden's justification for appropriating Shakespeare might equally serve as justification for appropriating Milton. His attitude toward Milton follows the same pattern. Just as the querulous Neander complains about "ruin'd Estates," Dryden starts with the frustration of feeling outdone by a predecessor: "This Man ... Cuts us All Out, and the Ancients too," he is said to have told Charles Sackville (later Earl of Dorset) when he first read *Paradise Lost*.[21] But the anxiety of impoverishment and belatedness gives way to the detection of flaws.

I agree with Vinton A. Dearing, Dryden's editor, who thinks he "had arrived at all his objections to Milton's epic before he undertook his opera and so wrote with the conviction that by using rhyme and omitting the rest of what he objected to he was succeeding where Milton had failed."[22] The criticisms that he specifies later, after the fact, correspond to his "improvements" to Milton's epic. In 1685 he refers to Milton's "antiquated words, and the perpetual harshness of their sound" (*Works* 3:17). In 1693, he objects to Milton's subject as inappropriate for a heroic work: his conclusion "is not prosperous, like that of all other Epique Works; his Heavenly Machines are many, and his Humane Persons are but two"; moreover, he cannot "Justify *Milton* for his Blank Verse" (4:15). Finally, writing specifically about epic versus tragedy in 1697, he declares that only Homer, Virgil, and Tasso are great epic poets: "After these three are entred, some Lord Chamberlain should be appointed, some Critick of Authority shou'd be set before the door, to keep out a Crowd of little Poets who press for Admission and are not of Quality" (5:275). Among these little poets, the Lord Chamberlain mentions Milton: "And *Milton*, if the Devil had not been his Heroe instead of *Adam*; if the Gyant had not foil'd the Knight and driven him out of his strong hold, to wander through the World with his Lady Errant; and if there had not been more Machining [divine] Persons than Humane, in his Poem" (5:276). One can raise the obvious objections: if Milton's narrative was to be true to Genesis, the "giant" had to foil the "knight," and so on. But Dryden's criticisms indicate the changes he makes to Milton's poem: writing in rhyme and contemporary idiom, he diminishes the stature of Satan, makes Adam the hero, slashes the number of divine characters, and gives the story a dubious but relatively "prosperous" ending.

The distance between the man who "cuts us all out" (like an improvident father) and the "little poet" trying to slip past the chamberlain is immense. How does Dryden navigate his way from the anxiety of belatedness to the correction of literary eminence? His collaborative rewriting with Davenant had pointed the way out of literary powerlessness and scarcity.

Free Will versus Determinism: The Heroic Adam

In the essay accompanying *The State of Innocence*, Dryden describes the use he makes of Milton's epic:

> I cannot without injury to the deceas'd Author of *Paradice Lost*, but acknowledge that this POEM has receiv'd its entire Foundation, part of the Design, and many of the Ornaments from him. What I have borrow'd, will be so easily discern'd from my mean Productions, that I shall not need to point the Reader to the places: And, truly, I should be sorry, for my own sake,

that any one should take the pains to compare them together: the Original being undoubtedly, one of the greatest, most noble, and most sublime POEMS, which either this Age or Nation has produc'd. (*Works* 12:86)

With Welch, I read Dryden's rehearsal of the modesty topos as an attempted intervention in the reception of Milton's poem—he wants to discourage people from reading *Paradise Lost*. He probably did think the epic was sublime, but the high praise glosses over the "faults" in the poem that he "corrects" in *The State of Innocence,* corrections that go beyond transforming epic into drama. Dryden says he uses the epic's plot, but his description of his dependence on Milton is disingenuous: he reconfigures bits and pieces of *Paradise Lost* into a mosaic work that is the antithesis of Milton's epic. Just as a sculptor is said to see the statue imprisoned in a block of stone, Dryden sees a heroic drama hidden within *Paradise Lost*: instead of the universal battle of good and evil, he sees a heroic trial of love. The Adam and Eve Dryden deems more relevant than Milton's to Restoration culture are more interested in their own sensual drama than in God.

The best subjects of heroic drama are love and valor. Eugene M. Waith specifies that heroic drama exalts loyalty and valor as the attributes of the protagonist who differs from the epic hero "in the importance he attache[s] to the experience of love and in his idealization of the object of his affections."[23] This protagonist does not necessarily behave prudently or ethically, but his greatness of spirit is never in doubt; his actions "might be open to question, [but] there is admiration for his courage."[24] Thus, in some plays, "actions that people might judge as reprehensible" are presented as heroic; others test their characters with "painful choices between such values as love and religion or friendship and patriotism."[25]

In *Paradise Lost,* as in the Bible story, Adam and Eve are to obey God by not eating from the forbidden tree, and Adam errs because he is "overcome with Female charm."[26] The commandment and Adam's response to it are the same in *The State of Innocence,* but everything else is different in Dryden's bold rewriting. Stephen Fallon suggested some time ago that by "writing monism into

Paradise Lost so consistently and so extensively," Milton partici-
pates in the mid-century controversy about free will versus determinism that gained impetus from the 1651 publication of Hobbes's
Leviathan.[27] That *The State of Innocence* is also related to the
controversy was suggested by Bruce King.[28] Just as free will is the
linchpin of Milton's theology in *Paradise Lost,* determinism is at
the heart of Dryden's *State of Innocence.*[29]

Paradise Lost as a whole is the creative catalyst for Dryden's
opera, but the author capitalizes on passages that can be made
congruent with determinism: Eve's "narcissistic" experience
and Adam's remark to Raphael that she was created with too
much beauty; the Father's explanation of free will in book 3 (and
Raphael's comments on the subject), and Adam's complaint that
God's "terms [were] too hard" (*PL* 10.751); and, chiefly, Eve's
speech regarding what she calls Adam's "glorious trial of exceeding Love" (9.961). As we shall see, Milton is aware of the problems
these passages might create. Consequently, he treats them with
great tact, trying to anticipate and (as far as possible) circumvent
readings that would compromise the moral doctrine of his poem.
But Dryden deliberately takes just those paths before which Milton
deliberately sets roadblocks. He rewrites the passages to suggest
that matters look different to people living in the age of reason.

Too Much of Ornament

Like the protagonists of heroic drama, Adam in *Paradise Lost*
idealizes Eve's beauty, which is so "absolute" (*PL* 8.547) that it
captivates even herself. Much has been made of Eve's reaction to
her image in the "Smooth Lake" (4.459). The "looks / Of sympathy
and love" that she believes the reflected image returns (4.464–65)
engender keen "desire" (466). In another passage stressing Eve's
beauty, Adam confides in Raphael that he is

> in all enjoyments else
> Superior and unmov'd, here only weak
> Against the charm of Beauty's powerful glance.
> Or Nature fail'd in mee, and left some part

> Not proof enough such Object to sustain,
> Or from my side subducting, took perhaps
> More than enough; at least on her bestow'd
> Too much of Ornament, in outward show
> Elaborate, of inward less exact.   (8.531–39)

Milton's Adam goes on about Eve's beauty until line 559, after having already enthused about it in lines 470–85. Eve and Adam are both idealized characters. But since Eve's beauty figures in her disobedience and Adam's, Milton prescribes: what would amount, in fallen characters, to her narcissism and his passion do not constitute sin or necessitate their falls.

Had Milton not given his characters emotions and qualities like anger, passion, pride, and ambition, neither they nor their actions would be interesting or comprehensible (supposing that Milton or anyone could describe perfect but dynamic characters). But the appealing human characteristics that enable Satan, Adam, and Eve to act beyond the stasis of perfection cannot be morally determinant; they cannot seem to ordain the characters' movement from innocence to fallenness. So Milton, following the terse Scriptures, emphasizes that for Adam and Eve (who in this regard resemble other figures in pre-Law Genesis) innocence or error is determined entirely by obedience or disobedience of God, and, in their case, obedience of only one commandment. Five times, *Paradise Lost* refers to the "Sole" or "Single" command that defines their moral state.[30]

In addition, to preserve the essential moral distinction between motivation and compulsion, between possibility and destiny, Milton employs a simple (but brilliant) strategy. When his unfallen human characters exhibit what readers may be inclined to see as fallen thought or behavior, the author provides them with explicit instruction. At the pool, for instance, Eve is taught by her Creator that she is unsatisfactory as the object of her own longing, whereas Adam, being "no shadow [that] stays / Thy coming, and thy soft imbraces," can satisfy her desire (*PL* 4.470–71). From Adam, she gets more instruction, learning that her beauty is excelled by "grace / And wisdom" (490–91). It is the same with Adam. Above beauty, he knows, are "higher knowledge," "Wisdom," and "Authority and Reason" (8.551–52, 554). But because Adam's emotions do not reflect the truth his mind acknowledges, Raphael lectures him about the relative merits of his own attributes and Eve's fair "outside" (8.568). The clear implication of such instruction is that attitudes, emotions, or behavior that would mark other creatures as fallen or imperfect are to be construed as radical ignorance or inexperience in Adam and Eve. Milton thus provides the motivational potential so necessary to narrative and, at the same time, preserves the semblance of moral self-determination for his characters. They are "perfet, [but] not immutable" (5.524), and their mutability is latent in their human qualities.

In *The State of Innocence,* Dryden rewrites ignorance as imperfection. He takes his cue from Eve's self-love; but instead of declaring it blameless as Milton does, he demonstrates that it is definitive. Eve says, in Dryden's play, that the beasts gaze "as if I were to be obey'd" and "I my self am proud of me."[31] When she tries to embrace her own image, she complains, "Ah, fair, yet false; ah Being, form'd to cheat, / By seeming kindness, mixt with deep deceit" (*Innocence* 2.3.26–27). This reads as a negative description, with the added implication (in "form'd") that Eve was *made* to be a trap.

No one steps forward, as in *Paradise Lost,* to declare Eve "yet sinless" (*PL* 9.659), to correct her or to instruct her in truer values. It is the same with Adam, whose passion Dryden rewrites as inevitable surrender. When he first joins Eve, it becomes evident that Dryden's inspiration is Adam's suggestion to Raphael in *Paradise Lost* that Eve was created with too much beauty (*PL* 8.534–39). Everything Dryden's Adam says on his first sight of Eve reinforces her overweening sense of self:

> Thou fairest of thy great Creator's Works;
> Thee, Goddess, thee th'Eternal did ordain
> His softer Substitute on Earth to Reign:
> And, wheresoe'r thy happy footsteps tread,
> Nature, in triumph, after thee is led.
> Angels, with pleasure, view thy matchless Grace,
> And love their Maker's Image in thy Face.
>
> (*Innocence* 2.3.29–35)

Students of *Paradise Lost* may hear echoes of Satan's temptation in book 9 in Adam's words, and worse follows:

> *Eve.* I, next myself, admire and love thee best.
> *Adam.* Made to command, thus freely I obey,
> And at thy feet the whole Creation lay.
>   . . . .
> If not to love, we both were made in vain:
> I my new Empire would resign again,
> And change, with my dumb slaves, my nobler mind;
> Who, void of reason, more of pleasure find.
>
> (*Innocence* 2.3.45–47, 60–63)

As Laura Knoppers observes, "Dryden's Eve exercises exaggerated and temporary sovereignty as a love object."[32] Adam agrees with her that she is "to be obeyed," reinforces her self-love, and fails to teach her that wisdom and reason trump beauty. Giving more weight to pleasure than to the whole creation, Adam immediately resigns his authority.

Although Dryden's Adam indicates clearly that he will fall, readers cannot judge him too harshly. Raphael gives him only the briefest instruction about his marital relationship: Eve "is design'd" as "an equal, yet thy subject," and "thy stronger soul shall her weak reason sway" (*Innocence* 2.1.64, 66). According to *The State of Innocence*, Milton's Adam is correct: Eve *was* created with too much beauty for her own good or for Adam's. Absent a delimited definition of sin or heavenly instruction whereby Adam and Eve's innocent ignorance is first indicated and then corrected, Dryden's first parents are flawed from the beginning.

One Easy Prohibition

Milton's Adam finds it unimaginable that he *can* disobey God. The first time Satan sees him, Adam is discussing "This one, this easy charge" (*PL* 4.421) with Eve before advising her, "Then let us not think hard / One easy prohibition" (4.432–33). Later, he feels "Assur'd" that "we never shall forget to love ... and obey him whose command / Single, is yet so just" (5.550–53).

Adam's stress on the "easiness" of obeying the sole command changes the instant the fallen Eve stands before him: "I feel / The Link of Nature draw me" to Eve and sin, he thinks in book 9.913–14. If there is ever a moment in Milton's poem when Adam's moral freedom seems questionable despite the author's best efforts, this is that moment, as Adam describes an almost visceral compulsion to follow his love into disobedience:

> However I with thee have fixt my Lot,
> Certain to undergo like doom; if Death
> Consort with thee, Death is to mee as Life;
> So forcible within my heart I feel
> The Bond of Nature draw me to my own,
> My own in thee, for what thou art is mine;
> Our State cannot be sever'd, we are one.
> One Flesh; to lose thee were to lose myself.   (PL 9.952–59)

Adam's view of God's commandment is utterly different after he falls: he believes then that he was "unable to perform / Thy terms too hard" (10.750–51). Attributing opposing ideas to Adam at different points in his short history, Milton gives the situation experiential validity: something that seems easy in theory proves to be difficult in actuality. At the same time, he endorses Adam's unfallen view—the sole command *is* easy to keep for one who is not deceived—but also indicates that, finally, this is not the test Adam faces. To obey the divine command is easy; to obey that command and thereby risk separation from Eve is altogether different.

Primarily, Dryden rewrites the easy/hard opposition to show Eve's ignorance and to sow doubts about the freedom of Adam's will. In *The State of Innocence*, it is Eve who blithely imagines obedience to be easy: "he merits [death] who disobeys / That one command, and one of so much ease," she declares (*Innocence* 3.1.74–75). Her desire to work alone is inspired partly by her mistaken views: "I know my self secure," she tells Adam, "and long my little trial to endure" (4.1.177–78). After she falls, her attitude changes: "The laws were hard; the pow'r to keep 'em, weak" (5.4.119).

Conversely, Adam's immediate reaction when Raphael tells him of the angelic fall is to suppose that keeping God's law is practically impossible:

> If such could fall from bliss, who knew and saw
> By near admission, their Creator's Law,
> What hopes have I, from Heav'n remote so far,
> To keep those Laws, unknowing when I err?
>
> (*Innocence* 2.1.25–28)

In a striking indication of the relative unimportance to *The State of Innocence* of the "one command," Dryden's Raphael does not instruct Adam at once when he expresses ignorance of God's laws. The reader is never told when Adam is informed (or reminded) of the Creator's Law. Not until 3.1.68–71 does he tell Eve about the forbidden tree, "(Our proof of duty to our Maker's will)." Dryden's parentheses speak volumes.

Dryden's Adam laments the apparent impossibility of obedience again after discussing free will with Raphael and Gabriel:

> Hard state of life! since Heav'n fore-knows my will,
> Why am I not ty'd up from doing ill?
> Why am I trusted with my self at large,
> When he's more able to sustain the charge?
> Since Angels fell, whose strength was more than mine,
> 'Twould show more grace my frailty to confine.
> Foreknowing the success, to leave me free,
> Excuses him, and yet supports not me.
>
> (*Innocence* 4.1.113–20)

As Lewalski writes, "Dryden's Cartesian Adam" is not swayed by the angels' arguments for free will: their "best efforts to persuade Adam that God's foreknowledge does not amount to predestination leave him dubious, and with an uneasy foreboding that he will certainly fall."[33] Nevertheless, before he eats of the fruit, Adam says, "Not cozen'd, I, with choice, my life resign" (5.1.69). The demands of Dryden's genre force him to give a momentary (and inconsistent) emphasis to Adam's experiential sense of freedom. Without the sense of deliberate volition (which is, of course, incompatible with determinism), he could not be the hero of the contest between love and godliness that is the heart of Dryden's heroic drama.

The Glorious Trial of Matchless Love

Eve's fallen celebration of Adam's love in Milton's epic is the main impetus of Dryden's creativity and artistic vision in *The State of Innocence*. Dryden's Eve is beautiful and vain: his uninstructed Adam, helpless before her, lays everything at her feet. Immediately after Eve has fallen — at the precise point in the story when the consequences of her choice must be reckoned — Dryden rewrites some of the key terms of the religious narrative in the register of love. In act 5, "Eden," "death," and "Sin" are given new meanings.[34] For example, Adam says to the newly fallen Eve, "While you were absent, *Eden* was no more" (*Innocence* 5.1.18), and Eve declares that separation from Adam was "a short death" (5.1.24–25). Adam redefines "sin" after falling:

> What e're shall be the event, the lot is cast:
> Where appetites are giv'n, what sin to tast?
> Or if a sin, 'tis but by precept such:
> Th' offence so small, the punishment's too much.   (5.2.77–80)

Adam makes a casuistic (and anachronistic) distinction between *genuine* "sins" and those that are so-called according only to God's order. Dryden also gives him a mechanistic explanation for his behavior — God did, after all, make him with the appetites that create temptation.

To encourage Adam's disobedience before he eats the fruit, Milton's Eve exclaims, "O glorious trial of exceeding Love" (*PL* 9.961). But Dryden's Eve celebrates Adam's love *after* he eats, praising his heroic valor:

> O wond'rous pow'r of matchless love exprest:
> Why was this trial thine, of loving best?
> I envy thee that lot; and could it be,

> Would venture something more than death, for thee.
> Not that I fear, that death th'event can prove;
> W'are both immortal, while so well we love.
>
> (*Innocence* 5.1.71–76)

To highlight the exaltation of love, Adam expresses the carpe diem sentiment in words reminiscent of Marvell's "To His Coy Mistress":

> And death, by fear, shall not be nigher brought:
> If he will come, let us to joyes make hast;
> Then let him seize us when our pleasure's past,
> We'll take up all before; and death shall find
> We have drain'd life, and left a void behind.
>
> (*Innocence* 5.1.86–90)

How insignificant death seems to those who have "drain'd life" of all the sexual pleasure it has to offer!

As Dryden's Adam earlier described their unfallen life together, it was a sexual paradise, an endless cycle of undiminished desire and gratification: "Thou young and beauteous, my desires to bless; / I, still desiring, what I still possess" (*Innocence* 3.1.25–26). But the relationship changes as soon as the first parents fall, just as it does in *Paradise Lost*. As Dryden's first couple awaits judgment, the emphasis is on the relationship between the sexes. In a conspicuous anachronism that parallels Adam's complaint about women in *Paradise Lost,* a prescient Eve looks into the future to limn the trajectory of courtship and marriage: "Curs'd vassalage of all my future kind: / First Idolis'd, till loves hot fire be o're, / Then slaves to those who courted us before" (5.4.26–28). She wishes bitterly that she had not been paired with Adam:

> Better with Brutes my humble lot had gone;
> Of reason void, accountable for none:
> Th'unhappiest of creation is a wife,
> Made lowest, in the highest rank of life:
> Her fellow's slave; to know and not to chuse:
> Curst with that reason she must never use.   (5.4.56– 61)

Adam and Eve express guilt, fear, and anger in the aftermath of sin, but Dryden's account is so compressed that it cannot account clearly for Eve's description of the radical alteration of their relationship. Before disobedience, desire and gratification followed upon each other in an ecstatic loop; now, Eve simply knows that satiated appetite has devalued her. She predicts female "vassalage" to men not on account of her sin, but because of the nature of desire and lust in a fallen world.

Furthermore, Eve laments that her error makes her "her [husband's] slave." As a wife, "curst with that reason she must never use," she is now in the undesirable condition that Milton's Father describes as serving "necessity / Not mee" (*PL* 3.110–11). Dryden's Adam seconds Eve's view that her reason must now be passive, regretting that he was "fondly kind" "When force [was] lawful" (*Innocence* 5.4.38). He should have exercised "an absolute restraint" to keep Eve from leaving him, to keep her from falling (5.4.36). At the same juncture in the plot of *Paradise Lost*, when Milton's Eve argues that if Adam had "been firm and fixt in [his] dissent" she would have remained by his side (and unfallen), Adam replies that he did all he could, since "force upon free Will hath here no place" (*PL* 9.1160, 1174). But Dryden uses their experience to endorse Adam's earlier, unfallen complaints that he should be "ty'd up from doing ill," and that "'Twould show more [divine] grace [his] frailty to confine" (*Innocence* 4.1.114–18).

Dryden's Raphael eventually arrives to announce the penalties for disobedience. Adam's sentence of toiling in "painful sweat" (*Innocence* 5.4.143–45) is unchanged from Genesis and *Paradise Lost*. But love continues to be the focal point when Raphael turns to Eve. His prescription of the woman's place in marriage merely reiterates Eve's description, quoted above. But Dryden rewrites her biblical punishment: "And he shall rule, and she in thraldome live; / Desiring more of love than man can give" (5.4.148–49). Genesis 3:16 reads, "I will greatly multiply thy sorrow and thy conception; in sorrow thou shalt bring forth children; and thy desire shall be to thy husband, and he shall rule over thee."[35] First and most obviously, Dryden omits any mention of childbirth, presumably because infants are superfluous in heroic love. More interesting is the change he makes to the biblical sentence about desire. The curse in Genesis 3:17 implies a shift in the balance of power

between men and women, a logical adjustment considering that
Adam disobeyed because he idolized Eve and "hearkened unto
[her] voice." Dryden's version comprehends and adds to that shift.
Henceforth, declares Raphael, women are condemned to perpetual
dissatisfaction in the qualified love that is the most a man can
give a subordinate. The change in the female experience of love
is perhaps implicit in the biblical curse, but Dryden expresses the
frustration that the traditional, unequal relationship of the sexes
creates in modern women.

In the play's conclusion, Dryden brings his materials into conformity with the ethos of heroic drama. I have already mentioned
the significance the author gives to Adam's "freely-chosen" decision to disobey and die with Eve. In addition, within 42 lines of
the end of the play, Dryden crowds in a number of positive gains
from human disobedience, the first of which is heavenly bliss.
Before Milton's Adam exclaims, "O goodness infinite, goodness
immense" (*PL* 12.469), he is instructed about the need for a savior to pay the price of human sin. He learns that bliss will be the
"reward / [of] His faithful" (12.461–62) and soon leaves behind
the paradox of the "happy sin," realizing that God's people must
still live among "the enemies of truth" (12.482). Raphael does not
minimize the challenge, either, saying that the faithful will be
equipped "with spiritual Armor, able to resist / *Satan's* assaults,
and quench his fiery darts" (12.491–92).

Dryden's Adam and Eve are given no such sobering information
along with Raphael's vision of heaven and immortality. Adam was
told about sin, punishment, and reward in act 4, scene 1. In the conclusion of the play, Raphael tells the couple simply that, in spite
of their mortality and error, their race will eventually "revive" and
live "in deathless pleasures" when "the blest" are crowned "with
immortality" (*Innocence* 5.4.222–25): in Dryden's version of the
felix culpa, Adam and Eve celebrate a seemingly unconditional
gift. Adam speaks first, describing the blessed in heaven:

> O goodness infinite! whose Heav'nly will
> Can so much good produce, from so much ill!
> Happy their state!

Pure, and unchang'd, and needing no defence,
From sins, as did my frailer Innocence.
Their joy sincere, and with no sorrow mixt:
Eternity stands permanent, and fixt,
And wheels no longer on the Poles of time:
Secure from fate, and more secure from crime.
Eve. Ravish'd, with Joy, I can but half repent
The sin which Heav'n makes happy in th'event.   (5.4.226–36)

The apparently unqualified gift of heaven seems to reward Adam
and Eve for their disobedience in the sense that they are given what
the unfallen Adam desired: a place where "grace [his] frailty [would]
confine" (4.1.118). Raphael's vision seems to vindicate Adam's earlier complaints—God finally supplies what, all along, Adam knew
he needed: a secure place where his frailty could not betray him,
subjecting him to consequences he did not deserve.

When Raphael tells them they must leave paradise, Adam puts a
brave face on it and, after some regret, Eve follows suit:

> *Adam.* Then farewell all; I will indulgent be
> To my own ease, and not look back to see.
> When what we love we ne'r must meet again,
> To lose the thought, is to remove the pain.
>   . . . .
> *Eve.* Farewell you flow'rs, whose buds with early care,
> I watch'd, and to the cheerful sun did rear:
>   . . . .
> A long farewell to thee, my nuptial bow'r,
> Adorn'd with ev'ry fair and fragrant flow'r.
> And last, farewell, farewell my place of birth;
> I go to wander in the lower earth,
> As distant as I can; for dispossest,
> Farthest from what I once enjoy'd, is best.
>   (*Innocence* 5.4.243–59)

Both express a practical acceptance of exile not unlike Satan's
acceptance of hell as his new domain in *Paradise Lost*, since
"fardest from [God] is best" (*PL* 1.247). Adam, particularly, seems
to share Satan's faith in the power of the mind to create ease or pain.
He and Eve are undaunted, and Raphael's final words, the last in

the opera, dispel any idea of significant loss: "But, part you hence in peace, and having mourn'd your sin, / For outward *Eden* lost, find *Paradise* within" (*Innocence* 5.4.266–67). The internal paradise is the crowning touch of the "prosperous ending" of Dryden's heroic drama.

Conclusion, with Metaphors

The State of Innocence is Dryden's effort to close the door on the *weltanschauung* represented by *Paradise Lost* and its generic expression. Heroic drama presents a particular view of flawed human nature in a world complicated by competing values and priorities. This is far from the world of *Paradise Lost,* which is a pendant of the numinous reality beyond itself, a reality that orders values and priorities clearly, and from which supernatural heroes are dispatched to accomplish what exceeds human capacity. There is no sense in *The State of Innocence,* either, as there is in Genesis and in Milton's epic, that, indisputably, the hero's priority should be to obey God. In Dryden's opera, the choice that a character confronts is difficult and seems tragic because no single choice is recognized as superior or privileged. Whatever he does, the protagonist chooses at least partial failure.

Dryden does not emphasize Adam and Eve's innocence or the commandment that God requires them to observe. His first parents are endowed with ordinary, flawed human nature, with qualities that not only account for but also dictate their actions and choices. The commandment they are to keep is almost irrelevant since, their nature being what it is, it is a foregone conclusion that they will not be able to obey it. In the end, however, the determinism that dictates Adam and Eve's choices is theologically innocuous because they are not punished severely for doing what they cannot help doing. Adam certainly does not blame God for his actions: "Seek not, in vain, our maker to accuse," he scolds Eve, "Terms were propos'd; pow'r left us to refuse" (*Innocence* 5.4.126–27). Moreover, any idea of divine injustice is blunted by Raphael's vision of heavenly bliss and his injunction to Adam and Eve to "find *Paradise* within."

In Dryden's play-opera, any elevation of character or spirit Adam and Eve experience arises from their passion for each other. In each other's arms, they feel immortal; in absence, they taste death. When Adam makes the choice between godly obedience and love in *Paradise Lost,* he shows his weakness; when he makes the same choice in *The State of Innocence,* he shows his greatness of spirit. The reader might register such domestic heroism as relatively modest, but there is no greater heroism in *The State of Innocence* to compare with it. When Milton's Adam follows his love into sin and mortality, he learns, from the Son's heroic payment of the penalty that should be borne, properly, by Adam, that God's grace abounds above human error. Dryden's Adam, having proved himself heroic by following his love into error and death, is prepared to suffer the consequences but finds, astonishingly, that God's grace abounds above weak human nature. Ultimately, Dryden's description of determinism, as well as his portrayal of human nature as imperfect from creation, has no serious implications for theodicy.

Nothing could show Dryden's antagonism to *Paradise Lost* and its author more clearly than his radical repurposing of Milton's materials to celebrate the same moral choice that Milton laments for the length of 12 books. Stripped of the conservative, educational, or patriotic motives that writers previously used to justify their incursions into the works of others, rewriting emerges in Dryden's *The State of Innocence* as the hostile challenge from a self-conscious "modern" to the deliberate adherent to a different cultural orientation. But Dryden was not inspired to rewrite *Paradise Lost* because he thought it could not speak meaningfully to a segment, at least, of Restoration society—when it came to Christian teaching, how much discontinuity could there be between 1667 and 1677? It could hardly be the case that overnight, so to speak, all of England became a culture that valued sex and romantic love over the spiritual righteousness taught by the Bible.

The State of Innocence is not an investigation of past versus contemporary values. Or, rather, it is and is not—for Dryden was absolutely correct in reading and placing *Paradise Lost* as the last great work of the age before the one he called his own, correct that "the Genius of every Age is different" (*Works* 17:73).

Milton deliberately aligned himself with the "ancients," and there can be no doubt that the taste of the contemporary book-buying public ratified the perspective of the "modern" Dryden: the first edition of *Innocence* "was followed by eight others" before 1701 (*Works* 12:325). Milton's age and genius *were* different from Dryden's, and especially so when seen from the totalizing distance of a few centuries. But this is not the bloodless clash of two cultures, of the old naturally giving way to the new. In terms of literary history, the great interest of this situation is in Dryden's unique sensitivity to the still unfolding contemporary situation and his manipulation of it to further his literary ambitions. An important aspect of *The State of Innocence* is that it is, among other things, the author's transparent stratagem to forge a literary past that appears to engender his own "modern" work. Rewriting *Paradise Lost*, Dryden does as Terry says "great authors" do—he casts the poem as the "antecedent tradition out of which [his] own writings arise";[36] and, as epic gives way to heroic drama, Milton, his contemporaneity occluded, is succeeded by the new man. Dryden's genius was to erect the concept of "ages" between Milton and himself.

Some years ago, Christopher Ricks suggested that Milton, "giant-like in all his power to enable or disable," was Dryden's "literary father."[37] "Within ten years of Milton's death," Ricks wrote, "Dryden had magnificently come into his [poetic] inheritance," as evidenced by the "imitative and allusive mode" that "recognized Milton's genius by making it serve [Dryden's] purposes in allusion."[38] It is true that Dryden made some of Milton's work his own through allusion. And it is also true that he sometimes gave Milton his due, as in the well-known epigram from the 1688 edition of *Paradise Lost* (though the compliment casts the epic poet back into the antiquity of Homer and Virgil). But "allusion" does not begin to cover the extent of Dryden's use of *Paradise Lost* in *The State of Innocence*. Ricks's suggestion of an untroubled filial relation of younger to elder poet depends on his elision of the opera, which he disposes of with half a sentence: "And then there is the bizarre endeavour that converted *Paradise Lost* into *State of Innocence.*"[39] Moreover, Ricks's concept of succession depends on the paternal metaphor Dryden employed in 1667.[40] But a later figure, I believe, better conveys the rewriter's ongoing preoccupation with, and attitude about, Milton, *Paradise Lost,* and succession.

Before and after *The State of Innocence* was published, Dryden visited and revisited the matter of his relation to the literary past as he strove to position imitation/rewriting alongside primary invention as worthy literary work. He was as invested in claiming achievement as in justifying appropriation. He used two metaphors, as previously mentioned, to describe literary succession; three others negotiate the difference between them. All of them involve scarcity of resources (including the limitation of Dryden's own talent) or of prestige, and this insufficiency informs Dryden's view of literary history and his place in it. His first metaphor for succession, quoted above, features improvident fathers who have "ruin'd" or "sullied" their sons' inheritance: "There is scarce an Humour, a Character, or any kind of Plot, which they have not us'd" (*Works* 17:73). Four years later, in 1671, Dryden used a couple of metaphors that rate aspects of literary work. He was answering the charge of plagiarism when he appealed to readers to consider his contribution in rewriting a foreign work: "When I had finished my Play, it was like the Hulk of Sir Francis Drake, so strangely alter'd, that there scarce remain'd any Plank of the Timber which first built it" (*Works* 10:211). A few paragraphs below this, Dryden complains that his critics do not understand the "work of a Poet": "But in general, the employment of a Poet, is like that of a curious Gunsmith, or Watchmaker: the Iron or Silver is not his own; but they are the least part of that which gives the value: The price lyes wholly in the workmanship" (10:212). Subsequently, in the preface accompanying his adaptation of Shakespeare's *Troilus and Cressida* (1679), there is another relevant figure: "There appear'd in some places of [this play], the admirable Genius of the Author, [so] I undertook to remove that heap of Rubbish, under which many excellent thoughts lay wholly bury'd" (*Works* 13:226). In the inheritance metaphor, Dryden lamented the scarcity of seemingly finite material, which had been used up by selfish forebears. The past deprived the present writer of materials.

But the last three metaphors reveal that the materials Dryden thought depleted are only "sullied"; consequently, they are available to him for correction—they have become his resources. In the ship metaphor, external resources are primary (the foundation of the ship/play); Dryden appropriates someone else's plot but, together with it and in larger proportion, he declares, there is his own invention, which produces a play almost entirely new. Following this, however, Dryden astutely (if only implicitly) assesses his gift as a poet. The ship and the gunsmith metaphors concede his lack of original invention: the hulk, iron, or silver of independent creativity is "not his own." But the gunsmith metaphor effects a shift: the rewriter's lack of inventive power is insignificant because it is his artistry that endows nearly worthless preexistent material with value. The metaphor of salvage, which may be Dryden's frankest, is in line with the previous one: he is the poet who transvalues "rubbish."

The salvage metaphor appears in the preface accompanying Dryden's adaptation of Shakespeare's *Troilus*, two years after the publication of *The State of Innocence*. The preface opens with reflections on the Greeks, who venerated Aeschylus but acknowledged the "imperfections" of his works. Dryden adds that the Greeks "ordain'd an equal reward to those Poets who could alter his Plays to be Acted on the Theatre, with those whose productions were wholly new, and of their own" (*Works* 13:225). The parallel that Dryden suggests with Shakespeare is obvious, as is his assessment of his chosen literary mode: Dryden equates rewriting (which he calls "imitation") with original invention. The merit of his work, he means, is equal to Shakespeare's, or Milton's, for that matter.

These comments and metaphors trace Dryden's mastery of the literary past and the resolution of any concern he might have had about his scarce powers of invention: daunting authors and work have become uneven writers of trash mixed with brilliant bits that only a superior talent can mine and translate into excellence. But if this description suggests that the rewriter accomplishes something *for* the original author or work, Dryden quashes the idea with another powerful metaphor. The preface to *Troilus* concludes with a quotation from Longinus's *On the Sublime,* which includes Dryden's second metaphor for literary succession: "We ought not to regard a good imitation as a theft; but as a beautifull Idea of him who undertakes to imitate, by forming himself on the invention and the work of another man; for he enters into the lists like a new wrestler, to dispute the prize with the former Champion. This sort of emulation, says Hesiod, is honourable...when we combat for Victory with a Hero, and are not without glory even in our overthrow" (*Works* 13:228). The differences between Dryden's first metaphor for succession and this one are tremendous. In the parent/inheritance metaphor, the historical priority that threatens scarcity or depletion ensures, at the same time, a natural, nonviolent progression. Time guarantees that fathers, however wasteful, will be succeeded by sons, who need only wait to assume their parents' places (if not their fortunes). But chronological order is irrelevant in the second metaphor. It is important to note, however, that, as in the "Gunsmith, or Watchmaker" figure, "the invention and the work" of the champion himself become the raw material the new wrestler reworks to "dispute the prize" with him.

Though Dryden suggests that emulation is without heat, the image of a wrestler contradicts that idea by characterizing rewriting as the expression of equal parts of admiration and aggression. Speaking through Longinus, Dryden declares that emulation is unpredictable in its outcome. A new wrestler may take the prize from "the former champion"; but in the last sentence above, the challenger is overthrown by the experienced "Hero." Still, no one enters the lists without the hope of victory—no one rewrites without expecting to surpass the first work—so perhaps the wrestler tips the scale toward aggression. Though the two metaphors for literary succession differ in important respects, scarcity figures in both. In the first, an insufficiency of material threatens; and in the literary agon Dryden describes, there can be only one

champion, one prize. Ultimately, victory belongs not to the origi-
nator of a work but to the author whose version of that material
excels. Potentially, rewriting is empowerment and victory over the
past, even the very recent past of John Milton and *Paradise Lost.*
The State of Innocence is John Dryden's effort to erect an "Age"
between Milton and himself, and to reverse the vagaries of mere
chronological priority.

University of North Texas

NOTES

I am grateful to Barbara Lewalski, John Leonard, and the anonymous readers of *Milton Studies* for their helpful comments and questions on an earlier version of this essay.
   1. John Aubrey, "Minutes on the Life of Mr. John Milton," in *The Early
Lives of Milton,* ed. Helen Darbishire (London, 1932), 7.
   2. Louis Martz, "Dryden's Poem of Paradise: *The State of Innocence,
and Fall of Man,*" in *John Dryden (1631–1700): His Politics, His Plays,
and His* Poems, ed. Claude Rawson and Aaron Santesso (Newark,
Del. 2004), 192; Steven Zwicker, "Milton, Dryden, and the Politics of
Literary Controversy," in *Culture and Society in the Stuart Restoration,*
ed. Gerald MacLean (Cambridge, 1995), 138.
   3. Sharon Achinstein, "Milton's Spectre in the Restoration: Marvell,
Dryden, and Literary Enthusiasm," *Huntington Library Quarterly* 59
(1997): 17; Nicholas von Maltzahn, "Dryden's Milton and the Theatre of
Imagination," in *John Dryden: Tercentenary Essays,* ed. Paul Hammond
and David Hopkins (Oxford, 2000), 39, 42.
   4. Anthony Welch, "Losing Paradise in Dryden's *State of Innocence,*"
in *Uncircumscribed Mind: Reading Milton Deeply,* ed. Charles W.
Durham and Kristin A. Pruitt (Selinsgrove, Pa., 2008), 222.
   5. Barbara K. Lewalski, "*Paradise Lost* and the Contest over the Modern
Heroic Poem," *Milton Quarterly* 43 (2009): 157.
   6. Joad Raymond, *Milton's Angels: The Early-Modern Imagination*
(Oxford, 2010), 335.
   7. Especially while they were unpublished, many plays were appropriated and rewritten in one way or another. See Wendy Wall, "Dramatic
Authorship and Print," in *Early Modern English Drama: A Critical
Companion,* ed. Garrett A. Sullivan Jr., Patrick Cheney, and Andrew
Hadfield (Oxford, 2006), 1–11, for an incisive account of the many

factors contributing to the typical playscript: "Plays were seen as provisional scripts for performance, subjected to numerous creative forces—annotators, actors, revisers, copyists, censors, compositors, later adapters, and publishers" (1). For a detailed treatment of appropriation in drama, see Paulina Kewes, *Authorship and Appropriation: Writing for the Stage in England, 1660–1710* (Oxford, 1998).

8. Marcie Frank, *Gender, Theatre, and the Origins of Criticism: From Dryden to Manley* (Cambridge, 2003), 45.

9. John Dryden, "Prefatory Letter to William, Duke of Newcastle," in *An Evening's Love; or, The Mock Astrologer* (London, 1671). The quotation comes from *The Works of John Dryden*, 20 vols., ed. H. T. Swedenberg Jr. et al. (Berkeley, 1956–89), 10:210. All citations from Dryden's prose are to this edition, cited in the text hereafter by volume and page number.

10. Lara Dodds, "'To change in scenes and show it in a play': *Paradise Lost* and the Stage Directions of Dryden's *The State of Innocence and Fall of Man*," *Restoration* 3 (2009): 10.

11. Frank, *Gender, Theatre*, 42; Welch, "Losing Paradise," 223; Gordon Campbell and Thomas Corns, *John Milton: Life, Work, and Thought* (Oxford, 2008), 371.

12. Nicholas von Maltzahn, "The First Reception of *Paradise Lost* (1667)," *Review of English Studies* 47 (1996): 479–99.

13. Joseph Wittreich, *Why Milton Matters: A New Preface to His Writings* (New York, 2006), 120.

14. Dustin Griffin, *Regaining Paradise: Milton and the Eighteenth Century* (Cambridge, 1986), 137.

15. Frank, *Gender, Theatre*, 53.

16. Gerald MacLean, "Literature, Culture, and Society in Restoration England," in *Culture and Society in the Stuart Restoration*, ed. Gerald MacLean (Cambridge, 1995), 9.

17. Ibid.

18. Earl Miner, "Introduction: Borrowed Plumage, Varied Umbrage," in *Literary Transmission and Authority: Dryden and Other Writers*, ed. Earl Miner and Jennifer Brady (Cambridge, 1993), 3.

19. Cedric D. Reverand II, "Dryden and the Canon: Absorbing and Rejecting the Burden of the Past," in *Enchanted Ground: Reimagining John Dryden*, ed. Jayne Lewis and Maximillian E. Novak (Toronto, 2004), 212–13.

20. Richard Terry, *Poetry and the Making of the English Literary Past, 1660–1781* (Oxford, 2001), 149–50.

21. John Dryden, "Explanatory Notes and Remarks on Milton's *Paradise Lost*," in Darbishire, *Early Lives of Milton*, 296.

22. Vinton A. Dearing, commentary on *The State of Innocence* (*Works* 12:342).

23. Eugene M. Waith, *Ideas of Greatness: Heroic Drama in England* (New York, 1971), 26.

24. Ibid., 6–7.

25. Ibid., 132, 161.

26. John Milton, *Paradise Lost*, in *Complete Poems and Major Prose*, ed. Merritt Y. Hughes (New York, 1957), 9.999. All subsequent references to Milton's poetry are from this edition and are cited in the text.

27. Stephen Fallon, *Milton among the Philosophers: Poetry and Materialism in Seventeenth-Century England* (Ithaca, N.Y., 1991), 244.

28. Bruce King, "The Significance of Dryden's *State of Innocence*," *SEL* 4 (1964): 371–91.

29. Dryden came to Milton's epic with settled views on the matter of free will versus determinism, as is evident in a prefatory letter he wrote to Roger, Earl of Orrery, in 1664:

> All your Heroes are more than your Subjects, they are your Creatures. And though they seem to move freely, in all the Sallies of their Passions, yet you make Destinies for them which they cannot shun. They are mov'd (if I may dare say so) like the Rational Creatures of the Almighty Poet, who walk at Liberty, in their own Opinion, because their Fetters are invisible; when indeed the Prison of their Will, is the more sure for being large; and instead of an absolute Power over their Actions, they have only a wretched Desire of doing that, which they cannot choose but do. (*Works* 8:97)

30. See *PL* 3.94–95, 5.551–52, 7.47, 8.329–30, and 9.652–53. In a similar vein, 4.421: "This one, this easy charge" and 4.428: "The only sign of our obedience." In 8.635, Milton refers to "His great command."

31. *The State of Innocence and Fall of Man*, 2.3.13, 15 (*Works* 12:80–146, 320–82). All subsequent quotations of the opera are from Dryden's *Works* and are cited by act, scene, and line numbers.

32. Laura Knoppers, *Politicizing Domesticity from Henrietta Maria to Milton's Eve* (Cambridge, 2011), 160.

33. Lewalski, "Modern Heroic Poem," 159.

34. Dryden has already identified immortality (another of the fundamental terms and issues of the Genesis story) with the sexual rapture of the unfallen Adam and Eve in *Innocence* 3.1.43–44.

35. Biblical citations are from the King James (Authorized) Version.

36. Terry, *Poetry*, 142.

37. Christopher Ricks, *Allusion to the Poets* (Oxford, 2004), 33, 35.

38. Ibid., 35, 33.

39. Ibid., 34.

40. Despite describing Dryden's allusive mode as decorously filial, Ricks several times acknowledges an underlying tension: There is "a further, complicating, strain in Dryden's relationship with Milton. For

while Milton stood in something of a paternal role to Dryden as a poet, the strain was exacerbated by the fact that Milton stood too in the role of an elder brother. He was, after all, not quite twenty-three years older than Dryden" (ibid., 38). One of Dryden's editors recognizes his lingering competitiveness. George Watson, ed., *Of Dramatic Poesy and Other Critical Essays*, 2 vols. (London, 1962), remarks that an apposite reference in 1693 to *Paradise Lost* "seems long delayed": "Dryden is reluctant to admit that his proposal for an epic combining classical and scriptural imagery has already been fulfilled" (2:91).

Galactic Milton:
Angelic Robots and the Fall into Barbarism in Isaac Asimov's *Foundation* Series

Ryan Hackenbracht

If you read John Milton's *Paradise Lost* you will find that his Heaven is described as an eternal sing-along of praise to God. It is no wonder that one-third of the angels rebelled. When they were cast down into Hell, they *then* engaged in intellectual exercises...and I believe that, Hell or not, they were better off. When I read it, I sympathized strongly with Milton's Satan and considered him the hero of the epic, whether Milton intended that or not.

—Isaac Asimov, *I, Asimov: A Memoir* (1994)

In 1974, science fiction writer Isaac Asimov published an anno-tated edition of John Milton's *Paradise Lost*, which he titled *Asimov's Annotated "Paradise Lost": An Original Interpretation of Milton's Epic Poem.*[1] What happens when science fiction meets Renaissance poetry, and the author of humanity's epic interstellar future meets the author of its epic biblical past? An "original interpretation," to be sure, and one that offers fascinating

293

(and entertaining) insight into Milton's influence on the grand master of science fiction.[2] For instance, when God the Father sends the archangel Raphael to warn Adam and Eve about Satan, Asimov points out that it would have taken Raphael one hour and 19 minutes to travel from Saturn to Earth—assuming, he says, that angels travel at the speed of light.[3] When Satan and his rebel angels consider the journey from hell to Earth, Asimov praises them as astronauts who were braving "interplanetary travel across space."[4] In another instance, Asimov seems to respond to the premise of Stanley Fish's *Surprised by Sin: The Reader in "Paradise Lost,"* which had appeared in print a few years earlier.[5] Declaring himself an "unregenerate reader," Asimov attempts to sway other readers toward a diabolic interpretation of Milton's text and suggests that "there is something wrong with Milton's Heaven."[6] "There is no question but that Satan is by far the most interesting character in *Paradise Lost*," he says in Empsonian fashion, and he claims we sympathize with the archangel because we "admire the underdog who doesn't know when he's beaten and who won't give up."[7]

Despite the combativeness of these annotations and in part because of them, Asimov's fascination with *Paradise Lost* raises important questions about Milton's influence on Asimov's *Foundation* series, which sold millions of copies worldwide. In a 2005 essay in the *Guardian,* Margaret Atwood asserted that "science fiction as a form is where theological narrative went after *Paradise Lost*" and that "extraterrestrials have taken the place of angels" in our cultural imagination.[8] Atwood's statement can serve as a heuristic for imagining the relationship between Milton and science fiction, and it encourages us to ask if Asimov's superhuman robots bear comparison to Raphael and his superhuman brethren, whose extraterrestrial descent dazzles Adam's eyes like "another Morn / Ris'n on mid-noon"?[9] When Asimov rewrites the biblical Fall in his seven *Foundation* novels, is he also rewriting Milton? If we consider the *Foundation* series as epic science fiction, how does Asimov engage his predecessors Milton, Virgil, and Homer?[10] When Asimov offers us visions of a wondrous world to come, can we hear in his narrative the whispers of Satan and his infernal crew, warning us that "long is the way / And hard, that out of Hell leads up to light" (*PL* 2.432–33)?

Those whispers are indeed audible, and by charting Milton's influence on Asimov and science fiction, I hope to further the conversation on Milton and popular culture begun by Laura L. Knoppers and Gregory Colón Semenza, who show how the appropriation of Miltonic ideas "give[s] new currency to Milton, making his works a vital, living part of contemporary culture."[11] Scholars continue to uncover new instances of Milton's presence in modern society. Noting that "reading Milton in light of pressing political and intellectual concerns is a practice as old as reading Milton," Feisal Mohamed demonstrates Milton's relevance to crises of ethics and violence in our post–9/11 world.[12] In his study of Milton and film, Eric Brown shows how *Paradise Lost* is central to our "cinematization of rebellious warrior angels" that began with Ridley Scott's *Blade Runner* (1982) and continues today.[13] Pointing out that Milton's Satan holds a special place in our political consciousness, Reginald Wilburn documents how Malcolm X and other African American writers "forge[d] rhetorical affiliations with Milton through the infernal hero of *Paradise Lost* and his tradition of poetic fallenness."[14] With regard to science fiction, Lara Dodds notes that *Paradise Lost* traffics in theories of the "plurality of worlds" of the mid-seventeenth century.[15] Showing how Atwood's *Oryx and Crake* (2003) reinvents the Miltonic Fall, Dodds asserts that "it is less useful to label *Paradise Lost* as science fiction than to ask how Milton's poem enables the creation of new literary forms."[16] As these studies indicate, Milton's works continue to shape the literary landscape of our society. In their own generic transformations, those works contain the formulae for the further reinvention of genres, forms, and modes in a given historical milieu.

However, mainstream science fiction of mid-twentieth-century America is largely absent from the discussion on Milton and popular culture, and the objective of this essay is to explore the ways in which Asimov's *Foundation* series appropriates and reinvents concepts from *Paradise Lost*. I suggest that we read the *Foundation* series as a work in conversation with *Paradise Lost*—that is, as a literary and ideological response to Milton's poem that not only borrows from its epic predecessor but also attempts to "fix" the places where Asimov believed Milton went wrong. Asimov's reworking of *Paradise Lost* is apparent in his superhuman robots, who prepare humanity for an oncoming Fall, much like Raphael. Like Milton's Adam, Asimov's protagonist Hari Seldon is supplied with an angelic instructor, the robot Daneel, who teaches him about an ancient interstellar civil war. However, Daneel is not only a teacher but also a renegade robot who rebelled against his makers. He channels Satan's attitude of *non serviam*, which Asimov rewrites in the *Foundation* series as the means of humanity's salvation—not its downfall. Asimov's revision of Miltonic narrative also extends to his treatment of gender and sexuality, and the female robots Dors Venabili and Bliss suggest Asimov's attempt to correct Milton's representation of women by granting Eve an uninhibited sexuality. As new Eves, Dors and Bliss exercise their sexual freedom through interspecies intercourse with humans, although (as we shall see) this ultimately others them as unknowable, inferior, and alien.

A broader understanding of how Asimov borrows from *Paradise Lost* uncovers the Miltonic character of mid-twentieth-century mainstream science fiction. As a science fiction pioneer and professor of biochemistry, Asimov was responsible for much of our modern thinking about robots—a fact noted by the *Oxford English Dictionary*, which credits him with having coined the term "robotics."[17] Asimov's notion of a robot revolution is still a powerful imaginary in modern American culture. It is evident in films like *Blade Runner*, the *Battlestar Galactica* franchise (1978–80, 2003–09), the *Terminator* franchise (1984–2015), *The Matrix* (1999), and *I, Robot* (2004), which may owe to *Paradise Lost* by way of Asimov their anxieties of a creation overpowering its creators. Milton's influence on science fiction is far-reaching, and on the page and the screen, we catch glimpses of the infernal crew, who first dared to think, "Our puissance is our own, our own right hand / Shall teach us highest deeds, by proof to try / Who is our equal" (*PL* 5.864–66).

1. "Perhaps we can learn from the past": The Adamic Education of Hari Seldon

In the manner of *Paradise Lost*, Asimov's *Foundation* series synthesizes Judeo-Christian and Greco-Roman literary traditions and constructs an epic about the Fall. As C. S. Lewis discerns, epic from Virgil to Milton is concerned with the "enlargement" of its subject, and as David Quint observes, the *Aeneid* "decisively transformed epic for posterity into both a genre that was committed to imitating and attempting to 'overgo' its earlier versions and a genre that was overtly political."[18] Milton seeks to supersede Homer and Virgil by writing an "argument / Not less but more Heroic than the wrauth / Of stern *Achilles*...or rage / Of *Turnus* for *Lavinia* disespous'd" (*PL* 9.13–15, 16–17). In Adam and Eve, Milton documents the rise of the faithful throughout history, a community far greater than Greek and Roman nations. Asimov was well read in Milton and Virgil, and his *Foundation* series engages both Renaissance and classical epic traditions.[19] In its own enlargement of epic, the *Foundation* series creates a cosmic version of Manifest Destiny and takes as its subject no less than the expansion of humanity into a massive empire spanning 25 million worlds.[20]

Written during the dual crises of World War II and the Cold War, the *Foundation* series offers an optimistic vision of *homo aeternus* at a time when the preservation of the species was in jeopardy.[21] Asimov, an American Jew born in Russia, was horrified at both Nazism and the possibility of nuclear fallout, and the *Foundation* novels were one response to these cataclysmic events. The first two *Foundation* stories, "The Encyclopedists" (originally "Foundation") and "The Mayors" (originally "Bridle and Saddle"), were written in 1941 and published in *Astounding Science-Fiction* in May and June of 1942. Asimov later explained in a 1979 interview that—in response to the seeming indestructibility of Nazism—he began the series "with the Foundation bound to win, no matter what the forces arrayed against it. I suppose that was my literary response to my own feelings...[and] to the inevitable victory of the anti-Nazi causes, although they seemed to be steadily losing."[22] His biographer, James Gunn, notes that the Foundation's military and political triumphs were "for Asimov a way to make Hitler's persistent victories bearable—[so that] no matter what initial successes the Nazis managed, the logic of history (psychohistory) would eventually bring about their defeat."[23] The later novels—*Foundation's Edge* (1982) and *Foundation and Earth* (1986)—continue Asimov's method of political engagement and play out Cold War anxieties about an Earth made radioactive through nuclear explosions. Consequently, by theorizing a future in which humanity has overcome the hazards of both nuclear war and Nazism, Asimov's fiction reconceives his own historical moment in twentieth-century America as the precursor to a desired, fictional future in which humanity has burgeoned into a galactic civilization.[24]

In its treatment of history, the *Foundation* series exhibits considerable generic self-awareness and epic revisionism. In the mathematician Hari Seldon, Asimov presents an epic hero who will prove victorious in his moment of crisis. Genesis and Revelation are key source texts for science fiction's cosmological crises, which often feature the revival of a lost paradise.[25] In the *Foundation* series, the oncoming struggle Seldon faces is described in biblical terms as a "Fall" into barbarism, in which humanity will exist in a Hobbesian state of "universal war and anarchy" for 30,000 years.[26] The prologue to *Foundation and Empire* (1952) states, "it was too late to stop that fall, but not too late to close the gap of barbarism. Seldon established two Foundations at 'opposite ends of the Galaxy' and their location was so designed that in one short millennium events would knit and mesh so as to force out of them a stronger, more permanent, more quickly appearing Second Empire."[27] Like Milton's Adam, Asimov's Seldon labors on behalf of the future of humankind. However, unlike *Paradise Lost*, the *Foundation* series posits that humanity can indeed learn from the past to forge a better and brighter future.

Like Milton's Adam, Asimov's hero is instructed by an angelic teacher who prepares him for the Fall by offering an education in ancient history. In *Paradise Lost*, God the Father commissions Raphael to warn Adam about Satan's intentions:

> tell him withall
> His danger, and from whom, what enemie
> Late falln himself from Heav'n, is plotting now
> The fall of others from like state of bliss;
> By violence, no, for that shall be withstood,
> But by deceit and lies; this let him know,
> Least wilfully transgressing he pretend
> Surprisal, unadmonisht, unforewarnd.   (*PL* 5.238–45)

Raphael's task is to not to stop the Fall but to make Adam accountable for it, which he does by teaching Adam about the celestial civil war and the fall of the rebel angels. Raphael concludes the history lesson with the admonition, "firm they might have stood, / Yet fell; remember, and fear to transgress" (6.911–12). Remembrance of the past is central to Raphael's strategy of preparing Adam for his epic conflict.

This mentoring relationship is replicated in the *Foundation* series in the friendship between Seldon and R. Daneel Olivaw ("R" for "robot"). Created in the early years of human expansion into the galaxy, Daneel is a synthetic being who is indistinguishable from a human, has superhuman mental abilities, and (by virtue of being 20,000 years old) is a near-immortal historian. When he first meets Seldon, Daneel introduces himself as a journalist named Hummin (a play on "human") who busies himself with recording the "downward spiral" of civilization (*PF* 21). This is not unlike Raphael, who tells Adam that he watched the rebel angels as "headlong themselves they threw / Down from the verge of Heav'n" (*PL* 6.864–65) and fell nine days to hell. However, unlike Raphael, Daneel will be successful in his tutelage. Under Daneel's instruction, Seldon will learn from the past, mitigate the Fall, and triumph in his epic conflict.

In this regard, the *Foundation* series invites being read as Asimov's attempt to correct what he sees as Adam's helplessness before an inevitable Fall. In his *Annotated Paradise Lost*, Asimov expresses outrage over the Father's statement, "if I foreknew, / Foreknowledge had no influence on their fault" (*PL* 3.117–18).

Asimov writes, "God had to be pictured as knowing in advance that Adam would fall and that mankind would therefore pass thousands of years of misery. Why, then (since God was also perfectly good), did God not create Adam strong enough to resist temptation?"[28] In writing his own epic, Asimov creates a hero who *is* strong enough to resist temptation. Initially, however, Seldon balks at the Sisyphean task before him:

> Hummin [i.e. Daneel] said, "Well then, you're part of the decay. You're ready to accept failure."
>
> "What choice have I?"
>
> "Can you *try*? However useless the effort may seem to you to be, have you anything better to do with your life? Have you some worthier goal? Have you a purpose that will justify you in your own eyes to some greater extent?"
>
> Seldon's eyes blinked rapidly. "Millions of worlds. Billions of cultures. Quadrillions of people. Decillions of inter-relationships.— And you want me to reduce it to order."
>
> "No, I want you to *try*. For the sake of those millions of worlds, billions of cultures, and quadrillions of people. Not for the Emperor. Not for Demerzel. For humanity."
>
> "I will fail," said Seldon.
>
> "Then we will be no worse off. Will you try?"
>
> And against his will and not knowing why, Seldon heard himself say, "I will try." And the course of his life was set. (*PF* 55)

Under Daneel's guidance, Seldon develops the science of psychohistory, a branch of mathematics that predicts the actions of human masses and enables Seldon to establish the Foundation. "We cannot stop the Fall," Seldon says in *Foundation* (1951), but this new empire will "shorten the period of Barbarism that must follow."[29] In order to do that, Seldon must gain an education in galactic history and learn about another fall—an interstellar civil war between Earth and its Spacer colonies, in which the rebellious Spacers were cast out of civilization.

The recourse to history is a significant aspect of epic form in the *Foundation* series, and it suggests the extent to which Asimov's saga mirrors the narrative structure of *Paradise Lost*. *Paradise Lost* learned from the *Aeneid* that history fails as a corrective to the present, and Adam partakes of the fruit despite Raphael's teachings.[30] Upon seeing fallen Eve, Adam silently soliloquizes, "How can I live without thee, how forgoe / Thy sweet Converse and Love so dearly joyn'd, / To live again in these wilde Woods forlorn?" (PL 9.908–10). Adam's knowledge of the fall of the rebel angels is suddenly displaced by another kind of historical knowledge: the painful memory of when he inhabited "these wilde Woods forlorn" and the fear that he might "again" live thus lonely.[31] The scene evokes the final moment in Virgil's epic, when Aeneas spies the belt of Pallas slung over Turnus's shoulder and succumbs to *furiis accensus et ira / terribilis*, just as Achilles had done before him.[32] As Craig Kallendorf observes, "a sinful Adam parallels a 'sinful' Aeneas," and like his precursor, Milton's hero "loses sight of his proper priorities [and] makes a mistake."[33] By contrast, in Asimov's *Foundation* series, the knowledge of past events is successful in prioritizing public concerns over private ones and consequently ensuring the well-being of a people yet unborn.[34]

Asimov engages both Virgilian and Miltonic epic traditions when exploring the relationship between history and virtue, but whereas Aeneas and Adam fail to benefit from prior examples, knowledge of the past successfully enables Seldon to vanquish barbarism. Asimov's historical optimism is evident in *Prelude to Foundation* (1988), which recounts Seldon's Aenean voyage to the oldest regions of the empire as he learns about the ancient civil war. He is accompanied by Dors Venabili, a professor of ancient history and a female robot indistinguishable from a human being. In his journeys, Seldon meets a resistance fighter, Davan, who shares a vital principle that will form the backbone of psychohistory. Davan says,

> "Even if you can't predict with—what do you call it?—psychohistorical accuracy, you've studied history and you may have a certain intuitive feeling for consequences. Now, isn't that so?"
>
> Seldon shook his head. "I may have a certain intuitive understanding for mathematical likelihood, but how far I can translate that into anything of historical significance is quite uncertain. Actually, I have *not* studied history. I wish I had. I feel the loss keenly."

Dors said evenly, "I am the historian, Davan, and I can say a few things if you wish."

"Please do," said Davan, making it half a courtesy, half a challenge.

"For one thing, there have been many revolutions in Galactic history that have overthrown tyrannies, sometimes on individual planets, sometimes in groups of them, occasionally in the Empire itself or in the pre-Imperial regional governments." ...

Davan, listening intently, said, "I'm aware of that. We all are. Perhaps we can learn from the past and know better what to avoid." (*PF* 318–19)

The conversation with Davan helps Seldon realize that studying the tyranny of the interstellar civil war, and thus "learn[ing] from the past," will allow him to predict future sociological trends. In turn, those predictions will become humanity's defense against the Fall into barbarism. Davan's seemingly simple statement exemplifies Asimov's thoughtful treatment of history as well as the epic revisionism of his series. In the *Aeneid* and *Paradise Lost*, the juxtaposition of past and present in a moment of crisis creates an opportunity to exercise free will and, essentially, to improve oneself morally through choice. Aeneas has the opportunity to grant Turnus the *clementia* Achilles denied Hector, but he does not take it, and Adam disregards Raphael's lesson of a prior Fall and eats the fruit Eve offers him.

In its own exploration of history's moral value, the *Foundation* series gestures toward both Virgilian and Miltonic moments but offers a positive outcome.[35] Seldon does in fact heed Daneel's lessons about the past. He is successful in developing psychohistory, and as a result, the impending "thirty thousand years of human misery and agony...[is] decreased to a single millennium."[36] The *Foundation* series thus registers Asimov's complex engagement with the idea of the past in the epic tradition. Virgil and Milton construct visions of future community around an act of *culpa*, whether the unjust slaughter of Turnus or "Mans First Disobedience" (1.1). In their moments of testing, Aeneas and Adam succumb to personal pain, and they fail. By contrast, Asimov relates the rise of a galactic community that triumphs in its time of crisis and thrives under the watchful eye of Daneel, whose remembrance of things past helps to prepare humanity for the things to come.

2. "Renegade" Robot and "Apostate" Angel: *Non Serviam* and the Salvation of Humanity

In addition to Raphael, Asimov's Daneel suggests an affinity with Milton's Satan, whose attitude of *non serviam* is rehabilitated in the *Foundation* series as nothing less than the means of humanity's salvation. Daneel originated in Asimov's *Robot* series (1953–83), and with his first appearance in the *Foundation* series in *Foundation and Earth* (1986), Daneel assumes an angelic role as humanity's guardian. When we first meet him, Daneel is working for humanity's well-being within the orbit of Earth, which has become so radioactive that—as one character says—it is "uninhabitable. The last bacterium, the last virus, is long gone."[37] On a small settlement on the moon, Daneel labors with a handful of fellow robots to "care," as he puts it, "for the Galaxy; for Earth, particularly" (*FEarth* 346) and its dispersed quadrillions of descendants. Daneel's stewardship of this radioactive Earth and of humanity at large identifies him as an imaginative response to Cold War fears in the 1980s about imminent nuclear war. As Cyndy Hendershot observes, "the non-realistic framework of science fiction allowed it to create a fantasy space for the cultural paranoia of the Atomic Age," and David Seed points out that "the unique urgencies of the Cold War, and particularly fear of nuclear war, affected writers' perceptions of the changed status of science fiction."[38] Science fiction suddenly became very relevant to world politics, and Asimov, who stated that "the dropping of the atomic bomb in 1945 made science fiction respectable," was one of the first writers to mark this shift. In his *Foundation* series, Asimov allays widespread fears about nuclear fallout through the idea that humanity is being guided by Seldon, who is in turn being guided by Daneel.[39] In our time of greatest need, Asimov seems to say, humanity's guardian angel will look homeward to Earth and lead us into a brighter world.

Furthermore, Daneel's satanic characteristics, as well as epic's method of surpassing its predecessors, promote reading the *Foundation* series as Asimov's attempt to give Satan a sporting chance in the form of this new angelic hero. In his *Annotated Paradise Lost*, Asimov expresses frustration when God the Father abandons Satan "to his own dark designs, / That with reiterated crimes he might / Heap on himself damnation" (*PL* 1.213–15). Complaining, as Empson did, that Satan is being unjustly baited, Asimov writes, "I find it is as hard to admire Milton's God as I find it easy to sympathize with Milton's Satan."[40] He anticipates the recent arguments of Peter Herman, who claims that the Father "shares some responsibility for the results of doing a poor job of confining Satan," and Richard Strier, who avers that "the attempt at theodicy — whether one regards it as successful or not — produces most of the aesthetic and religious failures of the poem."[41] In his science fiction epic, Asimov imparts to Daneel the best (or worst) characteristics of Milton's Satan. No longer damnable vices, these characteristics are now virtues to be praised as the instruments of humanity's salvation from the Fall into barbarism.

Asimov was fascinated with myths of cosmic rebellion, and the ancient interstellar civil war between Earth and the Spacer worlds in the *Foundation* series can be traced to classical theogeny and to *Paradise Lost*.[42] In a 1978 essay titled "The Myth of the Machine," Asimov hinted that his robot insurrections had their origins in "supplantation myths," such as Zeus overthrowing the Titans and "the one in which Satan tried to supplant God and failed; a myth that reached its greatest literary expression in John Milton's *Paradise Lost*."[43] As part of Daneel's instruction, Seldon learns that the Spacer colonies, led by the planet Aurora, developed robot technology and "despised their ancestral world..., and consequently they waged war against Earth" (*FEarth* 107). However, one robot betrayed his Auroran makers and came to the aid of Earth. His actions mimicked those of the biblical Lucifer, who likewise rebelled against his maker and said, "I wil bee like the most High."[44] In *Prelude to Foundation*, Seldon asks Daneel about this "renegade" robot, musing:

"Where Aurora was in question, one robot was spoken of as a renegade, a traitor, someone who deserted the cause. Where Earth was in question, one robot was spoken of as a hero, one who represented salvation. Was it too much to suppose that it was the same robot?...I imagine that Aurora, whether first or second, was nevertheless the one that was more advanced, the one that could produce more elaborate robots, even ones indistinguishable from human beings in appearance. Such a robot was designed and devised in Aurora, then. But he was a renegade, so he deserted Aurora. To the Earthpeople he was a hero, so he must have joined Earth. Why he did this, and what his motives were, I can't say." (PF 390)

Unlike Milton's "Apostate" angel (6.100), who intends to subject Adam and Eve to his own misery, Asimov's "renegade" seeks only humanity's well-being, and he is willing to defy even his own creators to accomplish it. Obedience is the most important principle in Milton's universe.[45] However, in rewriting this aspect of *Paradise Lost*, Asimov transforms disobedience into the greatest of virtues. Daneel's choice to defy his masters continues 20 millennia later, when he helps Seldon and the descendants of Earth who now populate the galaxy. Daneel's name, moreover, alludes to the biblical Daniel, who espoused an attitude of *non serviam* toward his Babylonian oppressors and—like Milton's Satan—refused to worship the king before him (Dan. 6:1–28).

The association between Asimov's Daneel and Milton's Satan is also evident in their extraordinary abilities of persuasion. In book 1 of *Paradise Lost*, for instance, Satan employs a rhetoric of mutuality to downplay his leadership role in the fall. He speaks of their "mutual league," "United thoughts and counsels," "equal hope," and "equal ruin" (PL 1.87, 88, 91). The "demonic attraction" of Satan's rhetoric, as Fish calls it, is apparent when the angels flock to their leader:[46]

> Dark'n'd so, yet shon
> Above them all th' Arch Angel: but his face
> Deep scars of Thunder had intrencht, and care
> Sat on his faded cheek, but under Browes
> Of dauntless courage, and considerate Pride

> Waiting revenge: cruel his eye, but cast
> Signs of remorse and passion to behold
> The fellows of his crime, the followers rather
> (Far other once beheld in bliss) condemn'd
> For ever now to have thir lot in pain,
> Millions of Spirits for his fault amerc't
> Of Heav'n, and from Eternal Splendors flung
> For his revolt, yet faithfull how they stood,
> Thir Glory witherd.   (*PL* 1.599–612)

Satan's eye, though "cruel," is careful to dissemble a seeming pity for the fallen angels. As the poetic narrator clarifies, contrary to Satan's rhetoric of inclusivity, the angels are not "The fellows of his crime, [but] the followers rather." The passage exemplifies Satan's uncanny capacity for compelling others to do his bidding through his seductive rhetoric and personal charisma.

In the *Foundation* series, Satan's manipulative tendencies are reborn in Daneel and ensure humanity's preservation. In *Prelude to Foundation,* Seldon asks about Daneel's psychic abilities. "I am not so much a romantic," Seldon says, "as to think that one robot, by switching from one side to the other, can alter the course of history. A robot could not make Earth's victory sure, nor Aurora's defeat certain—unless there was something strange, something peculiar about the robot" (*PF* 391). Daneel admits that he has "the ability to detect and affect human emotion" (*PF* 395), and he explains that this ability gave rise to his stewardship of humanity:

> "I am governed by the Three Laws of Robotics that are tradition-ally put into words—or once were, long ago. They are these:
> "'One. A robot may not injure a human being or, through inaction, allow a human being to come to harm.'
> "'Two. A robot must obey the orders given it by human beings, except where such orders would conflict with the First Law.'
> "'Three. A robot must protect its own existence, as long as such protection does not conflict with the First or Second Law.'
> "But I had a...a friend twenty thousand years ago. Another robot. Not like myself. He could not be mistaken for a human being, but it was he who had the mental powers and it was through him that I gained mine.

> "It seemed to him that there should be a still more general
> rule than any of the Three laws. He called it the Zeroth law,
> since zero comes before one. It is:
> "'Zero. A robot may not injure humanity or, through inaction,
> allow humanity to come to harm.'" (*PF* 397)

In the first civil war, Daneel used his mental powers to secure the
victory of the Earthmen and pave the way for their expansion into
the galaxy. At present, he uses his abilities to pave the way for Seldon, who will develop psychohistory to alleviate the Fall into barbarism. Daneel's commitment to the Zeroth law that "a robot may
not injure humanity or, through inaction, allow humanity to come
to harm" combines his two Miltonic roles as humanity's helper.
He is a history teacher in the fashion of Raphael, but he is also a
rebel in the manner of Satan. Daneel's cause in presuming to save
civilization is itself something borrowed from Satan, who likewise
seeks "League...and mutual amitie" (*PL* 4.375–76) with humanity and fancies himself the savior of his people. In the *Foundation*
series, the idea of the transgressive android resurfaces in the female
robots Dors Venabili and Bliss. Their feminization and sexualization as angelic teachers suggest that in writing them, Asimov is
rewriting Milton's Eve.

3. "How would you feel about making love to a robot?": Eve and Interspecies Intercourse

Asimov's practice of rewriting and (as he saw it) improving
Milton's epic also extends to his treatment of gender and sexuality,
and his female robots represent an attempt to bring Eve into the
twentieth century, so to speak, and liberate her from what Asimov
saw as Milton's puritanical oppression of women. Put another
way, Asimov's female robots are versions of a new and improved
Eve and an attempt to solve the problem of Milton's misogyny. As
with the historical optimism of his science fiction epic, Asimov's
rewriting of *Paradise Lost* reflects the social anxieties of his day.
But in his attempt to free Eve by granting her uninhibited sexual

freedom, Asimov rewrites Eve into a mid-twentieth-century notion of gender that Simone de Beauvoir, writing around the same time as Asimov, famously characterized as the "second sex."[47] As "the absolute Other," de Beauvoir writes, woman is never fully human but always an "angel, demon,...[or] a sphinx."[48] Asimov's robot women, too, are hybrid creatures. Occupying a nebulous space between being and identity, they are neither human nor nonhuman, but they are fully foreign and inferior.

In his annotations on *Paradise Lost,* Asimov expresses frequent frustration at Milton's portrayal of Eve, mocking his predecessor as "the rigidly Puritan Milton."[49] When Raphael looks with pleasure at Eve, Asimov notes with obvious scorn, "the only time a Puritan can with propriety praise female nudity is in the case of Eve in the garden of Eden, and Milton makes the most of it every chance he can. Eve may have been unaware, in her innocence, of the attractiveness of her body, but Milton isn't."[50] Later, when Eve leaves the conversation, Asimov notes, tongue-in-cheek, "obviously her feeble mind cannot understand such matters; she prefers to have them explained to her by Adam with kisses and (presumably) baby talk. Nothing in the poem, not even God's self-praise, is as irritating as Milton's view of women."[51] However, the idea of "baby talk" is absent from the passage, and in an act of eisegesis, Asimov reads into *Paradise Lost* the misogyny he expects Milton to harbor. In doing so, he anticipates the complaints of Sandra Gilbert and Susan Gubar, who would accuse *Paradise Lost* a few years later of promoting a traditional misogyny that Milton's text actually complicates and resists, as scholars have recently shown.[52]

Asimov's attempt to save Eve centers on the idea of intercourse between humans and their robotic teachers, which evokes one of the oddest moments in *Paradise Lost*: when Raphael looks with pleasure at Eve's body. The early modern period was fascinated with the notion of sexual relations between angels and humans.[53] They were particularly intrigued by the biblical myth of the Sons of God, those angels who "saw the daughters of men, that they were faire, and they took them wives" and begat the Nephilim (Gen. 6:2). Christopher Marlowe's Helen of Troy, whose "lips suckes forth"

Faustus's soul, and Thomas Middleton's succubus, who invites Master Penitent Brothel to "rouse thy amorous thoughts and twine me," speak to the place of such fantasies within the early modern imagination.[54] In *Paradise Lost*, Milton taps into popular interest in angelology by stating that Raphael might have found Eve sexually appealing—if only he had a libido:

> Mean while at Table *Eve*
> Ministerd naked, and thir flowing cups
> With pleasant liquors crown'd: O innocence
> Deserving Paradise! if ever, then,
> Then had the Sons of God excuse to have bin
> Enamour'd at that sight; but in those hearts
> Love unlibidinous reign'd, nor jealousie
> Was understood, the injur'd Lovers Hell.   (*PL* 5.443–50)

Milton's reference to the Sons of God draws a comparison between his two archangels: the unfallen Raphael, who is "enamour'd" at Eve but does not lust after her, and the fallen Satan, who in book 9 will see Eve's "Heav'nly forme / Angelic" and burn after her with the "fierce intent" of rape (9.457–58, 462). True to its early modern roots, the idea of interspecies intercourse figures prominently in science fiction. Critics in the field have long recognized that sex across species is one of the genre's tools for investigating gender, agency, and bodies.[55] The idea of interspecies intercourse is central to Asimov's revision of Miltonic gender, and Milton's angels supplied Asimov with ideas for alien sexuality in his own science fiction works.[56]

Asimov's view of *Paradise Lost* as blatantly misogynistic can be seen in how he handles Milton's idea of interspecies intercourse. When glossing the passage above, for instance, Asimov notes, "Raphael, seeing Eve, almost had [an] excuse for feeling libidinous desire, and [wished] that he could make love to earthly women with the same ease with which he could eat earthly food."[57] This is significant because in the *Foundation* series, superhuman beings do just that—make love to humans. Milton later returns to the myth of the Nephilim and the Sons of God when Michael tells Adam how beings of a "different sort" came, "ey'd" human

women, and "Fast caught" them as wives (*PL* 11.574, 585, 587).
Asimov believes that Milton is tweaking the scriptural account
to justify his own misogyny. "In Milton's version," he complains,
"the women are active seductresses, so once again the crime of Eve
is committed, this time en masse, and men, the more innocent, are
lured and cajoled into sin. Once again, Milton shoves the blame
onto women."[58] Asimov's distaste for Milton's misogyny is yoked
to his own enchantment with the idea of interspecies intercourse.
In Asimov's reworking of *Paradise Lost,* this idea would become
his tool for "fixing" Milton's problematic treatment of women.

In the *Foundation* series, the figures of Raphael and Eve cohere
in the humanoid robots Dors and Bliss, in whom the fantasy of
interspecies intercourse is played out through Asimov's feminization and sexualization of Milton's angelic teacher. Dors is a professor of ancient history, and as a teacher on the ancient civil war, she
channels Raphael in a manner similar to Daneel. However, Dors
is also a new Eve who demonstrates her sexual liberty by choosing partners from another species. The convergence of these two
Miltonic roles is apparent in *Forward the Foundation* (1993), when
Hari observes, "his friend—a robot [i.e., Daneel]—had provided
him with a protector—a robot [i.e., Dors]—to ensure that psychohistory and the seeds of the Foundations were given a chance to
take root. The only problem was, he had fallen in love with his
protector—a robot."[59] As one of only three female protagonists in
the *Foundation* series (the other two are Bliss, also a female robot,
and Arkady Darell, a child), Dors is an important case study for
exploring Asimov's representation of gender. Asimov others his
synthetic beings, and the Romeo and Juliet–style tale of forbidden love between Dors and Seldon casts women as inhumanly and
unquestionably foreign.[60]

Dors's female foreignness is articulated through her sexuality, and before he knows that she is a robot, Seldon sees her as a
body to be used. When they first meet in *Prelude to Foundation,*
Seldon immediately defines Dors in terms of her appearance and
sex appeal—a fact that does not go unnoticed by her:

He studied her. . . . She was not amazingly beautiful, but was quite
pleasant to look at, this being helped by full lips that seemed to
have a slight humorous curl to them. She was slim, well-built,
and looked quite young. (Too young, he thought uneasily, to be
of use perhaps.)

"Do I pass inspection?" she asked. (She seemed to have
Hummin's trick of guessing his thoughts, Seldon thought, or
perhaps he himself lacked the trick of hiding them.)

He said, "I'm sorry. I seem to have been staring, but I've only
been trying to evaluate you." (*PF* 69–70)

Seldon's crude aside that Dors might be "too young . . . to be of use"
indicates that he sees her as an object for sexual consumption.
His eyes roam across her body, and he notices that she is "well-
built"—an instance of irony on Asimov's part, since Dors is indeed
a manufactured being. The true irony of the passage, however, is
that Seldon does not yet know that Dors is a machine, but because
she is a pretty woman, he treats her as though she were one. Under
the scrutiny of Seldon's dehumanizing gaze, Dors becomes an item
for his personal "use." With her joking question, "Do I pass inspection?," Dors is made complicit in her own dehumanization, since
she encourages the reader to normalize Seldon's "staring" as nothing more than a humorous incident.

In attempting to liberate Eve from Milton's puritanism, Asimov
inadvertently transforms her into an erotic object—literally, a
machine—whose purpose is to satisfy male sexual desire. Nowhere
is this clearer than in the humanoid robot Blissenobiarella in
Foundation's Edge. Bliss jokingly informs her male admirers,
Golan Trevize and Janov Pelorat, that she goes by the name "Bliss"
because "once this body is attained, all sighs become sighs of
ecstasy" (*FEdge* 340). From her initial appearance, when Trevize
and Pelorat ask her, "are you human?" (*FEdge* 339), Bliss's experience as a woman is othered and dehumanized, and she is defined in
terms of a sexual body that is repeatedly subjected to male gazes.
The first thing Trevize and Pelorat notice about Bliss is that she
is "pretty," "small-breasted," and "narrow-waisted, with hips

rounded and full" (FEdge 339). Instead of the ambiguous gaze of the sexless Raphael, this new Eve is subjected to fallen gazes we have encountered before in *Paradise Lost*. Satan looks at Eve as a novelty to be obtained, and Adam casts "lascivious Eyes" (PL 9.1014) on her and encourages Eve to sin as he does — that is, to read bodies as objects, not selves. Coincidentally, that is exactly what Trevize and Pelorat do to Bliss.

Like Dors, Bliss channels Raphael, and her purpose throughout *Foundation and Earth* is to help humanity learn about the ancient civil war between Earth and the Spacer worlds. In an awkward moment between lovers, Bliss confronts Pelorat, who does not yet know that she is a robot. Bliss asks,

> "How would you feel about making love to a robot?"
>
> Pelorat snapped the thumb and mid-finger of his right hand, suddenly. "You know, there are legends of women falling in love with artificial men, and vice versa. I always thought there was an allegorical significance to that and never imagined the tales could represent literal truth. — Of course, Golan and I never even heard the word 'robot' till we landed on Sayshell, but, now that I think about it, those artificial men and women must have been robots. Apparently, such robots did exist in early historic times. That means the legends should be reconsidered — "
>
> He fell into silent thought, and, after Bliss had waited a moment, she suddenly clapped her hands sharply. Pelorat jumped.
>
> "Pel dear," said Bliss, "you're using your mythography to escape the question. The question is: How would you feel about making love to a robot?"
>
> He stared at her uneasily. "A truly undistinguishable one? One that you couldn't tell from a human being?"
>
> "Yes."
>
> "It seems to me, then, that a robot that can in no way be distinguished from a human being *is* a human being. If you were such a robot, you would be nothing but a human being to me."
>
> "That's what I wanted to hear you say, Pel." (FEarth 49–50)

Pelorat's mention of ancient legends alludes to the Genesis account of the Sons of God and to the moment between Raphael and Eve in *Paradise Lost*. As with the relationship between Seldon and Dors, Asimov's portrayal of interspecies intercourse defines women in terms of a transgressive and exoticized sexuality. Bliss's *real* query in the passage—how would you feel about *me* if I were a robot?—is construed, along with her own identity, in terms of her non-normative sexuality: "how would you feel about making love to a robot?" Pelorat's response that "you would be nothing but a human being to me" does not eschew the ontological difference between them but amplifies it through a charade of sameness that Bliss knows is false, just like her humanoid appearance, and which Pelorat is beginning to suspect is, too.

Ironically, Asimov's attempt to liberate Eve from Milton's "rigidly Puritan" worldview transports her to a new prison of mid-twentieth-century sexism that objectifies women and posits their ultimate inferiority and unknowability. In doing so, Asimov may reflect science fiction in his historical moment more broadly. The idea of woman as both object and other was integral to male domination of science fiction at the midcentury.[61] In 1975, Ursula K. Le Guin declared that science fiction, despite its penchant for challenging social norms, was still a genre nonetheless dominated by "male elitism."[62] "Science fiction has either totally ignored women," she claimed, "or presented them as squeaking dolls subject to instant rape by monsters...or, at best, loyal little wives or mistresses of accomplished heroes."[63] Although she does not name them directly, Le Guin clearly has the "big three" of science fiction—Asimov, Robert Heinlein, and Arthur C. Clarke—in her crosshairs.[64] Asimov's robot women, with their perfect bodies and transgressive sexuality, are an interesting example of the phenomenon Le Guin describes. As sexy female robots, Dors and Bliss epitomize what Debra Shaw calls the "roboticising of the female body" that occurred following World War II, when American companies redirected their resources to manufacturing women's domestic care products.[65] Like Ira Levin's *The Stepford Wives* (1972), which plays with the idea that the perfect wife is a robot, Asimov's robot women personify contemporary male fantasies about wives who are utterly submissive and impossibly beautiful.

In contrast, identities and bodies in *Paradise Lost* are amazingly fluid and "Indu'd with various forms, various degrees / Of substance" (*PL* 5.473–74), as Raphael explains. Denying Miltonic bodies this mutability, Asimov relocates Eve to a body that—for 20,000 years since its creation—resists change, and which exemplifies male desire at the midcentury for a wife who is cosmetically and eternally perfect. By attempting to grant Eve a truly human experience, Asimov in fact relegates her to the status of a nonhuman other whose value is determined by male sexual desire. In moving from *Paradise Lost* to the *Foundation* series, we trade a complex picture of gender for a less complex one, and a fluid idea of the human for one that is rigid, unyielding, and—in the passionless sense of the word—simply robotic.

4. Conclusion: Milton's Modern Legacy

What does this analysis tell us about the nature of Milton's modern legacy? First, the Miltonic elements in Asimov's *Foundation* series complicate distinctions between highbrow and lowbrow literature, despite the erudition of the literary forms in which Milton himself wrote. In 1945, at the time Asimov happened to be writing the *Foundation* trilogy, Douglas Bush made an important observation that Milton has always been a "popular poet," a poet of the people.[66] I would add that it is specifically the difficulties of Milton's text—the hermeneutic tension regarding theodicy, gender, and the representation of women—that garner interest from readers of all skill levels and backgrounds. Milton's interpretive challenges do not dissuade readers; they attract them. Those challenges are why he bridges the gap between academic and popular cultures in our society. Asimov's engagement with Milton is a testament to the way in which *Paradise Lost*, with its own agenda of epic revisionism, engenders new literary expressions and furthers the evolution of established traditions. As that engagement indicates, science fiction and epic are genres in dialogue with each other, and both work tirelessly to explore new possibilities for their own condition.

Additionally, much of the Miltonic revision taking place in science fiction focuses on Satan as a political rebel and refuge. From Asimov's *Foundation* series to Scott's *Blade Runner* and beyond, Satan's diabolical politics prove useful to science fiction because of science fiction's own political coding and its penchant for cultural subversion. In a well-known 2005 essay in *Milton Studies*, Stanley Fish argued against the historicist trend in Milton scholarship, which he claimed put "political concerns" first and "literary form second."[67] He asserted that "if Milton's value—the degree to which he matters—stands or falls on his contribution to English and European political thought, it will fall."[68] On the contrary, as we have seen, Milton's politics are the very thing that made *Paradise Lost* useful to Asimov and to science fiction. Political concerns are intrinsic to the aesthetic structures of both speculative fiction and epic. In a sense, to study the literary form of Milton's epics *is* to study his politics. Milton's Satan appealed to Asimov precisely because the fallen angel demands to be read in relation to tyranny as a historical phenomenon in seventeenth century England. That particular political conflict informed later ones, and Milton's struggle against Stuart oppression equipped Asimov with the tools necessary for carrying out his own struggle against Nazism and Soviet aggression.

Finally, this essay proposes that Milton is a major source of religious information in science fiction, and that the genre owes to *Paradise Lost* some of its speculation on theodicy, machine ethics or the ethics of creation, and the nature of alien life. Atwood, I believe, is only partly right in claiming that "extraterrestrials have taken the place of angels." Like Milton, we harbor a fascination for the nonhuman unknown, but to say that aliens are to us what angels were to him is a false analogy. For Milton, angels were a historical reality, inasmuch as they spoke to the Hebrew prophets, and an eschatological certainty, inasmuch as their presence would soon be revealed at the Last Judgment. In our own time, *Paradise Lost* continues both to provoke speculation on "the substance of things hoped for, the evidence of things not seen," as St. Paul put it (Heb. 11:1), and to supply science fiction with the Judeo-Christian vocabulary for expressing that speculation. Like modern science fiction authors, Milton too sought to tell "Of things invisible to mortal sight" (*PL* 3.55), and it is unsurprising that Asimov and others turned to him when doing the same. In *Paradise Lost* they found a language of religious belief adaptable to their own cosmic sagas, as they wrote of humanity's ascent out of darkness and into the new light of a galactic civilization.

Texas Tech University

Notes

I am indebted to Sarah Banschbach Valles, Michael Faris, Leah Orr, and Paul Zajac for reading early drafts of this essay and offering helpful recommendations. I am also grateful to David Ainsworth, Lara Dodds, Stephen Fallon, Everett Hamner, and other audience members at "Heavens Above: Envisioning Religion in Science Fiction," the panel organized by TC Religion and Literature at MLA 2016 in Austin, Texas, for their thought-provoking questions on a conference form of this essay.

1. *Asimov's Annotated "Paradise Lost": An Original Interpretation of Milton's Epic Poem,* ed. Isaac Asimov (Garden City, N.Y., 1974). The epigraph to this essay is from Isaac Asimov, *I, Asimov: A Memoir* (New York, N.Y., 1994), 333.

2. Michael White, *Isaac Asimov: A Life of the Grand Master of Science Fiction* (New York, 2005). Asimov has been called one of the "big three" of science fiction, along with Robert Heinlein and Arthur C. Clarke. In 1972, Neil Goble declared him "America's foremost writer of popular science," and Frederik Pohl, editor of *Star Science Fiction Stories,* stated in 1967 that "in the alphabet of science fiction, 'A' is for Asimov"; both in Neil Goble, *Asimov Analyzed* (Baltimore, 1972), 3.

3. *Asimov's Annotated "Paradise Lost,"* 224n336.

4. Ibid., 78n132.

5. Stanley Fish, *Surprised by Sin: The Reader in "Paradise Lost"* (New York, 1967).

6. *Asimov's Annotated "Paradise Lost,"* 207n319, 46n100.

7. Ibid., 14n25.

8. Margaret Atwood, "'Aliens have taken the place of angels': Margaret Atwood on Why We Need Science Fiction," *Guardian,* June 16, 2005, para. 9, http://www.theguardian.com/film/2005/jun/17/sciencefictionfan tasyandhorror.margaretatwood (accessed March 30, 2016).

9. John Milton, *Paradise Lost*, ed. Barbara K. Lewalski (Malden, Mass., 2007), 5.310–11. References to Milton's poem are to this edition and are hereafter cited in the text.

10. See Donald E. Palumbo, *Chaos Theory, Asimov's "Foundations" and "Robots," and Herbert's "Dune": The Fractal Aesthetic of Epic Science Fiction* (Westport, Conn., 2002).

11. Laura Lunger Knoppers and Gregory M. Colón Semenza, eds., *Milton in Popular Culture* (New York, 2006), 6.

12. Feisal G. Mohamed, *Milton and the Post-Secular Present: Ethics, Politics, Terrorism* (Stanford, Calif., 2011), 10.

13. Eric C. Brown, *Milton on Film* (Pittsburgh, 2015), 252.

14. Reginald A. Wilburn, *Preaching the Gospel of Black Revolt: Appropriating Milton in Early African American Literature* (Pittsburgh, 2014), 5.

15. Lara Dodds, "Milton's Other Worlds," in *Uncircumscribed Mind: Reading Milton Deeply*, ed. Charles W. Durham and Kristin A. Pruitt (Selinsgrove, Pa., 2008), 178. See also Frédérique Aït-Touati, *Fictions of the Cosmos: Science and Literature in the Seventeenth Century*, trans. Susan Emanuel (Chicago, 2011).

16. Lara Dodds, "Death and the 'Paradice within' in *Paradise Lost* and Margaret Atwood's *Oryx and Crake*," in *Milton Studies*, vol. 56, ed. Laura L. Knoppers, 115–50 (Pittsburgh, 2015), 142. On Milton and science fiction, see also Sanford Schwartz, "Reconstructing Eden: *Paradise Lost* and C. S. Lewis's *Perelandra*," in Knoppers and Semenza, *Milton in Popular Culture*, 23–34.

17. *Oxford English Dictionary Online* (2016), s.v. "robotics," 1.

18. C. S. Lewis, *A Preface to "Paradise Lost"* (Oxford, 1942), 35; and David Quint, *Epic and Empire: Politics and Generic Form from Virgil to Milton* (Princeton, N.J., 1993), 8.

19. Asimov's familiarity with classical epic is evident in his *The Roman Republic* (Boston, 1966), and references to Virgil and Homer litter his many interviews and autobiographies.

20. See Jari Käkelä, "Asimov's Foundation Trilogy: From the Fall of Rome to the Rise of Cowboy Heroes," *Extrapolation* 49, no. 3 (2008): 432–49.

21. On contemporary science fiction responses to World War II, see Andrew Pilsch, "Self-Help Supermen: The Politics of Fan Utopias in World War II–Era Science Fiction," *Science Fiction Studies* 41, no. 3 (2014): 524–42; Edward Wysocki, "Wartime Stories in *Astounding*," *Science Fiction Studies* 39, no. 3 (2012): 556–58; Wysocki, "*Astounding* and World War II," *Science Fiction Studies* 39, no. 1 (2012): 162–65; M. Keith Booker, *Monsters, Mushroom Clouds, and the Cold War: American Science Fiction and the Roots of Postmodernism, 1946–1964* (Westport, Conn.,

2001); Chris Hables Gray, "'There Will Be War!': Future War Fantasies and Militaristic Science Fiction in the 1980s," *Science Fiction Studies* 21, no. 3 (1994): 315–36; and H. Bruce Franklin, *War Stars: The Superweapon and the American Imagination* (New York, 1988).

22. Carl Freedman, ed., *Conversations with Isaac Asimov* (Jackson, Miss., 2005), 47.

23. James Gunn, *Isaac Asimov: The Foundations of Science Fiction*, rev. ed. (Lanham, Md., 1996), 37.

24. Istvan Csicsery-Ronay, in *The Seven Beauties of Science Fiction* (Middletown, Conn., 2008), notes that science fiction investigates "a complex hesitation about the relationship between imaginary conceptions and historical reality unfolding into the future" (4).

25. See Edward James, "Rewriting the Christian Apocalypse as a Science-Fictional Event," in *Imagining Apocalypse: Studies in Cultural Crisis*, ed. David Seed (New York, 2000), 45–61; and Tom Moylan, *Demand the Impossible: Science Fiction and the Utopian Imagination* (Bern, 2014), 31.

26. Asimov, *Prelude to Foundation* (New York, 1988), 55, 53; hereafter cited in the text as *PF*. Asimov's idea of the fall into barbarism also draws on Edward Gibbon's *The History of the Decline and Fall of the Roman Empire* (1776–88), which is discussed in Gunn, *Isaac Asimov*, 40, 44.

27. Asimov, *Foundation and Empire*, in *The Foundation Trilogy* (New York, 1974), v.

28. *Asimov's Annotated "Paradise Lost,"* 119n193.

29. Asimov, *Foundation*, in *The Foundation Trilogy*, 74.

30. Quint points out that Virgil introduced a pattern of "narrative circularity" and repetition to epic, such that the "past must be both buried and forgotten, and then reinvented in the 'memory' of the present" as a means of protecting *patria* in the future (*Epic and Empire*, 56, 62). E. M. W. Tillyard notes in *The English Epic and Its Background* (London, 1954), "Virgil, in turning his panegyric of Augustus into a poem on Rome, merged the present into a process of evolution" (71) stemming from an unforgettable past.

31. The inimical resurfacing of the past in Western epic is discussed, among other places, in Jonas Grethlein, "From 'Imperishable Glory' to History: The *Iliad* and the Trojan War," in *Epic and History*, ed. David Konstan and Kurt A. Raaflaub, 122–44 (Malden, Mass., 2010).

32. Virgil, *Aeneid*, in *Opera Vergili*, ed. R. A. B. Mynors (Oxford, 1969), 12.946–47. Charles Martindale, *John Milton and the Transformation of Ancient Epic* (Totowa, N.J., 1986), notes, "Milton owes much to Virgil for the organisation of his epic with respect to time [and] its incorporation of flashback" (144).

33. Craig Kallendorf, *The Other Virgil: Pessimistic Readings of the "Aeneid" in Early Modern Culture* (Oxford, 2007), 161–62.

34. On Asimov's historical optimism, see Peter Bergethon, "Landscapes of Change: Science, Science Fiction, and Advances in Biology," in *New Boundaries in Political Science Fiction*, ed. Donald Hassler and Clyde Wilcox, 3–16 (Columbia, S.C., 2008).

35. Joseph Patrouch asserts in *The Science Fiction of Isaac Asimov* (Garden City, N.Y., 1974), 107–08, that the question of free will is the primary theme of the *Foundation* series. The topic is taken up more recently by Andrew Milner, who argues for a purely deterministic view of Asimov's universe in *Locating Science Fiction* (Liverpool, 2012), 109.

36. Isaac Asimov, *Foundation's Edge* (New York, 1982), xi; hereafter abbreviated as *FEdge* and cited in the text.

37. Isaac Asimov, *Foundation and Earth* (New York, 1986), 330; hereafter abbreviated as *FEarth* and cited in the text.

38. Cyndy Hendershot, *Paranoia, the Bomb, and 1950s Science Fiction Films* (Bowling Green, Ohio, 1999), 2; and David Seed, *American Science Fiction and the Cold War: Literature and Film* (Edinburgh, 1999), 8. On contemporary science fiction responses to the Cold War, see also David Seed, *Under the Shadow: The Atomic Bomb and Cold War Narratives* (Kent, Ohio, 2013), 60–61, 95–111; Doug Davis, "Science Fiction Narratives of Mass Destruction and the Politics of National Security," in Hassler and Wilcox, *New Boundaries*, 145–56; Darko Suvin, "Of Starship Troopers and Refuseniks: War and Militarism in U.S. Science Fiction, Part 1 (1945–1974: Fordism)," in Hassler and Wilcox, *New Boundaries*, 115–44; Joseph F. Brown, "Heinlein and the Cold War: Epistemology and Politics in *The Puppet Masters* and *Double Star*," *Extrapolation* 49, no. 1 (2008): 109–21; M. Keith Booker, "Science Fiction and the Cold War," in *A Companion to Science Fiction*, ed. David Seed (Malden, Mass., 2005), 171–84; Booker, *Monsters, Mushroom Clouds*; Franklin, *War Stars*; and Paul Brians, *Nuclear Holocausts: Atomic War in Fiction, 1895–1984* (Kent, Ohio, 1987).

39. See John Clute, "Isaac Asimov," in Seed, *Companion to Science Fiction*, 365.

40. William Empson, *Milton's God* (Westport, Conn., 1961), 42; and *Asimov's Annotated "Paradise Lost,"* 21n35.

41. Peter C. Herman, "'Whose fault, whose but his own?': *Paradise Lost*, Contributory Negligence, and the Problem of Cause," in *The New Milton Criticism*, ed. Peter C. Herman and Elizabeth Sauer, 49–67 (Cambridge, 2012), 56; and Richard Strier, "Milton's Fetters; or, Why Eden Is Better than Heaven," in Herman and Sauer, *New Milton Criticism*, 25.

42. On Milton and the tradition of angelic war, see Stella Revard, *The War in Heaven: "Paradise Lost" and the Tradition of Satan's Rebellion* (Ithaca, N.Y., 1980).

43. Isaac Asimov, *Asimov on Science Fiction* (Garden City, N.Y., 1981), 160.

44. Isaiah 14:14. References to scriptural text are from *The King James Bible, Quatercentenary Edition,* ed. Gordon Campbell (Oxford, 2010); hereafter cited in the text.

45. See Michael Schoenfeldt, "Obedience and Autonomy in *Paradise Lost,*" in *A Companion to Milton,* ed. Thomas Corns (Malden, Mass., 2001), 363–79.

46. Stanley Fish, *Surprised by Sin,* 22.

47. Simone de Beauvoir, *The Second Sex,* trans. H. M. Parshley (New York, 1989). *Le Deuxième Sexe* was first published in French in 1949.

48. Ibid., 253, 257.

49. *Asimov's Annotated "Paradise Lost,"* 3n6.

50. Ibid., 235n355.

51. Ibid., 351n504.

52. Susan Gilbert and Sandra Gubar, *The Madwoman in the Attic: The Woman Writer and the Nineteenth-Century Literary Imagination* (New Haven, Conn., 1979), 188. See Laura Lunger Knoppers, *Politicizing Domesticity from Henrietta Maria to Milton's Eve* (Cambridge, 2011), 140–64; Shannon Miller, *Engendering the Fall: John Milton and Seventeenth-Century Women Writers* (Philadelphia, 2008); and Catherine Gimelli Martin, ed., *Milton and Gender* (Cambridge, 2004).

53. See Karma deGruy, "Desiring Angels: The Angelic Body in *Paradise Lost,*" *Criticism* 54, no. 1 (2012): 117–49; and Joad Raymond, *Milton's Angels: The Early-Modern Imagination* (Oxford, 2010), 76–78, 152, 269, 282–83, and 338–39.

54. Christopher Marlowe, *Doctor Faustus,* in *The Complete Works of Christopher Marlowe,* vol. 2, *Dr. Faustus,* ed. Roma Gill (Oxford, 1990), 12.84; and Thomas Middleton, *A Mad World, My Masters,* in *Thomas Middleton: The Collected Works,* ed. Gary Taylor and John Lavagnino (Oxford, 2007), 4.1.45.

55. See Sarah Lefanu, *Feminism and Science Fiction* (Bloomington, Ind., 1989), 76–83; and Marleen S. Barr, *Alien to Femininity: Speculative Fiction and Feminist Theory* (New York, 1987), 104.

56. Asimov's debt to *Paradise Lost* is further documented in his annotated edition, when Raphael describes to Adam how the angels "mix, Union of Pure with Pure / Desiring" (8.627–28) and Asimov comments: "I cannot resist a personal note here. A year and a half ago (as I write this), I wrote a science-fiction novel entitled *The Gods Themselves,* in which one major portion dealt with other-worldly creatures who enjoyed a completely non-human sex life. It wasn't until I began to study *Paradise Lost* line by line in order to prepare this book that it occurred to me that I had, more or less unconsciously, borrowed part of my other-worldly sex life from this very passage in the epic—a passage that, of course, I knew well" (*Asimov's Annotated "Paradise Lost,"* 385n540).

57. Ibid., 236n355.

58. Ibid., 552n759.

59. Asimov, *Forward the Foundation* (New York, 1993), 290.

60. In addition to its sexism, Emily Auger notes that Asimov's robotic othering also borrows from "power hierarchies based on racism and class-based elitism" of the midcentury, in "Robots and Representation in Asimov's Detective-Science Fiction Novels," *Foundation* 38, no. 107 (2009): 32. William Haney makes a similar point in *Cyberculture, Cyborgs and Science Fiction: Consciousness and the Posthuman* (New York, 2006), 73–74.

61. See Lefanu, *Feminism and Science Fiction*, 4.

62. Ursula K. Le Guin, "American SF and the Other," *Science-Fiction Studies* 2 (1975): 208.

63. Ibid. Michael LeBlanc notes that Asimov held only "moderate liberal sentiments" for his time, which made him "an oddity among his fellow sf fans and writers. Many people in science fiction belonged to polarised or radical political grounds in this period, particularly within the ranks of the Futurians, a group with which both he and [Judith] Merril rapidly became associated." Michael LeBlanc, "Judith Merril and Isaac Asimov's Quest to Save the Future," *Foundation* 35, no. 98 (2006): 60.

64. Jason Bourget offers an account of male chauvinism in contemporary science fiction in "Biological Determinism, Masculine Politics and the Failure of Libertarianism in Robert. A. Heinlein's *The Moon Is a Harsh Mistress*," *Foundation* 37, no. 104 (2008): 10–22.

65. Debra Shaw, *Women, Science and Fiction: The Frankenstein Inheritance* (New York, 2000), 73–74.

66. Douglas Bush, *"Paradise Lost" in Our Time: Some Comments* (Ithaca, N.Y., 1945), 108.

67. Stanley Fish, "Why Milton Matters; or, Against Historicism," in *Milton Studies*, vol. 44, ed. Albert C. Labriola, 1–12 (Pittsburgh, 2005), 2.

68. Ibid., 2–3.

INDEX

Abano, Pietro d', 257n27
Abdiel, 81–83
Achilles, 189–91, 199, 206
Achinstein, Sharon, 92n62, 263–64
Adam: and creation of Eve, 106–08;
    death and, 114; difference and,
    158–59, 161–62, 165, 168–70,
    174–75; Eve as, 169; Eve's beauty
    and, 271–73; friendship and, 165–66;
    likeness and, 168–69; love of, for
    Eve, 174, 277–82; "now" and,
    101–09, 112–14, 117n15; obedience
    of, 274–75, 279–80; self-knowledge
    of, 155–56, 161; solitude and,
    155–60, 164–65, 170, 172; in *State of
    Innocence*, 269–71, 273–74, 276–82;
    time and, 96–98, 101–02
Adam Unparadized (Milton), 205
Addison, Joseph, 211
Aeneid (Virgil), 297, 300–01
Aeschylus, 197–98, 200, 208n19
African Americans, 295
Agamemnon, 189
Agrippa, Marcus, 258n50
Ainsworth, David, 51, 91n52
air, 234–40, 245, 247–48, 255nn10–11,
    259n53
Albertus Magnus, 240, 243
alchemy, 121–22, 149n27, 152n69, 246,
    257n23
Alexander, Elizabeth Shanks, 35–36
Altmann, Alexander, 56n9
Amory, Hugh, 42
Amphitheatrum sapientiae aeternae
    (Khunrath), 245–46, 258n50
Anatomia hepatis (Glisson), 123–24,
    126–27, 129–30, 132, 138, 140
Andronicus Comnenus, 14

animal, 160–62
animism, 121, 124
Antigone (Sophocles), 199–200, 209n24
Anxiety of Influence, The (Bloom), viii,
    xivn10
Apollonius, 193, 195
Apology against a Pamphlet, An
    (Milton), 77–78, 81
Apology for Smectymnuus (Milton),
    44–45
appropriation, 264–66, 288n7
Areopagitica (Milton), 50–51
Argonautica (Apollonius), 195
Aristophanes, 188, 201
Aristotle, 126–27, 181n6, 243; change in,
    99–100; conception in, 119–20, 134;
    exhalation theory, 257n26; friendship
    in, 157; Greek and, 188, 208n19;
    metal in, 239, 256n22; "now" in, 96,
    98–100, 116n3; solitude and, 181n2;
    Supplices and, 200
Arnold, Matthew, 32, 55n6
Art of Logic (Milton), 135, 151n50
Asimov, Isaac, x, 316n2; Eve in,
    307–09; Fall in, 294–95, 298–300;
    history in, 298, 300–02; Nazism
    and, 297; on *Paradise Lost*, 293, 304;
    salvation in, 303–07
*Asimov's Annotated "Paradise Lost":
    An Original Interpretation of
    Milton's Epic Poem* (Asimov),
    293–94, 299–300, 320n56
"At a Vacation Exercise" (Milton), 225
Athanasius, 248
Attie, Katherine, 70
attraction, theory of, 138–40
Atwood, Margaret, 294–95
Aubrey, John, 19, 195, 237

323

Latin, 187–88, 207n3, 207n7, 212, 239n18
law, Mosaic, 33
Lear, Jonathan, 116n3
Leavis, F. R., 18
LeBlanc, Michael, 321n63
Le Comte, Edward, 217
Le Guin, Ursula, 313
Leonard, John, 230n31, 231n36, 254n3
Leviathan (Hobbes), 65, 86n7, 271
Levin, Ira, 313
Lewalski, Barbara, 66, 68, 76, 79,
    91n56, 182n19, 264
Lewis, C. S., 114, 297
Lewis, Jayne Elizabeth, 255n11
Lieb, Michael, 128
Life of St. Anthony (Athanasius), 248
Lightfoot, John, 33, 56n11, 59n36
likeness, 158–59, 166–67, 182n7
liminality, 115–16
linguistic purism, 226n5
literary appropriation, 264–66, 288n7
literary identity, 266–69
literary past, 265–69, 285
liver, 131–32. *See also Anatomia
    hepatis* (Glisson)
Lives of Wives (Riding), 12
London, theater in, 267
Long, Mary Beth, 158
Longfellow, Henry Wadsworth, 244–45
Longinus, 188, 205–06, 287
love, 174, 277–82, 307–14
Lowell, James Russell, 254n3
Luke 4, 41
Luxon, Thomas, 159–60, 165, 182n7
Lyly, John, 231n41
lyric: in *Apology against a Pamphlet,*
    77; critique of, 77–81; occasions of,
    71–77; *Paradise Lost* and, 71–85;
    politics and, 74, 77–79; politics
    of, 81–85; in *Reason of Church-
    Government,* 73; royalist authors
    and, 88n33; Satan and, 81–83

Maclean, Gerald, 266
Maimonides, 33
Malcolm X, 295
Map of Misreading, A (Bloom), viii
Marjara, Harinder Singh, 256n23
Marlowe, Christopher, 308–09
marriage, 157, 167–69, 177–79
Martz, Louis, 263
Masque of Augurs (Jonson), 14
materialism, 121, 124
Mathematical Magick (Wilkins), 241–43
matter, 128–29, 145, 148n13
Matter of Revolution (Rogers), 122–23

Matthew 23, 37–39
McColley, Diane, 171
McCormick, Ian, 20
mechanics, 241–43
medical model, of conception, 119. *See
    also* conception
Memoirs of an Infantry Officer
    (Graves), 6–7
Mersenne, Marin, 247, 251
metal, 238–40, 243, 245, 256n22–23,
    257n27
Metamorphoses (Ovid), 208n14
Milner, Andrew, 319n35
Milton, Deborah, 208n14
Milton, John (works). *See individual
    works*
"Milton controversy," 254n3
Milton in Popular Culture (Knoppers
    and Semenza), 28n3
Milton's Eve (McColley), 171
*Milton's Languages: The Impact of
    Multilingualism* (Kale), 211–12
mind: "now" and, 109–10; recognition
    of, in other, 109; time and, 98–99
Minear, Erin, 235, 255n4
Mirandola, Pico della, 168
Mohamed, Feisal, 295
Montaigne, Michel de, 184n35
morality: time and, 114–15
More, Henry, 134, 150n46
Morus, Alexander, 202–03
Mosaic law, 33
Mueller, Janel, 48–49
Murry, Middleton, 18
music, 240–41, 243–52, 254n3, 257n30,
    258n50
Musurgia universalis (Kircher), 251

Nazism, 297
nearness, 168
New Arcadia (Sidney), 80
Newman, William R., 126, 149n27
New Testament, 188, 202–03, 208n19
Newton, Isaac, 148n13
Newton, Thomas, 211, 230n35
Nicholls, Charlotte, 152n65
Nicholson, Catherine, 231n41
Nimrod, 219, 230n31
Norbrook, David, 83
Norton, David, 228n17
"Note on the Verse of John Milton, A"
    (Eliot), 233
"now": Adam and, 101–09, 112–14,
    117n15; in Aristotle, 96, 98–100,
    116n3; in Augustine, 98; and
    creation of Eve, 106–08; Eve and,